Revisionism and Empire

Revisionism and Empire

Socialist Imperialism in Germany 1897–1914

ROGER FLETCHER

London
GEORGE ALLEN & UNWIN
Boston   Sydney

George Allen & Unwin (Publishers) Ltd,
40 Museum Street, London WC1A 1LU, UK

George Allen & Unwin (Publishers) Ltd,
Park Lane, Hemel Hempstead, Herts HP2 4TE, UK

Allen & Unwin, Inc.,
9 Winchester Terrace, Winchester, Mass. 01890, USA

George Allen & Unwin Australia Pty Ltd,
8 Napier Street, North Sydney, NSW 2060, Australia

First published in 1984.

British Library Cataloguing in Publication Data

Fletcher, Roger
    Revisionism and empire.
1. Germany—Foreign relations—1888–1918
I. Title
327.43   DD228.6
ISBN 0–04–943031–9

Library of Congress Cataloging in Publication Data

Fletcher, Roger.
    Revisionism and empire.
Bibliography: p.
Includes index.
1. Germany—Politics and government—1888–1918.
2. Imperialism.   3. Germany—Foreign relations—1888–1918.
I. Title.
DD228.5.F58   1984   327.43'009'041   84–2989
ISBN 0–04–943031–9

Set in 10 on 11 point Plantin by
Inforum Ltd, Portsmouth
and printed in Great Britain
by Mackays of Chatham

Contents

Acknowledgements

My thanks are due to a great many people and institutions whose assistance was invaluable in the preparation of this work. Among the libraries and archives which have generously granted me the use of their facilities and permission to quote from their archival resources are Professor Werner Jochmann's Institute for Social and Labour History in Hamburg, the Staatsarchiv and Staatsbibliothek in Hamburg, the International Institute of Social History in Amsterdam, the Bundesarchiv in Coblenz, the Friedrich-Ebert-Stiftung in Bonn, the Verein für Geschichte der Arbeiterbewegung in Vienna, the National Library of Austria, the Austrian Arbeiterkammer in Vienna, the Norfolk Record Office (for permission to quote from the Massingham Collection), the Central Library of the University of Queensland and the National Library of Australia. I am also indebted to several scholars who gave advice, criticism and encouragement on various aspects of this study. To name but a few, my sincere thanks go to Professors Fritz Fischer, Christoph Schröder, Werner Jochmann, James Joll and Paul Kennedy, to John Moses for originally suggesting this topic, to Markku Hyrkkänen, Frau Freya Eisner, Frau Marianne Hirsch (for transcribing some of Karl Leuthner's correspondence) and to Carolyn, who patiently listened to Bernstein, Bloch, Leuthner and company for several years. With gratitude I acknowledge the indispensable financial and material aid provided by the German Academic Exchange Service, the Federal Ministry of Science and Research of the Republic of Austria, the Department of Education of the Commonwealth of Australia and the History Department of the University of Queensland. For permission to use material from some of my previously published journal articles I wish to thank the editors and publishers of the *Australian Journal of Politics and History*, the *Americal Historical Review*, *Central European History*, the *Canadian Journal of History*, the *Canadian Review of Studies in Nationalism*, *International History Review*, *European Studies Review*, the *Review of International Studies*, *Internationale wissenschaftliche Korrespondenz zur Geschichte der deutschen Arbeiterbewegung* and *Militärgeschichtliche Mitteilungen*.

Naturally, all errors are entirely my own responsibility. Thanks to my copy-editor, Carole Fries, these are far fewer than would otherwise have been the case.

For Louise, Richard and Carolyn

Preface

The aim of this book is to identify the foreign policy attitudes of German revisionism as manifested in the views expressed by prominent revisionist spokesmen and in the revisionist organ, the *Sozialistische Monatshefte*, between the turn of the century, when Eduard Bernstein's return to Germany roughly coincided with the inauguration of both the *Monatshefte* and Wilhelmine world policy, and the outbreak of the First World War in August 1914, which brought in its wake major changes in factional alignments. That it is not a study of the German socialist masses or of class but, as an attempt to recover the world view of significant persons who lived at a particular time in the past, is concerned primarily with leaders and ideas may stamp this work as contrary to present historiographical fashion. Yet this in no way removes the need for such a study.

This need, it seems to me, derives from two main sources. In the first place, there has been far too much facile and misleading generalisation about the nature of revisionism, or reformism, as it is often called, in part because factional polemics of the period have cast a long shadow and, in part, because of 'the enormous condescension of posterity', to borrow E. P. Thompson's vivid phrase (1963, p. 12). Today, as then, terms like revisionist, reformist, opportunist, social imperialist, pragmatist[1] and ethical socialist tend to be used in an unreflected way as if all those socialist dissidents who were identifiable as belonging to the right wing of pre-1914 German Social Democracy were essentially cut of the one cloth, the differences between such heterodoxies being insignificant by comparison with the chasm which reputedly divided them all from the centre-orthodoxy or the radical left. This assumption is a grossly misleading oversimplification. It is nevertheless a working hypothesis which is still to be found in a great deal of what is written on pre-1914 German labour history. Its longevity may be attributable, in part, to intellectual sloth, but one suspects that it is equally the product of the ideological blinkers which distort the vision of so many labour historians, for the majority of those who write on labour history undoubtedly see themselves as committed revolutionaries, or at least feel they ought to be something of the sort. Although most realise that insurrection is a fantasy and that the ballot box will not bring the fundamental and irreversible social transformation they desire, many focus their attention on the radical worker or, failing that, on radical consciousness. They are simply uninterested in the plodding right. Such historians might do well to recall the words of Edmund Burke:

> Because half a dozen grasshoppers under a fern make the field ring with their importunate chink, whilst thousands of great cattle, reposed beneath the shadow of the . . . oak, chew the cud and are silent, pray do not imagine that those who make the noise are the only inhabitants of the field; that, of course, they are many in number; or that, after all, they are other than the little, shrivelled meagre, hopping, though loud and

troublesome, insects of the hour. (Burke, *Reflections on the Revolution in France*, 1790)

In the second place, there has been very little serious study of German socialist foreign policy views in the pre-1914 era. Virtually all we have on the subject is a few digressions in biographical work and a great many studies which have treated particular aspects of the problem, such as nationalism, the colonial question, the imperialism debate and the disarmament controversy. Even work of this kind typically proceeds from the assumption of the 'primacy of domestic politics', as if foreign policy issues were not among the major preoccupations of prewar German Social Democracy. Yet it is well known that in all sections of the German Social Democratic Party (SPD) there were important exceptions to this rule. In the party centre (August Bebel, Karl Kautsky and Georg Ledebour), on the revolutionary left (Rosa Luxemburg, Karl Liebknecht, Paul Lensch and Anton Pannekoek) and among the so-called revisionists there were a great many informed and concerned individuals who not only expressed views on particular foreign policy issues but also attempted to articulate a coherent socialist foreign policy alternative. A case in point is Eduard Bernstein, the 'father' of theoretical revisionism. Until the 1970s the best Bernstein studies were all the work of non-Germans. It is less than a decade since the Germans themselves began to rediscover Bernstein, but then almost exclusively in terms of his 'challenge to Marx'. The most thorough of these rediscoveries, a brilliant if excessively schematic attempt by Thomas Meyer (1977) to present Bernstein as the formulator of a coherent and feasible model of democratic socialist transformation, remains in the familiar mould: of some 400 pages, only 3 are devoted to a 'note' on Bernstein's attitude towards imperialism. The arch-heretic's thirteen years of exile in London, his notorious Anglophilia, his activity in the Reichstag, where he made foreign affairs one of his two chosen areas of specialisation, his prodigious publications on problems of international relations, his wartime social pacifism and his subsequent stand on the 'war guilt' question are as ignored by Meyer as they have always been. Yet such factors cry out for a re-examination of Bernstein as something more than a pioneer of democratic socialism. Indeed, they suggest that much of the conventional wisdom on his attempt to update the social and political thought of Karl Marx may well be founded on unduly narrow and misleading premises. More serious still, in my view, is the fact that Bernstein is still used as a synonym for revisionism when, in reality, he was never more than a symbol, and certainly not at any stage the 'leader' of the revisionist or reformist faction.

The person who aspired to this role and came nearest to realising his ambition was not Bernstein but Joseph Bloch, editor of the *Sozialistische Monatshefte*. Bloch and his journal have been even more seriously misrepresented and more thoroughly neglected than Bernstein. Although contemporaries recognised the importance of the *Monatshefte* and its editor, Bloch and his periodical are now all but totally ignored. On the rare occasions when the journal is mentioned, it is, as often as not, misjudged badly: J. P. Nettl has called it 'Bernstein's paper' (1966, Vol. 1, p. 164); Helmut Hirsch refers to it as 'a theoretical organ close to the revisionist position' (Introduction, Bernstein,

1976, p. 29); Robert S. Wistrich also considers it a 'theoretical review' (1982, p. 165), although it contained far more articles by trade unionists and other *Praktiker* than by reformist or revisionist intellectuals; Alex Hall dismisses it as 'far from socialist' (1977, p. 206, n. 73); and Susanne Miller describes Bloch and his 'continental Europe' crusaders as having presented their imperialist programme only 'during the war' (1974, p. 229). Hardly more helpful are the well-meaning but misguided apologetics which have been presented by Joseph Bloch's friends and family (for example, Siemsen, 1956; C. Bloch, 1974 and 1977). The real Joseph Bloch and the real significance of the *Sozialistische Monatshefte* have slipped almost entirely beyond the historian's grasp. One of the purposes of this study is to show that Bloch was a very different kind of revisionist from Bernstein, that he was no less deeply concerned with foreign policy issues, although not in a way shared by Bernstein, and that in the last decade before the First World War his practical political influence far exceeded that of Bernstein or any other revisionist.

My interest in these men stems not from a penchant for retrospective muck-raking but is prompted by the view that men do have ideas and that they do, at times, attempt to act on the basis of these. If I have thus condemned myself as a methodological troglodyte, there is more to follow: I would also insist that social movements do tend to produce leaders and that leaders are as likely to lead as followers are to follow. At the very least, I must concur with Richard Evans that 'working-class experience . . . does not, and cannot, remain unaffected by the ideology and politics of the labour movement itself' (Evans, ed., 1982, p. 33). I emphatically resist the claim, implicit – in some instances, all too explicit – in much recent writing on German labour history, that the history of socialist politics should be written exclusively from 'the bottom upwards', as if the ideas of socialist leaders can be inferred from the study of working-class behaviour, values and ideas or, if they cannot, are somehow of no consequence and of mere antiquarian interest. While there has been, in the past, too much attention focused on high politics to the exclusion of the masses, and there has been too much history written from the top down, as though the masses were simply 'also present' as decorative props, some social historians seem to want to throw out the baby with the bathwater. The history of ideas is a legitimate and useful branch of historical inquiry and far more than mere self-indulgence on the part of curious intellectuals. The study of ideas, prominent individuals and organisations on their own terms – rather than as appendages of, or irrelevant vehicles travelling alongside, the all-important masses – can be as rewarding in its results as the work of the quantifiers and the social scientists, who are as prone to getting bogged down in sterile methodological squabbles as they are productive of sorcery, or just plain wrong.[2] Any suggestion that German nationalism may be explained satisfactorily without reference to intellectuals is patently absurd, as Geoff Eley readily concedes:

In this . . . sense – the formation of nationalist ideology – the German nation was conceived in the minds of intellectuals and realized in a political movement . . . The contradiction between state and civil society ran through the centre of the national question in Germany. By contrast with the 'core' states of Western Europe, nationalities East of the Rhine lacked the advantage of an early acquired statehood. Of necessity the real labour of constituting the 'nation' had to be conducted by private rather than public bodies, by individual intellectuals and voluntary associations rather than governments . . . Moreover, once political independence has been attained, . . . almost imperceptibly nationalism loses its character as a sectional creed articulating the aspirations of liberal and other tendencies within the bourgeoisie, and passes into the common heritage of a political culture . . . The process of national integration simultaneously, gradually, and subtly transforms the content of the national idea, universalizing its legitimacy, while endowing it with a vital plasticity. Thus, though drives for cultural uniformity within nations . . . may be vigorously state-directed, they are also subject to private initiative and political contestation, involving protracted struggles for leadership and control. (Eley, 1982, pp. 287–8)

Having said this, I would nevertheless suggest that the most fruitful means of getting at the nature and significance of revisionist foreign policy thinking is to approach the problem in the wider context of society, party and faction. State and society in Wilhelmine Germany, as well as the traditions of the labour movement, presented Wilhelmine Social Democrats with a number of choices – between integration and self-isolation, between reform and revolution – which previous generations of German socialists had not been obliged to confront with anything like the same sense of urgency. Those socialists who still felt constrained by the pressures of factory and state generally opted for the revolutionary immobilism of the party centre or for the radical activism of the emerging left, although, of course, not all radicals and militants took their cue 'from above'. But after 1890 a growing number of German socialists were favourably impressed by the possibilities of working-class integration into the political nation. These normally opted for the reformist tactic and are here designated revisionists, following the most widely accepted practice of the time. Whatever the choice, socialist tactics and socialist assessments of the surrounding societal terrain helped to condition Social Democratic attitudes towards foreign policy problems, but the reverse also applied. Yet factional labels have to be read with a measure of scepticism, for the most significant line of demarcation within this, the most heavily ideologised of labour movements within the Second International, remained that between intellectuals and the rest. Unless the former, whatever their factional allegiance, succeeded in presenting their programmes as reflecting the needs and aspirations of the socialist rank and file, they were unlikely to retain whatever hold they had acquired on the bureaucratic hierarchy of the movement or on the masses whom the hierarchy usually managed. Since Bloch and the *Sozialistische Monatshefte* group did this more effectively than Bernstein, the present book centres primarily on Bloch and his colleagues and only secondarily on the 'high priest of revisionism'. Although the revisionist foreign policy position which came closest to speaking for revisionism as a faction or movement was that of Bloch, not Bernstein, and probably enjoyed greater influence and support among the socialist rank and file than any other standpoint, it is none the less important to bear in mind that differences over the whither and how questions facing the Wilhelmine labour movement, together with fundamental disagreements on matters of principle, produced great variety in revisionist foreign policy views. Some effort will be made to do justice to this variety, although limitations of space necessitate concentration on the two major revisionist positions. While leaving open the question of the 'primacy of domestic politics', I have related foreign policy considerations to domestic political concerns wherever such a nexus seemed conducive to the clarification of revisionist foreign policy views and their impact on the Wilhelmine labour movement.

How to reduce such a study to manageable proportions has presented certain difficulties. Much has had to be compressed and much omitted. Worthy of a study in itself, for example, is the foreign policy position of South German reformism which, eluding the clutches of both Bloch and Bernstein, constituted a powerful independent force, virtually a faction in itself, no later than 1909. Specifically working-class foreign policy attitudes might also repay closer scrutiny, although lack of evidence is here a real obstacle. In fact, the paucity of archival sources has raised difficulties throughout this book. The private papers of Ludwig Frank, for example, turned out to consist of a mere handful of love letters containing only a few observations comparing Marx and Lassalle as readable theoreticians. Most of the revisionists of importance to this book (Leo Arons, Karl Leuthner, Max Schippel, Richard Calwer and Gerhard Hildebrand) left no known literary estates. Where private papers do exist, as in the case of Bloch, they are often fragmentary and incomplete. My endeavours to remedy such deficiencies have not always met with the whole-hearted co-operation of those on whom the historian is heavily dependent. The East Germans allowed me to see nothing of importance, while doing their utmost to tap my limited financial resources to ease the foreign-exchange problem of the 'German workers' and peasants' state'. Even in the Federal Republic, the foreigner working on German history is often greeted with little better than bemused contempt, occasionally with active obstruction. Members of the German historical *Zunft* (guild, for such a closed-shop mentality still prevails, especially in Austria) do not like to be questioned, much less corrected, by inquisitive foreigners, but then German historians by no means possess a monopoly on nationalist bias. In deference to such limitations, but also out of regard for my subject-matter, I have based this book very largely on the published work of my principal *dramatis personae*. As much of what I have to say flies in the face of received opinion (for example, the persistent refusal of most German historians to contemplate Bernstein in any but his German context, and the standard white-wash that Bloch and his spokesmen ventilated their nationalist and imperialist views only under the exceptional circumstances of the First World War), I have felt obliged to document my case more extensively than some readers might wish. If such argument from 'mere fact' invites charges of 'dense empiricism' and 'argument by citation' – according to David Blackbourn, 'a literal-minded (and conservative) way of addressing one's sources' (*Social History*, vol. 8, 1983, p. 119) – it is, in my view, a less objectionable failing than the modish theatrical rodomontade now so frequently perpetrated in the guise of 'Model Depiction, Terminological

Adaptation, Generalization Rush, Tangential Assertion, Dialectical Leap and Empirical Stretch' (Geoffrey Marshall, 'The containers and the contained', *Times Literary Supplement*, 28 January 1983, p. 90).

Preface: Notes

1   I prefer the German term, *Praktiker*, to its English translations, the most popular being 'pragmatist' and 'practicist', since no English equivalent really does justice to this term. The *Praktiker* were those socialists – almost all of them risen from the factory floor – whose prime concern lay with advancing the practical, ameliorative reform work of the labour movement and whose power base tended to be with the trade unions and the co-operatives, although many also branched into journalism and parliamentary work. Some were militant and a few were quite radical, but the overwhelming majority became party and trade union bureaucrats of the kind described by Günther Roth and others. As a species, they were generally reformist in ideology and conservative in function.

2   The quantifiers almost invariably allow their work to degenerate into positivism in new bottles, while the sociologically oriented practitioners of the new social history repeatedly make exaggerated claims on their own behalf and rarely turn their critical gaze on the limitations of their own methodology. For instance, Dick Geary's *European Labour Protest 1848–1939* (1981), for all its protestations of novelty, is neither based on original research nor a significant departure from the traditional emphasis on party, trade unions and leadership. Unable to agree among themselves on anything other than the error of all approaches but their own – thus Geary's claim that 'any explanation of working-class consciousness in terms of ideological and organisational factors is open to question' (1982, p. 223) – the devotees of *Alltagsgeschichte* (the history of everyday life) and social history in general tend to divorce social history from politics or, worse still, to generalise their political history from such phenomena as working-class experience of work and leisure, of family and factory life, or from occupational and regional peculiarities, in a manner which dismisses formal institutions and ideologies as external inputs and of *no* importance in the labour movement. While this bias is perhaps understandable in British labour historians, whose past contains few outstanding personalities and very little ideology, it is inappropriate when applied to the German context, where heroes and ideologies abounded.

PART ONE

The SPD and the Imperialism Debate

We must realise that at this point in time it is none of our business to speak of an ethereal concept of Weltpolitik. *It is not my object to enter into theoretical discussions of which* Weltpolitik *Social Democracy is called upon to promote. I think we can postpone the task until Social Democracy is in possession of political power and able to practise Social Democratic* Weltpolitik.

(Paul Singer, Mainz party congress, 1900)

Imperialism and imperialism are two quite different things.

(Eduard Bernstein, 1900)

In combating the imperialist plague in bourgeois society, we are unfortunately obliged to take into account that a few people in our own ranks are already infected by it. We have seen, in a publication distributed here, the Sozialistiche Monatshefte, *Comrade Bernstein holding a brief for this imperialist colonial policy . . . I believe it is no laughing matter that we are compelled actually to counteract within our ranks half-and-half supporters of such imperialism.*

(Georg Ledebour, Mainz party congress, 1900)

The discussion of questions of international politics is a completely novel matter for us German Social Democrats. We have no political tradition in foreign policy questions . . . Only in the last decade, and more especially over the last half-decade, has the grave pressure and constraint of the real world compelled the party, in the face of imminent conflict among the nations, to adopt a responsible position and thus to proceed from declamation to politics.

(Max Maurenbrecher, 1909)

The reply of the proletariat to the economic policy of finance capital, imperialism, can not be free trade, can only be socialism.

(Rudolf Hilferding, 1910)

1

Factional Alignments, Ideology and the Imperialism Debate in pre-1914 German Social Democracy

I have not the slightest intention of confuting Bernstein. Perhaps I cannot. In any case, I will not. I simply do not have the time to engage in theoretical hair-splitting.

(*Adolf Hoffmann, 1901*)

As far as I am concerned, I certainly have never described myself either as a Bernsteinian or as a Bebelite, nor even called myself a Marxist. I have no inclination or talent for such 'isms'. For me it is quite sufficient that I am a Social Democrat.

(*Georg von Vollmar, 1903*)

We are a party of class struggle and not of 'historical laws'.

(*Rosa Luxemburg, 1905*)

Germany is the only country in the world where the pharmacist cannot even fill a prescription without thinking about the connection of his activity with the fundament of the universe

(*Friedrich Albert Lange, 1866*)

When the Independent Social Democratic Party (USPD) was founded in April 1917, it appeared as a *mélange* of ultra-left Spartacists, former spokesmen of the party centre and centre-left, and a handful of renegade revisionists. Apart from their opposition to the war, they seemed to have little in common other than the fact that the new party attracted virtually all the leading theorists and intellectuals of prewar German Social Democracy. At first glance the wartime realignment on the extreme right wing of the German Social Democratic Party (SPD) was no less incongruous, comprising as it did not only erstwhile second-string revisionists but, more surprisingly, a number of ranking mavericks from the radical left. In the meantime, the leadership of the rump SPD seemed to have fallen entirely into the hands of revisionists or party practitioners who had previously been regarded as dupes or minions of the right. How had it come to this? Historians of the German labour movement have long recognised that these developments had their origins both in what Carl Schorske called 'the hammer blows of war' and in the cat's-cradle of prewar factional dispute going back to 1905 at least (1972, p. vii).

This fateful and seemingly paradoxical metamorphosis of the party that had once been the backbone of the Second International and a model to socialists the world over arose at least partly out of the maelstrom of fierce intra-party debate over domestic politics. But in the last years of peace foreign policy issues also became a significant determinant of factional allegiance, cutting across and blurring previously established distinctions between centre, left and right. By the Moroccan crisis of 1911, German Social Democrats of all factions had come to contemplate imperialism, in particular, as one of the most important problems darkening the political horizon. Those who had not already done so now felt compelled to confront the issue theoretically and within the framework of party tactics and organisation. Among the protagonists in this debate were Karl Kautsky and Rosa Luxemburg, both prominent theorists in their own right and spokesmen of the centre and left respectively. Their views, considered in the context of party faction, provide an illuminating prologue to the imperialism debate which rent the revisionist faction while demonstrating the fluid state of factional alignments within prewar German Social Democracy at large.

Factional Alignments: An Uneasy Triangle

The situation within the German Social Democratic Party on the eve of the First World War marked a sharp separation between appearance and reality. To outward appearances a monolithic juggernaut, the German party was in fact beset by serious fissiparous tendencies. A key element in the ideological and factional make-up of the party was the orthodox Marxist centre espousing an ideology which was, in essence, 'a synthesis of Enlightenment progressivism and Social Darwinism' that 'comforted itself with the label "Marxism" ' (Lösche, 1969, p. 523). Its sonorous trumpeting of revolutionary rhetoric masked a complete lack of revolutionary strategy coupled with a fierce organisational patriotism. The centre was faced with two 'revisionist' challenges: the revisionist right wanted theory brought into line with the realities of the party's reformist practice; the nascent left demanded that party practice be made to conform with the professed revolutionary ideology. The centrist faction responded defensively by adopting a precarious and ramshackle consensus policy. *Vis-à-vis* the hated bourgeois state, the position of the party centre in 1914 was that of revolutionary *attentisme* (wait and see). In intra-party affairs it busied itself with an organisational fetishism that enabled internal differences to be ignored indefinitely rather than resolved.

At this time the radical left was hardly to be taken seriously. With virtually no press of its own, remote from the trade unions and mass organisations, its parliamentary representation minuscule, lacking even ideological consensus, its spokesmen being for the most part querulous intellectuals who owed their limited prominence more to the positions they held within the party machine than to the mass appeal of their views, the radical left scarcely deserved to be called a faction at all (Fricke, 1962, pp. 58–64, 108 ff., 237–50; Laschitza and Schumacher, 1965, p. 33; Groh, 1973, p. 496). Until 1911 this very powerlessness rendered it relatively 'safe', as did the fact that in matters of theory, if not of tactics, it generally shared with the orthodox centre a common loathing of the revisionist right and a mutually intelligible ideological patois (Petit, 1969,

p. 337; Groh, 1973, pp. 165–6). But the left ceased to be a *quantité négligeable* only when it was joined by the centre-left in the struggle to shake the party centre out of its tactical torpor and to compel general acceptance of the radical doctrine of mass action (Schorske, 1972, pp. 276–84).[1]

Far more serious was the threat from the right. Since Georg von Vollmar's El Dorado speeches in 1891, and more so following publication of Bernstein's 'bible of revisionism' in 1899,[2] the 'Marxist centre' was subjected to sustained and embarrassing theoretical pressure from the right. The innumerable 'Bernstein debates' notwithstanding (culminating in the resounding defeat of revisionism at Dresden in 1903), revisionism both survived and prospered as an ideological alternative to the official party line. It did so not because it was better organised than the left and the centre or because it evolved a common programme, which it never acquired, but principally because it found in the revisionist press (Joseph Bloch's *Sozialistische Monatshefte*, Bernstein's *Dokumente des Sozialismus* and *Neues Montagsblatt*, and Heinrich Braun's *Neue Gesellschaft*) a haven from party discipline and an ideological sanctuary. To a considerable extent the independence enjoyed by these publications, and by the *Monatshefte* in particular, enabled revisionism to affect an Olympian detachment from party debate and to elaborate its own theoretical position with little regard to the claims and counter-claims advanced by centrist and radical opponents. After 1905, when the party began to build up a centralised bureaucracy (conceived originally as a weapon against the right), the revisionist challenge quickly acquired solid organisational roots as well. By the outbreak of the First World War, the revisionists had become powerfully entrenched in the trade union and co-operative hierarchies, in the party press, among party functionaries, in the Reichstag party caucus or *Fraktion* and in other socialist parliamentary bodies. The dual ideological-organisational onslaught of the right triumphed ultimately because the revisionists were most nearly attuned to the needs and aspirations of the party rank and file. By 1914 diligent and capable party practitioners like Friedrich Ebert and Gustav Noske emerged as the legitimate spokesmen of the whole party because they sprang from the people, retained close contact with the grass roots, and instinctively shared their attitudes and outlook. To a large extent, it is true to say that 'reformism, gradualism and a "non-political" trade-union movement were all . . . the results of the need "to meet effectively the challenge of the social and industrial conditions" ' confronting ordinary German workers in an age of exceptionally rapid economic modernisation (Crew, 1979, p. 217; cf. Hickey, 1978, pp. 215–40).

In 1914, with the revisionist right occupying key positions and wielding enormous influence within Social Democracy as a whole, the party centre no longer dared to move openly to squash it. Since the revisionists, with few exceptions, preferred to work unobtrusively in the wings and eschewed theoretical debate after the Dresden fiasco, the 'Marxist centre' was content to let well-enough alone. In any event, the centre found its do-nothing tactic and its authority under heavy attack from the radical left after 1910. This encouraged the centrists to seek allies in the right and, in self-defence, to narrow the ideological chasm that had formerly separated right and centre. The upshot was a paradoxical situation in which orthodox paragons like Kautsky and

Bebel strutted centre-stage, as they had always done, while revisionist mummers like Eduard David, Albert Südekum, Philipp Scheidemann, Ebert and Noske increasingly, yet unobtrusively, assumed total responsibility for the scenario.[3]

Such, in brief, was the factional line-up within Wilhelmine Social Democracy. A far cry from the monolith it pretended to be, the German party more closely resembled a rickety triangle. Two of its sides were usually in uneasy alliance against the third. In 1900 the faction most under pressure from within the party had been the revisionist right wing. By 1914 it was the radical left.

Party Marxism and Radicalism: The Irrelevance of Theory

Labour Leadership and Revolutionary Attentisme

It is debatable whether German Social Democracy in 1914 was still, or ever had been, a truly Marxist party. There can be no doubt that until the adoption of the Erfurt Programme in 1891 the SPD had not been Marxist in any meaningful sense. Throughout the period of the anti-socialist law (1878–90) the party had been exposed to a variety of influences, including those of Lassalle, Dühring, Schäffle, Rodbertus, F. A. Lange, Höchberg and the followers of Darwin. It was only after 1878 when Engels's *Anti-Dühring* appeared that Bebel, Kautsky and Bernstein, as the principal proponents and popularisers of Marxism within the party, began to acquire a solid grasp of Marxist theory (Gustafsson, 1972, pp. 29–30; H.-J. Steinberg, 1972, pp. 23, 43). Thereafter, in competition with state and ethical socialism, and supported by Engels and rank-and-file radicalism, the Marxist coterie gradually overcame the party's right wing and the suspect Marxism of the *Gebildeten* (intellectuals) to establish their own theoretical position as the dominant and official party ideology.

At no stage in the following one-and-a-half decades did the now official ideology succeed in entirely supplanting its competitors. Lassalleanism survived, as did state and ethical socialism, and theoretically indifferent *Praktiker* (practitioners) like Ignaz Auer and Karl Grillenberger continued to occupy important positions within the party. Darwinism, in particular, remained a potent force in party theory. In part this was due to Engels's extremely influential *Anti-Dühring*, which went through numerous editions and, together with Bebel's *Die Frau und der Sozialismus* (published in English as *Woman under Socialism*) and Kautsky's theoretical works (*Karl Marx' ökonomische Lehren* [Marx's Economic Teachings] and his commentary on the Erfurt Programme), remained among the principal vehicles for the dissemination of Marxist thought in pre-1914 German Social Democracy. In his rebuttal of Dühring, Engels applied the dialectic as a universal law of nature and of history, thereby facilitating a Darwinist interpretation of Marxism. Kautsky, too, had been strongly influenced by positivistic and Darwinist tendencies long before he converted to Marxism, which he initially adopted in the early 1880s only as a 'more refined' and 'modified' prop to his Darwinism. Although he ceased to be a Darwinist in 1890, evolutionary theory continued to influence his thinking in the sense that he never succeeded in divorcing social from natural evolution (Steenson, 1978, pp. 18, 24–9, 65, 237; Salvadori, 1979, pp. 23–4). Indeed, all tendencies within the party applied the principle of evolution, in varying ways, as a vindication of their own policy and tactical views. Bebel so used it, as did Anton Pannekoek of the party left. Among the revisionists, Eduard Bernstein, Edmund Fischer, Wilhelm Kolb, Albert Südekum and, above all, Ludwig Woltmann made frequent appeal to Darwinism. This was all the more possible because few of the party's leading theoreticians had any understanding of Hegel and the dialectic (Irrlitz, 1966, pp. 49–50, 56–9; H.-J. Steinberg, 1972, pp. 43–4, 48, 50, 53–60).

Within party-affiliated organisations such as the trade union and co-operative movements there is even less reason to suppose that Marxism was either understood or popular. After 1890 the socialist or Free Trade Unions were organised through the General Commission under Carl Legien. This organisation accounted for the vast majority of all union-organised labour, although its membership represented only a small proportion of the work-force.[4] In numbers, organisation, wealth and power the trade unions quickly became a force to be reckoned with. From a total membership only slightly in excess of 200,000 in 1890, the trade unions succeeded in organising $2\frac{1}{2}$ million workers by 1914. At this time the SPD had barely a million members and its coffers were in much poorer shape than those of the union movement. During the 1890s the party regarded its trade union wing as a valuable 'recruiting school' for the movement whose supreme authority remained the party *Vorstand* (executive). At Mannheim in September 1906 these roles were reversed. The trade union movement won recognition of its independence and autonomy and gained a virtual power of veto over the party in the all-important question of the political mass strike (Langerhans, 1957, p. 187; Hermes, 1979, p. 44; Bieber, 1981, Vol. 1, p. 48).[5]

Ideologically, the trade unions professed to be neutral, a position which they defended as a tactical necessity if they were to recruit new members. Since trade union effectiveness depended on membership and organisation, they had a point. In fact, the unions were thoroughly reformist from the beginning. They saw their task as being unique and quite distinct from that of the party:

> The difference between the political activity carried on by the workers' party and the tasks of the unions rests on the fact that the former seeks to transform the organisation of existing society while the efforts of the latter, being circumscribed by law, are anchored in present-day bourgeois society. (Appeal to union members, 1891, cit. Grebing, 1970, p. 100)[6]

The primary concern of union leaders like Carl Legien was not with the realisation of socialism as expounded by Marx, Lassalle or any other theorist but with improving the lot of the workers in existing society and with sharpening the tools appropriate to this task. They had no intention of blunting these tools for the sake of what they regarded as nebulous enterprises such as the political mass strike.

What the party leaders professed in the name of Marxism was, in effect, a combination of fatalism and formal radicalism, what Dieter Groh refers to as 'revolutionary *attentisme*'. The development of capitalist society was viewed as a natural process which must culminate in the collapse of that society, at which point the organised proletariat had merely to take up the reins of power in order to implement socialism. Revolution was equated with the collapse of capitalist society, and the task of the party in the meantime was simply to organise the proletariat, which it endeavoured to do primarily by pitting its might against the bourgeois parties in the vote-catching exercises of the politically meaningless Reichstag elections. Until the great day of the socialist *Machtübernahme* or seizure of power, the Marxist orthodoxy was careful to avoid all action which might provoke what it feared above all else – a conservative coup designed to destroy the laboriously constructed socialist organisations. In practice, therefore, the SPD gradually acquired the character of yet another legal mass party; in reality it became a pressure group not much different from the non-socialist parties in Imperial Germany.

What seemed to set Social Democracy apart was its paradoxical adherence to a formal radicalism, to a revolutionary ideology which ostentatiously refused to have any truck with bourgeois society except on the day of its interment. This self-imposed isolation from society meant, on the one hand, that attention was focused constantly and primarily on the *Endziel*, the ultimate objective of socialism. A utopian concentration on the *Zukunftsstaat* (future socialist state) was combined with a rejection or devaluation of all reform work. The prospect of a peaceful and gradual transition to socialism was ridiculed as wishful thinking, and suggestions of possible compromise with bourgeois parties or governments were denounced as class treason. On the other hand, the self-imposed pariah status was deemed necessary to the maintenance of proletarian class consciousness.

It was not until 1910, in the context of the mass-strike debate, that the position of the Marxist orthodoxy was clearly revealed for what it was – a strategically bankrupt policy of immobilism. In the course of this debate, which first flared up in the wake of the 1905 Russian Revolution and then erupted in full fury in the campaign against the Prussian three-class suffrage, Rosa Luxemburg compelled Kautsky, as the spokesman of the party *Vorstand*, to articulate for the first time the position of what has become known as 'centrism'. Essentially this was not a Marxist position at all, however much it owed formally to Marxist categories. Centrism was, at bottom, neither more nor less than a defensive ideology of 'those who believed that society had irrevocably cast them out and that Socialist isolation was mainly the product of Government policies and attitudes' (Nettl, 1965, p. 70).

Rosa Luxemburg savagely attacked the party leadership for its preoccupation with vote-gathering parliamentary work and its organisational fetishism. To her mind, such activities had no legitimacy except as weapons in the class struggle. She urged on the party, as an invaluable adjunct to these weapons, the adoption of the political mass strike. In reply, Kautsky and the party *Vorstand*, supported by the trade union hierarchy, tried in vain to prevent debate on the possibilities of a practical application of the mass strike and to contain all such discussion at an abstract theoretical level. The centrists went no further than to admit, in principle, the validity of the mass strike as an ultimate weapon for use in defence of the labour movement and its organisations in unpredictable and unspecified crisis situations. For the centrists could not conceive of the mass strike as being other than synonymous with the revolution itself. They could not countenance its use as a weapon in the class struggle for the simple reason that in their eyes the class struggle had been supplanted by the mechanically and undialectically conceived laws of capitalist economic development. What the centrists offered in place of the mass strike as class struggle was the *Ermattungsstrategie* or strategy of attrition. Capitalist society was to be harried to its ineluctable and immanently determined doom by the continued piling-up of ever greater socialist electoral successes and an ever expanding SPD presence in the Reichstag. In short, for the party centre nothing had changed since 1890.

In Germany the extent to which the position of the pre-1914 centre-orthodoxy was fundamentally Marxist or a perversion of Marxism has been hotly debated between Social Democrats and Communists ever since (Irrlitz, 1966, pp. 55–6; Grunenberg, ed., 1970, pp. 5–6). Social Democrats have argued that the SPD had never been a truly Marxist revolutionary party. On this view, party ideology was not based on the theoretical work of Marx himself but was rather an inadequate interpretation of Marx at the hands of Kautsky and even Engels, who manipulated theory as an integrative ideology, as a force for welding together the increasingly differentiated components of the Wilhelmine labour movement (Matthias, 1957, pp. 151–97). Communist historiography has always insisted on the existence of an organic nexus between Marxism and the German labour movement, explaining the temporary rupture which occurred in August 1914 as the product of a great betrayal from within. The villain in the piece was opportunism in the form of revisionism à la Bernstein and the insidious centrism or crypto-revisionism of the 'renegade Kautsky' (Klein, 1976, pp. 268–77).

In one sense this debate is irrelevant, for Marx himself is, and always has been, notoriously amenable to interpretation. Leaving aside the fact that some of Marx's early and most important writings were quite unknown at the time, we are still confronted with the problem of a profound ambivalence in Marx's own theory of emancipation. In the entire Marxist *œuvre* there coexisted two distinct and irreconcilable models of emancipation. One derived from philosophy and postulated the unity of the individual and society, which was to become social reality through practical action. Overlaying this, and more characteristic of the mature Marx although Hegelian in origin, was a view of emancipation based on the logic of the objective historical process. Whereas the former model was inherently activist and voluntarist, the latter was implicitly quietistic. This dichotomy existed in Marx's thought from the beginning and was never resolved by him. It cannot be explained away by reference to the dialectic or by identifying as the 'real' Marx either the young Marx or the mature Marx.

In their understanding of Marx the epigones in German Social Democracy faithfully duplicated this dichotomy. The problem was less that the SPD leadership read too much or too little into Marx than that they took too literal a view of Marx's objectivism. In fact, the interpretation of socialism among all factions in the Wilhelmine labour movement was closely bound up with the objectivist position. This was especially true in the case of those problem areas which collectively comprised the revolutionary *attentisme* of the centre-orthodoxy, namely the belief in a natural, inevitable and even 'mathematically calculable' development towards socialism; the contemplation of the introduction of socialism in terms of the collapse theory as the mere 'bursting of an integument' rather than in terms of a positive strategy for socialist transformation; the application of the concept of revolution; the assessment of the value of reforms; the anticipation of declining social complexity; and the expectation that the proletariat was already capable of, and prepared for, self-management in a socialist society. Thus the excessively narrow and abstract interpretation of economic determinism which, above all else, characterised the philosophical position of the centre-orthodoxy in prewar German Social Democracy offers a partial answer to the question of the extent to which the party orthodoxy was, or was not, Marxist: it was Marxist in so far as it accurately reflected a basic anomaly in the original model.

On the other hand, it must be emphasised that the party Marxism of the centre-orthodoxy had not only to compete with external influences (Lassalleanism, state and ethical socialism, positivism and Darwinism) and to meet a succession of challenges thrown up by rival interpretations of Marxism (the radical *Jungen* in 1890, the revisionists at the turn of the century and the nascent radical left after 1905); it had also to perform certain specific social and political functions. Moreover, if it reached the masses at all, it did so only through the medium of a small number of personalities actively engaged in its propagation. The actual content of the official 'party Marxism' was therefore subject to a great variety of influences among which the thought of the master was not necessarily the first consideration or even the prime mover.

Under the anti-socialist law the principal exponents of Marxism within the SPD had been Engels, Kautsky, Bebel, Bernstein and Bruno Schönlank. By 1900 death and apostasy had narrowed the field to Kautsky and Bebel, with occasional support from tiros like Gustav Eckstein, Heinrich Cunow and Rudolf Hilferding. By 1910, when 'centrism' began to emerge as a clearly identifiable, concrete ideological and political position, Karl Kautsky was so obviously its preceptor that the term 'Kautskyanism' has gained currency as a synonym for the centre-orthodox position after that date.[7]

It is perfectly correct, as numerous scholars have maintained (Nettl, 1965, pp. 70–1; Irrlitz, 1966, pp. 47–8; Ratz, 1967, pp. 432–77; Gottschalch *et al.*, 1969, pp. 187–90; Schorske, 1972, pp. 186–7, 196; Groh, 1973, p. 60), that it is necessary to distinguish between the position of the party *Vorstand* and that of Kautsky. The pseudo-revolutionary Marxism of the former had degenerated well before 1910 into an integrative ideology, a mere theoretical prop to the official party tactic which, too, could only be comprehended as an integrative tactic. Kautsky, on the other hand, did not look on Marxism, as he understood it, as an integrative ideology. His quarrel with Bernstein, for instance, was not that he viewed his old friend's revisionist efforts as a disruptive and divisive factor within the party but arose rather out of the conviction that Bernstein had abandoned the materialist view of history, which for Kautsky was an article of faith (H.-J. Steinberg, 1972, pp. 76–7). Moreover, in several important respects Kautsky's views differed from those of the official ideology. First, the party's ideological aloofness from the burgeoisie was never shared by Kautsky, either privately or publicly. Secondly, in his attitude towards revolution, which was never a static one, he was in fact closer to Bernstein than to the party leadership. Kautsky acknowledged the need for violent revolution in Germany to overthrow the existing order and establish a bourgeois parliamentary democracy as the pre-condition for the realisation of socialism. Although he differed from Bernstein in that he saw no peaceful road to parliamentary democracy, he agreed with Bernstein that in this struggle Social Democracy would have to play the role of bourgeois democracy since the German bourgeoisie was too weak to accomplish what its counterparts in England and France had long ago won for themselves. One final point worth noting is Kautsky's increasing isolation within the party from the late 1890s onwards: Schönlank had parted company with him in 1894; he was under fire from all the leading thinkers in the party (Bernstein, Heinrich Braun, Franz Mehring and Rosa Luxemburg); the reformists and trade union leaders had no time for him and boycotted the *Neue Zeit*; and the party *Vorstand* was uninterested in Kautsky's version of Marxism and professed instead a barely concealed evolutionist ideology based on tacit acceptance of the status quo (H.-J. Steinberg, 1972, pp. 79–81, 85–6). After 1905 his relations with Bebel also cooled markedly, and it was not until 1910, when he took up the cudgels on behalf of centrism, that Kautsky was restored to grace as 'the guardian of the ideological tradition of the party' (Groh, 1973, p. 157).

And yet, by virtue of his position as editor of the party's theoretical organ and a popular and prolific author of countless Marxist primers, Kautsky was 'the unchallenged party theoretician' (Grunenberg, ed., 1970, p. 45). He reflected the implicit ideology of the party leadership, if not faithfully then certainly more coherently, volubly and abundantly than did any other party theoretician. More significantly, he was generally regarded as *the* interpreter of Marx. Kautsky's popular exposition of Marx's economic theories, for instance, was so widely accepted as the valid account of Marx's theory that many SPD librarians catalogued it under the name of Marx (H.-J. Steinberg, 1972, p. 136, n. 25).

If Kautsky was the chief cicerone to the revolutionary *attentisme* of the party leadership, Bebel was unquestionably its political champion and practitioner *par excellence*. In the words of J. P. Nettl, 'the personality of August Bebel . . . from 1875 onwards dominated the policy and spirit of the SPD' (Nettl, 1966, Vol. 1, p. 120).[8] Far more than Kautsky, Bebel therefore deserves to be held personally responsible for the triumph of centrism within the party on the eve of the First World War. In every sense a fatalist, Bebel was much more strongly influenced by Darwinism, which he considered to be 'in perfect harmony' with socialism (Bebel, 1904, p. 204).[9] As 'the most zealous advocate' of the concept of revolution as an inevitable and predictable outcome of linear, evolutionary development which Social Democracy was powerless to accelerate or otherwise modify (H.-J. Steinberg, 1972, p. 61), Bebel repeatedly told his many audiences, socialist and non-socialist alike, that the party had merely to persist in its 'tried and tested' parliamentary tactic for power, and the millennium, to fall into its lap. In the meantime, nothing precipitate must be done to provoke the bourgeoisie into repressive action against the cherished party organisations. He loved to harp on such themes as the injustices and indignities heaped on the working class during the period of the anti-socialist law. By underlining simultaneously the certainty of ultimate victory and the futility of present collaboration with Lassalle's 'one reactionary mass' (the non-socialist classes), Bebel more than any other individual cemented the political immobilism of the party while preserving the revolutionary ideology and phraseology which now served almost exclusively social-psychological functions. Among these functions was the maintenance of proletarian *élan* and loyalty to the party *Vorstand*. In marked contrast to Kautsky, whose dogmatism inclined him to ignore or exacerbate inter-factional dissension (as in the agrarian question), Bebel was vitally concerned with the problem of party unity. To ensure its preservation he strained every nerve and sinew, threatening fractious elements with isolation, appealing to their sense of party discipline and, where necessary, as in the case of the February 1906 agreement with the trade union leadership, placating them with formal concessions. Above all, Bebel understood the value of the Marxist orthodoxy as an integrative ideology and consciously applied it as such (H.-J. Steinberg, 1972, p. 74).

Bebel's authority rested less on his capacity or productivity as a theoretician than on his enormous prestige as a veteran, shrewd and brilliantly persuasive public speaker, on his unparalleled organisational abilities, his position as party chairman, and above all on his great popularity with the masses. Wherever and whenever he spoke, Bebel filled halls to capacity. Hours before he was due to appear crowds would gather and mill about chanting his name. On one such occasion, a policeman was heard to observe, 'one would almost think you were waiting for the Kaiser', to which the crowd replied, 'he *is* our Kaiser!' Thereafter, 'Emperor Bebel' remained one of his nicknames. 'Like no other Social Democratic leader before or after him, Bebel personified the German Social Democratic Party' (Groh, 1973, p. 188). Within the party, his person was sacrosanct, and even such a determined iconoclast as Rosa Luxemburg bore him a grudging respect (Nettl, 1966, Vol. 1, p. 121). As a popular and accomplished politician, Bebel exerted an influence which reached into every nook and cranny in the party. By contrast, Kautsky, like Bernstein, was a mere intellectual, and acutely conscious of the limits of his own influence.

Yet there were also limits to even Bebel's influence. In the last five years of his life ill-health, his advancing years and family problems kept him increasingly out of touch with party affairs. Paul Singer was in a similar situation and died two years before Bebel in 1911. This left the practical direction of the party in the hands of three cautious and timorous members of the *Vorstand* – Richard Fischer, Herman Molkenbuhr (both over 60) and Hermann Müller. Acting with the apparent blessing of 'Emperor Bebel', these three did much to confirm the party in its tendency towards a centrist-based preoccupation with day-to-day practical affairs, a tendency which gained an added fillip with the election of Friedrich Ebert to the *Vorstand* co-chairmanship in 1913 (Schorske, 1972, pp. 212–13; Buse, 1973, pp. 129–40, 150–2; Groh, 1973, p. 186).

To sum up the functions served by the centre-orthodox ideology of revolutionary *attentisme*, it is apparent that, regardless of Kautsky's own position, the official Marxism of Bebel and the party *Vorstand* had an important integrative effect both internally and, albeit in a negative fashion, *vis-à-vis* Wilhelmine society at large. Party theory as expounded by the centre-orthodoxy provided a common jargon and a body of canon law to which even revisionists and reformists (Bernstein, Joseph Bloch, Vollmar and Grillenberger) could, and did, appeal when seeking legitimation of their policies and philosophy. For this reason the party left was slow to perceive the grave tactical and philo-sophical differences which separated it from the party centre. At the same time, the official ideology helped to explain the actual political impotence of the party while seemingly vindicating its immobilist tactic and quietistic *Praxis*. This was no minor advantage, as Bebel and other party leaders were well aware, in that the SPD had no prospect of ever wielding real political power in Imperial Germany. Under these circumstances, the revolutionary *attentisme* of the party centre afforded an excuse for its organisational fetishism, itself, in a sense, a substitute for both action and ideology and a pretext for its concentration on its, by definition meaningless, parliamentary vote-catching activities. The intransigent verbal radicalism of the party leadership benefited both the masses and the party leaders. To the socially alienated rank-and-file membership it offered a much-needed psychological support and sense of identity. To the party leaders it provided an invaluable aid to the maintenance of party discipline, while helping to perpetuate the status quo of self-imposed isolation by frightening away potential allies among the *Kathedersozialisten* ('socialists of the chair' or liberal academics) and the non-socialist parties. Inadvertently, this combination of formal radicalism and tactical 'standing pat' facilitated the revisionist conquest of the party from within. As the mass-strike debate revealed, the centre-orthodoxy could never sanction the radical demand for mass action and vigorous prosecution of the class struggle without jeopardising the unity and the survival of the party. But the centre-orthodoxy could, and did, allow the revisionists to do more or less as they pleased, provided they kept mum on the glaring incongruity between their parlia-mentary and trade union activities and the official party line. Under the aegis of this revolutionary *attentisme* a nominally revolutionary Marxist party became, by degrees, merely yet another pressure group competing for favours as a mass party which looked no further afield than to the creation of a bourgeois democracy, which it could only envisage as an act of God.

That the official ideology of the SPD assumed the form of a revolutionary *attentisme* which continued to play such a dominant role in the life of the party between the turn of the century and the First World War cannot be explained adequately by reference to a single 'central division'. The only satisfactory explanation is to be found in a reference to a combination of influences including ideological constraints, conditions within the party and the role of individuals. If one factor deserves to be emphasised above all others, this must surely be that of the objective conditions prevailing in Wilhelmine Germany.

The ideological deficiencies of this 'party Marxism' derived, in part, from the dichotomist and ambiguous character of the original model and, still more, from its incomplete assimilation within the SPD at the hands of cicerones like Kautsky and Bebel. Not only was it a mish-mash of such conflicting and ill-digested elements as Lassalleanism, state socialism, ethical socialism, Darwinism, positivism and Enlightenment progressivism, but at its core there remained an irreducible kernel of inherited bourgeois radicalism which was only thinly disguised by its radical Marxist verbiage (Mandelbaum, 1926, pp. 36–7, 45, 51; Victor, 1928, pp. 158–64, 167, 178; Grunenberg, ed., 1970, pp. 20–1; H.-J. Steinberg, 1972, p. 150; Schröder, 1975, pp. 89, 102, 137–81).

Within the party the experience of the anti-socialist law long exerted a powerful influence on the thinking of its leaders. The heroic period of persecution and proscription had done much to radicalise the party rank and file. As the steamship subsidies dispute had demonstrated in the mid-1880s (Lidtke, 1966, pp. 193–204), the mood of the masses could not be ignored, but it could be tempered and manipulated by an appeal to a radical rhetoric such as Marxism. On the other hand, the fear of renewed repression taught all too well the habit of caution in practical affairs. Also constantly on the minds of party leaders was the problem of party unity. No sooner had the quarrel between the Eisenach and Lassallean factions been shelved than the party had been obliged to fight for its very existence. The radical *Jungen* were easily brought to heel in 1891 (Müller, 1975, pp. 46–109), but the revisionist threat was too hydra-headed to be disposed of lightly. As the radical challenge gained momentum after 1905, throwing up a centre-left orientation as well (later to become the nucleus of the USPD), the centre-orthodoxy could see no way out of its dilemma other than to continue practising revisionism while preaching revolutionary Marxism. This tendency was strengthened after 1912 by the growing importance of the SPD Reichstag *Fraktion* within the party and by the apparent growth in the importance of the Reichstag itself (Mandelbaum, 1926, p. 17; Nettl, 1965, pp. 83–5; Rauh, 1977, pp. 17–285). Although most socialist deputies were either revisionists or centrists, few could resist the temptation to frighten conservative opponents by indulging on occasion, as in the 1913–14 Zabern debate (Wehler, 1970*b*, pp. 65–82; Schoenbaum, 1982), in outbursts of revolutionary flights of fancy. The centrist ideological position was further buttressed by the growing bureaucratisation of the party and by the power of the trade unions, although the pressure exerted by party and trade union functionaries was more symptomatic of existing developments than productive of novel tendencies.

The role of personalities as a significant element in the establishment and maintenance of the official ideology has already been alluded to. First among these personalities was Engels who, as the right hand of Marx, enjoyed an authority that was without equal. On at least two occasions Engels intervened decisively in favour of the centre-orthodoxy: one was his *Anti-Dühring*, the other his introduction to the 1895 edition of Marx's *Class Struggles in France*. In the latter he endorsed the parliamentary and electoral policy of the party while legitimising the Kautsky–Bebel view of revolution as a natural occurrence (G. Mayer, 1936, pp. 278–81; Grunenberg, ed., 1970, p. 22; Lehnert, 1977, pp. 106–23). The contribution of Kautsky and Bebel, who held key positions within the party and therefore provided continuity and immediacy as well as authority, was undoubtedly far greater. Each in his own way was the personification of revolutionary *attentisme*.

The most important reason why the centre-orthodoxy stubbornly adhered to this ideology long after economic circumstances had rendered it superfluous and obsolete must be sought in objective conditions in the *Kaiserreich* (Second Empire). These conditions affected Social Democracy in two ways. First, the pariah status of the German socialists owed at least as much to their utter rejection *by* society as it did to their own aloofness *from* society. In discussions of German revisionism and its prospects, historians have often been tempted to assume that the social structure of Wilhelmine Germany was at least potentially more flexible than was in fact the case. The German bourgeoisie had never had a 1789. Having been tried and found wanting in 1848, if indeed it can be said to have tried at all (Krieger, 1957, p. 329 ff.; Sheehan, 1978, pp. 59–76, 272–83), German liberalism traded its ideals and ultimately its class interest for the immediate morsels of national unity à la Bismarck and material prosperity born of a belated yet hothouse industrialisation on a scale and of such rapidity unknown in Europe before Stalin (Pollard, 1981, p. 223). Germany literally changed overnight from a semi-absolutist, Junker-dominated agrarian society into a modern industrial state. But the values and socio-political structures of a traditionalist society did not keep pace with economic development. Wilhelmine Germany was a fragile historical absurdity – a mighty industrial power still ruled by a semi-feudal, pre-industrial élite which grudgingly admitted a weak but prosperous bourgeoisie to associate membership in society on condition that the bourgeoisie kept their place and did not presume to practise more than sound business principles. Even the greatest steel barons were effectively never more than *Hofjuden* (court Jews) to East Elbia. In reality, the monarch himself was merely the first servant of the Junker class state. His position was accurately summed up in the Old Prussian satirical couplet:

> Und der König absolut,
> Wenn er unsern Willen tut.

In other words, the king might rule absolutely provided that he ruled in the interest of East Elbia. Wilhelmine society was both too rigid and too delicate a structure to accommodate any serious social engineering. It was, as Dieter Groh described it, 'an economic colossus with political feet of clay' (Groh, 1973, p. 20). In a situation where the Junkers flatly refused to share more than the trappings of power, even with the big bourgeoisie, where the spiritually disinherited and denatured bourgeoisie had derogated to mere myrmidons of Junkerdom, where an anachronistic socio-political structure showed itself increasingly incompetent to deal with the problems of industrial society, there was no chance of Social Democracy ever wielding real power in the Reich. The Junkers would not, and could not, tolerate the transformation of the Reich into a fully fledged parliamentary democracy – on the English or any other model.[10]

The constitutional structure of the Reich, state policy after 1890 and the political weakness of the bourgeoisie all conspired to perpetuate the isolation and impotence of Social Democracy before the First World War. There was no ministerial responsibility in the Reich, not even formal constitutional provision for the existence of political parties. Above all, there was no chance of a liberalisation of the restrictive Prussian suffrage. Since Prussia was the backbone of the Reich and the bastion of agrarian conservatism, parliamentary government had first to be made a reality in Prussia before any progress was possible in the Reich. Until this objective was achieved, the Reichstag and South German parliamentary and electoral successes of the SPD counted for nothing. But the Junkers and Wilhelm II were prepared to employ all methods, including a *coup d'état*, to ensure that in Prussia 'as things have been, they remain'. Moreover, it would be quite incorrect to interpret the lapsing of Bismarck's anti-socialist law in 1890 as portending an end to repressive measures against the socialists or a major change in policy towards the *vaterlandslose Gesellen* (unpatriotic vagabonds). Despite limited gains in the area of social policy, harassment and persecution continued on a wide front and Draconian repression was again seriously mooted on a number of occasions. As for the possibility of Social Democracy acquiring non-socialist allies in a broadly based campaign for the parliamentarisation of Prussia-Germany, the crux of the matter was that such allies simply did not exist in Wilhelmine Germany. The career of Franz Mehring is a case in point. As a liberal intellectual he had once been an active opponent of socialism and had worked as a journalist under Eduard Bernstein's uncle, Aron Bernstein, on the left liberal *Berliner Volkszeitung* (1884–90). Mehring finally joined the SPD at the age of 45 after the collapse of the Democratic Party in 1887–8 (the last attempt to found a radical democratic party in Imperial Germany) drove home to him the conclusion that there was nowhere else for a radical democrat to go (Höhle, 1958, p. 178).[11] This experience was repeated by many others, including half the membership of Friedrich Naumann's National Social Association.

The hopelessness of the SPD predicament, its practical impossibility of ever achieving a position of real power in the Reich, was no secret to hardened campaigners like Bebel and Kautsky. Changed economic conditions certainly favoured the revisionist case, but the centre-orthodoxy cleaved to its outworn revolutionary phraseology and insisted on keeping the party remote from society while at the same time focusing the attention of the masses on their allegedly inevitable ultimate victory. This course presented itself to the party leaders largely because it was the best available expedient for maintaining the loyalty and morale of the masses in a situation where the socialist movement had nothing to offer the faithful but faith itself. Alternatively, the party leaders dared not offer the masses anything more concrete for fear of provoking the premature trial of strength with the formidable Prusso-German state against which no less an authority than Engels had warned. The isolation which society thereby imposed on Social Democracy served to justify and reinforce the self-isolation of the SPD from that society.

The second way in which Social Democracy reacted to the pressures of the *Kaiserreich* was to emulate the spirit and structure of Wilhelmine society. In the last decade of peace, the socialist movement transformed itself into a state within a state and became, in the process, a mirror image of Imperial Germany (Nettl, 1965, pp. 76–85; Schorske, 1972, pp. 118–36). If rejection by society helped to perpetuate the profession of an isolationist, rejectionist ideology, it also compelled the party to look to its own devices organisationally. Here Marx was a poor crutch, having suggested neither a blueprint for socialist organisa- tion nor guidelines of any practical utility. He had merely predicted that the course of the class struggle would forge the necessary and appropriate organisational tools commensurate with objective social conditions. Among the German epigones this was interpreted as an injunction to duplicate what were perceived as the organisational strengths of the class enemy. By 1914 the SPD and its trade union auxiliary had therefore evolved a comprehensive and heavily bureaucratised complex of political, social and cultural institutions and services which catered to almost all needs of all sections of the proletarian and rural workforce (Schönhoven, 1980; Guttsman, 1981, pp. 149–52, 167–270). In their preoccupation with such organisational work the party leaders found an excuse for not confronting the class enemy. Organisation became an end in itself and a substitute for class struggle. It vindicated the party leaders' immobilism *vis-à-vis* the bourgeois state and registered their satisfaction with the status quo of isolation. Socialist revolution came to mean, for the centre orthodoxy, organising for the millennium which they believed and hoped would never really eventuate.

Imitation did not stop at structures. Something of the spirit of Wilhelmine society also percolated through to Social Democracy. One instance of this was the growing nationalisation of German socialism. Pride in the widely recognised organisational superiority of the German party – a point which gave it much authority within the Second International – together with fear of the reactionary Russian colossus gave credence to the idea, manifest in both leaders and followers, that in the event of war the German proletariat had a great deal to lose from a German defeat as well as from conservative repression at home (Wehler, 1962, p. 116). The party's organisational emulation of the Prusso-German state had the further effect of reproducing within the party a strong oligarchic tendency which, to the chagrin and frustration of the left, thoroughly negated the external appearance of democracy and reinforced the power position of centrism and revisionism (Michels, 1911, *passim*; Nipperdey, 1961, pp. 315–92; Mittmann, 1976, pp. 67–74). Even culturally, as the fate of the *Freie Volksbühne* demonstrated, Social Democracy was content to trail in the wake of its bourgeois class enemy (Roth, 1963, pp. 212–43; Lidtke, 1974, pp. 22–8). At the political level, actual points of contact, interaction and collaboration between Social Democracy and Wilhelmine society broadened and deepened in the last years of peace – through the SPD Reichstag *Fraktion*, in the field of social policy and elsewhere (Nettl, 1965, pp. 83–5; Grebing, 1969, p. 73; Groh, 1973, pp. 114, n. 119, 581, 628–9, 632–4).

By emulating the structure and spirit of Wilhelmine society while preserving a clearly defined distance from that society, pre-1914 German Social Democracy achieved, almost unnoticed at the time, a substantial measure of negative integration into the status quo. By and large, the party leadership was not dissatisfied with the results. The creation of a closely structured, inward-looking party at least distracted attention from its failure to come to grips with the real task of confronting bourgeois society. It also enhanced the value of the official ideology, which now functioned as a refuge from reality, a necessary face-saving mask for its immobilism and an indispensable psychological counterpoint to the centre-orthodoxy's immersion of the labour movement in a quagmire of humdrum and inconsequential parliamentary and organisational wool-gathering.

The ideological supremacy of the centre-orthodoxy persisted in the face of changing economic reality and the demonstrable tactical bankruptcy of the party leadership, not because Social Democracy had become subverted by opportunist elements but largely because society left it no option. The party was in no position to adopt a collision course with society. That way led to political suicide. To do as the revisionists recommended was equally impossible. Emancipation from Marxist theory could be achieved only at the cost of demoralising and alienating the party membership. In view of ruling-class intransigence and the complete absence of potential liberal fellow-travellers, the possible compensations in terms of concrete progress towards social reform and parliamentary democracy were bound to be disappointing. Just as Wilhelmine society sought escape from the insoluble dilemma created by a burgeoning industrialism battened on to an ossified and antedeluvian socio-political structure by giving free rein to a hopelessly illusory ambition to imperial grandeur, so Wilhelmine Social Democracy clung with an equally purblind tenacity to its private Cloud-cuckoo-land of revolutionary phraseo-logy, fatalistic immobilism and organisational fetishism. Societal pressures effectively shepherded the party into this cul-de-sac. Circumstances within the party, inherited ideological pulls and the impact of key personalities func-tioned as important back-up drives to this primary impetus.

Followers: Theoretical Indifference and Popular Radicalism
If the relatively small number of intellectuals comprising the party leadership and its radical and revisionist critics demonstrated, in general, great theoretical diversity and a very limited grasp of Marxism, the vast majority of those who made up the membership of the various socialist organisations demonstrated very little at all in the way of a clearly definable ideological disposition. There exists, unfortunately, a notorious and apparently irremediable paucity of reliable evidence as to what the organised workers or socialist rank and file thought about the where, why and how questions concerning the direction being taken by the Wilhelmine labour movement. The testimony of their more prominent and articulate comrades of the party mandarinate or *Bonzentum* – as often as not, non-proletarian in origin, which helps to explain why they all tended to speak down to, rather than with, the factory floor – is a guide of dubious utility in that the spokesmen of the leadership caste, regardless of factional allegiance, often badly misjudged the mood of the masses and varied enormously in their assessments of what the masses actually thought. A more profitable method of gauging the ideological position of the organised workers is that employed by Hans-Josef Steinberg, who has attempted to identify the outlook of the masses by analysing available statistics on workers' reading habits before 1914 (Steinberg, 1976, pp. 166–80; see also Langewiesche and Schönhoven, 1976, pp. 135–204). This approach is certainly preferable to such alternatives as generalisations from strike demands and statistics – from a number of standpoints, a highly question-begging procedure that may not present an accurate picture of even working-class militants – for in a highly literate society like Wilhelmine Germany, not all workers drank, pilfered, struck, or, indeed, were organised to strike, whereas it may be assumed that almost everybody read something, even if only a newspaper.

Before discussing the results of Steinberg's analysis it is necessary to dis-tinguish between radicalism and Marxism. For it is not true, as Marxist historians often assume, that an increase in popular radicalism necessarily implies greater receptivity to the tenets of theoretical Marxism, whether 'imported' or of the home-grown variety. At no stage in the history of the pre-1914 German labour movement where the masses more radical and bloody-minded than under the anti-socialist law. At that time, Marxism was struggling to establish itself as the ideological base of the movement. Popular radicalism, as it happened, did contribute to the Marxist victory signalised by the adoption of the Erfurt Programme, but the radicalism of the masses was neither Marxist in inspiration nor necessarily conducive to the acceptance of Marxism as such. In essence, the popular radicalism of the 1880s was a knee-jerk response to the oppressiveness of early industrialism and the Bismarckian state. Its ideological manifestations scarcely went beyond anti-monarchism, anti-clericalism and a fanatical hatred of Bismarck and the state which he personified (H.-J. Steinberg, 1972, p. 30).

The mood of the masses in the Wilhelmine period is probably beyond historical reconstruction (Geary, 1981, pp. 110, 120). Even so, there are lessons to be learnt from available strike statistics, incomplete and variable as these may be (Fricke, 1976, pp. 757–70). Throughout the period 1890–1914 strikes increased in number and scale. Yet the statistics clearly show that the incidence of strikes and lockouts, as well as the types of strikes (whether offensive or defensive, successful or not, of long or short duration), closely reflected fluctuations in the business cycle (Bry, 1960, p. 143). In brief, strikes were determined in origin and outcome more by social and economic than by political factors. The first political strike to take place in the *Kaiserreich* occurred in Hamburg in January 1906. More followed in 1910 but the political mass strike was generally a rare phenomenon, in practice, before 1914, however much radical intellectuals loved to talk about it (Fricke, 1976, p. 758).

The mood of the masses was nevertheless increasingly radical after 1905. By the summer of 1913 the party *Vorstand* and the General Commission were experiencing serious difficulty in containing and diverting (for suppression was now out of the question) the tide of anger and discontent that rose spontaneously from the factory floor and the local party organisations.[12] Rank-and-file unrest expressed itself not in 'discouragement and indifference' (Schorske, 1972, p. 257) but in an unprecedented wave of 'wildcat strikes, in discussions of the problem of the "masses" and "leaders" and of appropriate organisational structures, in a recrudescence of syndicalist tendencies and in discussion of the political mass strike arising from the "base", i.e. from the local organisations and factories, and not from the party intellectuals' (Groh, 1973, p. 498). Particularly significant was the large number of wildcat strikes in 1913 – a time of growing unemployment and deepening economic recession. This phenomenon flatly contradicted the customary relationship between strikes and the business cycle (ibid., pp. 497–8). Its fundamental cause was structural: the masses were growing impatient at the glaring discrepancy between the power potential and organisational strength of the party, on the one hand, and its inability to deliver concrete political successes on the other. What aggravated the situation at this particular time was the onset of another economic recession, an unprecedented decline in party membership and subscription numbers, disappointment at the meagre results of the 1912 Reichstag electoral victory and at the result of several *Landtag* or state elections since the summer of 1912.

The masses were undoubtedly becoming progressively more radicalised in the last decade of peace. But this cannot be cited as evidence of growing rank-and-file awareness of, or receptivity to, Marxism. In the first place, the mood of popular radicalism was largely spontaneous and did not reflect left-wing inspiration. What it represented, above all, was a protest against worsening external circumstances (economic recession, a hardening in employer organisation and government intransigence) and a cry of rage and despair at the unfulfilled hopes aroused by a do-nothing party and trade union apparatus. In the second place, mass-strike discussion was a very different thing from the mass strike itself. The masses, like the centrist leadership, indulged in a strictly verbal radicalism that was far removed from revolutionary intent and political action. Although the rank and file were frequently willing to discuss and to agitate in favour of radical action (as in 1905, 1910 and 1913), when obliged to vote 'yes' or 'no' on a specific proposal for implementation of the political mass strike the masses invariably rejected radical action with an overwhelming majority (ibid., pp. 559–61, 568–75). Their radicalism, in short, was largely a means of giving verbal expression to pent-up frustration. It was also spasmodic, fickle and of short duration. The massive peace demonstrations of late July 1914, for example, easily converted a few days later into the no less massive patriotic demonstrations of the 'August experience'.

The example of Bremen is instructive. Since 1910 the old Hanseatic city had been one of the strongholds of radical power within German Social Democracy. Yet it is apparent that even here left-wing predominance was by no means indicative of Marxism triumphant among the party rank and file. In Bremen, as in other parts of the Reich, local party branches, the labour secretariat, the trade unions, the co-operative movement and socialist local government representation were all in the hands of revisionists. The power of the radicals or party left rested exclusively on their control over the local party press, the formidable *Bremer Bürgerzeitung*, and on radical manipulation and monopolisation of key positions in the Bremen party organisation (Moring, 1968, pp. 130–3). There is no evidence to suggest that here, more than elsewhere, radical supremacy reflected greater rank-and-file awareness or mastery of Marxist theory.

The masses' ignorance of, and apathy towards, all theory is fully apparent in their reading habits. No doubt Noske was exaggerating in his memoirs when he boasted of his own ignorance of Marx:

> It was years before I heard anything of Karl Marx and Frederick Engels as the founders of a socialist movement. Not until 1903, while in prison, did I read Marx's *Capital*, after I had been a Social Democratic newspaper editor for six years. Even then I read only the first volume . . . Only a handful of semi-educated people discredited the labour movement by prating about Marxism in the propaganda work of the party. I do not believe that I ever made mention of Marxism either in a speech or in an article. (1947, pp. 7, 27)

He described this disruptive minority as consisting of pretentious, dogmatic and schoolmasterish Jewish bourgeois *déclassés* and starry-eyed idealists from Poland and Russia. Noske's remarks, coming from one of the new breed of apparatchiks which rose from the factory floor, exemplify an attitude of which

Kautsky complained in 1896 when he referred to a widespread 'silent hatred' of Marxism within the party. If, as applied to the rank and file, 'hatred' is perhaps also something of an exaggeration, ignorance and indifference are indisputably valid characterisations of rank-and-file attitudes towards Marxism. Such is the only possible inference to be drawn from an examination of workers' reading habits in the period from 1900 to 1914.

Statistics on borrowings from workers' libraries – these applied principally to union-organised labour – show that the libraries were used by only a small proportion of the workers for whom they catered. These statistics also indicate a steady decline in borrowings from all categories other than literary fiction, which was by far the most popular, accounting for 75 to 80 percent of all borrowings (Kliche, 1911, p. 316). Serious party literature was not at all popular, least of all among workers recruited to the movement after 1890. Much of the party's propaganda literature was not even to be found in the workers' libraries. Unquestionably, the work most in demand in this category, and also the most widely serialised as well as a perennial bestseller, was Bebel's *Die Frau und der Sozialismus*. Its popularity was enhanced by its non-theoretical character and by the massive publicity it received in 1910, when the author's seventieth birthday coincided with the publication of its fiftieth edition. Marx himself was hardly ever borrowed and was usually returned unread (Kliche, 1911, p. 318; Stampfer, 1957, p. 14). However, if the categories 'history, philosophy and social sciences' are added to the rubric 'serious party literature', Bebel's popularity was put in the shade by Corvin's anti-clerical *Pfaffenspiegel*, a scurrilously unscholarly work on a par with Zimmermann's *Gekrönte Häupter* and sought after for similar reasons. Works purchased by the socialist reading public evidently reflected, rather than complemented, the material borrowed from the workers' libraries. In other words, sales of serious party literature, with such rare exceptions as Bebel's book, were well below those of light-entertainment reading and other categories.

If the socialist rank and file did not gain a sound theoretical grounding through the books which they either borrowed or purchased, they assuredly did not acquire it through the party press (Nitschke, 1913, p. 367). Of the newspapers and periodicals produced by the party, the workers showed a strong preference for news above theory (Wurm, SPD A.C., 1902, p. 263; Fricke, 1976, pp. 410–16; Hall, 1977, p. 26). Theoretical publications, like Kautsky's *Neue Zeit* or Clara Zetkin's ultra-radical women's periodical, *Die Gleichheit*, did not enjoy a circulation even remotely comparable to that of papers like *Vorwärts*. The latter, in turn, did not sell nearly as well as lighter publications such as *Der Wahre Jacob*, *Postillion*, or the *Neue Welt-Kalender* (Haenisch, 1899/1900, p. 696). Relative to the increase in the number of socialist-organised workers, the real growth in the party press was in fact negative (Hall, 1977, p. 37).[13] The problem was one which greatly concerned party leaders. The solution customarily recommended was a reduction in both the price and the theoretical content of the party press, a broadening of its news coverage, particularly that of local news, and the inclusion of more human-interest and entertainment material. Since the workers did not find what they wanted in the socialist press, they turned in growing numbers to the bourgeois press (ibid., p. 36). And this at a time when the socialist share of the vote in Reichstag, state and other elections showed a progressive and dramatic increase (see Figures 1.1 and 1.2).

While more people were voting socialist, most socialists were showing a declining interest in discovering what socialism might be. As one observer lamented in 1913:

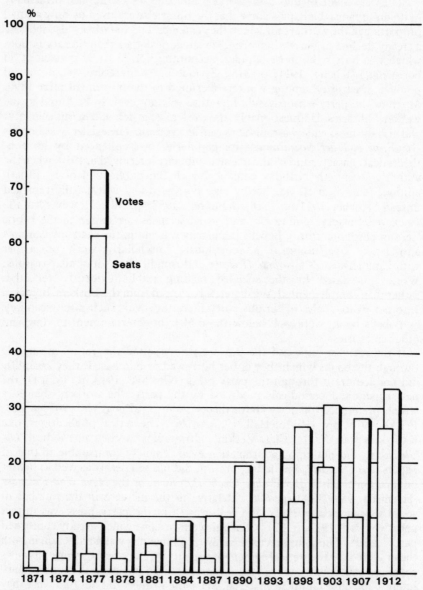

Figure 1.1   SPD share of the Reichstag vote and seats in percentage terms, 1871–1912.

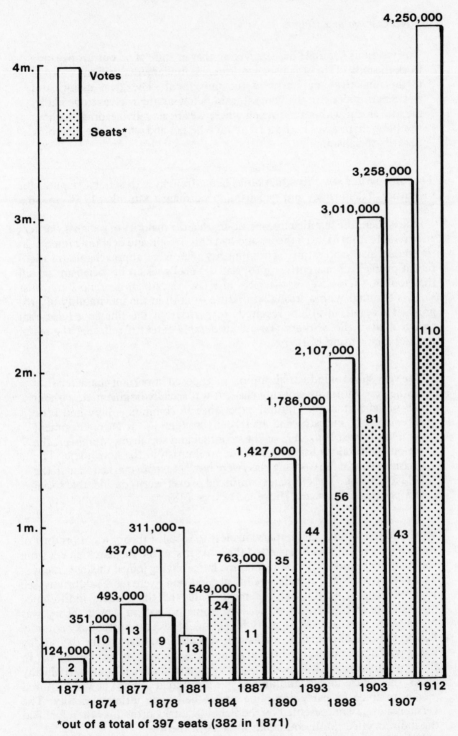

Figure 1.2 SPD share of the Reichstag vote and seats in numerical terms, 1871–1912.

Every serious comrade has the feeling that in spite of all our propaganda work the bulk of the organised workforce is fundamentally ill-informed as to the objectives and tasks of the movement. The great majority of workers trot along in the general train, allowing themselves to be led by the movement without inquiring where we are actually heading, without troubling themselves in the least about whether and why we are marching towards socialism.

The same writer saw this situation as being fraught with serious 'dangers for the future of democracy and socialism' in Germany (Nitschke, 1913, pp. 367, 369).

One is therefore justified in concluding that the majority of socialist workers were remote from Marxist theory and had only a slight and declining interest in theoretical party literature. The minority who were approachable on theoretical problems apparently appropriated Bebel's vision of socialism, which they took to themselves in the form of a few Marxist or anarcho-syndicalist slogans together with a strong admixture of faith in the inevitability of progress. This state of affairs resulted, in part, from the limited educational background of the workers. To a considerable extent it reflected the social realities confronting workers:

The very speed of industrialisation . . . imposed important characteristics on the newly forming working class. It was socially fragmented, without any broad historic or cultural experience in common. Many had little experience of industry and had been brought up in an environment profoundly hostile to ideas of class conflict and socialism. Moreover, the various cultural traditions continued to flourish in the new home. The divisions within the working class were nowhere more marked than in the field of religion. The churches continued to exert very considerable social and political influence. (Hickey, 1978, p. 218)

Partly, too, working-class imperviousness to socialist theory was a product of the generation gap which separated the 'old salts' of the Bismarckian era from the post-1890 generation of workers, the latter having joined the movement at a time when economic as well as political conditions were more salubrious (see Figures 1.3 and 1.4). But it also seems probable that the workers' indifference to theory proceeded in large measure from the way in which theory was presented to the masses. The party Marxism of the centre-orthodoxy not only flew in the face of economic reality but was also irrelevant to the day-to-day issues which most concerned the average trade unionist or party member. In these circumstances it was hardly likely to pique the worker's curiosity. In any event, theoretical understanding was not demanded of him: he was required merely to abide by party discipline and to believe in ultimate victory. The version of Marxism presented by the Bebel–Kautsky orthodoxy therefore had the indirect effect of discouraging interest in theory.

In fact the masses remained indifferent to, or hostile towards, all theoretical

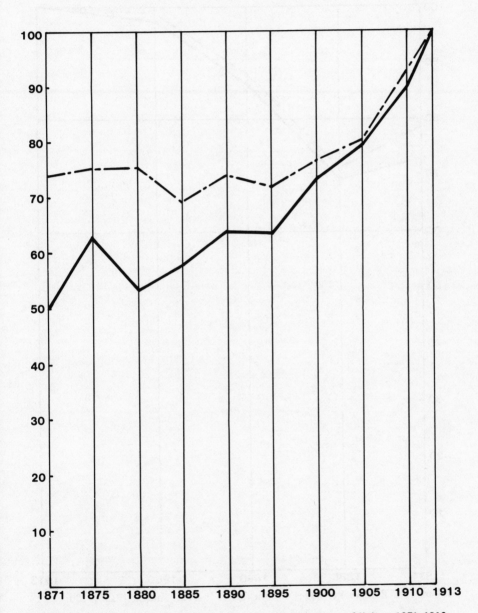

Figure 1.3 Nominal weekly wages in industry and the cost of living, 1871–1913.
(Index: 1913 = 100)

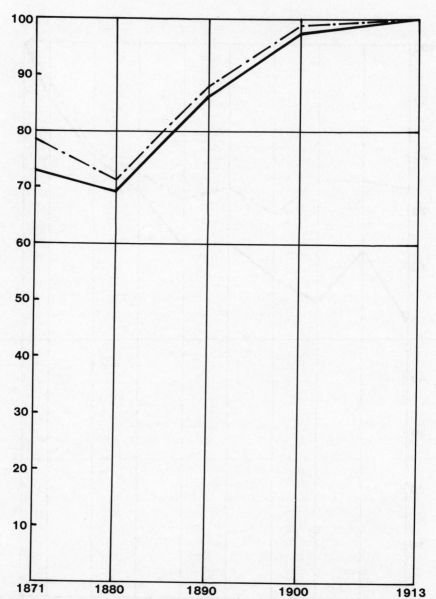

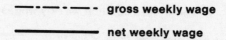

- — · — · — gross weekly wage
- ——————— net weekly wage

Figure 1.4 Real weekly wages in industry, 1871–1913. (Index: 1913 = 100)

discussions within the party. They regarded it as a waste of time and a distraction from the real work of the party. At Munich in 1902, for instance, one delegate rose to complain of yet another Bernstein debate. Pointing an accusing finger at the party intellectuals, he suggested it might be advisable in future if these held their own separate congress a few days in advance of the general party congress (Leyendecker, SPD A.C., 1902, p. 131). At Lübeck the previous year another delegate, Adolf Hoffmann, had voiced the same complaint: 'I have not the slightest intention of confuting Bernstein. Perhaps I cannot. In any case I will not. I simply do not have the time to engage in theoretical hair-splitting' (Hoffman, SPD A.C., 1901, p. 138). That the masses viewed all theoretical debate as 'hair-splitting' was well known to the party leaders. In 1899 Kautsky informed Bernstein that, in his view, Bernstein's heresies were unlikely to create much of a stir in the party 'because the masses simply do not bother themselves about our discussions' (KP, C 229: Kautsky to Bernstein, 29 June 1899).[14] Spokesmen of all factions endeavoured to use this attitude for their own ends. Thus Bebel tried to discredit Bernstein by branding him a finicky, hair-splitting intellectual who was fond of whetting his sagacity by inventing ever-increasing criticisms of the party (Bebel, SPD A.C., 1901, p. 168). Ignaz Auer liked to curry favour with the masses by feigning total ignorance in all theoretical matters (Auer, SPD A.C., 1899, p. 208; cf. H.-J. Steinberg, 1972, p. 116). Similarly, Vollmar declined to be labelled a Bernsteinian, a Bebelite, or even a Marxist, claiming that for him it was quite sufficient that he was a Social Democrat (Vollmar, SPD A.C., 1903, p. 342). Even Rosa Luxemburg – surely one of the worst offenders against the masses' poor digestive capacity for theory – implied that a surfeit of theory might be a bar to action. In 1905 she insisted that 'we are a party of class struggle and not of "historical laws" ' (cit. Schröder, 1973, p. 111, n. 85). Indeed, her view of tactics and mass action was posited on the assumption that theory must issue from *Praxis* rather than vice versa.

The ideological position of the party rank and file may therefore be summed up as comprising, in essence, a simple and uninformed faith in the inevitability of the millennium (Mandelbaum, 1926, p. 13; Grunenberg, ed., 1970, p. 20; H.-J. Steinberg, 1972, pp. 141–2). Whereas rank-and-file radicalism fluctuated in response to changing political and economic conditions, the masses remained constant in their ignorance of, disinterest in, and even aversion to Marxism. In fact, the organised socialist masses manifested a deep and growing apathy towards all theory, be it Marxist, revisionist or whatever.

Where all this leads is still debatable. Where it does not necessarily lead is to the conclusion that workers in prewar Germany were 'concerned with political change and social revolution' (Geary, 1982, p. 237). Economic grievances and alienation may be transformed into political struggles, as they eventually were under the devastating burdens of four years of war, but there is no reason to suppose that in the prewar period they were already resulting in revolutionary militancy. In 1914

Bochum and other industrial towns like it did reflect essential characteristics of the specific stage in the development of capitalist society Germany had reached by the late nineteenth century. In that stage of large-scale, heavy-industry-based, 'organised' capitalism the link between liberal ideology and social reality must have seemed far more tenuous, not only in Bochum, but in Germany as a whole, than perhaps it had during the early phases of the English Industrial Revolution. (Crew, 1979, p. 223)

If, for the Wilhelmine working class, social reality proved inhospitable to liberal ideology and the 'imported' theories of the socialist leadership, it did not render the working class immune to the various manifestations of illiberalism which abounded in Wilhelmine society. Although the workers did not succumb to the populist nationalism of the Navy League and similar non-socialist agitational groups, the aggregate impact of traditional values, uprooting, material and status deprivation, structural change, the work experience and social controls undoubtedly made many workers more susceptible to the kind of nationalist fare offered by avowedly socialist organs like the *Sozialistische Monatshefte* than historians have hitherto cared to contemplate. This was not a case of workers being betrayed or misled by opportunistic leaders so much as a matter of autonomous working-class radicalism seeking, and to some extent finding, an outlet for its grievances in an avenue that was compatible with social reality as it appeared to the ordinary shop-floor worker.

Foreign Policy and the Imperialism Debate: The Primacy of Domestic Politics?

Before 1914 German Social Democracy generally evinced as little interest in foreign policy as in party theory, although actual interest in foreign affairs was probably far greater than that overtly displayed. *Weltpolitik* and imperialism – the terms were used synonymously in party parlance until 1905 at least (Owtscharenko, 1970, p. 547) – appeared on the agenda of party congresses only twice between 1900 and the outbreak of the First World War (at Mainz in 1900 and at Chemnitz in 1912). It is worth remembering also that Hilferding's great study *Das Finanzkapital*, though written in 1906, did not appear until 1910, while Rosa Luxemburg's contribution to the debate, *Die Akkumulation des Kapitals*, which attracted much less attention at the time even among the left (Victor, 1928, p. 167; Nettl, 1966, Vol. 2, pp. 474, 529),[15] was not published until 1913. Indicative of the general apathy was Paul Singer's key-note address on *Weltpolitik* at Mainz, where he declined to offer a definition of imperialism, which he regarded as a 'nebulous concept', and confidently predicted that Social Democracy could well afford to postpone the elaboration of a socialist foreign policy alternative until it was in possession of political power (Singer, SPD A.C., 1900, p. 158).[16] It was not until the second Moroccan crisis hammered home the imminence and urgency of the threat of world war that this general indifference, punctuated by largely formal, hyperbolical and desultory forays against imperialist excesses, gave way to serious attempts to comprehend, explain and combat the imperialist syndrome.

Such interest as was expressed in foreign policy problems was usually vague and woolly-minded, reflecting a clear ambivalence in Social Democratic thinking. Like Marx and Engels before them, German socialists in the Wilhelmine era customarily thought of foreign policy as an autonomous sphere governed as

much by strategic, diplomatic and power-political factors as by purely economic considerations (Victor, 1928, pp. 147–52; Schröder, 1975, pp. 89, 92).
Alternatively, they treated the subject not uncommonly as a mere by-product
of domestic politics or as a projection of tactical and theoretical differences
within the party. Thus they frequently contemplated foreign policy in the light
of its probable implications for the 'inevitable' socialist accession to power or in
relation to the on-going quarrel with the revisionists. After 1907 especially, the
party centre was ever mindful of the need to tread warily in the presence of the
national question. In short, it would be quite misleading to speak of a socialist
foreign policy before 1914. Socialist Russophobia in fact represented 'the one
foreign policy constant of German Social Democracy and an old legacy from
the 1848 democracy and from Marx and Engels' (Groh, 1973, p. 724).[17]
Otherwise, the only consistent factor in the foreign policy thinking of pre-1914
Social Democracy was provided by the variable, tactically dominated guidelines laid down by its 'pope' and expounded in the Reichstag either by
Kautsky's parliamentary vicar, Georg Ledebour, or by 'Emperor Bebel'.

Curiously enough, there is virtually no evidence to support the often-made
assertion that pre-1914 socialist theories of imperialism were strongly influenced by the views of J. A. Hobson, who has the unique distinction of having
anticipated both Hilferding and Lenin as well as J. M. Keynes.[18] Even in the
1890s, it is true, Hobson's unorthodox economic views – he was, like
Rodbertus, an underconsumptionist – were known to Continental socialists,
including Kautsky, Bernstein and Rosa Luxemburg. Yet Hobson's pioneering
1902 study of British imperialism, entitled simply *Imperialism: A Study*, was
reviewed only once in prewar Germany (in 1908 by G. Brodnitz in the *Jahrbuch
für Nationalökonomie und Statistik*, p. 391) and had no noticeable impact in
socialist circles. One is obliged to conclude that although socialist theorists –
Hilferding being the best example – often reached strikingly similar conclusions, they arrived at their views quite independently of Hobson. Lenin, of
course, was the exception, his wartime study being based explicitly and
extensively on both Hobson and Hilferding, but before 1914 Lenin and his
Bolsheviks were 'generally ignored' within the German party (Reisberg, 1970,
p. 116).

The position of the party centre on the question of imperialism faithfully
mirrored the confused and inchoate state of Social Democratic foreign policy
thinking generally. By 1909, when Kautsky's controversial *Der Weg zur Macht*
first appeared, 'A good many Marxist ideas on the subject were already floating
in the air, but the task of working them out and fitting them together was taken
up slowly – and never completed before 1914' (Kiernan, 1974, p. 9). From the
turn of the century onwards, Social Democratic discussion of the problems of
imperialism served a variety of purposes: above all, it sought to offer a
non-revisionist explanation of the unexpected longevity of capitalism while
providing a platform for combating revisionist heresies. The answer to these
problems was found in pointing to overseas expansion as having given
capitalism a new but temporary and finite lease of life. In this way, socialist
theorists of the centre and the left sought to account for recent changes in
capitalist development while, at the same time, vindicating and corroborating
their own previously held convictions and tactical concepts.

Within the Second International, as within the German party, Karl Kautsky was widely acknowledged as 'the most authoritative interpreter of Marxism in the generation after Marx and Engels' (J. H. Kautsky, 1961, p. 103). As 'the official party spokesman and "Pope of socialism" ', Kautsky spoke with far greater weight than did intellectually more imposing theorists like Hilferding (Joll, 1974, p. 91).[19] Kautsky's analysis of imperialism, as enshrined in *Der Weg zur Macht*, may therefore be taken as representative of the position of the party centre. In 1909, at the pinnacle of his 'radical' phase (Irrlitz, 1966, pp. 52–3), Kautsky laid considerable stress on the disintegrative effects of imperialism, whose origins he attributed in large measure to the expansion of railway construction and of trade into the whole world. As the bourgeois classes gained in solidarity and self-assurance, pressing the proletariat into total isolation, the choice for Social Democracy lay between imperialism and socialism. Imperialism, nevertheless, provided the means for the destruction of capitalism. Within the imperialist states the arms race, with its crushing financial burdens and its ever more acute and frequent threats of war, was inexorably intensifying class antagonisms. Further, by exporting the capitalist means of production to Asia and Africa, imperialism was creating for itself new competitors and opponents, awakening the national consciousness of non-European peoples and providing them with the material and intellectual weapons for their own emancipation.[20] Kautsky perceived definite revolutionary possibilities in the anticipated national liberation movements of colonial peoples. For instance, he believed that political unrest in Asia and Africa would transfer back to Europe and significantly enhance the danger of world war, which must inevitably bring socialist revolution in its wake. Secondly, the independence struggles of colonial peoples would ultimately deprive capitalism of its last escape hatch: they could not but sap the economic and psychological vitality of the colonialist powers, finally obliging the capitalist system to confront socialism directly in its historic moment of truth. In this study, Kautsky repeated his earlier description of Social Democracy as 'a revolutionary but not a revolution-making party' (K. Kautsky, 1910, p. 52). Whatever the revolutionary implications, Kautsky's message was essentially as it had always been: Social Democracy must condemn colonialism while passively awaiting the inevitable collapse of the capitalist order.

By 1911 the attitude of the party centre towards imperialism had undergone a pronounced shift to the right as apocalyptic prognoses of collapse, war and revolution retreated before a much more benign interpretation of the imperialist phenomenon. Claiming that the bourgeois classes were only in part identifiable with imperialism, centrist spokesmen like Kautsky now strove to emphasise countervailing pacifist tendencies which merited Social Democratic support. For Kautsky, in particular, the period between spring 1910 and the close of 1911 marked a watershed in his intellectual development for, at this point, 'the differences between "centrism" and official revisionism disappeared almost completely' (Ratz, 1966, p. 216, n. 1). Thereafter, in arguments reminiscent of his 1898 position, he fulminated against the party left that militarism and war were not a necessary or inevitable feature of imperialism but merely an optional and mutually ruinous method of capitalist expansion, other methods being both possible and more truly reflective of the natural interests of the capitalist classes. Kautsky now went further and argued that imperialism itself was not a necessary feature of mature capitalism but rather an ephemeral aberration foisted on capitalism by pre-industrial social groups. He predicted that capitalism would soon outgrow its perverse flirtation with imperialism and that imperialist rivalries would give way to a 'cartel situation' in the world market or, as it might be termed today, the multi-nationalisation of the world economy (K. Kautsky, 1911/12, p. 108).

Kautsky's views during this post-radical, crypto-revisionist phase of the last years of peace were fully shared by other centrist leaders such as Ledebour (Ratz, 1969, p. 115). They were certainly shared by Bebel, at least publicly. Privately, Bebel was convinced by 1910 that the insatiable Prussian Junkers would sooner or later unleash a war of conquest upon Europe, a war which German Social Democracy was powerless to prevent or oppose. Here Bebel's thinking clearly owed little to Marxist categories and was obviously much more power-politically oriented than that of Kautsky. Believing such a war to be a catastrophe not only for European civilisation but, above all, for the cause of socialism and democracy within Germany, Bebel embarked on a private and secret diplomacy with Sir Edward Grey in the hope of persuading Britain to adopt a firmer stand against Germany, thereby either deterring lupine German imperialism from war or ensuring its defeat in the event of war (Crampton, 1973, pp. 218–32; Bley, 1975).

To a degree, Bebel's secret diplomacy with Britain was indicative of the true situation within the party centre. Whatever theorists like Kautsky might avow – and much of this theorising on the part of the left and centre alike was little more than rationalisation of tactical differences (Schröder, 1973, p. 40) – attitudes changed substantially after 1907. Outwardly and superficially the centre held fast to its official negativism towards imperialism and colonialism. But the realities of centrist practice were pragmatic acceptance of the status quo and growing collaboration with the policies of the imperialist state. In fact, by 1914, the majority of centrists, like the revisionists, thought of war not in the context of Marxist theory of imperialist rivalries but rather from the vantage-point of tacit faith in the power and invincibility of the Prusso-German state. They contemplated war as an avoidable catastrophe, but not as a catastrophe which Social Democracy by its own exertions was in a position to prevent or terminate. Should the unthinkable eventuate, the party majority was prepared to meet this contingency in the confident hope that Germany would emerge victorious. Meanwhile the party centre had 'come to regard the Triple Alliance as the policeman of Europe and the best deterrent to war' (Maehl, 1973, p. 5; cf. Victor, 1928, p. 178).

On the question of imperialism, the radical left adopted an unwaveringly militant and rejectionist position from the turn of the century onwards. In their polemical confrontation first of the revisionists and later of the party centre, a host of radical spokesmen (Rosa Luxemburg, Karl Liebknecht, Karl Radek, Paul Lensch, Anton Pannekoek, Franz Mehring, Parvus, Karski and others) adumbrated their implacable, after 1911 almost fanatical, hostility to imperialism which, like Kautsky, they perceived as an advanced and terminal stage of capitalist development. But, unlike Kautsky, they grasped the problem of imperialism essentially at its political roots, and always with a tactical purpose: their unrelenting demands for vigorous mass action against imperialism were a function of their voluntarist conviction – seemingly confirmed by the Russian experience of 1905 – that the way forward for German Social Democracy was to engage the masses continuously in active, aggressive and consciousness-raising class struggle culminating in socialist revolution:

> Having tried and failed to propagate the mass strike as an instrument for galvanising the party's thinking, Rosa Luxemburg began to look outward to society to provide the necessary solution. Like Canning she brought in one world to redress the balance of the other; in this case the old world of society to redress the ills of Social Democracy. (Nettl, 1965, p. 89)

Although radicals had been ventilating their opposition to imperialism at least since the suppression of the Boxer Rebellion in China, until Lenin wrote his *Imperialism: The Highest Stage of Capitalism* in 1916, the only radical leftist of note to attempt to underpin these preconceived political perceptions of imperialism with a Marxist economic proof was Rosa Luxemburg.[21] Her theory of imperialism, if it may be so called,[22] was enunciated in her *Accumulation of Capital*, which originated as an attempt to solve the problem (posed in Vol. 2 of *Capital*) of the extended reproduction of capital. More than 'a shot in the war between revisionists and anti-revisionists', her book was nothing if not an economically affirmed, massive attack on the tactical *attentisme* of the party centre (Kemp, 1967, p. 54; cf. Groh, 1973, p. 291).

In her anti-revisionist polemic of 1899 (*Sozialreform oder Revolution?*) Rosa Luxemburg had conceded that capitalism had not yet reached full maturity. It would do so, she predicted, only when it had expanded into and absorbed the whole globe, which would happen inevitably sooner or later. In another essay of the same year, entitled 'Shifts in world politics' (1899b), she saw the opening up of China as marking the beginning of the end for capitalism, China being the last remaining sphere of activity for capitalist expansion. At the International Socialist Congress at Paris in 1900 she also referred to the probability 'that the collapse of the capitalist order will proceed not from an economic crisis but from a political crisis induced by *Weltpolitik*' (MISC, 1900, p. 27). Her *Accumulation of Capital* was conceived partly as an intellectual exercise, partly as an attempt to provide the requisite economic proof of these theses, and above all as a theoretical vindication of her call to arms to the masses.

In this work of 1913 Rosa Luxemburg sought to demonstrate that by absorbing pre-capitalist societies and social strata – necessary for the realisation of surplus value and without which capitalism could not survive – imperialism was both 'the historical method for prolonging the career of capitalism' and 'a sure means of bringing it to a swift conclusion' (Luxemburg, 1963, p. 446). The assumption – evident in 1899 – that the maturation of the revolutionary proletariat might lag behind that of capitalism was now abandoned. In 1913 she emphasised the necessity of proletarian revolution to overcome capitalism before it reached the stage of collapse, which she limned in lurid doomsday colours as 'a period of catastrophe, . . . [of] ever more violent contortions and convulsions'. Since militarism, the growth of armaments and war were an integral part of the imperialist phase of capitalist development, she sounded the un-Marxist tocsin that imperialism in its death throes might well bury civilisation beneath its ruins. Veering back to Marx, she predicted an economic end to capitalism: 'The more ruthlessly capitalism sets about the destruction of non-capitalist strata at home and in the outside world, the more it lowers the standard of living for the workers as a whole'; terminal-stage capitalism 'becomes a string of political and social disasters'. Enter the revolutionary proletariat! All this was 'not to say that capitalist development must be actually driven to this extreme', for 'even before this natural economic impasse of capital's own creating is properly reached it becomes a necessity for the international working class to revolt against the rule of capital' (ibid., pp. 446, 453, 466–7). Here Rosa Luxemburg differed fundamentally from left-wing colleagues like Lensch, Pannekoek and Radek. Whereas the latter took the fatalistic view that collapse must precede revolution and was to be welcomed on that account, Rosa Luxemburg saw the mere tendency towards collapse as sufficient grounds for revolution.

Theoretical and tactical implications aside, Rosa Luxemburg's analysis of imperialism 'offered no specific recommendations for policy'. Least of all did she recommend any specifically colonial policy to the SPD (Nettl, 1966, Vol. 2, pp. 531, 535). Indeed, the efforts of colonial peoples to resist their exploitation and so hasten the collapse of capitalism were either ignored or rejected as reactionary and utopian. Like Marx and Engels (Schröder, 1975, p. 99; Wehler, 1971, p. 21; Lipgens, 1974, pp. 529–83), Rosa Luxemburg firmly believed that history was on the side of the big battalions, of large-scale, multinational political and economic entities. For her, the principle of national self-determination had no universal validity and could not be applied in the cases of small, economically backward or non-viable nations either in or beyond Europe. Furthermore, she saw behind national liberation movements merely the reactionary class claims of indigenous exploiters against those of foreign capitalist exploiters (Nettl, 1966, Vol. 2, pp. 535, 842–62). In practical terms, the position of Rosa Luxemburg on *Kolonialpolitik* – and of the left generally – therefore closely paralleled the indifference and negativism of Kautsky and the party centre.

But there was more to the emergent left than Rosa Luxemburg's contribution to Marxist economics cum clarion-call to the masses. Well before the advent of *Die Glocke* in September 1915, the party left also evinced traces of incipient social imperialism.[23] It was not uncommon, for instance, as at Chemnitz in 1912, for left-wing spokesmen like Paul Lensch and Anton Pannekoek to argue from the standpoint of historical materialism that Social Democracy should permit, even encourage, imperialist antagonisms to run their full and natural course, whatever the attendant risks and evils, as the shortest and necessary route to revolution and the socialist millennium (SPD A.C., 1912, pp. 415–19, 421–3). By arguing that imperialism was the historic-ally necessary and inescapable precursor to revolution and socialism, that German capitalists were serving the general interest in challenging Britain's industrial monopoly and maritime supremacy, that socialist opposition to imperialism and war was futile, utopian and un-Marxist, such writers lent powerful support to the cause of Wilhelmine expansionism. After August 1914 this radical chauvinism was to become all too explicit (Ascher, 1961, pp. 555–75; Sigel, 1976).

One concrete example of left-wing endorsement of social imperialist tendencies within prewar Social Democracy was the idea of a European federation or United States of Europe. From time to time this Saint-Simonian legacy, expressed in non-imperialist form, received the imprimatur of most centrist spokesmen, including Kautsky, Ledebour, Bebel and Max Beer. In sections of the party left, however, the idea of a German-dominated central European free-trade zone directed against the USA, Britain and Russia – as expounded by writers like Parvus-Helphand and Heinrich Cunow from the turn of the century onwards – acquired unmistakable overtones of the social imperialism which was the stock-in-trade of the revisionist right (Cunow, 1899/1900, p. 242; Parvus-Helphand, 1900, pp. 708–16, 738 ff; idem, 1907, p. 21 and *passim*).[24]

As Joseph Bloch complained to Karl Leuthner in 1907 (SMP, vol. 8: Bloch to Leuthner, 5 March 1907), the revisionists, too, were generally little interested in foreign policy and imperialism (Miller, ed., 1966, pp. xxx–xxxi; Owtscharenko, 1970, p. 566; Schorske, 1972, pp. 68–9). But there were two revisionist tendencies which rated foreign policy as a problem of the highest importance, and these two tendencies were themselves of the highest importance to revisionism. One was the moderate, rather amorphous free-trade imperialism represented by Eduard Bernstein, with occasional and limited support from patriots like Kurt Eisner and Eduard David; the other was the blatantly social imperialist current championed by Joseph Bloch, Richard Calwer, Karl Leuthner, Max Schippel, Gerhard Hildebrand, and other *Sozialistische Monatshefte* writers. The nature and significance of this dualism within the revisionist camp forms the substance of this study and will be elaborated in subsequent chapters. For the present it is worth noting that the ambivalence which characterised prewar revisionist attitudes towards imperialism was reflected in all factions well before the catalyst of war provoked a complete and enduring realignment of socialist forces.

From the above discussion of party theory and the imperialism debate in the dog-days of German Social Democracy just prior to the First World War it is apparent that in both the party centre and the radical left the nexus between theory and faction was indeed a tenuous one, and that neither theory nor faction offered a reliable guide to positions actually held on the imperialism problem. Very often theory was more a weapon in the struggle over tactics than a serious issue in its own right. Similarly, factional dispositions tended to reflect a preoccupation with tactical concepts: while the revisionists wanted a bourgeois alliance for parliamentary government and democracy, the left demanded mass action as part of a revolutionary learning process leading to social revolution, and the centre tried to conceal its tactical bankruptcy by insisting on the need to sit tight and wait for the millennium. Factional allegiance was certainly a poor indicator of the degree of receptivity or hostility towards imperialist ideas. Although present in all factions, social imperialist tendencies were manifestly most strongly rooted at either extreme of the socialist spectrum – in the illiberal nationalism of the right and in the impatient activism of the left. On the party as a whole the imperialism debate had both a disruptive and an integrative effect. While permanently alienating the left and setting it on the path leading to Spartacus, the KPD and the SED, it drove the party centre into an enduring symbiotic relationship with the right. This alliance was possible because there already existed a latent compatibility of outlook despite obvious surface antipathies. What the centre shared with radical or Bernsteinian revisionism in its foreign policy thinking – but not only on this terrain – was a substantial indebtedness to the assumptions of bourgeois and particularly English Radicalism. The gap, or rather the historical lag, between the party centre and revisionism was further bridged by the fact that by 1914 the centre had already been captured organisationally by the revisionists and their allies. Although the party and trade union rank and file played no direct part in this debate, the heat thereby generated added significantly to the fissionable material which in August 1914 drove the German masses not to the barricades but to a *furor teutonicus* and the massive destruction that followed in its wake.

Notes: Chapter 1

1   Some recent studies of working-class militancy on the eve of the First World War (Tampke, 1978; Geary, 1981, pp. 115–26) suggest that the left was much more influential, but the available evidence tends to confirm that 'the demands of the extreme left . . . elicited only a limited response within the party in the period immediately before the outbreak of war, [and] there is no reason to believe that the decisions taken by the party leadership did not reflect fairly accurately the state of public opinion among the rank and file of the SPD' (Guttsman, 1981, pp. 305–6).

2   *Die Voraussetzungen des Sozialismus und die Aufgaben der Sozialdemokratie* (The Presuppositions of Socialism and the Tasks of Social Democracy) (Stuttgart, 1899). All page references in my book refer to the 1921 edition, which omits nothing of importance from earlier editions and often expands on and defends controversial points made in the first edition. The only English translation, entitled *Evolutionary Socialism* (1909), is not a good one and omits the key chapter on Blanquism and the dialectic.

3   This was illustrated by Noske in his description of the party's activity in the Reichstag: 'In practice, things worked as follows: Ledebour or the Bremenese Henke would make a so-called theoretical speech. It then fell to me, as the party's second speaker, to get up and repair the damage wrought by their twaddle' (Noske, 1947, p. 35).

4   Whereas 80 per cent of all organised workers belonged to the Free Trade Unions, this figure represented only 20 per cent of the total workforce (Groh, 1973, pp. 482–3; Fricke, 1976, pp. 718–33). To date, the only English-language study of the German trade unions is Moses, 1982, 2 vols.

5   Groh believes that whereas an important precedent was established in 1906, the real trade union victory over the party came later, in 1913 (1973, p. 502).

6   For a Marxist account of the origins of trade union reformism, see Lison, 1978. Cf. Moses, 1982, pp. 1–13, 112–76.

7   Although most scholars appear to have accepted the Korsch–Matthias view of 'Kautsky-anism' as an integrative ideology, some have expressed reservations (Abendroth, 1964, pp. 36–7; H.-J. Steinberg, 1972, pp. 75–86; Meyer, 1977, pp. 35–7).

8   Kurt Mandelbaum considered Bebel 'the most consummate embodiment of all [the] contradictions' which collectively defined the party centre (Mandelbaum, 1926, p. 17, n. 33). Grunenberg sees Bebel as exemplifying as early as 1905 'all elements of that position subsequently described as "centrism" ' (Grunenberg, ed., 1970, p. 27).

9   Of the serious party literature available to German workers before 1914, Bebel's *Die Frau und der Sozialismus* (published in English as *Woman under Socialism*) was the most frequently purchased and widely read book, far outstripping in popularity any single work by Kautsky

or other party theorists (Haenisch, 1899/1900, p. 694; H.-J. Steinberg, 1972, pp. 129–42). On Bebel's theoretical position, see Grunenberg, ed., 1970, pp. 27, 30; Schorske, 1972, pp. 42–4; H.-J. Steinberg, 1972, pp. 18–19, 29, 56, 61–2, 69–72, 74–5; Groh, 1973, pp. 58, 74–8, 133, 156–7, 185–95; Lehnert, 1977, pp. 66–82.

10   This account might be objected to as being excessively 'Kehrite', a term which has been used (erroneously, as it happens) to encompass the supposed failings of scholars as diverse as Eckart Kehr, Hans Rosenberg, Fritz Fischer, Hans-Ulrich Wehler, Jürgen Kocka, Dirk Stegmann, Hans-Jürgen Puhle, Heinrich-August Winkler, Volker Berghahn, Fritz Stern and Karl-Dietrich Bracher. The principal deficiency discerned in the work of such scholars is that they have presented an allegedly distorted picture of modern German history by proceeding on the assumption that the British, French and North American experience of modernisation may be taken as the norm, in which light German industrialisation and its social and political consequences appear as a deviation and a perversion. Early criticism of the 'Kehrite' approach (e.g., Kennedy, 1972, pp. 134–41; W. Mommsen, 1973, pp. 3–43; Zmarzlik, 1975, pp. 62–71; A. Mitchell, 1977, pp. 181–99) has more recently given way to a concerted, full-scale assault on the part of a group of gifted and prolific young British social historians (e.g., Evans, ed., 1978; idem, 1982; Blackbourn, 1980; Eley, 1980; Blackbourn and Eley, 1980). Although the provocative and stimulating work of these determined 'anti-Kehrites' has produced valuable results, it is generally marred by a tendency to ignore or underrate high politics, and the role of the Junkers in particular (see Eley and Nield, 1980, pp. 249–71). To a greater degree than elsewhere, the work of the 'anti-Kehrites' has manifested that tendency, of which Arno Mayer recently complained, 'to neglect or under-play, and to disvalue, the endurance of old forces and ideas and their cunning genius for assimilating, delaying, neutralizing, and subduing capitalist modernization' (1981, p. 4). More seriously, it has failed to offer convincing proof that the German *Sonderweg* (separate or unique path to modernity) was no more than a myth. After all, numerous informed contemporary observers believed Germany to be significantly different from the West (see Ritter and Kocka, eds, 1982, especially chs 3, 7, 8 and 12) and German conservatives, then and since, have celebrated such putative divergence as a positive virtue. At this stage in the debate it therefore seems to me that the more reliable models, whatever their shortcomings, are still those of the German rather than the British school (see Wehler, 1973; Fischer, 1979).

11   This view of the impossibility of a gradual and peaceful transition to parliamentary democracy in Wilhelmine Germany is supported by Braunthal, 1961, Vol. 1, pp. 275–8; H.-J. Steinberg, 1972, pp. 145–50; Groh, 1973, pp. 21–33; Saul, 1974, p. 10; Steenson, 1978, pp. 119–20. Eley also concedes that there were 'definite limits to a decisive reforming departure before 1914' (Eley, 1980, p. 16).

12   Schorske maintains that 'pressure for action [came] not primarily from politically motivated, radically-minded Social Democrats . . . but from an economically dissatisfied and impatient rank and file'. At the same time, he insists that 'the mass strike discussion of 1913 . . . arose neither out of a strong popular wave of radicalism nor out of the tense atmosphere of constitutional crisis, but from the worried heads of the second echelon party leaders', for the working class 'was more indifferent than incendiary in the year 1913' (1972, pp. 262, 275, 276). Yet the substantial body of evidence adduced by Groh and others suggests that in 1905, 1910 and 1913 the masses were, in fact, in a highly radical frame of mind.

13   In the year 1912/13 the number of subscribers to the official party press showed an actual decline which was only barely made good in the following year (Schorske, 1972, p. 269; Groh, 1973, pp. 472–3; Fricke, 1976, p. 403).

14   Noske was of the same opinion: 'The German workers in their great majority listened to all kinds of speeches about the downfall of capitalism and the construction of a new order, but all these speeches meant to them was that they might eat their fill and enjoy a little pleasure in life' (1947, p. 5). For a non-socialist view of the irrelevance of theoretical disputation to the concerns of the rank and file, see Sombart, 1908, p. 254.

15   Neither study was very clearly understood at the time (H.-J. Steinberg, 1972, p. 85).

16   On his position within the party – he was, with Bebel, co-chairman of the SPD – see Gemkow, 1969, pp. 106–13.

17   For an introduction to Marx's views on this subject, see Wehler, 1971, pp. 17–33; H. Mommsen, 1979, pp. 61–80; Talmon, 1980, pp. 21–66. Once again, the master offered only limited guidance to those who would act in his name.

18   In recent years there has been a long-overdue revival of interest in the work of J. A. Hobson,

an important and influential thinker whose early economic studies were widely translated and avidly read, in Eastern Europe in particular, from the 1890s onwards. See Lee, 1970; Cain, 1978; idem, 1979*b*; Clarke, 1978; Freeden, 1978; Allett, 1981.

19　Hilferding's study is not considered here – partly for reasons of space and partly because of its irrelevance to this discussion, for Hilferding normally aligned himself with the party centre, although his theoretical work was grist to the radical mill (Ratz, 1966, pp. 220–1). For an overview of the prewar imperialism debate within German Social Democracy, see Schröder, 1975; H.-H. Paul, 1978, pp. 121–86; Walther, 1981, pp. 250–97.

20　Although *Der Weg zur Macht* has been praised as 'one of the summits of theoretical achievement on the part of the German labour movement, a true document of the revolutionary application of Marxist theory' (Irrlitz, 1966, p. 52), this prognosis of tumult in the non-European world was no more than mere prediction. At bottom, Kautsky was still wedded to the traditional, quietistic collapse theory (Ratz, 1967, p. 435; Schröder, 1973, pp. 32–4).

21　Hobson was not a Marxist; Hilferding was, though an Austro-Marxist. Despite his *Militarismus und Antimilitarismus unter besonderer Berücksichtigung der internationalen Jugendbewegung* (Militarism and Anti-militarism) (1907), Karl Liebknecht was not a theoretician, never aspired to recognition as such, and was always more popular with the rank and file than with the party intellectuals, who regarded him as something of a crank. In common with other radical spokesmen, he was much more concerned with action than with theory, of which, in his view, the party already had an excess (Trotnow, 1975, pp. 171–91; idem, 1980).

22　Even Nettl, whose sympathetic identification with his subject is beyond question, entertains doubts on this score. See Nettl, 1966, Vol. 2, p. 529, where he defends his use of the term 'physiognomy' in preference to 'theory'. In his later, abridged edition (1969, p. 165), he drops the term 'physiognomy' but still declines to accept her characterisation of imperialism as a theory.

23　The term 'social imperialism' is customarily employed to designate a manipulative and diversionary tactic designed to neutralise or co-opt internal liberation movements through external expansion (Bracher, 1964, p. 359; Eley, 1976*a*, pp. 265–90; idem, 1976*b*, pp. 71–86). It is here used to describe all attempts, including those emanating from within these movements, to link external expansion with the interests of such movements – in this case, with proletarian class interest or the interest of the labour movement.

24　See also Deutscher, 1954, pp. 103–5; Ascher, 1957, pp. 267–79; idem, 1961, pp. 555–68; Scharlau and Zeman, 1965, pp. 41–2, 62–4, 103–5, 113–20. One of the first to draw attention to such tendencies within the German party, although he focused mainly on the *Sozialistische Monatshefte* group, was Charles Andler, a French socialist intellectual who in 1913 made himself extremely unpopular (he was attacked by Jean Jaurès, Rosa Luxemburg and others) by lumping the likes of Hildebrand and Leuthner together with Lensch, Pannekoek and even Bebel (Andler, 1918).

PART TWO:

The Pursuit of National Integration: Joseph Bloch and the Sozialistiche Monatshefte

One must be an optimist if one wishes to remain a Social Democrat. Fortunately, this optimism is not entirely groundless. For as long as we have politicians like Schippel and Leuthner the differentials of progress are at least on hand; perhaps we will yet succeed in effecting real integration.

(Joseph Bloch to Leo Arons, 1908)

Even from a socialist standpoint, the acquisition of colonial domains has become a present economic necessity . . . We Germans, severely disadvantaged and repressed for decades by France and England, must, if it comes to the crunch, unanimously stand up for the long-term vital interests of our people . . . Only by means of a consolidation of Western Europe through final resolution of its internal difficulties will it be possible to present a solid counterbalance to the Russian advance in the East and the North American advance in the West . . . The socialist labour movement must decide on its fate. If it makes the wrong decision, it condemns itself to opposition and impotence. If it does what is necessary, it can rapidly win undreamt-of success in the domestic arena as well. Here there is only an either-or.

(Gerhard Hildebrand, 1911)

Indeed, it is precisely the Eisner–Stampfer tendency which is conducting no less than the most calamitous foreign polemics afflicting us, a heavier burden than Vorwärts *or the* Leipziger Volkszeitung.

(Joseph Bloch to Karl Leuthner, 1909)

For a long time the journal [the SM] used Bernstein as a decoy

(Dieter Fricke, 1974)

2

The World View and Politics of Joseph Bloch, 'Impresario of Revisionism'

You know how terribly important it is to me to create awareness of the issues of national politics. It is high time that people got to read an article beyond the customary ranting about crazy Junkerdom.

(*Joseph Bloch to Karl Leuthner, 1908*)

The socialist ideal is no longer a consumer ideal. It does not seek the greatest good of the greatest number but rather the highest attainment of all . . . True socialism is productive socialism. Productive socialism revolutionises world politics. The revolution in world politics occurs not for the sake of humanity but for that which has yet to be created.

(*Joseph Bloch*, Revolution der Weltpolitik, *1938*)

The opportunist phrases about positive work mean in many cases working for the liberals, *in general working for others, who hold the reins of power, who set the course of the given state, society, community. And Bebel drew this conclusion frankly, declaring that 'in our Party there are no few National Liberals of this kind, pursuing a National-Liberal policy'. As an example he mentioned* Bloch, *the well-known editor of the so-called* (so-called *is Bebel's word*) Socialist Monthly (Sozialistische Monatshefte)

(*V.I. Lenin, 1910*)

In May 1909 Rudolf Hilferding identified as the true 'impresario of German revisionism' not Bernstein but Joseph Bloch (1871–1936), editor of the principal revisionist organ, the Berlin-based *Sozialistische Monatshefte* (Hilferding, 1908/9, p. 165). From its inception as the *Sozialistische Akademiker* in 1895 until its suppression in 1933, and especially in the years 1907–14, Bloch's *Monatshefte* served as the main forum of both German and international revisionism and reformism.[1] If Bloch by no means escaped the attention of his contemporaries, he has since passed into an obscurity more complete and undeserved than that which has for so long shrouded the person of Eduard Bernstein. What is now known about Bloch and his publication, about his world view, political philosophy, strategic concept and attitude towards imperialism, suggests that he was a man of considerable influence within pre-1914 German Social Democracy and that this influence was used to proselytise on behalf of a position which was much further to the right than that of Bernstein or any other leading revisionist theorist of the time.

Joseph Bloch: Background and Training

Born in Lithuania and apparently brought up in an orthodox Jewish environment, Bloch received a classical humanist education in Königsberg and
studied mathematics and physics in Berlin, where he obtained his doctorate.
He began his association with the *Monatshefte* in 1896 while still a student and
thereafter supported himself with the assistance of his wife's dental practice
and by giving mathematics tuition. In 1933 he went into exile in Prague, where
he died three years later. Although capable of forming strong personal attach-
ments and of forceful advocacy of causes, Bloch normally abhorred public
appearances. He neither sought nor attained high office in the party or in
public life. He was, none the less, socially well-connected and an *habitué* of the
fashionable Café des Westens. A lifelong Francophile and a man of strong
intellectual inclinations, he cultivated an avid interest in the arts and in
learning, which interest he expressed in a variety of ways including active
membership of the *Freie Volksbühne* and his close attention to the review
section in each issue of the *Monatshefte*.

This publication was certainly far more widely known and read than were
the theoretical works of intellectuals like Bernstein. Yet the task of giving
precise definition to Bloch's world view or programme and to his influence
within prewar German Social Democracy has been rendered difficult by
Bloch's preference for anonymity. Bloch himself wrote only four substantial
articles out of some 4,000 contributions published by the *Monatshefte*. There is
no Bloch archive, and the Bloch correspondence which has survived is only
fragmentary. In his one and only book, posthumously published, *Revolution
der Weltpolitik*, Joseph Bloch expressed through Felix Stössinger[2] his basic
ideas on liberalism, nationalism and the Germans, in fact on all the great issues
which for so long had formed the mainstay of his political existence. The
following passage exemplifies Bloch's position in the mid-1930s when the book
was written:

> The immortal ideas of 1789 lead from humanity to the nation, which
> utilises this differentiation to solve discrete problems of human develop-
> ment. In Germany, Lutheranism prevented the development of an
> Erasmian humanity and a Cartesian civilisation, so that the Germans,
> while availing themselves of the same vehicle, travelled beside the path of
> evolution rather than along it. They proceeded not from humanity via
> nationality to universality but instead from Lutheranism via nationalism
> to racism. This progression is the work of the German educated class; it
> has determined the fate of the Germans as human beings in the twentieth
> century. (Stössinger, 1938, pt 3, p. 84)

Bloch's book (actually the work of Felix Stössinger 'in collaboration with
Joseph Bloch'), subtitled 'Joseph Bloch's legacy', offers an accurate compen-
dium of Bloch's post-1933 political position.

Stössinger's exegesis of Bloch's ideas needs to be read in the light of two
important qualifications. First, it is probable that in several respects the voice

speaking through Stössinger is not invariably the authentic Bloch but rather the revised and embellished version refracted through his devoted factotum, Bloch having died without having an opportunity to edit or approve the manuscript. His widow, Helene Bloch, did avail herself of this opportunity, and her emendations were apparently made in the same apologetic spirit as the Stössinger original. Secondly, in the author's zeal to display his mentor as a philosophically coherent whole and to plead Bloch's case before posterity by underlining whatever positive and durable elements were contained therein, Stössinger unjustifiably neglected to periodise the thought of the master. For the intellectual development of Joseph Bloch spanned four distinct phases. Until about 1905 he was a revisionist who took his stand on the now famous letter he received from Engels in September 1890. Then he became primarily a partisan of a socialist world policy. In the Weimar period, like Stresemann, he trimmed his sails and flew the ensign of the 'good European', until the onrush of anti-Semitic barbarism left him so disillusioned and embittered that he grasped at the very liberal straws he had once so egregiously despised. The Bloch who concerns us here is manifestly the revisionist social imperialist of prewar vintage.

Like so many assimilated German Jews, Joseph Bloch had developed an intense and cultivated pride in his links with German culture. He regarded himself as a German first and his religion, in accord with the Erfurt Programme, as a private matter beyond the purview of politics. He was therefore deeply shocked and mortally offended to see the German working class apparently acquiescing in the race theory of National Socialism which disinherited him politically, intellectually and culturally. It was at this point that Bloch turned to 'the immortal ideas of 1789' as providing a suitable theoretical framework for his counter-attack on the 'Germanic ideology'. In the prewar period, and beyond, incongruous as it may seem, he had been both a Zionist of sorts and a Pan-German nationalist while professing also a reformist rather than revisionist form of socialism. Like the British Fabians, Bloch had never been a Marxist. He was, therefore, able to devote his energies to the propagation of a positive programme of his own devising without, like Bernstein, having first to vindicate his apostasy.

As a Jew and as an intellectual acolyte on the fringe of theoretical revisionism, Bloch was something of a marginal figure. Yet he neither attached great importance to his Jewishness nor evinced a strong personal interest in Zionism or Jewish nationalism before 1914. He was certainly interested in, and well informed on, the plight of Jews throughout the world. He was also sensitive to anti-Semitism, particularly to Jewish anti-Semitism, and, like Eduard Bernstein, he complained of those socialist Jews who flirted with anti-Semitism in order to demonstrate their 'freedom from prejudice' (J. Bloch [Catilina], 1895c, p. 295).[3] Bloch was also opposed to anti-clericalism and insisted that the party maintain strict neutrality in matters of religion. He further expressed keen interest in the Bible as a document of Holy Scripture and in 1912 welcomed signs of a revival of religious sentiment. On such evidence it would seem not impossible that Joseph Bloch was, even before 1914, a religious Jew, most probably an adherent of reform Judaism. Although he published pro-Zionist articles, he personally wrote nothing on the Jewish question before the

First World War and he did not openly support Zionism until much later. An important guide to Bloch's prewar position is to be found in a remark he made in 1907, when he urged socialists to undertake a closer study of the Jewish question 'in its uniqueness'. As a worthy beginning in this area, Bloch commended to his readers an important Austro-Marxist study, *Die National-itätenfrage und die Sozialdemokratie* (1907*b*), by Otto Bauer, an assimilated Viennese Jew who, while denying the Jews any future as a nation, faithfully applied Marx's dictum (from his famous essay 'On the Jewish Question') that 'the social emancipation of the Jew is the emancipation of society from Judaism' (SMR, 1907, vol. 2, pp. 792–3. Cf. Bauer, 1907*b*, pp. 366–81; Wistrich, 1976*b*, pp. 115–24). In 1908, when one of Bloch's favourite *Monatshefte* contributors drew a parallel between the social and political function of Viennese anti-Semitism and the German socialists' abuse of the Junkers as a scapegoat for all the ills afflicting the German Reich, Bloch endorsed the absurd comparison as 'completely apt' (SMP, vol. 8: Bloch to Leuthner, 11 June 1908). In so doing, he was not, as Kurt Eisner objected, confusing the class concept with 'racial drivel'; Bloch was simply expressing his conviction that anti-Semitism and socialist Junker-baiting were equally products of a false consciousness that must vanish as man progressed in enlightenment. As an assimilated, enlightened Jew who identified strongly with German *Kultur*, Bloch at this time contemplated the Jewish question in Western Europe from an exclusively religious vantage-point. In so far as he acknowledged the necessity of Zionism, he did so as one born in Riga and hence in full awareness that the Jewish question in Eastern Europe was so manifestly a national question that Jewish emancipation there was virtually synonymous with emigration (Vital, 1975, pp. 71–2; Leuschen-Seppel, 1978, pp. 95–6). His post-1933 position (combining passionate Zionism with a bitter, blanket condemnation of the whole German people) arose, like his belated discovery of 'the immortal ideas of 1789', from an altogether different source – his spurned German nationalism – and represents an inversion of his earlier, culturally optimistic, Germanophile dichotomy of assimilated Western Jews and hopelessly oppressed and benighted *Ostjuden* (Wistrich, 1982, p. 165).

Bloch's World View

Joseph Bloch's world view bore unmistakably the marks of his background and training, his thinking being thoroughly imbued with the ethos of German idealism. The stamp of the German mandarin can be seen in his veneration of theory and the philosophical spirit which produced it, of the abstract values of *Kultur* and *Bildung*, in his anti-materialism, his contempt for mundane practicality, his ranting against philistinism, and his uncompromising hatred of liberalism. It can also be seen in his holistic turn of mind which yearned for the universal, for harmony and consensus in place of pluralistic discord, and in his susceptibility to Caesarism and the blandishments of national pride and national hope. Paradoxically, the mandarin caste was no less firmly attached to the principles of *Realpolitik*. Through this caste all Germany had become Prussianised, and the Prusso-German, as Bloch noted, was 'still a Machiavellian', a person who despised 'moralistic gibberish', used the lie as a weapon of war and 'cheerfully confesses to successful lies like Bismarck's falsification of the Ems dispatch' (Stössinger, 1938, pt 3, p. 57). The Joseph Bloch of prewar vintage was by no means remote from this tradition.

Where Bloch diverged from the mandarin tradition was his conversion to socialism, which he derived more from Ferdinand Lassalle than from Karl Marx. Bloch rarely supported his position by direct and explicit reference to Lassalle, although he had no qualms about playing off Lassalle against Marx, hailing the former as the true 'founder of German Social Democracy' and so branding Marx, by implication, as an interloper and an aberration (SMR, 1908, p. 249). Despite the obvious parallels (their idealism, statism, *Realpolitik*, nationalism, and so on), one cannot emphasise often enough two important qualifications. First, Lassalle was by no means the exclusive property of the right. Secondly, one cannot hold a thinker responsible for the excesses and false interpretations of his disciples and epigones. To accuse Lassalle, as does Leszek Kolakowski (1978, Vol. 1, p. 243) of being 'a pioneer of national socialism' is a gross exaggeration, although one could probably go further than Hartmut Stirner, who sees Lassalle as having merely 'paved the way for [socialist] recognition of Prussian militarism and the undemocratic unification of Germany from above' (1979, p. 125). In Bloch's view the foremost theoretician of the day was Conrad Schmidt (SMP, vol. 1: Bloch to Arons, 2 March 1908). What Bloch esteemed in Schmidt was his scholarship and theoretical competence, which contrasted starkly with the theoretical indifference of the 'revisionist' rank and file, as well as his undogmatic and critical approach to Marx, which made Schmidt, as one of the party's few trained and original economic thinkers, an invaluable weapon against the party radicals (see Osterroth, ed., 1961, p. 267; Sandkühler and de la Vega, eds, 1974, pp. 15–16).

But Bloch also expressed great admiration for the 'hyper-opportunistic' Austrian Social Democrats, whom he applauded less for their theoretical achievements than for demonstrating by their actions what had to be done by German revisionism once it transcended mere proselytising (SMP, vol. 8: Bloch to Leuthner, 16 August 1907). As a young man he had written to Engels seeking clarification of the relationship between economic substructure and socio-political superstructure. Engels's reply (MEW, vol. 37, pp. 462–4) was pounced upon as an excuse for treating economic determinism in a quite arbitrary and cavalier fashion. (While not denying the decisive importance of the economic factor, Engels stressed the reciprocal nature of the interaction between economic and non-economic forces, including contingency, and went so far as to declare that 'we make our history ourselves'.) Bloch did not hesitate to use this doctrine as an *ad hoc* prop to his own foreign policy views if necessary, but he ridiculed it as a 'funny notion' when revolutionaries like Trotsky enlisted it in the service of class struggle. What socialism meant to Bloch was a moral ideal – absolute and conceivable independently of economic conditions (Stössinger, 1938, pt 1, p. 11). It was not merely a theoretical structure but 'above all a complex of feelings having its ultimate justification in the personality of the respective individual' (SMP, vol. 1: Bloch to Arons, 24 October 1908). This suggested, on the one hand, 'the necessity of a consistently reformist policy' (Bloch, 1906, p. 883); on the other, the pursuit of an abstract ideal with specific implications:

> The socialist ideal is no longer a consumer ideal. It does not seek the greatest good of the greater number but rather the highest attainment of all . . .
> True socialism is productive socialism.
> Productive socialism revolutionises *Weltpolitik*. The revolution in *Weltpolitik* occurs not for the sake of humanity but for that which has yet to be created [*für die zu schaffenden Dinge*]. (Stössinger, 1938, pt 1, p. 20)

What he understood by productive socialism was a curious compound of individualism, democracy and mutual aid, anarchism being one of his earlier and continuing interests.[4] It had little to do with Marxism, for he saw Social Democratic politics as being, 'strictly speaking, anti-Marxist' (SMR, 1913, p. 1186). Although he subsequently claimed to have applied the Marxian method 'without adhering to the letter of Marxism', Bloch interpreted this method as 'nothing but the application of the evolutionary idea to social theory' (Stössinger, 1938, pt 1, p. 40). It is arguable that Bloch's idealism referred to 'the will to overcome oneself' in the tradition of St Paul, Spinoza and Schopenhauer. It is also arguable that it inclined heavily to Nietzsche's 'will to power'. What is not arguable is that it had anything to do with Kant. Bloch had no time for Enlightenment progressivism and disdained 'humanitarian chimeras' (SMP, vol. 8: Bloch to Leuthner, 1 June 1909). He insisted on a strict separation of politics and morality, regarding politics as being beyond good and evil and national interest as the only valid criterion of international policy (ibid., 12 February 1908).

In fact, the world view of Joseph Bloch owed a great deal to the thought of Friedrich Nietzsche, although the evidence does not point unequivocally to a close relationship. Writing in 1895 under his Catilina pseudonym, Bloch already demonstrated an acute awareness of the ambivalent uses to which Nietzsche might be put (1895b, pp. 121–7), and his reticence in publicly acclaiming such a resolute foe of democracy, socialism and nationalism was undoubtedly reinforced by the understandably widespread unpopularity of Nietzsche within the labour movement. Yet there are grounds for believing not only that Bloch had a thorough knowledge of Nietzsche but also that he retained an abiding affection for the man repeatedly condemned by Mehring as the philosopher of big capital. Catilina's 1895 anti-Bismarck article clearly showed that Bloch knew his Nietzsche at least as well as most Nietzscheans and that his reservations applied not to the master but to his disciples. When Nietzsche died in 1900 Bloch marked the occasion by publishing his portrait in the *Monatshefte* together with an article attempting to claim Nietzsche for the labour movement (Gystrow [W. Hellpach], 1900, pp. 630–40). At the outbreak of the First World War in 1914 Bloch defended the German cause in arguments that were the more strikingly Nietzschean for never having direct recourse to the philosopher. In his posthumously published *Revolution der Weltpolitik*, Bloch referred to Nietzsche several times, invariably with approval and usually in the company of such creative genius as Goethe, Heine,

Beethoven, Voltaire, Lassalle and Napoleon. Significantly, Marx was never mentioned in any configuration of this pantheon.

Nietzsche's cultural standard, his critique of morals and his superman myth were all paralleled in Bloch's thought. Like the young Nietzsche, Bloch entertained a profound and active interest in art, particularly in tragedy and music, and his cultural standard was no less fervently Greek and humanist (see Fletcher, 1980*a*, p. 463, n. 79). Reflecting Nietzsche again, he rejected all absolute moral systems in preference to a gradation of rank among different types of morals. In his article of September 1914, for instance, Bloch contrasted stale 'old' England with the vital, upwardly striving, young German nation. The Germanic superpower of the future had allegedly been subjected by the obstructionist and decrepit Entente powers to 'a mortal struggle for its national life, the highest moral entity yet produced by humanity'. To seek to impose restrictions on the growth of the German nation was denounced as nothing short of 'a crime'. This was no crime in the formal sense, for in the affairs of nations there was no judge to decide right against wrong. Technically, Bloch admitted, Germany had acted in breach of international law. But she did so with 'true ethics' on her side, since she fought for the 'transformation of all relationships' (*Neuordnung aller Verhältnisse*) among nations. At the same time, Bloch welcomed the internal solidarity of classes ushered in by the external menace of war. He saw the proletarian party as at last putting aside that petty, plebeian resentment which had hitherto weakened the whole and hindered the fruitful unfolding of national power. Now the domestic path was clear for the emergence of a true German greatness. Germany, he concluded, had the will to triumph, and Germany therefore would triumph (1914, pp. 1023–7). Bloch further mirrored Nietzsche in the supreme importance which he attached to the intrinsic worth of the hero or supra-historical personality. Thus, over a period of at least five years between 1906 and 1910, and at a time when the two men were in serious political conflict, Bloch persistently badgered Eisner for what he once termed 'a real article on the real Napoleon, a panegyric if you will, a hymn, just as long as it is not an allegory' (SMP, vol. 4: Bloch to Eisner, 7 February 1908). To get this 'art work drawn with love and enthusiasm' in the way Heinrich Heine might write on Napoleon, Bloch sent Eisner numerous books on the Corsican *Übermensch* (superman or, as Kaufmann insists, 'overman' [1974, pp. 308–31]). Some were borrowed from libraries, others from friends such as Scheidemann, and still others were obtained from publishers as review copies. Since Eisner neither returned the books nor delivered the promised article and ignored Bloch's pleas even when legal action threatened, Bloch must be credited with having demonstrated formidable patience and single-mindedness in the pursuit of a solitary article on a single 'higher-being'. This was by no means the only instance of Bloch's enduring interest in this phenomenon. The Nietzschean impact on Bloch's thought is conspicuous, even if not always identifiable as such. From Catilina the *popularis* to Bloch the 'liberal' Germanophobe and ardent Zionist, Nietzsche remained a constant intellectual companion.

Bizarre as it may now seem, Bloch's attempt at a synthesis of Nietzschean idealism and socialist politics was then by no means unique. Gustav Landauer, for example, maintained an equally deep-seated and enduring commitment to an anarchist variety of Nietzschean socialism, and others who sought some such reconciliation of Marx and Nietzsche included Bruno Wille (like Max Schippel and Landauer himself, formerly one of the Berlin *Jungen*), Erich Mühsam, Clara Zetkin and Ernst Bloch (Lunn, 1973, pp. 18–74; Bathrick and Breines, 1978, pp. 119–35). Within the Austrian labour movement, two of its founding fathers and most prominent figures, Victor Adler and Engelbert Pernerstorfer, were also strongly influenced by Nietzsche (McGrath, 1967, pp. 183–95; idem, 1974*a*, pp. 182–237; H. Mommsen, 1979, pp. 180–94). At any rate, Bloch saw no incompatibility between Nietzsche and socialism, as he understood that doctrine. He believed that socialism, or 'politics for the interests of the working class', was necessarily interventionist and therefore also, among other things, protectionist (SMP, vol. 11: Bloch to Edward Pease, 14 February 1910). Further, since socialism was collectivist it had a vital interest in the highest collectivity of all, which was not the proletarian class but the nation. Bloch considered the class struggle and national solidarity as being complementary and dialectically related, and he insisted that taking due cognizance of the general or national interest involved the adoption of a particular set of attitudes on specific issues such as the national question, world policy, *Kolonialpolitik* and *Englandpolitik* (SMP, vol. 1: Bloch to Arons, 24 October 1908). He was convinced that his own concept of socialism – and he himself used the terms revisionist, reformist and opportunist interchangeably – was the only valid one. But, in general, he was less concerned with explicating a coherent theory of either socialism or revisionism than with cultivating 'correct' attitudes and mobilising support for particular policies. Important as theory was, Bloch saw no need for the creation of a revisionist orthodoxy. He recognised the value of theory as a weapon in asserting the claims of revisionism against 'pseudo-theorists' of the left and centre but, in his view, theory had little value apart from this, unless it reflected and inspired *Praxis* or concrete political action of a positive sort, by which he meant the *Gegenwartspolitik* or day-by-day practical work of the party and movement. In this respect, he believed himself to be a true scientific socialist whereas the 'verbal revolutionism' of the orthodox and radical Marxists was mere disembodied dogmatism or utopian recidivism. The theorising in these quarters, so he complained to Eisner, was counter-productive because it 'generates no direct action while it hinders each and every kind of indirect action' (SMP, vol. 4: Bloch to Eisner, 2 August 1907). For all his patronage of theorists like Bernstein, Bloch was therefore, strictly speaking, a reformist rather than a revisionist.

The Programme of the *Sozialistische Monatshefte*

Illiberalism

The broad themes of idealism, *Realpolitik* and socialism set the parameters to Bloch's political thinking. Yet the central concerns of Bloch's world view, as these emerge above all from his correspondence with leading revisionists in the period 1897 to 1914, were his attempts to come to grips with the problem of liberalism, his absolute attachment to tariff protectionism, his Anglophobia, his commitment to German nationalism, his preoccupation with the problem of socialist tactics and strategy, and his conviction that German imperial expansion was desirable and necessary.

Unquestionably, the supreme bugbear of Bloch's political thinking before 1914 was liberalism. This canker, as he saw it, had its origins in classical economic theory and in the ideas of 1848. In his correspondence during these years Bloch repeatedly denounced liberal economic theory in the strongest possible terms. Free trade, he believed, was not only bad economics – bad for Germany and bad for the world economy – but it presupposed other evils which were at least as pernicious: it implied a pro-English foreign policy, renunciation of German *Weltpolitik*, internationalism in place of a 'healthy national policy' and the sacrifice of the 'productive classes' on the altar of sterile dogma (SMP, vol. 8: Bloch to Leuthner, 12 February 1908 and 18 May 1909). He was determined that Social Democracy should not be a party to any of this. As matters stood, it appeared to Bloch that the German labour movement, and especially its revisionist wing, was running the very real risk of 'duplicating all the mistakes and stupidities of its liberal predecessors to the point of self-annihilation' (ibid., 10 October 1909). Rather than court disaster in this way, Bloch wanted to see Social Democracy standing always to the right of bourgeois democracy on all important issues, including the national question (ibid., 21 May 1909).

Since liberalism and Prussianism were polar opposites, Bloch took it upon himself to defend the Junkers against 'the nonsense of 1848' (*Achtundvierzigerei*), which he later professed to admire as the only German uprising which had also served the cause of social liberation in accord with the ideas of 1789 (Stössinger, 1938, pt 3, pp. 61–2). He encouraged Leuthner's efforts to propagate 'Prussia's mission' and frequently expressed his irritation at the wrong-headed anti-Prussian outbursts of the perverse South German reformists. The reason the Junkers had to be tolerated and protected was that they had become an essential pillar of the Prusso-German social structure: their material interests were too intricately meshed with the state and society at large for the Junkers to be cast aside without serious detriment to the German nation (SMP, vol. 8: Bloch to Leuthner, 19 January 1910). German Social Democracy had no interest in weakening the nation, only in consolidating and strengthening the state by broadening its popular base so that state and nation became coterminous. By 1907 Bloch's statism had carried him a long way from the Catilinarian *popularis* of the mid-1890s.

Protectionism

His incessant and vociferous denunciation of free trade was matched by his equally insistent advocacy of tariff protectionism. Persuaded that protectionism was the wave of the future, even in liberal Britain, Bloch argued that it represented 'the class interest of the worker in the economic sense' and served the best interest of 'the actual producers' generally, in which category he also included the peasantry (SMP, vol. 1: Bloch to Arons, 24 October 1908). Protectionism was socially progressive as well as a tactical necessity for the realisation of parliamentary government through alliance with non-proletarian forces (SMP, vol. 8: Bloch to Leuthner, 3 March 1908; Bloch, 1910, pp. 941–5). 'Real socialism', he strove to persuade Edward Pease of the London

Fabian Society, 'can only be protective' (SMP, vol. 11: Bloch to Pease, 14 February 1910). Hence the vehemence with which he condemned the free-trade leanings of Bernstein, David and other revisionists. By defending free trade they were guilty of a quixotic tergiversation, of working to replace the barren Kautsky dogmatism with a pointless *Simplicissimus* dogmatism that was as devoid of hope as it was anachronistic and moribund (SMP, vol. 8: Bloch to Leuthner, 19 October 1909).

Anglophobia

No less vehement was Bloch's dislike of the British and his low regard for British culture and civilisation. In this he declared himself 'in complete agreement' with Leuthner: 'What you say . . . is the only correct view' (ibid., 14 April 1909). Bloch totally disapproved of 'the prevailing Anglomania' which he discerned in German society and politics, and not least within Social Democracy. This he denounced as 'detrimental to the interests of the German people' (*volksschädigend*) and downright unpatriotic (ibid., 1 June 1909). In any event, it was quite unwarranted in that the British had made no worthwhile contribution to civilisation, as he once sarcastically claimed:

> Even I recognise full well the significance of Anglo-Saxondom for civilisa-tion as a whole, and I shall never forget that it was the English who brought the bath-tub to the Continent. Yet I cannot summon up any warmth for this nation, possibly because of its inartistic nature. But even if I was infatuated with England, as is Bernstein for instance, I would consider it absolutely necessary to oppose with the utmost vigour this pernicious approbation and undignified apeing of all things English. Most emphatically in political life, of course (but not only in politics). And indeed the very manner in which our comrades are wont to play the role of English advocates in Germany can not be condemned too strongly. (ibid., 14 April 1909)[5]

Bloch was disposed to recognise that the British had, after all, certain accom-plishments to their credit. For example, he disagreed with Leuthner on the British administration of India, which he considered sound and beneficial even for the Indian people. But he stressed that such positive features of British achievement, rare as they were, flowed exclusively from the hard-headed pursuit of national interest; they were in no way attributable to such factors as the British Constitution, economic policy or national character, and they were on no account to be confused with the application of moral principles (ibid., 14 April 1909). Bloch fatalistically accepted the inevitability of Anglo-German conflict. Like his non-socialist contemporaries, he traced this antagonism to the harsh but ineluctable realities of competing economic interests and power-political objectives. In this view, Britain was everywhere standing in the path of Germany and had somehow to be thrust aside – for she would never budge voluntarily – if the youthful and yet friable German empire were not to go the way of the Spanish, Portuguese, Dutch and French empires.

Bloch therefore proselytised for greater Social Democratic interest in ques-tions of world policy and for deeper understanding of the larger problems of

Germany's future place in the world. Above all, he sought unswervingly to inculcate in his readers a lively awareness of the magnitude and seriousness of the 'English peril'. Hence his close attention to the fortunes of the British protectionist lobby. He did not overlook the possibility that a protectionist victory in Britain might prove damaging in the short term to Germany's export markets, but he nevertheless welcomed such a prospect in the belief that it must finally put all Germans on their mettle *vis à vis* Britain. He hoped that, at the very least, it would compel the doctrinaires within Social Democracy to open their eyes at last to their national responsibilities and abandon their misplaced deference to British models.

Revisionist Consensus Politics

In his attitude towards the state and the national idea Bloch revealed himself to have been the best Trojan horse the Pan-German reactionaries could have hoped for within Social Democracy. Traditionally, Social Democrats of the left and centre alike had contemplated the Prusso-German state as an impregnable and irretrievably satanic citadel which had to be smashed to its foundation-stones before the harbinger of the millennium, the socialist *Zunkunfts-staat*, could be erected in its place. As a 'revisionist', Bloch preferred to look on the semi-feudal bourgeois state as a crumbling fortress ripe for the taking and worth the taking because its foundations were essentially sound. Through Parliament, the Reichstag suffrage and the prospect of 'an extension of the basis of the movement through co-operation with all suitable elements' (ibid., 3 March 1908), Social Democracy had already forced the drawbridge of the semi-absolutist class state. Since he regarded parliamentary democracy as being almost a reality, Bloch felt that it was time for socialists to adopt a proprietorial or national view of the existing state. Social Democracy, he wrote, was 'a party with the highest interest in the body politic, and therefore the true bearer of the idea of the state' (ibid., 17 December 1908).

The kind of state Bloch had in mind as the ideal product of a bourgeois-socialist alliance (since the proletariat was considered incapable of attaining political power by its own exertions alone) had no connection either with proletarian dictatorship or liberal democracy. Insufficient evidence exists to enable us to piece together a precise and detailed picture of Bloch's concept of the state in the prewar period. It is clear that he favoured a strong executive power and had little faith in parliaments on the liberal-democratic model. Occasional remarks in his correspondence, juxtaposed with attitudes which may be inferred from articles by his favourite contributors, suggest that, for Bloch, democracy held scant appeal except in so far as it advanced the cause of security and efficiency. As a vehicle for expanding or preserving freedom and individual rights it seemed hardly to enter into his ken. According to Stös-singer, Bloch aimed at an 'organic socialist democracy in ascendancy over individualistic, head-count democracy'. This tells us very little in terms of concrete institutions, unless it refers to the abortive Weimar experiment in a *Reichswirtschaftsrat*, which Bloch evidently anticipated and approved (Stössinger, 1953, p. 514). Certain it is that Bloch had a low opinion of Parliament as a source of creative ideas and set little store by such institutions as ministerial responsibility (Bloch, SMR, 1908, pp. 442–3). In his view, democracy was not inherently desirable, merely expedient, and justifiable to the extent that it served the nation (SMR, 1913, p. 1186).

Even if political power were not within immediate reach of the working class, the proletariat and its party still had a vital stake in the national idea. The folk community or *Volksgemeinschaft* – Bloch chose to call it the 'solidarity of classes' – was for him at least as important as its complement, the class struggle. Service to the common weal was, after all, the essence of socialism (SMP, vol, 1: Bloch to Arons, 24 October 1908). Bloch saw this concept as being founded in the economic interests of nations and in the psychological vitality of peoples. The economic interests of the whole nation, he explained, formed a powerful determinant of the national idea in that they were decisive for the world standing of the nation which, in its turn, acted as a major generator of national sentiment among all classes. But the national idea was more than the sum total of the collective economic interests of the nation. It also had cultural and spiritual dimensions which transcended class and fostered a sense of national community among all classes. If the *Volkskraft*, or vitality of a people, was as potent as that of the Germans, socialists would be dogmatic fools to pretend that only the class struggle mattered to the worker (SMP, vol. 8: Bloch to Leuthner, 19 October 1908).

In brief, socialism demanded active support for German nationalism. Internationalism Bloch dismissed as mere 'cant'. He therefore called on Social Democracy to activate in the masses 'the German disposition' (*die deutsche Gesinnung*), which he defined as 'the national, non-monarchist interest of the German nation' (ibid., 30 November 1908). This attitude inclined him to favour each and every naval and military increase, for he believed that a strong Germany was 'the only guarantee of peace', by which he seemed to imply that a 'weak' Germany might actually have to go to war – a prospect which he genuinely deplored – in order to enforce her claims in Morocco and elsewhere (ibid., 17 December 1908).

The programme of action to which Bloch hoped to convert Social Democracy through the pages of his journal did not envisage an opportunistic 'hand-to-mouth' collaboration with non-socialist parties 'for the sake of bagatelles'. Bloch urged the adoption of 'a definite political plan founded on the premise: no perpetually changing constellations – these merely facilitate extra-parliamentary government – but the creation of a solid majority on the basis of common short-term objectives' (1910, p. 943). Although he aimed at the foundation of a stable, long-term parliamentary alliance between Social Democracy and 'all suitable elements', Bloch was emphatic that this must not be achieved at the price of concessions to liberal doctrine or policy. He expressed his basic attitude towards a bourgeois alliance as follows:

My programme has always been: in all purely political questions, collaboration with the bourgeois parties (not with the *Demokratische Vereinigung* but with real parties); in all questions of economic policy, strict representation of the worker's standpoint, which requires protectionism and therefore the protective tariff system as well – in this matter, in short, the strongest antagonism towards liberalism. Regrettably, the thinking of the [Social Democratic] party has been quite the reverse: in political questions it has hacked away at liberalism instead of making use of it. In economic questions it has trailed after a liberalism championing an interest inimical to that of the party. (SMP, vol. 4: Bloch to Eisner, 14 June 1909)

Vorwärts was therefore quite incorrect in accusing Bloch, as it did on 27 and 28 July 1910, of seeking to convert Social Democracy into a mere bourgeois party by recommending the adoption of bourgeois policies in order to enhance the alliance value of Social Democracy. (The real perpetrators of this heresy, in Bloch's view, were the party orthodoxy and the left.) What Social Democracy must do was first equip itself with the correct ideology and programmatic objectives which, as indicated, must always be to the right of bourgeois democracy and which must be rigidly adhered to. The basis of a bourgeois alliance followed naturally from this. Ideologically, the revisionist bloc policy of the *Monatshefte* was founded on support for the national idea (SMP, vol. 8: Bloch to Leuthner, 21 May 1909). Its practical basis was to be the pursuit of 'common short-term objectives'. Bloch evidently believed that no agreement could be reached on economic questions. These had, therefore, to be somehow eliminated or put in cold storage (*ausgeschaltet*). Clearly he believed the bourgeois parties, as a whole, to be still too much tainted by Manchesterism and 'the nonsense of 1848' (SMP, vol. 1: Bloch to Arons, 2 March 1908, vol. 4: Bloch to von Elm, 17 August 1907). In effect, Bloch was urging something very closely resembling Miquel's *Sammlungspolitik*, with the notable difference that Social Democracy was to form part of the *Sammlung* rather than serve as its whipping-boy.[6] The object of this strategy was to secure the integration of Social Democracy into the existing social order, to realise that solidarity of classes which he viewed both as a necessary complement to the class struggle and as in the general interest and hence in the interest of socialism (SMP, vol. 1: Bloch to Arons, 2 March 1908).[7] Since the Reich leaders were too incompetent to effect this from above, it behoved Social Democracy to do so from below by means of a parliamentary alliance (SMP, vol. 8: Bloch to Leuthner, 19 November 1908).

Revisionist World Policy
Bloch had nothing but scorn for the efforts of left-wing and orthodox Marxists to grope their way towards a coherent and consistent theory of imperialism. In his estimation, Hilferding, Kautsky, Luxemburg and the others were trying to make imperialism do the work of the revolutionary proletariat now that the collapse theory was so palpably unserviceable as the *deus ex machina* of revolution. Since its terms of reference were irrelevant to his concerns, Bloch held aloof from this debate. Before publication of either Kautsky's *Der Weg zur Macht* or Luxemburg's *Die Akkumulation des Kapitals* Bloch put his finger on what he regarded as the fundamental flaw in the thinking of orthodox and radical theorists alike when he ridiculed as a 'funny notion' Trotsky's insistence on 'the decisive character of the economic factor'. On Bloch's analysis, the problem of imperialism had a political-historical dimension which was at least as important as the laws of economic development pertaining to advanced capitalism. English imperialism, for instance, was much more than an

appendage of Watt's steam-engine. British expansionism, so he repeated again and again through his minions, had a pedigree and a dynamic which extended back to Elizabeth I and bore the hallmark of geography at least as strongly as it reflected transient social and political structures.

Taking a positive view of his role, Bloch disdained controversy with misguided Marxists and concentrated instead on the propagation of his own 'realistic' interpretation of imperialism together with the tasks that it devolved on German socialists. His view of imperialism (maintained to his dying day: *Revolution der Weltpolitik* contains a whole section, part 6, expounding 'the law of empire') was essentially that in vogue among non-socialist intellectuals of the period. This was the geopolitically oriented theory of the world empires which assumed that Germany was subject to an inexorable law which obliged her to confront, as a question of immediate practical politics, the stark choice between world power and irreversible downfall (see Fischer, 1969, pp. 68–77; Barkin, 1970, pp. 131–207). By 1907, at the latest, this theory had become the linchpin in Bloch's political thought. Thereafter his prime concern, and that of the *Monatshefte*, was to revolutionise the foreign policy thinking of German Social Democracy by winning over the masses and their party to an understanding of the urgent necessity of a German world empire.

During the prewar period Bloch himself was less directly preoccupied with the minutiae of German imperial policy, as it might or ought to be, than with the more fundamental task of inculcating in Social Democracy at large an appreciation of the importance of foreign policy as an issue in its own right. He complained repeatedly of a fault which he discerned in all tendencies within the party, but one which he deemed most reprehensible among the South German reformists. In fact, Bloch had little justification for impugning the patriotism of the Bavarian socialists. In 1907, for example, Vollmar informed the Stuttgart congress of the International:

> It is not true that internationalism means anti-nationalism. It is not true that we have no fatherland. And I say the word 'fatherland' without adding any hair-splitting declarations on the concept. Not for a moment can the love of humanity hinder us from being good Germans. (cit. Hirschfelder, 1979, vol. 2, p. 534)

Yet the source of Bloch's anxiety was not Vollmar so much as Kurt Eisner and his activity as editor of the *Fränkische Tagespost*. What concerned Bloch most was an alleged indifference to, and ignorance of, foreign policy issues which manifested itself in misguided and irresponsible attempts to make party-political capital out of the Imperial government's failures and lack of accomplishment in this field (SMP, vol. 8: Bloch to Leuthner, 5 March 1907 and *passim*). Bloch set himself the task of rectifying this situation.

The short-sightedness of Social Democracy was all the more deplorable in that the role of Social Democracy, as Bloch saw it, was to save the nation from its incompetent rulers through the establishment of parliamentary control over foreign policy. Bloch's Caesarism is here fully apparent:

> The truth is that I would have no serious objection to personal rule in

foreign policy if only the person of the ruler was in a position to provide the necessary guarantees of ability. Ultimately, foreign policy can not be made in Parliament. There must always be a great personality on whose decisions it hinges. To be sure, this personality must himself be only the objective embodiment of the whole nation (*des Volksganzen*). Whether this person holds the office of king or chancellor is of secondary importance. (ibid., 19 November 1908)

It need hardly be pointed out that Bloch's position on the conduct of foreign policy was in no way compatible with the inherited body of socialist thought, not even with Lassallean social monarchism. In its reference to the *Volksganze* it was far more redolent of the conservative romanticism of the extreme right. Bloch continued:

But all this is, of course, irrelevant because in our case the wearer of the crown has not only failed to offer proof of ability but has done the reverse and proven his inability. It follows that for us, in the realm of foreign policy too, salvation lies in the transition to parliamentary government. (ibid.)

When he urged the people, through Parliament, to save the nation from its incompetent rulers, Bloch naturally referred to an aroused and properly informed Social Democracy, for there was no doubt in his mind that the irresponsible and muddle-headed liberals had nothing positive to contribute to this task. To realise this objective, Bloch waged a concerted campaign through the *Sozialistische Monatshefte* to promote the idea of a parliamentary alliance with all suitable non-socialist elements, the essential criterion of suitability being the extent to which the parties in question rejected liberal doctrines and deferred appropriately to 'national' values.

The core of Bloch's foreign policy programme was the concept of a 'continental Europe' united under German domination. Bloch himself did not begin to endorse this objective publicly until August 1914 (1914, pp. 1023–7),[8] but there can be no doubt that its exponents among the *Monatshefte* writers – Leuthner, Calwer, Hildebrand, Schippel, Maurenbrecher and Quessel being its most consistent advocates – spoke for Bloch on this question. To Kurt Eisner, Bloch frankly admitted that he and Calwer were of one mind on foreign policy issues (SMP, vol. 4: Bloch to Eisner, 29 January 1906). To Leuthner, he confided that in matters of *Kolonialpolitik* Calwer championed 'the sensible, in my opinion, only possible viewpoint' (SMP, vol. 8: Bloch to Leuthner, 24 June 1907), and to others he confessed to being 'terribly depressed' over the treatment meted out to Calwer when the party declined to re-endorse Calwer as an SPD Reichstag candidate in 1907 (SMP, vol. 4: Bloch to von Elm, 12 August 1907). On numerous occasions he told Leuthner that he entrusted the cause of the *Monatshefte* in essence to him (Leuthner) and to Schippel (for example, SMP, vol. 8: Bloch to Leuthner, 5 January 1907). On matters of foreign policy generally, and on the continental idea in particular, Bloch therefore left it to his favourite authors to spell out in detail his imperialist programme. The manner in which they discharged their commission has been excellently summarised by Mandelbaum (1926, pp. 19–31).

The content of the continental idea, as expressed by Bloch's spokesmen without interruption from 1905 onwards (Stössinger, 1953, p. 516) and subsequently by Bloch himself, derived from the then popular assumption that the entire globe was in the process of being divided into vast economic and political power concentrations, designated world empires. Those already in being or under construction were the power conglomerates of Russia, Great Britain, the United States and East Asia. No single European power possessed a broad-enough economic or political base to be able to withstand indefinitely the pressure of these colossi. If Germany hoped to preserve an independent existence in the future, she must therefore create a world empire of her own. This new German imperium should take the form of a European consolidation, together with overseas colonies and Asia Minor, into an economically and politically integrated Euro-African power bloc under German leadership. This 'Greater Germany', as Calwer called it as early as 1900, could be realised peacefully after the manner in which Prussia united Germany through the Zollverein (1900, p. 1234). (In begging the question of Bismarck's wars, Calwer may well have been speaking with a Machiavellian tongue in cheek.) Bloch, Calwer and company were aware that the key to European union lay in a Franco-German understanding founded on mutual economic and political interests and cultural ideals, which prescribed an autarkic economic policy directed, above all, against Britain as the traditional and natural enemy of European integration. The projected union of Europe would be 'secured against all tempests only when Germany and France [had] buried the hatchet for all time', which would issue not from a momentary decision but from 'economic development over coming decades' (Calwer, 1908, p. 664). At the time of the Anglo-French Entente, Bloch had also urged such a *rapprochement* while acknowledging that the attainment of this desirable objective had been postponed by the conclusion of the Entente (SMR, 1904, p. 403). On the other hand, Gerhard Hildebrand, a former National Social whose heretical views finally led to his expulsion from the SPD in a *cause célèbre* of 1912, pleaded stridently for a 'United States of Western Europe' encompassing Britain as well, although he doubted whether anything short of war could induce Britain to acquiesce in, much less join, a united Europe under German leadership (1910*b*; 1911*b*). Yet even a Franco-German *entente* was difficult to visualise without an appeal to Mars, especially after 1904 but equally by virtue of the nature of the envisaged integration, which was not to be a partnership of equals but 'a closer commercial *Anschluss* to Germany' (Calwer, 1900, p. 1234). Several of Bloch's spokesmen argued quite openly that Germany should not shrink from any method, including a war of aggression, if her demands were not granted peacefully (for example, Maurenbrecher, another former National Social, 1907, p. 199; Hildebrand, 1911*b*, pp. 2–3, 58, 62–3). Others, such as Leuthner and Schippel, were more circumspect, confining themselves to veiled hints as to the inevitability of war. In any event, the anticipated five-part division of the globe was not expected to plateau into a state of equilibrium. The same dynamic which was producing this supranational, transcontinental and centripetal power concentration was expected to culminate in the restoration of the universal empire or, as Bloch put it, in 'a rebirth of the Roman imperium'. Naturally, as a German patriot, Bloch hoped that of the five contending superpowers the Germanic continental European imperium would ultimately emerge as the new cock of the walk enforcing a *pax Germanica* (Stössinger, 1939, p. 32). In 1953 Stössinger betrayed the truly revolutionary scale of his mentor's imperialist dream by referring to the projected European imperium in terms of a Euro-African restoration of the Carolingian empire that would 'neutralise the other imperia [Stössinger then had in mind the USA, the British Commonwealth, Soviet Russia and Maoist China] through its own power' (Stössinger, 1953, pp. 517–18).

What has been said with respect to Bloch's position on *Weltpolitik* and imperialism applies with equal validity to his position on *Kolonialpolitik*. Bloch merely insisted that the subject be treated from 'the higher standpoint of *Weltpolitik*' and then left it to Max Schippel and others to develop in detail the ideas which he wished to see accepted as the cornerstones of Social Democratic *Kolonialpolitik*. He was more than content with the fruits of Schippel's labour:

> Schippel's colonial articles reveal him at an even greater pinnacle than that on which he hitherto so consistently stood, and I am pleased that it was I who was able to secure their publication. If our comrades would appropriate to themselves even a small part of the abundance of lessons to be learned therein, then I would regard that in itself as a great service rendered by the *SM*. (SMP, vol. 8: Bloch to Leuthner, 3 March 1908)

After 1909 Gerhard Hildebrand was also given free rein as a colonial specialist of the *Monatshefte*. Bloch was of the opinion that Hildebrand and Schippel were basically of one mind on this issue. He was nevertheless critical of Hildebrand's methodology, which he considered too narrowly based on economic determinism to the exclusion of the all-important political factor, 'the higher standpoint of *Weltpolitik*' (ibid., 1 June 1909).

Well before the outbreak of war in 1914 writers of the Schippel–Leuthner school were striving to link this grandiose concept of imperial expansion to the class interest of the proletariat. Few did this more convincingly than Gerhard Hildebrand. All tended to borrow the jargon of the left. Thus a commonly advanced argument was that national capitalism must be permitted, even encouraged, to run its full and natural life-span before socialism could appear on the agenda of history. Social Democracy might, therefore, speed up the wheel of history not by obstructing German capitalism because of its present evils but by assisting its flight towards full maturity and socialist metamorphosis. This was often bolstered by subsidiary arguments, such as the view that socialism was viable only on the basis of large-scale economic entities. To hasten the maturation and ultimate demise of German capitalism, Social Democracy was urged, as the heir to German capitalism, to adopt a positive attitude towards such manifestations of imperialism as protectionism, colonialism, navalism and militarism. Frequently advanced *ad hoc* arguments in support of the latter were humanitarian considerations or the need to defend hearth and home against tyrannical Russian barbarism, French *revanchisme* or British commercial envy.

Bloch admitted that the editors of the *Neue Zeit* had quite correctly guessed his purpose: it was not a matter of coincidence that the views expressed by writers like Schippel, Leuthner, Calwer, Hildebrand, Maurenbrecher and others tended to converge in support of Pan-German nationalism; what the *Monatshefte* boiled down to was 'the unfolding of a new set of intellectual guidelines' (*das Werden eines neuen Gesichtsfeldes*) (ibid., 19 October 1908), which, as historians like Dieter Fricke (1973, pp. 1209–20; 1975b, pp. 454–68; 1975a, pp. 528–37) and Robert Wistrich (1976a, pp. 109–42) have described them, radiated from an epicentre of fervent German nationalism and self-conscious, if often cryptically expressed, social imperialism. The image of Joseph Bloch presented by his widow, Helene Bloch (in Siemsen, 1954, pp. 86–91), his colleague and pupil, Felix Stössinger, and his nephew, Charles Bloch, is therefore incomplete and misleading as it applies to that period of Bloch's life and work when the impresario of revisionism reached the apogee of his influence and success.

If opportunism means unprincipled behaviour, abandonment of principles in favour of momentary or partial successes, retreat in the face of difficulties and resistance, then Bloch cannot be regarded as an opportunist. Never having shared the aspirations and objectives of Marxism, this grey eminence of German revisionism nevertheless had a world view, an instrument and a strategy which he would under no circumstances compromise. His world view was that of a social imperialist and assuredly not that of a 'good European'; his instrument was the *Sozialistische Monatshefte*; and his strategic concept was that of a *Sammlung* or consensus of all the nationalist forces, united through Parliament in the cause of national integration at home and in the pursuit of imperial grandeur abroad.

Notes: Chapter 2

1   Readers interested in more detailed documentation or more extensive reference to the available literature are advised to consult Fletcher, 1980b, pp. 459–84.

2   At an early stage, Felix Stössinger (1889–1954) worked with Bloch as an editorial assistant on the *Monatshefte*. He then became a publisher and antiquarian and in 1933, like Bloch, went into exile, first in Prague, moving to Nice in 1938, and finally to Switzerland in 1942. After Bloch's death he fought and won a long, and apparently bitter, legal battle with Bloch's widow, Dr Helene Bloch, over ownership of *Revolution der Weltpolitik*, which is therefore here attributed to Stössinger rather than to Joseph Bloch. Stössinger had published his book in a *Selbstverlag* (private printing) at Prague in 1938. In Paris in 1939 Bloch's widow had reissued the book, attributing authorship to her late husband.

3   Friedrich Stampfer, also of Jewish origin, similarly remarked on 'many Jewish Social Democrats who granted anti-Semitism a certain relative justification' (1957, p. 86; cf. Leuschen-Seppel, 1978, pp. 162–82 and *passim*). This phenomenon probably had nothing to do with the fact that Bloch signed his early articles 'Catilina'. It is uncertain why Bloch should have chosen as his pseudonym the name of the famous Roman conspirator who, having once served the dictator Sulla, set out to save the republic – in a proletarian uprising which, had it succeeded, could only have ended in another military dictatorship – from selfish optimates and the moral decay which, according to Sallust, had begun to undermine the traditional republican virtues when Rome embarked on her path to imperial grandeur. Bloch's choice of pseudonym does, however, suggest a preference for conspiratorial methods and an ethical approach to socialism, both of which he retained. That he ceased to sign himself 'Catilina' after the turn of the century may indicate an early shift in his attitudes towards both the state and imperialism.

4   Writing under his Catilina pseudonym in 1895, he had argued in the *Sozialistische Akademiker* that 'all the anarchist systems are nothing but communism' and that the only real point at issue between anarchists and socialists was their differing assessments of the tactical worth of parliaments (1895*b*, pp. 273–6, 299–303, 360–2, 382–4, 474–7). In his subsequent *Monatshefte* Rundschau contributions, Bloch continued to take a close and informed interest in the fortunes of German anarchism and in Gustav Landauer, in particular, whom he – like Kurt Eisner – held in high regard.

5   Bloch denounced as 'barbarism' a proposal to substitute English for French in German school curricula. The greater practical utility of English, which he conceded, did not, in his view, commend it above a *Kulturgut* such as French (SMP, vol. 11: Bloch to Engelbert Pernerstorfer, 11 February 1908). In his low regard for all things British and his concomitant Francophilia Bloch maintained a stable position throughout his life (Wistrich, 1976*a*, p. 129).

6   If one disregards the (admittedly most important) anti-socialist dimension to official *Sammlungspolitik*, it becomes apparent that Bloch's *Sammlung* (consensus) ideal was not so very far removed either from that of Bülow, Tirpitz and the Navy League (Berghahn, 1971, pp. 146–52; Deist, 1976, pp. 126–7, 328–31; Winzen, 1976, pp. 228–30; Kitchen, 1978, p. 239), or from the rumbustious populist nationalism of Alfred Hugenberg, General Keim and some of the Young Turks of the Centre Party (Zentrum) (Chickering, 1979*a*, pp. 7–33; idem, 1979*b*, pp. 470–89; Blackbourn, 1980; Eley, 1980, p. 290 and *passim*).

7   In this letter Bloch expressed the hope that through Leuthner and Max Schippel 'we may yet succeed in bringing about a real integration'. His nephew Charles Bloch is therefore wide of the mark in interpreting Joseph Bloch as having striven consistently for the revolutionisation of society through socialism rather than as having aspired to working-class integration into some modified version of the existing capitalist social order (1977, p. 150).

8   Here Bloch equated 'true internationalism' with 'giving free rein to one's own nation to unfold its power'. While justifying the war against both Britain and Russia, he found it 'painful' that Germany was obliged to wage war against France, who had none the less brought this on her own head through her 'unhappy alliance with Russia' and the extravagant world-power ambitions of leading French politicians. Such ambitions he deemed inappropriate to a nation with a declining population and productivity growth rate. In this war, he claimed, Germany was 'acting also in the interests of France' in that she was laying the foundation-stones of a strong and united Europe. To Bernstein, Bloch expressed his belief that France ought to be drawn into an economic and political alliance with Germany, suggesting that the pill might be sweetened by the return of part of Lorraine to France in exchange for the whole of the French Congo (BP, D 61: Bloch to Bernstein, 9 December 1914). Thus the kind of Franco-German partnership envisaged by Bloch was a decidedly one-sided affair. His culturally oriented Francophilia plainly had little practical political import. It was no accident that during the First World War 'the only Majority Social Democratic group which possessed a clear foreign policy programme was the small revisionist circle around *Sozialistische Monatshefte*' (Matthias, 1954, p. 30).

3

The Organ of German and International Revisionism – Bloch's Sozialistische Monatshefte

The so-called Socialist Monthly *has deliberately placed itself outside the party press, it is subject to no party supervision, its financial backers are shadowy, unknown figures, and for years its tendency has been constantly directed against the views of the party . . . In fact, the views of our opponents have been represented in the SM (in trade policy, in naval and military matters, by Calwer and Schippel; in the imperialist furore, by Leuthner and Maurenbrecher) much more vigorously than in many of the organs of our antagonists.*

(Leipziger Volkszeitung, *1909*)

Enclosed, at last, the cheque for use by the Monatshefte; *you can simply write in the amount. Get the bank there to give you a cheque-book at once.*

(Leo Arons to Joseph Bloch, *1907*)

The SM offers seven sheets for 50 pfennig, whereas we [on the Neue Zeit] *charge one mark for eight sheets. We are not privy to that publisher's secret*

(Emanuel Wurm, Munich party congress, *1902*)

There is no doubt that the Neue Zeit *is considerably lacking in topicality, no doubt either that it has not always succeeded, to the extent that the* Sozialistische Monatshefte *has succeeded, in attracting new blood to its staff.*

(Clara Zetkin, Munich party congress, *1902*)

The Sozialistische Monatshefte *owes its flourishing condition to the fact that it publishes a great many articles on important topical issues, articles that would not have been published unless someone had appealed to the appropriate writers.*

(Wolfgang Heine, Munich party congress, *1902*)

Take the German magazine Sozialistische (??) Monatshefte *and you will always find in it utterances by men like Legien, which are thoroughly opportunist, and have* nothing *in common with socialism, utterances touching on* all *the vital issues of the labour movement. The 'official' explanation of the 'official' German party is 'nobody reads [the]* Sozialistische Monatshefte, *that it has no influence, etc.; but that is* not true. *The most prominent and responsible people, members of parliament and trade union leaders who write for [the]* Sozialistische Monatshefte *constantly and undeviatingly propagate their views among the masses . . . We must not try to play down the disease which the German party is undoubtedly suffering from, and which reveals itself in phenomena of this kind*

(V.I. Lenin, April 1914)

On the eve of the SPD annual congress held in Leipzig in 1909 there appeared a once-only satirical publication which was widely distributed among delegates attending the congress. Styling itself the *Also-Socialist Monthly Circus* and ruthlessly lampooning the *Sozialistische Monatshefte* and all associated with it, this model of scurrility not only went for the jugular vein but also tellingly revealed much of the pith and marrow of Bloch's latter-day Catilinarian conspiracy. Adorning its cover, for example, was a cartoon showing a frail and scholarly Bernstein as the revisionist Siegfried forging a sword bearing the name Dr Twaddle, or Tin (*Blech*), unmistakably a pun at Bloch's expense. The caption neatly reversed a line from Act 1 of Wagner's *Siegfried*, so that *'mit Bappe back' ich kein Schwert'* (I cannot forge a sword with pap) became 'Of pap I forge my sword'. Although decidedly wide of the mark in its depiction of the relationship between Bloch and Bernstein, this caricature alone captured several essential truths of German revisionism. In the first place, Bernstein was accurately portrayed as a Don Quixote figure: whatever his intellectual contribution to the movement, he was not a man of action but an artless, unworldly intellectual who often confused and exasperated his would-be followers by his apparent predilection for rushing at the impossible. Secondly, Dr Bloch and his publication did indeed serve the function ascribed to them by the anonymous Leipzig wits. As the needful 'sword of revisionism', Bloch saw to it that the *Monatshefte* did consistently 'champion the principle of taking the mickey out of everything officially endorsed by the party'. In the long term, too, Dr Twaddle/Tin, the sometime Catilina, did turn out to be a cardboard 'Nothung', for he never succeeded in forcing his programme on the party, and the men who inherited Bebel's mantle were not his own favourites but detested *Praktiker* like Friedrich Ebert.

The *Sozialistische Monatshefte* had originated in 1895 as *Der Sozialistische Akademiker* (Socialist Academician) (see Jarausch, 1982, pp. 357–9). In its third year of publication the red-covered journal changed its name to *Die Sozialistischen Monatshefte* (Socialist Monthly), apparently in order to broaden its appeal and 'to evade direct party supervision' (C. Bloch, 1974, p. 257). In 1908 it began to appear fortnightly, still styling itself the *Sozialistische Monatshefte*, and it remained in existence until 1933. It was published by a limited-liability company, the Verlag der Sozialistischen Monatshefte GmbH, which also put out occasional brochures and booklets. The business affairs of the *Monatshefte* were managed by Fräulein Martha Mundt.

The *Sozialistische Monatshefte* Image: Independent Socialist Scholarship

The character which Bloch tried to stamp on his creation was that of an independent, socialist and scholarly publication. With each issue the *Monat-shefte* proclaimed itself 'an independent organ for all viewpoints based on the common ground of socialism', Bloch's understanding of independence being absence of official party control or supervision. No more than Kautsky did he intend to tolerate *all* viewpoints within the socialist camp. Despite some token deference to the left around the turn of the century – even Rosa Luxemburg once published an article in the revisionist journal, and Paul Lensch offered his services, to his subsequent embarrassment – Bloch quickly established his publication as the mouthpiece of a motley crew of right-wing dissidents generally stigmatised in the party as 'revisionists'. This was hardly surprising since Bloch himself was clearly out of step with the centre-orthodoxy, and revisionist or heterodox writers virtually had nowhere else to go. After the suppression of the radical *Jungen* in 1891, the full weight of the party's anti-heresy witch-hunt apparatus bore down almost exclusively on unorthodox opinion of the right. By 1900 the *Neue Zeit* was closed to such writers, and in 1905 *Vorwärts* conducted a thorough anti-revisionist house-cleaning. Socialists were forbidden by party discipline from writing for non-socialist publications, and although this rule was not strictly enforced, transgressors ran a grave risk and were frequently taken to task at the party's annual congresses. Some, like Calwer and Schippel, were quietly shunted out of the movement; others, like Hildebrand, were unceremoniously expelled. Still others (Karl Leuthner, for example) either were beyond the clutches of SPD officialdom (Leuthner was an Austrian), or enjoyed a measure of immunity by virtue of their possession of independent power bases (in the local or regional party organisations, in the trade unions and co-operatives) or (like Eduard Bernstein) out of considera-tion for personal stature acquired through past services to the movement and general popularity. In fact, as Bebel reluctantly acknowledged, there were simply 'too many Bernsteins' within German Social Democracy for its ortho-dox oligarchs to risk provoking a party split by mounting a determined campaign to be rid of them. Anti-revisionist crusades therefore tended to be more desultory, perfunctory and ritualistic than persistent and resolute. Although some mavericks were driven out of the movement, many remained active within it, even if the official party organs did their best to silence or ignore them as mere noisome eccentrics. The party centre did not succeed in eliminating such heretics because, as Lenin, Luxemburg and others repeatedly objected, it did not really try to do so. In one sense, it would even be true to say that if the *Monatshefte* had not existed, it would have been necessary, or at least convenient, for the party centre to invent it. The point, however, is that the *Monatshefte* was very far from being, as was argued at the time and has been repeated ever since, merely an uninfluential gaggle of up-market intellectuals.

Although not an official party organ, the *Monatshefte* insisted on its claim to be socialist, a claim which Bloch took pains to emphasise against the innuen-does and calumnies of the official party press. The *Leipziger Volkszeitung*, for instance, invariably referred to the *Monatshefte* as 'the so-called *Socialist Monthly*', and in *Vorwärts* and elsewhere it was continuously alleged that the *Monatshefte* was published by a capitalist enterprise, that it was secretly financed by bourgeois benefactors (by implication, having a vested interest in discrediting Social Democracy), or that the journal accepted contributions from bourgeois writers (as if the official party press never did so). In reply, Bloch insisted that his publication was every bit as socialist as the official theoretical organ, the *Neue Zeit*, both by dint of its content – all social and political problems dealt with in the *Monatshefte* were discussed, so he contended, exclusively from a socialist standpoint – and in view of the high reputation of its contributors, all of whom were respected persons enjoying responsible positions in the party and trade unions or in the fraternal parties and organisations abroad. Indeed, Bloch maintained that he was guided by the principle that party discipline should be as meticulously adhered to by the *Monatshefte* as it was binding on the *Neue Zeit*. Bloch was so confident of his position that he challenged Bebel, as he did on subsequent occasions, to appoint an official inquiry into the affairs of the *Monatshefte* in respect of the accusations made by its critics (ABP, B68c: Bloch to Bebel, 29 October 1902).

Bloch's concern for the scholarly reputation of his journal was also apparent at its inception as the *Sozialistische Akademiker*, which had described itself as an 'organ of German-speaking socialist students and scholars'. In 1897 the only change, apart from its name, was that it became international as well, which then enabled the *Monatshefte* to broaden the basis of its claim to academic excellence and disinterested intelligence. 'One ought to appeal to the educated', Bloch confided to his closest colleagues (SMP, vol. 1: Bloch to Arons, 2 March 1908, vol. 8: Bloch to Leuthner, 3 March 1908). By so doing, Bloch hoped not merely to enhance the prestige and plausibility of the journal or to bolster its claim to independence of party control; here he was hinting at the highly ambitious *raison d'être* of the journal. For 'the task of the *SM*', as explained by his widow, 'did not consist in merely enlightening the *masses* but in showing their *leaders* the *practical* paths they had to tread, in providing them with the arguments *for* and *against* an action, *for* and *against* a *theory*, thus leading them in new directions' (Helene Bloch, cit. Siemsen, 1954, pp. 88–9).

Bloch's Editorial Dictatorship

Content with his role as a sort of socialist Baron von Holstein (Rich, 1965), Bloch functioned as a decidedly shadowy figure. Not only, as we have seen, did he rarely write articles himself, but he also, though a member of the party, normally shunned congresses, conferences and public appearances, which he found depressing and attended, if at all, merely as an observer. Only once did he run for public office and, in general, he neither sought nor attained prominence within the party or in public life. As an editor, he was not without certain idiosyncrasies. He attached great importance to enthusiasm and personal conviction. He esteemed brevity and disliked undue polemical acerbity, even where he shared the sentiments involved. A man of intense feeling, he could forgive almost any personal or political lapse in a writer for whom he had formed a fondness. Dieter Fricke has claimed (1973, pp. 1210–11; 1974c, p. 844) that the *Monatshefte* was strongly influenced by 'a small circle of revisionists' including Wolfgang Heine, Leo Arons, Eduard Bernstein, Adolf von Elm, Eduard David, Edmund Fischer, Otto Hué, Paul Kampffmeyer, Paul Löbe, Max Quarck, Robert Schmidt, Wilhelm Schröder, Friedrich Stampfer and Albert Südekum. But Fricke does not clearly indicate the nature or scope of this influence and admits that Bloch 'made sure that only those contributions appeared which were not at odds with his own views'. Moreover, some of those listed – Stampfer, for example – had no influence on the prewar *Monatshefte* and were, in fact, intensely disliked by Bloch. In reality, Bloch ran the journal almost as a fief and brooked no interference with his editorial policy. As Eduard David grumbled, no one but Joseph Bloch exerted any influence on the editorial policy of the journal (*Vorwärts*, 6 May 1909). Issues of the *Monatshefte* were normally planned two to three quarters in advance, where possible a year ahead of publication. Articles were solicited from contributors through a torrent of letters, telegrams, postcards, telephone calls, and reminders of every imaginable sort. Once a writer had been badgered, cajoled or bullied into promising an article, he was immediately deluged with suggestions as to subject and title, sources and reading material, points to be made or refuted, arguments to be utilised or attacked. As Arthur Stadthagen complained at the 1902 Munich party congress, there was simply no saving oneself from the man (SPD A.C., 1902, p. 137). Under Bloch's editorial pen, manuscripts submitted were often quite drastically altered and distorted, in which form they not infrequently went to press before the author had been consulted fully as to Bloch's deletions and amendments.[1]

This was one method of censorship employed by Bloch. Naturally he did not hesitate to reject outright, on one pretext or another, those articles whose content he deemed irreconcilable with his own political position but, as a rule, he was much more prudent and flexible in his handling of contributors than was Kautsky on the *Neue Zeit*. Rather than blacklist writers he disliked, Bloch made every effort to acquire and retain the services of notable authors, however uncongenial their opinions. To circumscribe their nuisance effect on the journal, Bloch preferred to guide their journalistic productivity into safe channels or to arrange in advance for an approved author to prepare an immediate counter-attack (SMP, vol. 8: Bloch to Leuthner, 6 May 1909).[2] In this way, he was able to keep on his staff and manipulate to his own advantage a variety of noted writers with whom he had little or nothing in common politically. For a long time, the revisionist organ could therefore profess to be what it was not – an independent journal for the propagation of all viewpoints and tendencies within the German and international socialist camp. Until about 1905 this fiction retained some plausibility (C. Bloch, 1974, p. 261; Fricke, 1974*a*, p. 455). Thereafter, Bloch discriminated more openly in favour of those writers whose views he considered to be in accord with what he termed 'the programme of the *Sozialistische Monatshefte*' (SMP, vol. 8: Bloch to Leuthner, 5 January 1907). According to Stössinger, by 1908 the *Monatshefte* had become the 'organ of Blochian revisionism', which was 'worlds apart' from Bernsteinian revisionism (Stössinger, 1953, pp. 507, 514). By 19 June 1909 *Vorwärts* and the *Leipziger Volkszeitung* could claim with justification: 'In fact, the views of our opponents have been represented in the *Sozialistische Monatshefte* (by Schippel and Calwer on trade policy and on the naval and military question, by Leuthner and Maurenbrecher on the imperialistic furore) much more vigorously than in many of the organs of our antagonists.' As Bloch gave more and more space to his favourite writers (Schippel, Calwer and Leuthner), the *Monatshefte* became an avowedly imperialist organ with a palpable bias towards Anglophobia, tariff protectionism and German nationalism after the Pan-German manner. In any event, Bloch had never valued freedom of expression *per se*. He tolerated views other than his own not out of principle but for reasons of expediency. As he put it to Karl Leuthner, toleration was to him a political tool, not an ideal (SMP, vol. 8: Bloch to Leuthner, 21 February 1907). Bloch, after all, could hardly expect his critics within the party to show forbearance in respect of his own heresies if he himself failed to make formal obeisance to the principle of toleration as applied to his own comrades within the revisionist fold. Much as he disliked them, he felt that the polemics of people like Bernstein, Eisner and David were harmless enough, even useful in that they provided a convenient foil to the Leuthner–Schippel viewpoint, which he believed was more than capable of holding its own in debate with Bernsteinian 'fantasies'.

Nothing Succeeds Like Secession

The Success of the Sozialistische Monatshefte
Despite occasional claims to the contrary – these were frequently an expression of wishful thinking on the part of anti-revisionists – Bloch's periodical struck root within a few years of its first appearance, soon outstripping in popularity and notoriety the party's official theoretical organ, the *Neue Zeit*. In the absence of reliable circulation figures for both publications, this impression cannot be adequately confirmed statistically. Nevertheless, the testimony of contemporaries indicates that the shaky fortunes of the *Neue Zeit* were a constant source of concern to the party, whereas the *Monatshefte* regularly sold out quickly (SMP, vol. 15: Mundt to Bloch, 13 September 1908), continued to increase its circulation among working-class subscribers even in times of higher subscription rates (SMP, vol. 4: Bloch to von Elm, 4 August 1908, vol. 10: Mundt to Bloch, 7 September 1904), and had no difficulty in attracting the collaboration of most of the leading literati within the prewar German and international labour movement, all of which alarmed and exasperated the party left and centre, and the partisans of the *Neue Zeit* in particular.

Certainly, Bloch and the friends of the *Monatshefte* had no doubts as to the success of the revisionist organ (SMP, vol. 4: Bloch to von Elm, 4 August 1908). This success is further reflected in the attacks to which it was subjected by its opponents within the party, in the judgement of non-partisan observers, and in the use made of the *Monatshefte* by the enemies of the labour movement.

At the Lübeck and Munich party congresses (1901 and 1902) several delegates complained vehemently that the *Neue Zeit* was already being undermined by Bloch's publication, pointing out that almost all the party's Reichstag deputies and even a member of the party *Vorstand* (Ignaz Auer) evidently preferred to write for the *Monatshefte* rather than for Kautsky's journal (SPD A.C., 1901, p. 189, 1902, p. 133). Bebel, too, protested that 'a considerable number of respected party comrades' had manifested a serious 'want of solidarity and comradely feeling' in this way (1901/2, p. 104). On another occasion, he called the journal the 'organ of party stupefaction', while Kautsky was equally adamant that it represented a 'scandal for the party' (see Schröder, 1978*a*, pp. 202–3). As a rule, organs like *Vorwärts* and the left-wing *Leipziger Volkszeitung* strove to ignore the *Monatshefte*, having learnt from experience that anti-revisionist tirades were futile and more likely to provoke a revisionist counter-offensive than to rally the faithful to a trial of strength with the citadel of right-wing heresies. When the party press could not refrain from delivering broadsides against the *Monatshefte*, the tenor of its invective served merely to underline the magnitude of the threat perceived in the revisionist journal. Thus, in its issue of 26 June 1908, *Vorwärts* felt compelled to admit that the *Monatshefte* writers were 'persons who not only play a certain role in the party but [were] arrogating to themselves, over and above this, the role of a supreme tutelary authority within the party'.

In 1914, in one of his many attacks on the 'model organ of opportunism', Lenin accused the German party leaders of covering up for the *Monatshefte* out of fear to move against it. He repeatedly branded as an untruth the claim that the *Monatshefte* was without influence within the party. Since such luminaries as Carl Legien regularly wrote for the *Monatshefte*, where they consistently propagated views which had nothing in common with orthodox Marxism, Lenin believed that the *Monatshefte* was having a decisive and wholly deleterious impact on the working-class reading public in Germany (Lenin, 1966, pp. 169–70 and *passim*). In 1913 a French socialist academic, well acquainted with the German party situation, issued a similar warning against the influence of the *Monatshefte*, which he yet considered 'the most lively and erudite socialist periodical in the world' (Andler, 1913, p. 452). More recently, Bloch's widow claimed that the *Monatshefte*, and its review section in particular, was widely used in universities and seminars, noting too that the *Handwörterbuch der Staatswissenschaft* described the publication as 'the most important socialist journal' (in Siemsen, 1954, p. 88n.)

The anti-socialist forces naturally found in the *Monatshefte* a veritable treasure-trove of information and opinions which they utilised to embarrass the party. Even Imperial Chancellor Bethmann Hollweg was not above quoting the *Monatshefte* against the SPD, and Admiral Tirpitz also took a favourable view of the journal (SPD A.C., 1913, p. 121; Tirpitz, 1919, p. 423). As early as 1902 a Social Democratic Reichstag deputy protested that 'we [socialist deputies] in the Reichstag have had to take issue with the *Sozialistische Monatshefte* in every session' (Stadthagen, SPD A.C., 1902, p. 138). The same complaint was voiced again and again in the party press. On 26 June 1908 the *Leipziger Volkszeitung* accused the *Monatshefte* of providing the enemies of Social Democracy with an arsenal of ammunition against the movement, a scandal which had been going on for years. According to the *Schwäbische Tagwacht* the revisionist journal was 'virtually living from its struggle against Social Democracy', and the Hamburg *Fremdenblatt* opined, in its issue of 7 May 1909, that the best weapons against Social Democracy were being supplied by the revisionists of the *Monatshefte*. There were times when even staunch supporters of the revisionist journal felt that the *Monatshefte* had gone too far in this direction, as when Adolf von Elm warned Bloch that a backlash appeared imminent – involving a possible boycott by both readers and writers – unless Bloch extended his criticism beyond Social Democracy so as to cover the sins of the non-socialist parties as well (SMP, Vol. 4: von Elm to Bloch, 1 August 1908).

Where the Sozialistische Monatshefte *Succeeded*

The influence acquired by the revisionist journal was exercised principally through such avenues as the party and trade union press, trade union official-dom, Reichstag and other parliamentary deputies, and through party func-tionaries like Ignaz Auer. After 1905 a large proportion of the regional party press came under the domination of revisionist editors (Fricke, 1962, pp. 132–9). Many of these editors themselves wrote for the *Monatshefte*. All were supplied with material by Bloch or were heavily dependent on other revisionist syndicated material, such as Friedrich Stampfer's *Privatkorres-pondenz* or Wilhelm Schröder's *Sozialdemokratische Parteikorrespondenz*. It has been estimated that four-fifths of the party press reprinted without alteration the articles supplied by Stampfer (Fricke, 1962, pp. 136, 180–1; Schumacher, 1964, p. 99; Nettl, 1969, pp. 312–14, 323). By contrast, the *Sozialdemo-kratische Korrespondenz* – launched as a left-wing alternative to the official party press in December 1913 and sponsored by Franz Mehring, Rosa Luxemburg and Julian Marchlewski after the centrists had forced their exclusion from the *Leipziger Volkszeitung* – had a very limited success: 'no more than four local papers ever reprinted any of the articles at any one time, and often whole issues appeared without any echo' (Nettl, 1969, p. 314). The trade union press fell under revisionist control still earlier and to an even greater extent than in the case of the regional party press (Fricke, 1962, p. 237).

Trade union officialdom was quick to align itself with revisionism, in which union leaders saw a natural ally and a theoretical vindication of their work and of their claims to status and autonomy within the labour movement. Through his close relations with individuals like Carl Legien and Adolf von Elm, Bloch therefore acquired a powerful foothold in the trade union and co-operative movements. The significance of this connection was nowhere better illustrated than at Mannheim in 1906, where the party was obliged to grant *de facto* recognition to the trade unions' independence of party control.[3]

No less firmly in revisionist hands was the parliamentary representation of the party. Indeed, the all-important Reichstag parliamentary *Fraktion* or caucus – party organisation closely paralleled the Reichstag electoral structure – had been under right-wing control at least since the steamship subsidisation quarrel of the mid-1880s. With the advent of theoretical revisionism in the late 1890s, the SPD *Fraktion* was easily captured by the emergent revisionist faction. In the 1912 Reichstag, for instance, no fewer than 36 of the 110 socialist deputies were trade union representatives. When Bebel died in August 1913 even the leadership of the parliamentary party became visibly revisionist, the decisive voices now being those of such notables as Südekum, David, Vollmar, Frank, Ebert, Scheidemann and Noske. In the provincial parliaments and local government bodies revisionist predominance was still more marked than in the Reichstag (ibid., p. 129).

Not so easily defined are the links between the *Monatshefte* and the new breed of party functionaries which emerged after 1905. Epitomised by Fried-rich Ebert, these men generally had no interest in theoretical questions, immersed themselves in the day-to-day practical work of the movement and its organisations and thus acquired the undeserved reputation of being above factions. Their sympathies unquestionably resided with the revisionists. Ebert, for one, may well have been a 'centrist' who 'personally rejected revisionism'. But however hard he 'tried to remain detached from the party factions by burying his reformist preferences', Ebert's actions revealed 'how much patriotic emotions affected his policies and prevented him from being "neutral" ', and it was Ebert, after all, who 'led the party to an openly reformist course' (Buse, 1973, pp. 83, 229, 232, 293). That the revisionism of such *Praktiker* was non-theoretical and derived more from the nature of their work and their contact with the masses than from the pages of the *Monatshefte* cannot obscure the fact that they came to represent, if not a tool then certainly an invaluable ally of Bloch's cause.

Why the Sozialistische Monatshefte *Succeeded*

Three factors explain the success of the *Monatshefte*. These were Bloch's skill in attracting and retaining the services of notable and respected writers; the greater popular appeal which he was able to impart to the journal by keeping it topical, down to earth, readable, varied and comprehensive in content; and, most important of all, the stable financial base enjoyed by the *Monatshefte*.

Bloch's success in winning an impressive list of reputable writers has already been noted. These included all the leading revisionists as well as notable 'liberals and renegades'. Indeed, a list of his regular contributors reads like an international socialist 'who's who'. Bloch's success in this area must be attributed to his aggressive soliciting, his comparatively even-handed editorial policy, the journal's independence of party control and, quite possibly too, to his more attractive remuneration of authors (5 marks a page). Bloch's proficiency in winning an ever-expanding circle of subscribers, especially working-class subscribers, was recognised even by Clara Zetkin and was attributed by Wolfgang Heine to the circumstance that the *Monatshefte* published a great many concrete articles on important day-to-day issues which would not appear if someone had not appealed to the right authors (Zetkin and Heine, SPD A.C., 1902, pp. 141, 145). Workers evidently found Bloch's publication more comprehensible and relevant to their concerns than Kautsky's *Neue Zeit*. One delegate to the Munich party congress expressed this view by asserting that 'the articles which Auer and others have written for [the *Monatshefte*] are better understood by the workers than the articles in the *Neue Zeit*, which are too theoretical' (Leyendecker, SPD A.C., 1902, p. 131). But the *Monatshefte* was by no means pitched exclusively at a working-class readership. Bloch saw to it that the journal offered something for everyone, and intellectuals were not overlooked. He proudly pointed out, for example, that his journal was first in the field with an issue dedicated to the twenty-fifth anniversary of Marx's death. Of the articles which appeared in this issue he particularly favoured one by Conrad Schmidt and took pains to ensure its maximum exposure and distribution. A special feature of the *Monatshefte*, and one which appealed even to bourgeois intellectuals, was its review section, covering all aspects of cultural life under as many as thirty-five different rubrics.

After 1905, and still more so after 1910, the survival and growth of the

Monatshefte were increasingly favoured by the confusing internal situation of the party. Far from being simply divisible into a neat factional triangle of centre, left and right, with each faction standing on a permanent war-footing with the other two, the party threw up factional alliances which varied greatly in accordance with the issues. If the centre and the left tended to unite against the right on questions of political theory, the centre normally joined forces with the right to isolate the left on matters of political practice. On some issues, above all on the need to find some means of bringing theory into line with practice, left and right were both highly critical of the party centre and, at times, even joined hands against the centre, the mass strike issue being a case in point, for revisionists like Bernstein and Ludwig Frank here adopted a position that had far more in common with the radicalism of the left than with the cautious quietism of the party centre. Indeed, on most questions of political practice the party centre was conspicuously vulnerable, as each new success at the polls further underlined the glaring disparity between its revolutionary ideology and its wait-and-see attitude in practical politics. In short, the party situation was sufficiently fluid to afford considerable elbow-room to revisionism and its principal organ, the *Monatshefte*. By going to ground whenever theoretical squalls darkened the party horizon, by giving maximum exposure to problems of practical politics and by attacking the party centre at its weak point, Bloch and his colleagues were therefore in a position to appeal successfully to allies or potential converts in all factions within the party.

An important reason why Bloch was able to do all this was the solid financial basis of his publication, which was secured by the extensive financial backing provided primarily, but not exclusively, by Dr Leo Arons, son-in-law of the banker Julius Bleichröder (brother of Bismarck's financial adviser) and a brilliant physicist who had been deprived of his livelihood under the infamous 'lex Arons'. From the turn of the century onwards Bloch's financial sources formed the subject of a great deal of speculation in party circles. In 1901, for instance, Arthur Stadthagen maintained that the *Monatshefte* had been taken over by 'a capitalist entrepreneur, a certain [Dr John] Edelheim' (*Vorwärts*, 15 September 1901). At the Munich party congress Kautsky claimed that the journal had 'a rich man behind it paying its deficit' (SPD A.C., 1902, p. 258). Another delegate (Emanuel Wurm, co-editor of the *Neue Zeit*) wondered how it was possible that the *Monatshefte* could offer seven sheets of paper for 50 pfennigs while the *Neue Zeit* had to charge twice as much for eight sheets while still operating at a loss (ibid., p. 263). Most damaging of all was the charge that the revisionist journal received money from non-socialist quarters which could only have an anti-socialist purpose in funding a revisionist organ (*Vorwärts*, 2 September 1908; *Leipziger Volkszeitung*, 11 June 1909). There was fire behind this smoke. The *Monatshefte* did consistently sell at prices below production costs (Helene Bloch, in Siemsen, 1954, p. 86). It did receive substantial financial support from Leo Arons. And it did, on at least one occasion, solicit and accept financial support from a non-party person known to have connections with a bourgeois party. Most suspect of all was the fact that Bloch and the journal's supporters for a long time either denied or endeavoured to conceal both Arons's involvement in the journal and that of its non-socialist benefactors (David, SPD A.C., 1901, p. 162; Joseph Bloch,

SMR, 1908, p. 1250).[4] Not until 1909 did Bloch acknowledge Arons as his Maecenas of long standing (SMR, 1909, p. 746), and this only when the Hallgarten donation of 1905 became public knowledge.

The extent of Arons's generosity towards the *Monatshefte* is indicated by the fact that it encompassed the entire annual deficit of the journal until Arons's death in 1919 (BP, D 746: Verlag der Sozialistischen Monatshefte to stock-holders, 15 April 1926). The requisite annual injections of Arons's capital must have been of astronomical proportions, almost beyond the resources of a private individual, given that the rival *Neue Zeit*, which did not sell at dumping prices, needed an annual party subsidy of 10,000 marks to keep it afloat. Since the *Monatshefte* was not the sole beneficiary of Arons's generosity, and since this largesse was distributed to the journal through Gebrüder Arons, the possibility exists that this banking firm was a conduit for funds raised from sources other than Leo Arons's private fortune, sources which might have been an acute embarrassment to the revisionist movement had they become known.[5]

The plausibility of such conjecture is heightened, first, by Arons's lack of secrecy in respect of his own revisionist sympathies and his lavish financial support of other party and trade union worthy causes and, secondly, by the magnitude of Arons's financial commitment to revisionism. The latter included the granting of large personal loans to indigent revisionist writers such as Karl Leuthner. In 1910, for example, a loan amounting to the then princely sum of 10,600 Reichsmarks was arranged through Bloch in such a way that Leuthner was unaware of the identity of his rescuer until he received Arons's cheque. For years prior to that loan Bloch had been trying to acquire a financial stake in Leuthner by offering what he termed a twelve-month scholarship tenable in Berlin, the prospective donor of the proffered scholar-ship being Leo Arons. Subsidies, private loans, scholarships: it would appear that Arons set no limits to his support for the *Monatshefte*, provided always that his anonymity was preserved.

The only known condition attached by Arons to his patronage of the *Monatshefte* was his insistence that all other donations to the journal should be approved by him before being accepted. Until at least June 1909 Arons had not had occasion to reject any donation made to the *Monatshefte* (Joseph Bloch, SMR, 1909, p. 746). This cannot be taken as implying that the journal benefited exclusively from Arons's generosity. In 1901, for example, the *Monatshefte* received 1,000 Reichsmarks from Perles of Vienna, a further sum from Wertheim of Berlin and 3,500 Reichsmarks from 'a few others' (SMP, vol. 10: Mundt to Bloch, 27 September 1901). In this instance, both persons named were stockholders of the Verlag der Sozialistischen Monatshefte GmbH and presumably also party members. It is not clear whether the payments referred to were private donations or represented amounts collected from other persons or organisations. The same source mentions two other possible bene-factors, W. Friedländer from Berlin and an unnamed young jurist and former civil servant from Altona. In 1903 Bloch also approached a certain Dr Lind-heimer, the only son of a very rich father, and a man who had contemplated supporting Heinrich Braun's venture, the *Neue Gesellschaft* (1903–7), to the tune of 50,000 Reichsmarks (Fricke, 1974*b*, pp. 1060–1).

Assuming these persons were all Social Democrats, we are still left with the Hallgarten episode, a clear and proven case of Martha Mundt canvassing funds from non-socialist quarters. In 1905 Martha Mundt visited Frankfurt-on-the-Main where she called on a number of well-to-do party members from whom she obtained the names of local philanthropists who might be approached for a donation to the *Monatshefte*. In Frankfurt Fräulein Mundt collected the sum of 5,000 Reichsmarks from Charles Hallgarten, a wealthy Jewish German-American banker known to be associated with the left liberals in that city.[6] At least one other individual, a wealthy Frankfurt Social Democrat named Louis Opifizius, was approached at the same time.

The precise nature of Martha Mundt's errand is still unclear. She herself subsequently maintained in a letter to *Vorwärts* that she had been *en route* to the trade union congress in Cologne and had availed herself of the opportunity to 'visit some *Sozialistische Monatshefte* writers resident in the Rhineland', which purpose had also led her to Frankfurt (*Vorwärts*, 26 June 1909). Yet those whom she met in Frankfurt interpreted her visit as a fund-raising trip involving several German cities. Also unclear is the exact number and identity of the persons approached by her. Since several sources referred to a 'list of names' in her possession, it appears likely that Hallgarten and Opifizius were not the only persons called on to offer financial aid to the revisionist journal. As Opifizius pointed out (in a letter to Bebel later published in *Vorwärts*), moneys collected in this way, and quite possibly originating from persons decidedly hostile to Social Democracy, could well have been laundered through the simple device of having them entered in the *Monatshefte*'s ledgers under the names of party members ibid., 20 June 1909). Under these circumstances, Bloch could well afford such gestures as his offer to open the journal's 'management, its expenditures and receipts, and everything else which might be desired of it' to inspection by the party *Vorstand* or agents thereof (SMR, 1908, p. 1250).

Was Hallgarten the only bourgeois benefactor of the *Monatshefte*? Probably not, because Bloch admitted in 1908, before the Hallgarten incident came to light, to having received contributions from 'a few personalities outside political life'. Since Arons did not exercise his right to veto the Hallgarten donation, which was accepted by Martha Mundt, acting presumably with the knowledge and approval of Bloch and Arons – on all important matters she acted in close consultation with Bloch – it seems probable that, as a matter of policy, the revisionist journal did seek and obtain financial assistance from non-socialist sources. But why all the secrecy and subterfuge? After all, as a private or non-official publication with no aspirations to official status, the *Monatshefte* was not subject to the party's ban on acceptance of 'bourgeois gold'. It was perfectly entitled to take its sustenance from whatever source it chose. One is tempted to wonder whether, in fact, Bloch and Arons had more to conceal than the extent of Arons's involvement or their readiness to accept financial aid from non-socialist quarters. It is not impossible that government funds might also have made their way into revisionist pockets. To weaken and divide the socialist movement had been a perfectly natural and long-standing objective of official policy. To this end Bülow had quashed the warrants preventing Bernstein's return to Germany in late 1900. The government had no qualms about entering into secret arrangements with shady characters like Parvus-Helphand, nor did it balk at assisting Lenin, the high-priest of revolution, to return to Russia in the famous 'sealed train' of 1917. From the government point of view it would have made good sense to foster dissident elements within Social Democracy. However, there is no proof that it actually did so.

Until more is known about the finances of the *Monatshefte*, no further inferences can be drawn. Available evidence does not indicate that bourgeois patrons like Hallgarten exerted any significant direct influence on editorial policy. Nor is there any evidence of fundamental disagreement between Bloch and Arons, or of Arons compelling Bloch to adopt a policy or position that Bloch otherwise would not have adopted of his own volition. Yet Arons did play a more active editorial role than Bloch admitted: he freely expressed his opinions on articles both before and after publication, demanded the rejection of articles of whose content he disapproved, instructed Bloch what to write to correspondents and *Monatshefte* contributors, tendered advice on hiring policy, and at times used Bloch almost as an errand boy. Over a four-year period between 1906 and 1909 he is known to have written to Bloch no fewer than ninety-four communications. Whether because of his financial leverage over the publication or despite it, Arons was the one person apart from Bloch who enjoyed a major voice in the conduct of the affairs of the *Sozialistische Monatshefte*.

Still more significant was the indirect influence exerted by people like Arons. At a purely personal level, the fees paid by the *Monatshefte* to its contributors must have been quite attractive. Bernstein, for one, was by all accounts in straitened circumstances by 1903, having lost his position both on the *Neue Zeit* and as the *Vorwärts* English correspondent.[7] Six years later Bernstein claimed that the income he derived from his literary activity had risen to four times the amount he had received from *Vorwärts* (*Vorwärts*, 29 August 1909), which put him in an income bracket then matched by very few other socialist writers. Since the *Monatshefte* was Bernstein's main journalistic outlet until 1914 – he himself described it as his 'literary home' (BP, C 40: Bernstein to Wurm, 2 October 1903) – it seems likely that Bernstein's vastly improved earning capacity was chiefly related to his work for the *Monatshefte*. One of the additional advantages of such work was the fact that it afforded writers like Bernstein an *entrée* to more respectable non-socialist publications offering much higher honorariums and status. Despite the party's official disapproval of socialist collaboration on the bourgeois press, Bernstein had, by 1914, acquired both regular and occasional outlets in a wide variety of non-socialist publications. Nor was Bernstein's an isolated case of 'capitalist superprofits' making their way to members of the 'labour aristocracy'. It may be assumed that the protectionist and military heresies of Max Schippel – in Bebel's view, a still greater nuisance to the party than Bernstein (SPD A.C., 1904, p. 239) – which, however polite and circumspect in expression, resulted in his being elbowed out of the party's Reichstag *Fraktion* in November 1905 (Heilmann, n.d. [1912], pp. 295–301), survived and flourished for exactly the same reason. Through his continued active association with the *Monatshefte* Schippel managed to remain a highly effective exponent of Blochian revisionism while pursuing a successful career, first with Legien's trade union General Commission and finally as an academic.[8] If even left-wing writers like Paul Lensch, one of Rosa Luxemburg's closest colleagues and later editor-in-chief of the *Leipziger Volkszeitung*, approached the *Monatshefte* with offers of articles, it may be assumed that they did so less in obedience to the call of ideological compatibility than out of considerations such as the fees paid by the *Monatshefte*. Journalists who wrote for the *Monatshefte*, as the Arons loan to Leuthner indicates, were financially well cared for. Had it not been for the haven represented by the *Monatshefte*, many a revisionist might have been constrained by party discipline either to keep silent or to run the gauntlet of extreme personal hardship.

Without the financial stability provided by Arons, Hallgarten and others, the *Sozialistische Monatshefte* could not have survived. Without the *Monatshefte*, German revisionism might have gone to the wall. As a tendency or faction within the party, revisionism lacked both organisation and a common programme. This disunity was not compensated for in terms of strong leadership. For a variety of reasons, including age and personal unsuitability, Eduard Bernstein could not fill this role (see Fricke, 1974c, p. 1346). Vollmar might have done so, but was hampered by chronic ill-health. Other possible revisionist leaders in the prewar period – Albert Südekum, Eduard David, Ludwig Frank – had too narrow a power base or lacked national standing. In this situation, where even Bloch lived in constant anticipation of an imminent crisis in revisionism, the *Monatshefte* was not merely a literary focal point but a factor which gave the entire revisionist movement its essential, perhaps sole, unifying force and coherent direction. But for the editorial prowess of Joseph Bloch and the patronage of persons like Leo Arons, the revisionist wing of prewar German Social Democracy might well have disintegrated into its diverse and individually innocuous component parts in the face of concerted centre and left-wing pressure. This returns us to the *Also-Socialist Monthly Circus* mentioned at the beginning of this chapter. The wits of Leipzig had clearly misinterpreted the revisionist scenario to the extent that the smith who welded together the splinters of 'Nothung' was Bloch rather than Bernstein. On the other hand, they correctly identified as the sword of revisionism not the theoretical writings of Eduard Bernstein but the journalism of the *Sozialistische Monatshefte*.

Notes: Chapter 3

1   Thus Engelbert Pernerstorfer, in respect of an article submitted to the *Monatshefte*, wrote to Bloch (SMP, vol. 11: Pernerstorfer to Bloch, 4 August 1907), '*I insist absolutely on seeing the proof-sheets*' (italics in original). Similar phrases are to be found in letters from Bernstein and other contributors.
2   A striking example of Bloch's temerity in this regard is his attempt to enlist the services of Edward Pease, secretary of the London Fabian Society and a staunch free-trader, for the cause of German protectionism by making a circuitous appeal to Pease's patriotism (SMP, vol. 11: Bloch to Pease, 14 February 1910 and 23 February 1910). Pease's response can have done nothing to assuage Bloch's Anglophobia.
3   On the esteem which the *Monatshefte* claimed to enjoy in trade union circles, see SMR, 1908,

p. 958. Although many trade union leaders, Legien included, regularly wrote for the *Monatshefte*, this nexus has thus far been commented upon only by East German historians.

4   On at least one occasion, Bloch was prepared to publish a statement on the *Monatshefte's* financial backers which he knew to be false. Arons strongly urged him against such a course (SMP, vol. 1: Arons to Bloch, 14 September 1908).

5   Even before Bernstein's return to Germany in 1901, Democrats in Frankfurt were 'discussing the possibility of stimulating revisionist trends within the Socialist Party in order to build a bourgeois working class alliance' (Rolling, 1979, p. 62). On the availability of 'bourgeois gold' for revisionist purposes, see Braun-Vogelstein, 1967, pp. 115–16.

6   On Hallgarten's philanthropic activities and his connection with Friedrich Naumann, see Struve, 1973, pp. 86–7; Rolling, 1979, pp. 173–4, n. 181. One of the sources discussed by Struve (Theodor, 1957, p. 46) refers to a 'corruption fund' allegedly administered by Hallgarten. That Hallgarten was a valued friend of the *Monatshefte* is apparent from Paul Kampffmeyer's obituary (SMR, 1908, p. 643).

7   Under an arrangement of 2 August 1895 Bernstein received 100 Reichsmarks a month for his *Vorwärts* work, making a total party stipend of 4,800 Reichsmarks, which was then 'a comfortable income, though not high' (Steenson, 1978, p. 90). His revisionist apostasy was a courageous step in that it threatened him with financial disaster while also severing the friendships of a lifetime. His election to the Reichstag in 1902 did nothing to ease his financial situation, for Reichstag deputies were not paid until 1906, and in the following year (in the famous 'Hottentot' elections) he lost his Reichstag seat, which he did not regain until 1912. Eventually, in view of the regularity of his contributions to the *Monatshefte*, Bernstein was put on the payroll of the journal, receiving a monthly salary instead of the more customary fee per article (BP, D 61: Bloch to Bernstein, 2 January 1915 and 5 January 1915).

8   Like Max Quarck, Conrad Schmidt, C. A. Schramm and Hermann Bahr, Schippel was a former Rodbertus enthusiast (Lidtke, 1964, pp. 202–25; idem, 1966, pp. 171–2; Schröder, 1975, pp. 109–10; Höhn, 1969, vol. 3, pp. 567–88, 612–15; H.-J. Steinberg, 1972, pp. 22, 35). He had also been a prominent member of the Berlin *Jungen* and an admirer of Eugen Dühring (Osterroth, ed., 1961, p. 264). In several respects Schippel's career and views found a close parallel in those of Richard Calwer (Mrossko, 1972, p. 373). Both made effective use of the *Monatshefte* and the trade union movement as a sanctuary for their economic and imperialist heresies and retraced their steps to their middle-class origins.

4

Karl Leuthner as Spokesman of the Sozialistische Monatshefte

I turn to you in particular because your political views, as I understand them, are also my own, and because I therefore prefer to see them, above all others, expressed in the SM

(*Joseph Bloch to Karl Leuthner, 1906*)

Karl Leuthner is nothing more than a Treitschke who ventilates in the SM *what he is not permitted to write in the Viennese* Arbeiter-Zeitung

(*Kurt Eisner to Joseph Bloch, 1908*)

The enemies I have acquired in the party were, as is so often the case, my best friends . . . For me, they are the more dangerous antagonist.

(*Karl Leuthner, 1909*)

I have already written to you on several occasions of my most ardent desire to have you right here in Germany itself.

(*Joseph Bloch to Karl Leuthner, 1908*)

The 'revisionist' tendency is a not inconsiderable segment of the party, and if the impression is created that all or even many 'revisionists' share those views [of Leuthner, Schippel and Calwer], then the latter acquire an importance beyond their due as the eccentricities of particular individuals.

(*Eduard David, 1909*)

As we have seen, one of Bloch's favourite and most voluble spokesmen was Karl Leuthner. Between 1906, when Leuthner began writing for the *Monatshefte*, and the outbreak of war in 1914 Leuthner's contribution of articles was exceeded in number only by those of Bernstein and Max Schippel. Since Bloch rarely published his own beliefs, in the *Monatshefte* or elsewhere, detailed consideration of Leuthner's views (his *Weltanschauung*, socialist reformism and foreign policy outlook), together with an examination of the influences which inspired these views, enables us to acquire a clearer picture of precisely what the revisionist organ stood for and propagated among its working-class and intellectual readership. For the sake of brevity, Leuthner alone will be considered here, but it is important to note that a similar examination of the views and backgrounds of others among Bloch's favourite and more prolific writers would reveal an almost identical ideological position and a very similar impact, in so far as Leuthner's impact can be gauged at all accurately. This presents something of a problem. Obviously, there were no surveys done at the time. But expressions of contemporary opinion all suggest that this impact was considerable, and they all clearly indicate that the message conveyed was a reformist one which linked the pursuit of working-class integration into a modified and improved version of the existing social order with a strong appeal to radical nationalism.

Leuthner: Background and Biographical Data

Karl Leuthner was born on 12 October 1869 in Padechau, Moravia, where national antagonisms were particularly strong. The son of a mining engineer who died when Leuthner was 3 years old, he attended the *Gymnasium* in Brünn (Brno) and later studied law in Vienna. Attracted to socialism by his reading of Lassalle, Rodbertus and Marx, he made his début as a public speaker in March 1893 when invited by Victor Adler to address a socialist meeting. When the Viennese *Arbeiter-Zeitung*, the central organ of the Austrian Social Democratic Labour Party, began to appear daily in January 1895, Leuthner joined its editorial staff, becoming its foreign affairs editor in 1897, which post he retained until the suppression of the paper in 1934. As a journalist, he distinguished himself by his erudition, his widely admired literary talent and his incisive polemical style. In 1911 he entered the Austrian Parliament as a socialist deputy after an electoral upset in which he defeated Dr Robert Pattai, a leading Christian Social, for the inner-city constituency of Mariahilf II. In Parliament, Leuthner attracted attention as a fiery orator and a quick-witted, trenchant debater. He quickly established himself as a military specialist and a vehement anti-clericalist with an interest and expertise in education and cultural affairs. Although he retained his parliamentary seat until 1934, and was widely regarded as a leading socialist right-winger even before the First World War, Leuthner never attained high office either in government or in the party. In February 1934 he was arrested and interned for six months. After his release he retired from political life, spending his last ten years in bitter regret that he had not pursued an academic career.

As a Sudeten German, he had grown to manhood proudly conscious of his roots in German *Kultur*, which commitment intensified rather than abated over the years. A lifelong admirer of Nietzsche, Wagner and Goethe, he loathed the Habsburgs, clericalism, neo-Kantianism, revolutionary Marxism and, above all, the doctrinaire high liberalism prevailing in late-nineteenth-century Austria. His anti-liberal nationalism was suffused by a passionate attachment to *Realpolitik* as the essence of all true politics. His was a solitary temperament which did not easily develop close personal relationships. He was a hypochondriac, a non-drinker and a non-smoker. His wife, Klara Tatiana Leuthner née Berlin, was a Russian revolutionary intellectual of wealthy Jewish parentage. The marriage, which was vigorously opposed by his wife's family, produced no children but did arouse in Leuthner an informed interest in Russian literature and politics. Early in life he went heavily into debt, and among his guarantors was Victor Adler. What leisure his journalistic and political activity permitted him was apparently given over entirely to his love of literature and of learning.[1]

Leuthner's World View

Leuthner's ideological square one was 'the primacy of the idea' (Leuthner, 1911*b*, p. 366) and his favourite philosopher was 'the divine Nietzsche' (SMP, vol. 8: Leuthner to Bloch, 3 October 1908), whom he reflected in his emphasis on the need for passion in politics, his élitism, his underwriting of the 'superman' myth, and in his forthright application of the will to power as the primary determinant of relations among parties, classes and nations. Heeding 'the eloquence of the facts' (1902, p. 27) as well as Nietzsche, he also took as his lodestar an anti-intellectual and morally unprejudiced tactical opportunism which recognised power politics as the true and only valid basis of all political endeavour. A major component of this neo-idealist *Realpolitik* was a profound animus against Enlightenment progressivism. Proclaiming himself 'cool to the marrow towards all the humanitarianism, irenics and benefactions of men and peoples that would lead us via the committee system and the soirée to ultima Thule, weaning wolves from slaughtering and cats from mouse-hunting in the empire of the Turks as in darkest Africa' (1909*h*, p. 755), Leuthner condemned this debilitating tradition for its lack of realism, its individualism, cosmopolitanism, particularism and, above all, for its liberalism. He was convinced that 'there [had] possibly never existed an intellectual current that [was] so bereft of healthy political insight as the Manchester liberal world view' (1907*e*, p. 225) and that this world view had permanently blighted the political perceptions of the Germans as a people and of the Social Democrats as their authentic voice. Until liberal economic and political doctrines had been eradicated, he saw little hope of the German people attaining popular sovereignty at home or political maturity in the global community (1906*d*, p. 5; 1913*e*, p. 1089).

His concept of nationality, another central component of his world view, certainly owed nothing to Nietzschean or Hellenistic inspiration. Although he was less interested in nationality in general (SPÖ A.C., 1911, p. 243), in so far as he contemplated the phenomenon as such he did so, like Otto Bauer, from the perspective of cultural differentiation rather than ethnic bias (Leuthner, APD, 27 May 1913, p. 7266), which is not to say that his attitude towards the Slavs in general, and the Czechs in particular, was invariably free of racist bigotry. What interested him far more than the nationalist phenomenon was its German particularity, *Deutschtum*, which he prized for its uniqueness and for its universality. Leuthner extolled as extraordinary the distinctive features of the German language and *Kultur*, exemplified in creative genius such as Goethe, Wagner and Nietzsche, which had elevated it to a global language or *Weltsprache*, its universality consisting also in the ready access to German *Kultur* enjoyed by all Germans, regardless of social class or geographical location. Yet his concept of *Kultur* also had a materialistic dimension – he was immensely proud of Germany's economic achievements in the post-Bismarckian generation (1912*c*, p. 213; 1912*g*, p. 1123) – and here his romantic nationalism took a Hegelian–Lassallean turn, for he contemplated the German spirit not as a supra-territorial entity in the sense of Hellas but as requiring for its fulfilment a specific political dimension in the form of the nation-state (1911*a*, p. 575). In his view, the quintessence of German civilisation and the embodiment of the German spirit was the Prussia of Frederick the Great, which he regarded as a sustained act of will (1908*c*, pp. 1251–8; 1908*i*, pp. 912–22; 1908*l*, pp. 773–8). Taking a highly positive view of the existing Prusso-German state, he believed it required for its completion only the attainment of popular sovereignty, which would bring state and nation into harmony on the basis of the *Volksgemeinschaft* or folk community (1907*h*, p. 625; 1911*g*, pp. 1157; 1913*d*, p. 22). But he was pessimistic about the capacity of the 'unpolitical Germans' to rise to the occasion by divesting themselves of their obsolete and unrealistic liberal baggage (1908*j*, p. 662; 1913*a*, p. 966).

Leuthner's Reformist Socialism

Leuthner's perception of socialism was as heterodox and eclectic as his neo-idealist, illiberal nationalist and 'realist' world view. To Leuthner, socialism meant a modern, class-based and scientific movement which aimed at liberating the industrial worker from the evils of wage-slavery. It was a product of the *Zeitgeist*, *Praxis*-oriented and above theory, though by no means a mere proletarian sounding-board, for the party had a clear duty to lead and educate the masses. The movement dated from the 1890s, which had seen the birth of a proletarian class or 'estate' consciousness (Leuthner's writings manifest an exceptionally pronounced preference for corporative and *völkisch* terminology), the quickening of a proletarian sense of mission and the efflorescence of the Marxian–Lassallean intellectual heritage. In respect of the latter, Leuthner repeatedly stressed the fecundity of the Lassallean over the Marxian inheritance while emphasising his firm belief that neither mentor, in terms of his real impact on the movement, had ever been more than first among such other equals as Wagner and Ibsen (1910*b*, pp. 417–23; 1910*h*, pp. 488–96; 1912*c*, pp. 210–15). Leuthner frankly admitted, indeed boasted, that he personally owed far more to Lassalle than to Marx, whom he criticised *inter alia* for moralising like an Old Testament prophet, for failure to allow for individual genius in his mischievous veneration of a false economistic monism, of an invalid theory of value, a negative and counter-productive doctrine of class struggle, and for seriously underestimating the role of the national factor in human affairs (1908*f*, p. 602; 1908*i*, p. 918; 1909*d*, pp. 10–13; 1909*e*, p. 1079; 1909*i*, p. 342; 1913*e*, p. 1089). With special vehemence Leuthner rejected the Marxist theory of revolution, for he considered the notion of class rule an otiose absurdity and regarded proletarian revolution as being at once superfluous, undesirable and impossible (1907*i*, pp. 57–63; 1910*e*, pp. 282–3; 1911*g*, p. 1156). Renouncing even revolutionary reformism, he aspired not to the radical transformation of the existing social order beneath the cumulative weight of piecemeal reforms but simply to the completion of the nation-state, interpreting this task as the gradual integration of the industrial working class into an improved, more socially modern and efficient status quo (1906*d*, p. 6; 1910*b*, pp. 420, 423; 1910*h*, p. 491; 1912*c*, p. 214). Indeed, he considered Marxism, as an historical relic, a 'subsequently vanished' ideology (1911*g*, p. 1157).

Unable to accept revolutionary socialism, Leuthner put in its place an anti-democratic, nationalistic opportunist tactic exhibiting both positive and normative aspects, at once a means and an end. As a thoroughgoing, self-confessed opportunist, Leuthner urged German Social Democracy – we are not concerned here with his prescriptions for the Austrian labour movement, which are dealt with in Fletcher, 1982*d*, pp. 27–57 – to concentrate on applying the opportunist tactic to the economically and politically rewarding trade union and co-operative struggles as well as in the parliamentary arena. Yet he showed little warmth for democracy *per se*. In his reformist parlance, the term 'democrat' often did duty as a pejorative for those whom he disliked, from Marxists and liberals to fellow-revisionists like Bernstein and Eisner (1908*e*, p. 463; 1909*c*, p. 475; 1909*h*, p. 754; 1909*k*, p. 562), and he habitually execrated parliamentary democracy for its inadequacies and weakness. The democracy to which he aspired must be national and effectively reflect the popular will, which might gain equally valid expression through extra-parliamentary institutions (1908*d*, pp. 402–8; 1909*e*, pp. 1078–82; 1910*d*, pp. 680–7; 1910*e*, pp. 279–83; 1911*g*, pp. 1156–60; 1912*g*, pp. 1415–25; 1913*e*, pp. 1089–93). He nevertheless expressed positive support for a vaguely defined but unmistakably Lassallean-inspired concept of socialist democracy, namely a centralised representative democracy based on the universal suffrage and under strong executive leadership (1907*h*, p. 629; 1908*d*, p. 405; 1908*e*, pp. 467–8; 1908*k*, p. 1511; 1910*d*, pp. 681–2; 1910*e*, pp. 279–83; 1913*e*, pp. 1090–1). He believed the realisation of this objective might be furthered in two ways. First, the German labour movement needed a more realistic and popular press policy, one that did not reinforce the ghetto-mentality foisted on the masses by their Marxist leadership but strove for real influence on public opinion. This was of crucial importance, for in certain situations (international politics, for example) *vox populi* could far exceed the impact of the Reichstag on government policy (1905, p. 308; 1906*d*, p. 5; 1908*a*, pp. 1127–9; 1910*c*, p. 98; 1910*h*, pp. 488–96; 1911*g*, p. 1159; 1912*e*, pp. 1555–61). On this point Leuthner was not only echoing Joseph Bloch but advocating the same style of mass politics as practised by the radical right – in Austria by Georg von Schönerer and Karl Lueger (Whiteside, 1975; Carsten, 1977; Kitchen, 1980; Schorske, 1980, pp. 116–46), in Germany by Alfred Hugenberg and General Keim (Guratzsch, 1974, pp. 183–350; Eley, 1980, pp. 218–26 and *passim*). Secondly, Social Democracy should actively cultivate all potential alliance-partners in the non-socialist camp. As he did not rule out collaboration even with the intransigent Junkers (the most imponderable of improbabilities),[2] one is tempted to question his sanity, but he was doubtless indulging in hyperbole in order to drive home the primacy of the Lassallean national, anti-liberal message (1908*e*, p. 468; 1908*k*, p. 1509; 1910*c*, pp. 92–8; 1911*e*, pp. 1073–7; 1913*e*, p. 1091). Leuthner's principal hope, however, lay in the prospect of socialist collaboration with the 'new middle class' or white-collar proletariat (1907*f*, pp. 234–5, 1909*d*, p. 13; 1909*e*, p. 1082), the very class which was being so successfully mobilised by the nationalist pressure groups (*nationale Verbände*) under men like Hugenberg and Keim. Both avenues to Leuthner's image of socialist democracy unequivocally demanded the abandonment of the quiescent ghetto-ideology of Marxist negation in favour of a self-consciously and aggressively 'national' outlook and programme of action.

Nationalism thus constituted a major ingredient in Leuthner's concept of

socialism. This was especially true of, but not exclusive to, his tactical opportunism. In the age of the mass market, of mass education, mass communications, mass armies, of impersonal and massively bureaucratic government,
when economic and political power had become irretrievably graduated and
dispersed in an intricate and complex web of reciprocal relationships,
Leuthner insisted that no political movement could hope to win power or
influence, by whatever means, if it appealed only to narrow class or sectional
interests. To be at all politically effective, the German labour movement could
not do otherwise than transform itself into a mass or people's party (*Volkspartei*) and place the national or general interest above class interests (1905,
p. 309; 1907f, p. 235; 1908e, p. 466; 1908k, p. 1509; 1910e, pp. 280–1; 1910h,
p. 494; 1913e, p. 1091).[3] Although it is not known whether he was familiar with
Durkheim's early work – true to his calling, he so larded his work with such
'great names' as to give the (in his case, misleading) impression of an astonishingly encyclopaedic mind – what clearly emerges is Leuthner's belief that
functional interdependence between classes and the solidity of everyday life
were sufficient guarantees against the triumph of a socially disruptive ideology
like Marxism. On the other hand, it is equally apparent that he fully grasped
and deliberately tapped the vast potential of nationalism as a vehicle of
working-class integration into the 'dominant culture'. Thus he pronounced
nationalism and socialism theoretical siblings, popular sovereignty being 'the
confluence of the nationalist and the socialist theoretical systems' (1911g,
p. 1157; see also Fletcher, 1982b, p. 76, n. 23). Both were adjudged dictates of
the *Zeitgeist* (1909b, p. 1477; 1909d, p. 13; 1909j, p. 1012), which enabled him
to deny the existence of any significant direct or causal nexus between nationalism and capitalism (as proposed by the emerging Hobson–Hilferding–Lenin
thesis) while facilitating a non-economic explanation of the alleged autonomy,
primacy and historical necessity of the national factor in human affairs. But
Leuthner made no secret of the fact that his nationalism was simultaneously an
intensely personal matter. So deep was his commitment, he informed Joseph
Bloch, that he would find it hard to remain a socialist if required to live in
Germany rather than Austria: 'Truly, if I were now living in Berlin I would
have to stretch every sinew of self-restraint in order to prevent myself from
becoming a Prussian Conservative or possibly, despite my well-nigh congenital
hatred of all things Catholic, a fellow-traveller of the Centre Party.' He
therefore urged Bloch to accept as 'a veritable honour' the National Liberal tag
which *Vorwärts* persistently attached to him (SMP, vol. 8: Leuthner to Bloch,
6 December 1910). Evidently, there are grounds for arguing that Leuthner's
prewar reformist socialism was not merely integrally related to his nationalism
but in fact a subordinate part of his overriding commitment to German
nationalism.

His socialism was plainly gradualist and majoritarian, and, to that extent
only, democratic. Decisively populist rather than pluralist, it was rationalist in
method, conspicuously lacking in any significant ethical or libertarian content,
egalitarian and even authoritarian in tendency. Recognising power alone as the
measure of all things, it emphasised the claims of the community to the almost
total exclusion of those of the citizen and perceived the collective impulse as
culminating in the nation-state, of which class or political allegiance formed a

subsidiary category, being of no greater significance than occupational grouping or place of residence (1911*a*, p. 576; APD, vol. 4[27 May 1913], p. 7266).

It is arguable that there was nothing exceptional in Leuthner's conflation of socialism and democracy (for which, read popular sovereignty) with nationalism. After all, Britain had her Hyndmans (Tsuzuki, 1961; Price, 1972), as did the socialist movements in other countries (Davis, 1967; Haupt, 1972; Talmon, 1980). Closer to home, Karl Marx has been accused of nationalist and even racist blind-spots (Bloom, 1941; Cummins, 1980; D. Paul, 1981, pp. 115–38); Engels was undoubtedly a Slavophobe (Rosdolsky, 1964, pp. 87–282); Lassalle, a Pan-German nationalist in the tradition of 1848 (Dayan-Herzbrun, 1967, pp. 195–200; Na'aman, 1970; Wehler, 1971, pp. 34–48; Wistrich, 1976*b*, p. 53; H. Mommsen, 1979, pp. 276–8), as was Bebel (Schieder, 1978, p. 133). In Leuthner's native Austria, Victor Adler and Engelbert Pernerstorfer had both come to socialism from a similarly tainted background (McGrath, 1967, pp. 183–201; idem, 1974*a*; Wistrich, 1976*b*, pp. 98–114; Kulemann, 1979, pp. 132–5; H. Mommsen, 1979, pp. 180–94). It may also be argued that patriotism did not necessarily preclude radicalism or a sincere commitment to socialism in domestic affairs. All this is perfectly true. But Leuthner was not of this species. Patriots or not, Marx, Engels, Lassalle, Bebel and Adler all subordinated their patriotic and other nostrums to their primary commitment to a socialist transformation of society. Pernerstorfer, the only one of these luminaries who was a died-in-the-wool reformist, explicitly disowned Leuthner's nationalism, proclaiming that whilst he regarded national sentiment as basic, he was 'opposed to all chauvinism . . . opposed to Leuthner's nationalism just as [he was] opposed to the internationalism of Kautsky or [Karl] Liebknecht' (AA, file 141: Pernerstorfer to V. Adler, 5 March 1916). Not only did Leuthner's patriotism owe much more to Fichte, Rousseau and Lassalle than to Marx, but his reformism was both inextricably bound to his nationalism and a subordinate category of the latter. Moreover, his foreign policy views reveal him to have been no ordinary patriot.

Socialist World Policy according to Leuthner

One of the few Austrian socialists to openly admit his 'revisionism', Leuthner none the less gave pride of place not to socialism, however interpreted, or questions of domestic politics but to what he called that 'subject of subjects' – Germany's place in the global community (SMP, vol. 8: Leuthner to Bloch, 4 April 1909). In his view, foreign policy might be susceptible to human will and the power of ideas, but it was definitely not a projection of domestic social structures or constitutional forms and it could not be conducted in accord with ethical, liberal and humanitarian principles (1907*h*, p. 629; 1908*d*, p. 405; 1909*b*, p. 1478; 1909*h*, p. 756; 1911*f*, p. 1384; 1913*f*, p. 483). At bottom, he saw foreign policy as an autonomous sphere governed by traditional, immanent forces 'in accordance with its own purposes and objectives' (1909*k*, p. 564), its basic determinants being 'brutal questions of power' (1907*e*, p. 225).

Leuthner's bailiwick was imperialism, which he defined, somewhat ambiguously, as a novel and unique phenomenon dating from the 1890s and popularised by 'a transformed patriotic and ethical nationalism animated by a new vitality derived from novel objectives adapted to shifting power relation-ships and economic change' (1910*b*, p. 421). He vigorously repudiated all variants of the Hobson–Hilferding–Lenin theory for their 'Manchester' ancestry and their economic determinism (1909*b*, p. 1478; 1913*d*, p. 20). This did not prevent him, however, from agreeing with Hobson, Hilferding and Bauer (virtually alone among socialists of the Second International, he seems to have been familiar with Hobson's early views on imperialism) that imperialism tended towards big government and profoundly altered the dominant ideology of the bourgeoisie in the direction of nationalism, tariff protectionism, colonialism, militarism and social imperialism – all changes for the better, in Leuthner's estimation. His own views, like those of Gerhard Hildebrand and others of Bloch's favoured interpreters, owed much to the protectionist patriotism of the neo-Listian economic thought then in vogue in the Wilhelm-ine intellectual establishment (see Ringer, 1969; Barkin, 1970; Fletcher, 1982*b*, p. 78, n. 45), for he explained the basic motivation of imperialism, and not merely its external form, by reference to nationalism and such traditional power factors as economics and geography, geographic considerations consti-tuting in his mind 'always the basic relationships' (1913*c*, p. 284). To the extent that the ideas of such geopolitical precursors of Karl Haushofer as Friedrich Ratzel, Halford Mackinder and Rudolf Kjellen were already 'in the air' before 1914 (Whittlesey, 1971, pp. 388–96), Karl Leuthner mirrored many of them while sharing much common ground with mainstream academic or 'mandarin' opinion.

Germany's dearth of colonies was not a subject on which Leuthner wrote extensively. His province was the broad sweep of international relations and the inculcation of the fundamental principles which Bloch wanted to see adopted as the guidelines of Social Democratic world policy. In any event, Leuthner did express views on the colonial problem. Denouncing anti-colonialist 'Manchesterism' as a British-imperialist fifth column (1907*e*, p. 226), he argued that an extensive German colonial empire was indispensable not simply for reasons of prestige but as an adjunct of national political and economic power and a vital necessity if the Germans were to avoid 'starvation and misery' (1911*f*, p. 1387), attributing the same view to August Bebel.[4] He recognised that colonial expansion, so essential to the survival of the Germans as a nation, was hardly to be had without recourse to violence, but he declined to accept this as a valid argument against empire (1906*a*, p. 292).

Militarism and war represented a subject which captured Leuthner's inter-est and on which he cultivated a special competence. (In the Austrian Parlia-ment after 1911, he functioned as one of the socialists' principal spokesmen on military affairs and educational policy, which brought him into close contact and sympathy with Professor Ludo Hartmann, another nationalist gadfly among the Austrian Social Democrats.) Consistently scorning liberal, pacifist and Marxist attitudes to war, he maintained that the principal threats to the peace of Europe stemmed from Pan-Slavism, British imperialism, liberal-humanitarian internationalism and the balance-of-power system, which was being manipulated by the Anglo-Russian 'transnational real-estate syndicate'

(*Länderverteilungssyndikat*). But he discussed issues like peace, arbitration and disarmament only 'with a certain embarrassment' (1910*a*, p. 1017), for he regarded war as the highest expression of state power, and the military strength of Germany as the surest guarantee of world peace (1913*d*, p. 18). German socialists, he insisted, 'must never contemplate even an unjust war as mere blood-letting and mass-murder without simultaneously comprehending it in the context of world-historical events' (1907*h*, p. 631). Praising universal conscription as 'the people in arms' and the embodiment of 'the warrior as compatriot (*Volksgenosse*) and citizen' (1907*h*, p. 625; 1910*a*, pp. 1017–18), he applauded 'the warrior spirit' as something deeply ingrained in the German people and proudly described the Prusso-German Empire as 'the most militaristic state in the world, the state with the richest tradition in military history' (1906*b*, p. 424; SPÖ A.C., 1913, p. 200). Since Leuthner's prewar writings and speeches afforded numerous examples of such sentiments, it was to be expected that the *Also-Socialist Monthly Circus* of 1909 should decline to take him at his word as 'a friend of peace' (1913*c*, p. 285) and attribute to him the view that 'the evolution to socialism will be achieved through militarism' (*Also-Socialist*, 1909, p. 26).

In almost every article that he wrote for the *Monatshefte*, Leuthner pilloried British and Russian popular imperialism as the gravest threat to the security and other vital interests of the German nation. He did not overlook the rising North American and Japanese world empires, but he evidently saw little polemical mileage in such remote, and as yet immature, imperial rivals (1911*b*, p. 371). Of the lesser powers, France alone was taken seriously enough to attract regular and systematic comment. Unlike Joseph Bloch, Leuthner was not a Francophile. Neither was he a Francophobe, but this merely reflected an *hauteur* that assessed the French as a nation of has-beens and therefore beneath contempt (1912*d*, p. 349). Only in so far as the French possessed powerful allies were they to be treated with caution (1907*e*, p. 228), although he did sound a note of concern, even of alarm, at the resurgence of French *revanchisme* after 1912. Leuthner's primary and abiding concern, however, was with the Anglo-Russian straitjacket which he believed to have been imposed on Germany by British and Russian nationalism. The future, the very existence of the Germans as a *people*, seemed to him to be imperilled by the aggressive spirit of the British and Russian *peoples*. This, above all, was the message which Leuthner sought to convey in the pages of Bloch's journal. Jingoism and Pan-Slavism were repeatedly portrayed as examples of a genuinely vital, vigorous popular nationalism (1908*a*, pp. 1128–9; 1909*c*, pp. 477–81; 1909*d*, pp. 8–10; 1909*k*, pp. 558–69; 1910*a*, pp. 1018–20; 1911*b*, pp. 365–72; 1912*b*, pp. 1033–8; 1912*g*, pp. 1120–2; 1912*h*, pp. 6–13; 1913*c*, pp. 283–7), each aiming at the subjugation of foreign peoples and ultimately determining official policy, despite the vastly different constitutional systems of both countries (1908*d*, p. 403; 1909*d*, pp. 7–14; 1911*f*, pp. 1384–6; 1912*g*, pp. 1119–24; 1913*e*, pp. 1089–93). Russian nationalism had allegedly been anti-German since 1878 because the Germans blocked the Russian steamroller in the Near East and in south-eastern Europe (1908*e*, pp. 463–4; 1909*d*, p. 9; 1909*i*, p. 347; 1909*k*, p. 565; 1912*a*, p. 1424; 1912*b*, p. 1036; 1913*f*, p. 478). British Germanophobia was explained as a function of imperial difficulties occasioned by the emergence of new rivals and centrifugal tendencies within the British Empire: the German bogey was invented by British imperialists in order to drum up support for electorally unpopular policies at home (heavy defence expenditure, for example), to recruit imperial dogsbodies abroad (Japan, France and then Russia) and to jostle the self-governing colonies into greater subservience to British imperial interests (1911*b*, pp. 365–72; 1912*g*, pp. 1121–2; 1912*h*, pp. 6–13). Although he did not deny the importance of Anglo-German commercial, colonial and naval antagonism, Leuthner was inclined to regard these aggravations as relatively superficial irritants. Although he did not deny the existence of Russo-German friction in consequence of such factors as Bismarck's *Lombardverbot*, German tariff policy, the 1909 Bosnian crisis and German penetration of the Ottoman Empire, these, too, were not the real bones of contention between Russia and Germany. The bedrock issue undermining German relations with both these superpowers was the force of popular nationalism in Britain and Russia.

The German predicament, in a nutshell, was that the German people were still a nation of 'poets and thinkers' and had yet to develop that healthy life-force which allegedly animated the Anglo-Russian drive to grow and expand. The situation, he argued, invited comparison with the fate of Carthage or, in more recent times, of Venice or Holland. 'Never before', he wrote in 1913, 'was a great people confronted with a more difficult task under more unfavourable circumstances.' As 'a people inextricably enmeshed in the fluctuations of Continental power relations and at the same time imperatively driven to the sea by their economic development, which impels them to meet both conditions of their existence' (1913*c*, p. 286), the Germans were driven by geography and economics into rivalry with a territorial colossus in the East and a maritime superpower to their west. In the wake of the Russian defeat at Port Arthur and the debilitating revolution of 1905, 'perfidious Albion' had seized the opportunity to hitch the Franco-Russian alliance to her chariot wheels and thus to complete the encirclement of Germany. As a result, German *Kultur* confronted 'the gravest danger that [had] threatened it since the days of the Napoleonic universal bureaucracy' (1907*e*, p. 228). Partial responsibility for this menace was sheeted home to the Germans themselves. The poor leadership they had suffered since 1871 (Bismarck's defensive diplomacy, weak and vacillating chancellors after Bismarck) had not helped matters. The gravamen of Leuthner's charge, however, was that the German people were excessively naïve, gullible, lacking in national sentiment and still attached to antiquated liberal-democratic traditions which impeded their political development. Hence their failure to draw the appropriate inferences from their unprecedented economic and population growth since the 1890s (1907*h*, p. 629; 1908*e*, pp. 461–8; 1909*b*, pp. 1473, 1477; 1909*c*, p. 478; 1909*k*, p. 561; 1912*b*, pp. 1037–8; 1912*g*, p. 1122; 1912*i*, p. 598). The best the bourgeois imperialists had come up with was to stimulate the imperial appetite of their countrymen without offering them anything solid to bite on (1912*i*, p. 598). In consequence of these international difficulties accentuated by the political immaturity of the German people, Leuthner in 1912 proclaimed Wilhelmine world policy totally bankrupt and impossible to continue (1912*b*, pp. 1037–8; 1912*g*, p. 1122).

The German problem required for its solution, so Leuthner consistently argued through the *Monatshefte*, the systematic and deliberate pursuit of three main objectives. One such goal was a united Europe under the political and economic leadership of 'Greater Germany' – usually referred to in his writings as '*Alldeutschland*' (1908*i*, p. 912; 1913*f*, p. 479). Incorporating German Austria but excluding all non-Germans, 'the united nation of 80 million' (1911*e*, p. 1077) might secure its Continental hegemony by creating a string of client states in the West and in the East. France must be separated from her British alliance and rendered a German vassal through indirect economic and political controls (1912*d*, p. 349; 1912*i*, p. 597; 1913*c*, p. 287), while Russia was to be expelled from Europe and contained through a *cordon sanitaire* of nominally autonomous buffer states bound economically and politically to Greater Germany and extending from the Baltic to the Black Sea (1912*a*, pp. 1416, 1424; 1913*a*, p. 966; 1913*d*, pp. 16, 20, 22; 1913*f*, pp. 481–3). This would solve the Russian problem and rid Germany of 'the nightmare of coalitions'. But Germany also needed, as a guarantee of her independence of the British-dominated world market and hence of her future economic security, an autarkic world empire comparable in size to that of the British. This entailed a massive colonial redistribution (1907*e*, pp. 225–9; 1909*c*, pp. 471–81; 1912*d*, p. 351; 1912*h*, pp. 6–13; 1913*c*, pp. 283–7), a credible German sea power (1909*c*, pp. 478–80; SPÖ A.C., pp. 205, 211), and the final abandonment of the balance-of-power concept in favour of a more dynamic and global view of international relations. This posed the all-important question of parity with the British, who thought of themselves as 'a predestined master race' (1909*h*, p. 758) and a new Rome (1908*d*, pp. 403–4; 1909*j*, p. 1012). With deliberate obtuseness and diabolical cunning, the British feigned an inability to comprehend that Germany must, for reasons of military security alone, unite Europe against Russia and, if the Germans were to have any economic future, force a renegotiation of global power relationships. Behind this indifference to Germany's 'to be or not to be' (1909*k*, p. 564) lay the traditional British pursuit of global hegemony (1907*e*, p. 227; 1911*b*, pp. 367–71; 1912*g*, pp. 1121–2; 1912*h*, pp. 10–12). This policy had taken such a giant step forward after the Russo-Japanese War that the Germans forfeited virtually all hope of a peaceful settlement with Britain (1908*a*, p. 1127; 1909*k*, pp. 562–3; 1912*d*, p. 347). For the Germans, however, there could be no compromise. The question before them was a simple either-or: world power or downfall.

With minor variations, this was the 'socialist foreign policy programme' which Leuthner and others propagated in the *Sozialistische Monatshefte* in the decade prior to the First World War. For most of this time, none of Bloch's foreign policy mouthpieces, Leuthner included, had ever really presented a very coherent or plausible set of guidelines as to how these imperatives might be realised. Under the circumstances, all of them regarded war as suicidal folly. Moreover, as socialists, they were hardly in a position to openly advocate a war of national aggrandizement without risking expulsion from the party, as happened to Gerhard Hildebrand in 1912. Some of the Blochian social imperialists may have been merely beating the nationalist drum for its integrative, heuristic effect on readers brought up in the ghetto-mentality of the quasi-Marxist subculture. This was not true of Karl Leuthner, as it was not true of other *Monatshefte* writers. In the last two years of peace, several of them came out of the closet and articulated what most had been hinting at, more or less heavily, over the preceding decade. In 1913, for example, Edmund Fischer wrote in the *Monatshefte*:

> And even Marx and Engels set their hopes on a world war . . . Old England, they said [in the *Neue Rheinische Zeitung*], could only be toppled by a world war . . . The next world war will wipe from the face of the earth not only reactionary classes and dynasties but also whole reactionary peoples. 'And that, too, is progress.' (E. Fischer, 1913, p. 606)

Something of the sort was undoubtedly in Leuthner's mind in November 1912 when he heard 'the bells of history ringing so loudly', and at last saw 'a real opportunity to tread new paths and attempt a completely new orientation in policy' (1912*a*, p. 1423). Actually, he had been hearing these bells since he first began writing for the German revisionist press (see 1905, p. 309), but until 1912 they had conveyed chiefly gloom and silence as to how Germany might bridge the gulf between aim and method, theory and practice – an intolerable situation for an avowed revisionist.

What had changed, and why? Briefly, Leuthner (and others) now began to advocate something hitherto consistently opposed as illusory, namely a limited Anglo-German naval agreement as the price of a free hand against France and Russia in Europe. The adoption of a Continental strategy willing to risk war for the sake of European hegemony was first endorsed in January 1912 (1912*h*, pp. 6–13) and remained a constant theme thereafter.[5] This, as is now well known, was also the policy of Chancellor Bethmann Hollweg (F. Fischer, 1969, pp. 106–13 and *passim*; Jarausch, 1972, pp. 94, 112–15, 126–30, 142).

A number of general factors probably contributed to, and strengthened, the conviction, shared by Leuthner with other *Monatshefte* imperialists, that the time was ripe for a 'Continental breakthrough'. First, like some of Bethmann's advisers and many British Radicals, he completely misread the signs of an accommodating spirit emanating from Britain (the Haldane mission, Churchill's naval holiday, the 1912–13 London ambassadors' conference, colonial negotiations, and so on) as an indication that Britain wished to cut her imperial losses (Persia, for instance) and concentrate on domestic reform. In North Africa and the Near East, Italy and the Balkan states were disrupting the peace and the European balance while the Triple Entente appeared unable or unwilling to act decisively against them. At home, national sentiment and national unity were clearly hardening, much of it directed against the reputedly weak and lack-lustre Bethmann government (the Leipzig 'cartel' of August 1913, for instance), and there were also new indications of government willingness to respond positively to such public pressure (fresh army and navy increases, Bethmann's reaction to the Zabern incident). Official as well as public opinion had clearly swung away from the Tirpitz plan in favour of a Continental priority. Finally, the SPD appeared to be progressing in the desired direction, the 1912 Reichstag electoral victory and the rising tide of revisionism within the movement (symbolised by the election of Friedrich Ebert to replace Bebel as party chairman in 1913) proving particularly encouraging to the right wing of German Social Democracy. All these factors were noted by Leuthner, who was also strongly influenced at this time – and not entirely favourably – by such writers as General Bernhardi and Paul Rohrbach (1913*c*, pp. 283–4).[6] Frankly admitting, in August 1912, that the only possible war for Germany was a war on all fronts (1912*b*, p. 1036), he drew the same 'now or never' conclusions as those arrived at, albeit for vastly different and at least partly anti-socialist reasons, in government and non-socialist circles (cf. F. Fischer, 1969, pp. 117 ff.; Groh, 1973, pp. 355–460, 577–652).

The foreign policy perspectives, goals and methods which Leuthner urged on the government of Imperial Germany through the German revisionist press in the last decade of peace were, of course, directed primarily at a socialist readership and proffered as meriting the full and active support of German Social Democracy. Why German socialists should support such a programme was therefore also explained. First, he stressed the matter of working-class self-interest, underlining 'how deeply the workers [were] rooted in their ethnicity, whose external and internal collective fate must touch them nearest as the most vital kernel of the whole' (1907*f*, p. 235). Like it or not, the workers shared their destiny with the German economy, *Volk* and *Kultur* (1908*a*, p. 1131; 1914*a*, p. 1218). Far from having anything to gain from national defeat and revolution, the triumph of the proletarian cause was directly dependent on German living space (*Lebensraum*), for socialism presupposed economic prosperity far more than it did a libertarian constitution (1906*c*, p. 184; 1912*g*, pp. 1123–4; 1913*d*, pp. 19–20). Given the uniqueness of Germany's development (American growth on an ancient cultural base), her defeat would deprive humanity of the enriching singularity of the German idea – a grievous loss to civilisation and progress, and not merely to the cause of socialism – but if the workers threw in their lot with the nation they would march in the vanguard of historical evolution (1912*g*, p. 1124). So far, so good: Leuthner was saying no more than Bernstein or even Bebel. But a second argument anticipated by a decade the 'war socialism' of extremists (and former radicals) like Lensch, Cunow and Haenisch, for Leuthner also maintained that the interests of socialism and *Deutschtum* were identical, in that socialism, both as an ideology and as a movement, was quintessentially German (1906*c*, p. 184; SPÖ A.C., 1911, p. 247; 1912*c*, p. 211). A third argument employed was the characteristically revisionist one of expediency. By adopting a nationalist foreign policy position, Social Democracy would not merely prevent the use of the army and the abuse of the national idea against itself but simultaneously win over public opinion and gain the confidence of the bourgeois classes. Genuine parliamentary government and socialist power would follow inevitably (1905, p. 308; 1907*h*, p. 628; 1912*c*, pp. 214–15). In this sense, Leuthner was anticipating the arguments of Eduard David and other exponents of the *Burgfrieden* or 'civic truce' during the war years.

Leuthner further explained what Social Democracy might do, or refrain from doing, to help realise the *Weltpolitik* to which he, Bloch and the *Monatshefte* were dedicated. One thing German socialism must avoid at all cost was the plague of internationalism, for this was merely a weapon used by the Entente imperialists to beat Germany in the war of words. Although German socialists might pay lip-service to anti-militarism, they must abstain from all peace resolutions and the like, insist on their right to national autonomy within the International and give unequivocal support to their own government in all crisis situations (1906e, p. 139; 1908a, p. 1130; 1908h, p. 1389; 1909b, p. 1481; 1909c, p. 477; 1909k, pp. 560–2; 1911f, pp. 1385–7). More positively, German Social Democracy needed to re-examine its press policy. Like Joseph Bloch, Leuthner was a firm believer in the power of the press, which he considered stronger than Parliament and especially effective in moulding public opinion and influencing the foreign policy decision-making process (1906d, p. 5; 1908a, pp. 1127–9; 1910h, p. 491; 1911f, p. 1385; 1911g, p. 1159; 1912e, p. 1556). He urged that this power be mobilised to mount an intensive propaganda campaign among the German working class in order to educate the workers to their national responsibilities and dangers (1909c, p. 481). At the same time, the socialist press should seek to influence public opinion in general. Only in this way would Social Democracy acquire the non-socialist allies and helpers that would bring it to power in a nationalist *Sammlung* (1910c, p. 98). This demanded the introduction of a more sensationalist *Klatsch* (trivial) element, a willingness to compromise party theory and, above all, a greater tactical flexibility in the socialist press. In brief, the socialist press needed more revisionism and greater freedom for revisionist journalists (1910h, pp. 488–96). Apart from a more flexible, more revisionist press, Social Democracy also stood in urgent need of younger blood at the helm. Leuthner considered Bebel a senile anachronism and repeatedly lamented the want of talent and genius in the SPD leadership (SMP, vol. 8: Leuthner to Bloch, 21 September 1910, 6 December 1910). Through the expertise of its spokesmen, through the power of an educated and reinforced public opinion (educated in the principles of *Realpolitik* and in the pursuit of national interest), Social Democracy might work miracles (1905, pp. 306–9; 1907h, p. 630).

In February 1907 he had been far from optimistic when he wrote to Bloch, 'Let us admit it: we [revisionists] are all of us, now and always, interminably incorrigible illusionists' (SMP, vol. 8, 18 February 1907). In 1910 he still believed that the party radicals had the masses with them (ibid., 21 September 1910). By 1912, however, he sang a different tune. In May 1912 he recorded his belief that the socialist movement was at last in a position to give German imperialism the programme of concrete objectives and sense of direction that were lacking in the work of non-socialist imperialists (1912i, p. 598; see also 1913e, pp. 1091, 1093). In January 1913 he again registered his pleasure at the degree of national sentiment manifest in the German proletariat (1913d, p. 22). He now saw a great future opening up to the labour movement. Because of its unparalleled economic development and population change, Germany occupied a position of great strength and hope for the future. For the same reasons, and because German Social Democracy was older than the Reich itself, the socialist movement was more powerful in Germany than anywhere else in the world. Here it faced a divided bourgeoisie which needed and sought a proletarian alliance. Political history and economic development had, therefore, placed German Social Democracy in a unique position of strength and opportunity, and socialism and democracy were both imminent (1912c, pp. 214–15). For Leuthner, this prospect, together with that presented by the presumed change of focus in British world policy, conjured up a vision of enormous promise. Both at home and abroad, all the cards appeared to be falling into place for his 'Greater Germany'.

Leuthner's Muses: Marx or Mammon?

In respect of Marx, Leuthner may have been, as his disciple Bruno Marek has described him, 'a knower but no believer' (*ein Kenner aber kein Gläubiger*), and there can be no doubt that Leuthner waged an unremitting struggle against all that was said and done in the name of Marx during his own era, but this does not tell us much about the precise inspiration underlying Leuthner's work for Bloch's revisionist publication. Whom did he acknowledge as his mentors? What did he read? For whom did he write? With whom did he have social intercourse? In so far as Leuthner's own writings enable us to answer such questions, it is possible for us to get at the nature of some of the influences which inspired both his revisionism and his social imperialism.

Following the death of his father, Leuthner grew up in the household of his maternal grandfather, a medical practitioner, in whose library he devoured works on art, classical history and literature and formed the ambition to become an historian (SMP, vol. 8: Leuthner to Bloch, 5 May 1910). In 1910 he summed up his legacy from the (for him) formative decade of the 1890s in terms of *Zarathustra* (Nietzsche), *Hyperion* (Hölderlin), *Faust* (Goethe) and the *Critique of Pure Reason* (Kant), adding that 'everything else comes and goes' (ibid.). As a mature revisionist, he described his interests and reading priorities as literary, historical and philosophical, with politics coming in fourth (ibid., 1 June 1909); his main interests in political history as Rome at the time of Cicero and in the early imperial era, together with 'particular parts of German history' (ibid., 4 April 1910); his main newspaper reading, in so far as he had time for such, as non-socialist rather than socialist. Of French newspapers, for instance, he preferred *Figaro* and *Le Temps* to the socialist *Humanité* (edited by the neo-Kantian Jaurès) and the Radical *Action* because the latter were 'too empty and [contained] absolutely nothing but exclamations' (ibid., 1 June 1909). What he gleaned from such reading is rather difficult to gauge. A remark made in a speech to the Austrian Lower House of Parliament in 1912 suggests that his reading of German history and philosophy had taught him to venerate only Frederician Prussia, the autonomy of the will and Herder's concept of the *Volksgeist* (APD, 21st session, vol. 3 [14 March 1912], p. 2776). To Joseph Bloch, he confessed an attraction to 'the laboriously held-at-bay siren voices of biology' (SMP, vol. 8, 5 May 1910). Apart from his bread-and-butter work for the Viennese *Arbeiter-Zeitung*, Leuthner evidently wrote only for German revisionist and non-socialist literary publications, although he did write one or two articles for the 'Austro-Marxist' *Kampf*. He wrote no books, and his few brochures (the longest was a wartime diatribe against Russian 'popular imperialism') dealt almost exclusively with his anti-clerical hobby-horse. His social contacts appear to have been confined to intellectuals like Ludo Hartmann and younger trade unionists like Bruno Marek.

The testimony of contemporaries confirms the impression that Leuthner's muses were those of the dominant 'bourgeois' culture rather than the socialist classics or the life of the movement. As early as 1894 Karl Kautsky objected to the Nietzschean influence on Leuthner's style (Adler, 1954, p. 155), and at Innsbruck in 1911 Victor Adler publicly upbraided Leuthner as a would-be *Realpolitiker* whose nationalist excesses made a mockery of his socialism (SPÖ A.C., 1911, p. 275). From the left, of course, Leuthner was repeatedly attacked in this vein – by Trotsky, Otto Bauer, Karl Renner, Hilferding, the *Leipziger Volkszeitung* and others (Trotsky, 1908/9, pp. 76–84; Bauer [Weber] 1909, pp. 540–1; Renner, 1911, pp. 103–9). On 25 April 1909 even the middle-of-the road *Hamburger Echo* branded him 'East-Elbian national' and a 'Pan-German nationalist "Social Democrat" '. On the party right, fellow-revisionists like Bernstein questioned his socialist bona fides (see below, Chapter 6, p. 137) and Kurt Eisner described him as Bloch's 'Old Prussian in Vienna' and 'nothing but a Treitschke' (SMP, vol. 4: Eisner to Bloch, 25 July 1908).

Subsequent scholarship has been kinder to Leuthner in that it has generally either passed him over in silence or buried his nationalism in polite and misleading hagiography. An example of the latter is Heinz Brantl's description of Leuthner as 'first and foremost a socialist much indebted to liberal-humanist ideas' (in Leser, ed., 1964, pp. 251–7; for further examples, see Fletcher, 1982*b*, p. 74, n. 1). Recently, a few scholars have been closer to the mark. Peter Kulemann, for instance, describes Leuthner as having gone 'a step beyond' Bebel's endorsement of wars of national defence to a completely un-Marxist and even racist apology for Wilhelmine imperialism (Kulemann, 1979, pp. 147–50, 181–2). Less harsh is Robert Wistrich's judgement of Leuthner as a 'Pan-German socialist' who was 'strongly influenced' by 'the Lassallean tradition of "national" socialism' (Wistrich, 1982, p. 302).

The best evidence of Leuthner's heavy intellectual indebtedness to the values and norms of bourgeois culture remains the internal evidence from his own writing. Whereas Marx and Engels are hardly ever mentioned, unless it is to underline their alleged shortcomings, Leuthner's writings are full of references to Schopenhauer, Wagner, Kant, Goethe, Lessing and Herder. What his journalism exudes, above all, is the influence of Nietzsche, albeit a selectively appropriated Neitzsche. The crucial importance of the 'will to power', for example, is fully apparent in Leuthner's articles. Thus his complaints against the 'personal rule' of Wilhelm II and his entourage were directed, like Bloch's, less against the institution than against the personnel in question: parliamentary control of foreign policy was impractical, after all, and Germany was in need of, but unlikely to get, a second Bismarck (Leuthner, 1908*k*, pp. 1510–11; SMP, vol. 8: Leuthner to Bloch, 6 December 1910). What Germany required was a Frederician superman; all she had was mediocrities and 'great deceivers'. The German entitlement to world power, in Leuthner's view, derived from the superiority of German *Kultur* and Germany's proven capacity to make effective, generally beneficent use of such power. All that was lacking was the will to power (1908*d*, p. 403; 1912*f*, pp. 893–7; 1913*b*, p. 30; 1915, pp. 38, 39, 71). Leuthner's ethical Darwinism also owed a great deal to Nietzsche, particularly in its consistent emphasis on conflict and its rejection of conventional morality as a denial of life, an impediment to survival and a precluding of greatness. Nietzsche's attacks on Christianity, socialism and democracy were closely paralleled in Leuthner's anti-clericalism and hostility to all manifestations of liberalism. Similarly, Nietzsche's abhorrence of anti-Semitism was faithfully mirrored in Leuthner. Indeed, this fidelity to 'the divine Nietzsche' extended much further, encompassing acceptance of the centrality of art and aesthetics, hostility to intellectuality, contempt for 'mere facts'; his rejection of system in preference to the unique, the singular and the exceptional; his partiality to the psychological approach and esteem for the unconscious, the natural and the instinctive as authentic modes of experience; his espousal of the doctrine of heroic commitment, the exaltation of a healthy, creative life instead of a merely intellectual knowledge of the world (for a few examples, see 1906*d*, p. 4; 1906*h*, p. 101; 1908*i*, p. 920; 1909*e*, p. 1081; 1909*g*, p. 1342; SPÖ A.C., 1911, p. 246; 1913*e*, p. 1093; 1915, p. 24).

Yet Nietzsche could not help him where the master's extreme individualism collided with the disciple's collectivism. Nietzsche's views on the state, history, socialism, democracy and nationalism, and his lack of interest in the transition from the enhancement of self to the enhancement of mankind, or a portion thereof, were plainly unserviceable in an avowed 'national' socialist. Nor could Leuthner accept Nietzsche's moral-existential nihilism. Instead of coming to terms with the full implications of a godless existence, Leuthner, in fact, made a god of the German nation. Here he drew some comfort and inspiration from the example of Ferdinand Lassalle. 'In the crisis years of the Wilhelmine empire', Lassalle's latest biographer has observed, 'the call "Back to Lassalle" was occasionally to be heard; what this referred to was a Lassalle who could be played off against Marx, a nationalistic "good German" ' (Na'aman, 1963, p. 23). Leuthner was a Lassallean in more than this super-ficial, tactical sense. For him, Lassalle's impact went much deeper, conditioning his belief in 'the primacy of the idea', his passionate commitment to a *grossdeutsch* or 'Greater German' nationalism inspired by Fichte, his Hegelian view of the state as 'the way of God in the world' and the supreme instrument for the realisation of human freedom, his flirtation with 'integral' democracy and contempt for Parliament, his rejection of class struggle in favour of national integration, his hatred of liberalism, his élitism and authoritarianism, and so on down to his emphatic rejection of Britain as an appropriate model. In essence, the philosophical substructure of Leuthner's journalism was Nietzsche eked out with Lassalle.

The flesh and blood of his commentary on international relations was drawn from neither. Here Leuthner reflected the dominant intellectual climate of Wilhelmine society. Although he had scant respect for the aristocracies of wealth and birth, he absorbed and utilised many of the ideas which were then common currency among the German educated élites. What did make an indelible impression on him was the ubiquitous and pervasive spirit of anti-Enlightenment, pseudo-Darwinist and neo-idealist Prusso-German patriotism which proclaimed the alleged cultural mission of the Germans, as the his-torically ordained heirs to the jaded Romance world, to champion the cause of Europe against Slavic barbarism. He was especially deeply affected by a variant of this missionary cult, the neo-mercantilist doctrine of the three (or four) world empires. It is not known whether, before 1914, Leuthner had read

Karl Haushofer (already in print with two books on Greater Japan) or such proto-geopoliticians and precursors as Friedrich Ratzel, Halford Mackinder and Rudolf Kjellen. But there is no doubt that Leuthner was familiar with, and much impressed by, the work of Heinrich von Treitschke, Theodor Schiemann, Paul Rohrbach, Friedrich von Bernhardi, Karl Lamprecht, Adolf Harnack, Hermann Oncken, Werner Sombart and Paul Nathan (1908*j*, p. 662; 1912*d*, pp. 350–1; 1913*c*, pp. 283–4; 1913*e*, p. 1089). Most were professors and historians. All were opinion-makers of the era. All were highly respected members of the certified intelligentsia. In varying degrees, they all reflected and influenced the ideology of Wilhelmine expansionism (F. Fischer, 1969, pp. 62–84; Ringer, 1969, pp. 128–80; McClelland, 1971, pp. 168–224; idem, 1980, pp. 314–21; Calleo, 1978, pp. 123–59) and most, like Leuthner, adhered to the neo-Rankean orthodoxy which asserted the primacy of foreign policy (Leuthner, 1913*e*, pp. 1091–2; Dehio, 1965, pp. 38–71; Moses, 1975, pp. 7–26). Even in his critical asides Leuthner betrayed the measure of his indebtedness to such doyens of the Wilhelmine intellectual establishment. In 1911, for example, in a barb directed at the Freiburg economic historian Gerhard von Schulze-Gaevernitz, Leuthner revealed that his own national-psychology account of British 'hegemonism' was identical with, if not a replication of, that presented by Schulze-Gaevernitz following his conversion to Schmoller's view of English history (Leuthner, 1911*b*, p. 367; cf. McClelland, 1971, p. 222).

If Leuthner's cultural milieu and intellectual inspiration owed virtually nothing to socialist inspiration or working-class culture, it is well to recall that it was not by chance that he emerged as the *Sozialistische Monatshefte's* principal foreign policy spokesman between 1907 and 1914. Leuthner accurately described his own position when he wrote to Bloch on 10 April 1909, 'it is not I but Bloch who is the Saint Sebastian' of revisionism (SMP, vol. 8).

Leuthner's Impact

At this point it is also worth recalling that in the late nineteenth and early twentieth centuries the press was *the* mass medium. In the absence of newer rival media, people at the time certainly believed in the omnipotence of the press. Thus Albert Südekum noted in his diary in 1912 his conviction that the press was the most effective means of influencing the masses, since people no longer read books, only newspapers and magazines (SP, no. 109). Leo Wegener, a friend and confrere of Alfred Hugenberg, was no less firmly persuaded that the popular press was 'the most influential and effective means of struggle' (cit. Guratzsch, 1974, p. 345). While technical advances on the production side improved the ability of the press to reach a larger audience, the demand for popular newspapers and periodicals grew enormously as Germany developed a national culture and in consequence of such other social and political changes as rising prosperity, rapid urbanisation, expanding literacy and the universal suffrage. All this brought more and more Germans – industrial workers and the lower middle classes, in particular – within the political pale. At the same time, however, the state severely restricted alternative forms of mass communication and working-class self-expression. The right of free association was strictly limited, while the Reichstag and other representative bodies provided most imperfect public forums as long as governments did not answer to parliaments, as long as the franchise was limited (as in Prussia and Saxony), and as long as elected representatives were unpaid. Since the official Social Democratic press found it increasingly difficult to compete successfully with the better-funded and better-organised bourgeois press, which amused and entertained rather than informed its readers, the relative success of Bloch's publication and the extraordinary effectiveness of Leuthner's journalism may be taken almost as a sign of the times.

Virtually the only other available guide to Leuthner's probable impact is that provided by the responses which his journalism elicited among his German contemporaries. First, let it be noted that he did evoke very definite responses throughout and beyond the organised labour movement. Leuthner reported to Bloch that the *Monatshefte* was read as far afield as the Austrian Parliament, where its audience allegedly included liberals as well as socialists (SMP, vol. 8: 11 November 1910). It was certainly read in Paris, for in January 1913 Charles Andler, writing in *La Revue socialiste*, named Leuthner as one of the most dangerous social imperialists at work in the German labour movement (Andler, 1913, p. 451). But the echo provoked by Leuthner was an ambiguous one. On the one hand, his nationalist views were regularly quoted approvingly in the non-socialist press, to such an extent that Otto Bauer accused him of 'contaminating broad sectors of the people with a cynical nationalist ideology of the overlord (*Herrenideologie*) which flies in the face of all ethics, abandons all cultural values and ceases to have anything but the name in common with the older [democratic] national idea' of 1848 (Bauer [Weber], 1909, p. 540). Within the socialist movement, on the other hand, Leuthner's journalism seems to have been appreciated only by Joseph Bloch and Leo Arons.

This '*enfant terrible* of revisionism' – as *Vorwärts* described Bloch on 27 July 1910 in a tirade entitled 'Negation of Social Democracy' – expressed only the highest praise for Leuthner's work. On 6 October 1906, in what was probably his first letter to Leuthner, Bloch wrote, 'I turn to you in particular because your political views, as I understand them, are also my own, and because I therefore prefer to see them, above all others, expressed in the *SM*' (SMP, vol. 8: Bloch to Leuthner). A few months later, on 5 January 1907, Bloch applauded Leuthner's contributions as being

> different from those of the others, not only from the main body but also from those of the intellectuals. You belong among the very few (Schippel, Calwer and a handful of rare cases). You consistently treat the other side of the question . . . and if only we had a greater abundance of brains that knew how to read [what you write] the programme of the *SM* would be fulfilled. For the present, we must be content with rejoicing over isolated swallows in the hope that they may yet bring the summer. (ibid.)

Almost two years further on, the revisionist 'impresario' wrote to his 'swallow' of his continued satisfaction:

At every new contribution with which you favour me I feel increasingly in congruence with your fundamental political position; and the way in which you express yourself, the manner in which you apply your inferences to particular cases, interrelate your points of view – otherwise beyond the grasp of our good comrades – repeatedly arouses in me not only a feeling of purely aesthetic satisfaction, but shows me afresh what a gain for the *SM* (and thus for the German party, or that part of it which can be reached) your collaboration represents. At the same time it is provoking good opposition. (ibid., 30 November 1908)

Specific qualities were singled out for similar encomia, and among these, of course, was Leuthner's exemplary stand on national issues (ibid., 23 January 1907, 27 March 1908, 28 December 1908). In fact, it was not Bernstein, nor even Conrad Schmidt, but Karl Leuthner who, in Bloch's estimation, was forming 'the crystals of that which is coming' (*Krystalle des neu Kommenden*) (ibid., 31 July 1908). What he expected of his Viennese paragon was that Leuthner might not only provide the still outstanding corrective to Marx but also go on to lay the foundations of the 'productive socialism' of the future.

Such a golden opinion did Bloch have of Leuthner that he tried repeatedly, initially at the suggestion of Leo Arons, to lure his champion to Germany, where he might exert a more direct impact on the reformation and integration of Social Democracy via the national question. At first he used the bait of a *Monatshefte* grant or stipend for a year's residence in Berlin (ibid., 12 August 1908, 28 September 1908, 19 October 1908, 19 November 1908). Then he offered Leuthner the editorship of the *Chemnitzer Volksstimme*, made vacant when Gustav Noske resigned to take up Schippel's Reichstag seat (ibid., 28 September 1908). When Leuthner refused to leave Vienna despite his professed wish to do so – pleading a variety of hindrances including debt and his personal unsuitability to the hurly-burly of German politics (ibid., Leuthner to Bloch, 3 October 1908, 2 November 1908) – Bloch left open indefinitely the invitation to Berlin (ibid., Bloch to Leuthner, 19 November 1908) and consoled himself with the thought that a Leuthner in Vienna was at least better situated to present the *Monatshefte* case boldly and unequivocally than were such Reich German 'swallows' as Calwer, Schippel and Hildebrand. Still Bloch persisted in his efforts to commit Leuthner more deeply to the cause of the *Monatshefte*. He endeavoured, for instance, to persuade Leuthner to take over (allegedly for six months only) the editorship of Schippel's *Monatshefte* review column and to secure from Leuthner an undertaking to contribute a minimum of twelve articles per annum to the *Monatshefte* (ibid., 30 November 1908, 1 February 1908). Leuthner politely but firmly rejected both propositions.

If Bloch could not get enough of him, others objected that Leuthner was altogether too much. In the official party press a Leuthner scandal (*Fall Leuthner*) had blown up as early as the spring of 1909. On 25 April 1909, for example, *Vorwärts* complained in an article 'On the Leuthner affair' that

Karl Leuthner . . . has already written numerous articles in the so-called '*Socialist' Monthly* and was previously considered as the beacon of international revisionism. He participated in every 'national' orgy and demands, so to speak, neither more nor less than that the Social Democratic press should support *every 'national' policy* even when it is criminal . . . Leuthnerism is nothing but Schippelism in a different guise. The system is that the one applauds [Chancellor] Bülow while the other reviles the Social Democratic press, and the whole is called 'reformist tactics'. (Italics in original)

A fortnight before, Leuthner had written to Bloch of 'my struggle, our struggle' (SMP, vol. 8: 11/12 April 1909). The *Vorwärts* analysis was correct. There *was* a concerted 'reformist tactic', and Leuthner's part in it, as Trotsky remarked, was to propagate 'consistent revisionism in the realm of foreign affairs' within the German party (Trotsky, 1908/9, p. 79). Bloch had chosen Leuthner for this role precisely because, as Kautsky complained to Victor Adler in July 1905, Leuthner's name had long been a byword for Anglophobia, contempt for the Slavs, 'German *völkisch* arrogance' and a 'Pan-German outlook, which in him outweighs other considerations' (Adler, 1954, p. 462). It was in full awareness of this fact that the party press – from *Vorwärts* and the *Leipziger Volkszeitung* to the *Hamburger Echo* – not only noticed Leuthner's work but regularly and repeatedly repudiated it as part of a plot to force the German labour movement to re-examine its options, choosing again between imperialism and socialism, between nationalism and internationalism.

Leuthner recognised that his views made him extremely unpopular in the German party, even with many revisionist colleagues (1909*f*, p. 607; 1909*h*, p. 754; SMP, vol. 8: Leuthner to Bloch, 10 April 1909). Some of his sternest critics were *Praktiker* like Adolf von Elm (SMP, vol. 4: von Elm to Bloch, 28 June 1909). Revisionists of all persuasions both disagreed with much of Leuthner's viewpoint and objected still more strongly to the manner in which it was presented. Many, like Eduard David, felt they were being used as stalking-horses:

The 'revisionist' tendency is a not inconsiderable segment of the party, and if the impression is created that all or even many 'revisionists' share those views [of Leuthner, Schippel and Calwer], then the latter acquire an importance beyond their due as the eccentricities of particular individuals. ('In Sachen Leuthner', *Vorwärts*, 6 May 1909)

When Kurt Eisner wrote to Bloch that 'Joseph Bloch is indeed educating a proletariat, albeit a bourgeois one' (SMP, vol. 4: 25 July 1908), he undoubtedly spoke for a great many revisionists who felt not only that they were being manipulated but that such manipulation served a purpose which was profoundly at odds with any meaningful definition of the socialist aim and movement.

Much harder to assess is Leuthner's impact on the rank and file, as opposed to the socialist leadership, revisionist and otherwise. It may well be the case that the militancy of the German masses was growing rather than declining by August 1914, and it is obviously true that radicalism in domestic affairs is compatible with patriotism. But such speculation not only flies in the face of the findings of existing scholarship; it is impossible to square with the fact that the German masses did flock to the colours in 1914. For four long years they fought against overwhelming odds, suffering and dying in their millions for the fatherland. In the East, German arms triumphed completely, while Germany twice came within a hair's breadth of victory in the West, which equally eluded the exhausted Allied powers. This German achievement cannot be attributed to any notable superiority in generalship or material resources, only to the morale of the German soldier. Nor can it be explained otherwise than in terms of the breadth and depth of patriotic feeling which by 1914 had gripped the whole nation, including the millions comprising the organised and unorganised industrial working classes. It would be absurd to claim that Karl Leuthner and the *Sozialistische Monatshefte* played a major part in this process, but it is highly improbable that Leuthner and Bloch played *no* part in helping to 'nationalise' the German industrial proletariat during the last decade of peace. Günther Roth, Carl Schorske, Dieter Groh, Klaus Saul and many others have explained in meticulous detail the process whereby the Wilhelmine socialist subculture became gradually, if 'negatively', integrated into the dominant culture to the point where the 'workers' culture, in spite of its emancipatory aspirations, was helplessly at the mercy of the dominant culture in both form and content' (Leuschen-Seppel, 1978, p. 287). However badly Chancellor Bethmann Hollweg miscalculated in respect of British intentions in 1914, he was right about the German workers and their movement. When given a plausible pretext, such as the Russian bogey, they would not, and did not, desert the fatherland in its hour of danger. To the extent that Joseph Bloch and Karl Leuthner had a hand in the taming of the Wilhelmine working-class movement, the cause of the *Sozialistische Monatshefte* may be said to have triumphed.

One does not have to be a Gramscian to recognise that among the major reasons for the ultimate triumph of revisionism – or, to be more precise, the conquest of the labour movement by its bureaucrats and *Praktiker* – was the failure of Wilhelmine Social Democracy to develop a genuinely autonomous, authentically working-class counter-culture. Recent caveats notwithstanding, the Social Democratic subculture has been shown, in my view convincingly, to have fallen prey to the 'hegemony' of the dominant 'bourgeois' culture. A myriad of empirical studies now exist which confirm the 'neo-Weberian or functionalist' view that the labour-movement subculture imitated and duplicated the institutions and values of the dominant culture without ever seriously aspiring to the construction of a counter-hegemony.[7] Leuthner's work for the *Sozialistische Monatshefte* affords a concrete example of one means whereby the consent of the working class was organised. Here we see an influential, ostensibly socialist journalist absorbing and propagating values and norms which were heavily indebted to the philosophical, moral and political ideals of the dominant culture. A parallel indebtedness and effect could as readily be demonstrated with regard to other standard-bearers of Bloch's instrument – Max Schippel, Richard Calwer, Max Maurenbrecher, Gerhard Hildebrand, Ludwig Quessel and others – many of whom, as former National Socials, had come over to

Social Democracy precisely because they recognised its increasingly reformist, integrationist character and for the specific purpose of advancing this process of *embourgeoisement* within the Social Democratic subculture (Düding, 1972; Struve, 1973, pp. 93–4, 101). In his appeal to his readers, Leuthner, like the others, consciously and deliberately combined a clear commitment to an unmistakably integrationist reformism with espousal of a populist nationalism which was only slightly different from that applied with such telling effect among the lower middle classes and in the radical-nationalist pressure groups by Keim and Hugenberg (see Guratzsch, 1974, pp. 90–1; Eley, 1980; Kocka, 1981). Although the effect which Leuthner and his colleagues produced on their working-class and intellectual readers is impossible to quantify, the general trend of their work was indisputably the promotion of integrationist, social-imperialist tendencies within prewar German Social Democracy.

It is not legitimate to dismiss Leuthner, and those like him, as uninfluential cranks. True, Bernstein wrote more. But Bernstein's work for the *Monatshefte* was confined almost exclusively to theoretical questions or issues of day-to-day domestic politics. On the all-important national question, it was writers like Leuthner who made the running for the *Monatshefte* and reached its readership. As previously noted, this readership was considerable, and there can be no doubt that the *Monatshefte* was read by workers as well as by intellectual opinion-makers.

Notes: Chapter 4

1   I am greatly indebted to Herr Bruno Marek, former mayor of Vienna and a one-time disciple of Leuthner, for an interview (6 April 1979) which added significantly to my understanding of Leuthner's personality and position within the Austrian labour movement. For literature on Leuthner – there is very little – see Fletcher, 1982*b*, p. 74, n. 1; idem, 1982*d*, pp. 28–9, n. 3, 4, 7.

2   As H. J. Puhle (1966), K. D. Barkin (1970), P. C. Witt (1970) and others have demonstrated, the Junkers were most reluctant to share power with even the steel barons and had no intention of admitting 'the great unwashed', whatever the colour of their collars, to any conceivable realignment of the ruling power bloc. Thus Eley is obliged to admit that in the formation of the 1913 'cartel of the productive estates' (allegedly an instance of the white-collar proletariat 'forcing a renegotiation of hegemonic class relations' and so gaining entry to the magic circle of power) 'the leaders of the petty-bourgeoisie were certainly not admitted to the *Sammlung* as full participating partners, for . . . certain key spokesmen of the *Mittelstand* were taken in, but only on sufferance, and with a clear manipulative intent' (Eley, 1980, p. 331). If Bloch and Leuthner appeared to underestimate this obstacle, other revisionists did not. Seven years after the death of Wilhelm von Kardorff, the Free Conservative leader, Südekum recalled with bitterness the latter's dictum, so typical of Junker intransigence: 'Important as is the struggle against syphilis, tuberculosis and foot-and-mouth disease, there remains the still more important struggle against Social Democracy' (SP, no. 101, pt I, February 1914).

3   He was especially fond of the term *Volksgemeinschaft*, referring to 'the sacred name of the folk community' (1906*c*, p. 184) and identifying the interests of the German folk community as 'the commandments of political progress' (1906*j*, p. 193). This term was subsequently to become a holy of holies to the Nazis (Schoenbaum, 1966, p. 55).

4   At the 1911 Jena party congress Bebel had claimed that German Social Democrats had a 'natural wish that Germany's trade and economic development [were] able to unfold in Morocco under the same conditions as those applying to every other country, in other words that all countries may uphold their interests in Morocco on a basis of complete parity, that none gains preference over the others, none abuses its position to dislodge others' (SPD A.C., 1911,

p. 336). Bebel's utterances on this occasion, especially when read in the context of his other patriotic pronouncements, can be interpreted in Leuthner's sense, as demonstrating the degree to which even the SPD's 'Marxist' leadership now felt obliged to make formal obeisance at the altar of national sentiment. Yet Bebel's cautious diplomatising may also be viewed as a plea for free trade, for he was now, through Bernstein, in contact with Alfred Fried of the German Peace Society (Chickering, 1975, pp. 277–8) and, through Sir Henry Angst, in touch with the British Foreign Office as well. If the private views of 'Emperor Bebel' gained public expression in a form which facilitated their appropriation by nationalists like Leuthner, this must surely be taken as an index of the manner in which the dominant ideology imposed its 'hegemony' on the socialist subculture, and as a pointer not simply to labour conformity or acquiescence but to ways in which 'the *consent* of the working class was organized' (Eley and Nield, 1980, p. 258).

5 Comparison of his article on 'Continental Germany' (1913*c*, p. 287) with 'Is it still the same war?' (1914*a*, pp. 1217–18) illustrates his view of a naval détente as no more than an expedient for keeping Britain neutral while Germany settled accounts with France and Russia. In the 1913 article Leuthner insisted that an Anglo-German naval agreement must leave Germany a free hand on the Continent. In the later article he ridiculed the notion that there had ever been any prospect of Anglo-German amity, thereby reverting to the position occupied in his 'Master race and rabble' article of 1909 (1909*c*).

6 In Leuthner's case, personal factors may also have clouded his judgement, for he appeared to suffer some kind of personal crisis at this time. His correspondence with Bloch in the last few years of peace reveals frequent complaints of overwork, financial worries and health problems as well as a marked deterioration in his intellectual powers. Even his published writings disclose a noticeable preoccupation with madness, angst and phobia of one kind or another. During the First World War he successfully evaded military service by pleading unsuitability because of a nervous disorder. A letter to Bloch dated 6 December 1910, in which Leuthner alternated his customary formal style of address with the familiar *tutoiement*, may serve to indicate his disoriented state of mind at the time: he ranted, 'Rather an end to terror than these endless terrors of [radical] moral and demagogic twaddle . . . Rise up against them! The elections will give you a roaring reply. In place of radical bawling impudence, demand a grain of reason and conscience for the woes of the nation. They will hail you in triumph for having, thank God, better understood the nation and what it is capable of'(SMP, vol. 8). In so far as he was sane at the time, which may be doubted, these exhortations also provide an example of a clear link, in Leuthner's mind, between nationalism and revisionism (or at least anti-Marxism).

7 A recent attempt to dismiss such work as misguided products of 'unreflected empiricism' and antiquated structural-functionalism apparently yielded little more than a sterile epistemological and philosophical squabble among Gramscian culturalists (arguing like good Narodniks that 'the cultural organizations of an apparently non-revolutionary working class . . . constitute the concrete terrain from which the working class can *force* a re-negotiation of hegemonic class relations and even *wrest* important public, moral and political space from the institutions of bourgeois society' [Eley and Nield, 1980, p. 265, italics in original]), 'economistic reductionists', residual and 'full-blown' Leninists, and other 'social scientists'. Out of this debate there emerged a determined effort to identify an 'authentic' working-class culture manifesting at least revolutionary possibilities. This endeavour turned out to be little more than an evasion, stressing the volatility of working-class thought and action and insisting that the context is everything. More importantly, it did not deal systematically with the working class as a whole but presented only an impressionistic, highly selective coverage of specific instances of 'deviant' behaviour and so extrapolated an image of an autonomous, 'authentic' working-class culture very largely from the idiosyncrasies of the *Lumpenproletariat* (Evans, ed., 1982).

5
Bloch at Bay: The Failure of the Catiline Conspiracy

It is generally agreed that opportunism is no chance occurrence, sin, slip, or treachery on the part of individuals, but a social product of an entire period of history.

(V. I. Lenin, 1915)

Opportunism is characterised by disregard of theory, and not a few party members who ranked as revisionists were simply opportunists who made no bones about the fact that they had little or no interest in theory. Almost without exception, the opportunist socialists in Germany have now, understandably, joined the nationalist forces.

(Eduard Bernstein, 1915)

Revisionism was the child of its time: the logical expression of the belief in progress which motivated wide circles in Europe before it was destroyed by the war.

(Peter Gay, 1952)

However thin and tenuous it may be, the connection exists between the liberal belief in progress, the march of science and Auschwitz.

(H. W. Koch, 1970)

During the world war the revisionist tendency dissolved into various groups. One part of the old revisionists, the circle around the Sozialist- ische Monatshefte, *thoroughly approved of national defence and was in this respect in agreement with the party Executive. At the same time, it condemned passive tolerance of government policy and demanded that Social Democracy pursue an independent and, if necessary, oppositional stance in all the vital issues concerning the German people. A second group of revisionists simply went over to the party executive. Finally, a third group, led by Bernstein, the actual theoretical head of revisionism, and by Eisner, seceded from the old party and, together with former members of the party executive, founded the new Independent Social Democracy.*

(Arthur Rosenberg, 1936)

The reformists gained power in the party quite independently of the Revisionist theorists.

(Peter Gay, 1952)

In another sense, Bloch's dual victory over fellow-revisionists and non-revisionists within the SPD must be judged to have been a Pyrrhic one. In terms of what he really hoped to achieve, his journalistic enterprise was a tragic failure, although this did not become fully apparent until much later. As the Bebel–Singer generation departed the Wilhelmine political scene, the men who picked up the mantle of leadership and the plums of office were neither Bloch's 'swallows' nor Bebel's 'crown prince', Ludwig Frank, but a mixed bag of reformists and *Praktiker* who owed no allegiance to Bloch and for whom the 'impresario of revisionism' had little but contempt. During the war years, Bloch's journal was eclipsed by better-funded and more extremist publications. After Germany's military defeat in 1918, Bloch had nothing more to say to his countrymen. Thereafter, his integrationist tactic, minus its now obsolete radical-nationalist opportunism, was applied by the Majority SPD with as much success as could be expected under the circumstances. Bloch was content to go along with this under the banner of 1789, a fall-back position long in use among all party factions. His only alternative, after all, was to stick to his nationalist guns and to enter into competition with Hugenberg and Hitler. For Bloch, this was not a realistic option, given the 1917 split in the German labour movement, the perceived threat of Bolshevism and the increasingly virulent *völkisch* anti-Semitism of the populist nationalists. (His more sympathetic attitude towards Zionism in the immediate prewar period suggests that even then he was beginning to realise where his German patriotism might terminate [see Wistrich, 1982, pp. 165–72].) In the Weimar period, Bloch finally recognised that politics is the art of the possible. Yet the seeds of his political demise had begun to sprout in the prewar years.

The Limits of Bloch's Success

Seeking to consolidate the various revisionist elements around the *Sozialistische Monatshefte* and 'Leuthnerism', to capture the SPD from within and to locate non-socialist allies to force a democratisation or 'popularisation' of Prussia and the Reich that would effectively terminate the pariah status of the working-class subculture, Bloch aimed at a reconstitution of the political nation via populist nationalism in a manner and a style not vastly dissimilar to that of Alfred Hugenberg. Whereas the patriotic societies and Centre Party radicalism functioned as agents for the political integration of the lower middle classes and Germany's Catholic minority under the slogans of populist nationalism and anti-socialism, Bloch's programmatic formula for working-class integration was populist nationalism and anti-Marxism. His strategy, too, bore a strong resemblance to Hugenberg's drive for 'power through organisation'. With populist nationalism and hostility to revolutionary Marxism as its ideological fundament, Bloch's strategy was to create the impression that Leuthner and kindred 'swallows' spoke on behalf of the entire revisionist camp, and so to promote the organisation and step-by-step creation of a new public opinion within Social Democracy and beyond. Bloch hoped to wield influence through personal contacts and co-optation. Using his network of bilateral contacts, Catiline–Siegfried hoped to manipulate all elements of revisionism and to consolidate his common ground with all possible allies, his minimum objective being to exert significant influence on opinion-makers within Social Democracy and thus to transform the mood of the masses. Hence his concern with secrecy, especially in regard to his network of contacts, his financial support and the fact that all threads led to Joseph Bloch. Only by posing as mediator among the various splinters of revisionism could Bloch hope to forge a united and cohesive revisionist 'Nothung' with a real cutting edge.

Viewed in the short term, Bloch's journalistic enterprise was unquestionably a success. He did succeed in establishing his publication as *the* organ of revisionism, and he did manage to enlist and retain the services of a wide range of writers whose ideological positions often diverged markedly from his own. In the prewar era, he was by no means as isolated or unimportant as generations of labour historians have assumed. His deliberate choice of a low profile, like that of Hugenberg, was a matter of policy; it is not evidence of isolation and impotence. A man who was in a position to offer Karl Leuthner the editorship of the Chemnitz *Volksstimme* was no mere cypher, as his contemporaries were only too well aware. That his influence declined after 1914 is beyond dispute, but it is no proof that he was also a non-entity *before* 1914. In the long term, however, Bloch's press policy failed to knit together a cohesive revisionist movement. He proved unable to preserve his anonymity and, with the public disclosure of his partisanship and his position as the 'impresario of revisionism', the credibility of his role as mediator was damaged beyond repair. Thus he succeeded in using the *Monatshefte* as an organ of populist nationalism only by alienating many of those whose support and collaboration were essential if he were to capture Wilhelmine Social Democracy for the reformist ideology and tactic which he propounded. Intellectuals as diverse as Bernstein, Kurt Eisner, Eduard David and Albert Südekum distanced themselves from his 'conspiracy' or publicly attacked it. Even *Praktiker* like Adolf von Elm voiced serious reservations about the activities of Bloch and his 'swallows' (see SMP, vol. 4: von Elm to Bloch, 1 August 1908). In the end, the continued allegiance of the practitioners was more apparent than real, reflecting their indifference to all theory rather than their acquiescence in Bloch's 'conspiracy'. His network of personal contacts therefore broke down, unable to bear the strains which he imposed on it.

This is not to say that Bloch's project was entirely unrealistic. On the contrary, the strength of revisionism as a movement derived from the fact that its feet were firmly planted in the ground of social realities. For one, it recognised, as some centrists and most left-wing Marxists did not, that revolution was impossible in Wilhelmine Germany. On the one hand, it is important to bear in mind that for all its anomalies and reactionary tendencies, Imperial Germany was significantly different from Tsarist Russia. The dismantling of the apparatus of official persecution in 1890 and subsequent socialist successes at the state and national polls, in municipal politics and in trade union activities after 1890 should not be allowed to obscure the fact that the very substantial economic and political controls exercised by employers and the state were still in place in 1914. These controls remained operative until defeat in war momentarily, and only temporarily, unnerved the ruling élites in 1918–19, and even then the political left proved incapable of establishing a viable German democracy, to say nothing of a socialist transformation of German society. In 1914 the morale of the ruling classes was not broken but as firm as ever. The army was loyal and efficient, 'determined to lead a war *à outrance* against the Social

Democrats' (Kitchen, 1968, p. 145), and even the 'unpatriotic vagabonds' obeyed orders when in uniform. On the other hand, conditions appeared to be improving after 1890, holding out some hope of a peaceful, piecemeal working-class integration into the political nation. In any event, such developments as the gradual bureaucratisation of the labour movement, the growth of a labour aristocracy and rising working-class affluence made a revolutionary upheaval increasingly improbable. When a revolution finally did occur in November 1918, its aim was not socialism. We have it on good authority that 'most of the revolutionaries in Germany in November 1918 simply demanded peace and democratic reform' (Geary, 1981, p. 162).[1] A second strength of revisionism as a movement was its firm foundation in German patriotism – a more potent force than revolutionary Marxism and a social reality which is recognised as such even by historians owning to a revolutionary Marxist bias. Here Bloch was on to a good thing and he knew it. Finally, Bloch's truculent anti-Marxism was equally in accord with existing social realities, for he correctly recognised that the basic line of demarcation within Wilhelmine Social Democracy was not that between *embourgeoisé* bureaucrats and an authentically proletarian rank and file but the great divide separating intellectuals from the rest. This was the meaning of Kautsky's previously noted reference to the 'silent hatred' of Marxism within the labour movement. Bloch tried to turn this sentiment to his own advantage while making no attempt to devise a new 'orthodoxy of opportunism', which he deplored as a 'monstrosity' (SMP, vol. 8: Bloch to Leuthner, 25 October 1907). Thus Bloch stood at least an even chance of rallying to the *Sozialistische Monatshefte* both the disenchanted reformist intellectuals and the working-class rank and file together with its pragmatic and theoretically disinterested leaders.

Yet Bloch's tactic of national integration was ultimately a failure. It miscarried, in part, because he overestimated the power of the socialist press in an overwhelmingly anti-socialist society. Bloch overlooked important differences between his own position and that of non-socialist counterparts like Alfred Hugenberg. The latter had access to power far in excess of anything to which Bloch and Leo Arons might reasonably aspire. During the war, for example, Bloch had little real hope of competing successfully with a journal like *Die Glocke*, which was funded by Hugo Stinnes and far more extreme and consistent in its social imperialism. In fact, Bloch's single-issue programme was not enough to secure the desired national consensus. Employers were not willing to accept the working class or its movement into a genuine partnership, and both official and unofficial non-socialist nationalism aimed as much at containing the working class and its political demands as at expanding German influence in the global community. As Eckart Kehr argued correctly more than half a century ago, the latter policy was neither conceived nor implemented independently of its domestic political function of containing the social and political consequences of economic modernisation (see Kehr, 1977). Another reason for the failure of Bloch's revisionist strategy was that reformism (or whatever one wishes to call it), as a movement, was essentially a social phenomenon thrown up by the conditions of advanced capitalism and beyond the control of any one individual. As such, it tended to bypass all ideologies and theories, although it might and did make occasional use of some of them. In the words of Geary,

Only a small group of intellectuals around Bernstein wanted to revise party *theory*, only a few intellectuals around Kautsky were devoted to it as theory; and only a few intellectuals around Rosa Luxemburg wanted to develop that theory in a more revolutionary direction . . . Reformists often voted for the party orthodoxy as it rarely interfered with their day-to-day activities and they disliked all theoreticians, as they caused unnecessary trouble in a party whose greatest need was unity. (1976, p. 306, italics in original)

To a considerable extent the revisionist phenomenon may be seen as a proletarian parallel to the kind of spontaneous mass revolt which Eley and Blackbourn allege to have taken place in the lower middle classes through the patriotic societies and among German Catholics in the Wilhelmine era. Demanding that they, too, be given a place in the 'magic circle of power', such movements produced their own leaders and institutions which, in the case of revisionism, were largely beyond the control of Bloch, as they were of Bebel, Kautsky or Luxemburg. South German reformists like Ludwig Frank, for example, were prepared to split the German labour movement after 1908 rather than accept dictation from the party centre; they were equally determined to preserve their independence of Bloch (SMP, vol. 4: Bloch to von Elm, 6 and 8 October 1908). The trade unions' assertion of their independence of the SPD at Mannheim in September 1906 is well known. It goes without saying that they were equally adamant that they would not be dictated to by Bloch, who pronounced them unreliable and vacillating (SMP, vol. 1: Bloch to Arons, 24 October 1908). On 6 May 1909, Bloch informed Leuthner that he regarded the *Sozialpolitiker* (social policy specialists) and the trade unionists as 'a particularly valuable circle of contributors' because 'in this of all spheres the *SM* exerts direct influence, which [he would] under no circumstances abandon, on matters of importance'. Although anxious at the prospect of losing these forces to the David group, Bloch was prepared to forego their collaboration rather than compromise the principles for which the *Monatshefte* had always stood (SMP, vol. 8). On several occasions Bloch was warned by his friend Adolf von Elm (Hamburg trade union and co-operative leader, SPD Reichstag deputy between 1894 and 1907 and, like Bloch, an admirer of Wagner) that Leuthner's articles and the obsessive anti-Marxism of the *Monatshefte* were so unacceptable to the working-class rank and file that Bloch had to face up to the possibility of a working-class boycott of his journal. Von Elm agreed with Bloch on the importance of drumming up support for revisionism both outside and within Social Democracy, but he warned that Bloch ran the risk of retaining the allegiance of no one but his non-socialist supporters (SMP, vol. 4: von Elm to Bloch, 1 August 1908, 28 June 1909). He, too, objected to Bloch's deletions and amendments to his *Monatshefte* articles, threatening to withdraw his contributions and his collaboration unless Bloch refrained from this practice. What this instance illustrates is that prominent *Praktiker* were as loath to be manipulated by Bloch as were the reformist and revisionist intellectuals.

Personal factors may also have played a part in Bloch's failure to create the revisionist phalanx which was to capture Social Democracy and then inflict a

Gaugamela on those who denied the working class its place in the political nation. Obviously, Bloch's Prussianism won him few friends in the south. Evidently a man of great sensibility, he was temperamentally unsuited and disinclined to the public platform, more a committee man or administrator than a charismatic leader. For reasons which remain obscure, he seems to have been personally disliked among many colleagues and allies. Even after the outbreak of the First World War, people like David and Südekum recorded in their diaries meetings with Bloch which they judged 'disagreeable' or 'unfruitful' (SP, no. 166: diary entry of 26 August 1914; S. Miller, 1974, p. 186, n. 13). It is not impossible that part of the reason for Bloch's personal unpopularity was anti-Semitic prejudice, for a great many of his closest colleagues were either Jews or (as in the case of Calwer and Leuthner) married to Jews. A number of recent studies has shown that although anti-Semitism was officially frowned upon and rarely expressed in Wilhelmine Social Democracy, in reality it was never far beneath the surface, and this applied to socialist intellectuals like Franz Mehring as much as to the masses (Leuschen-Seppel, 1978, p. 283; Wistrich, 1982, p. 126). Not all socialist anti-Semites were as frank as Noske, who spoke of 'a certain foreign influence' (*Ausländerei*) which got on his nerves and blamed 'semi-educated . . . Eastern Jewish "Marxists" ' for having discredited the pre-1914 German labour movement with their 'twaddle about Marxism' (Noske, 1947, pp. 26, 27).

For these reasons the *Sozialistische Monatshefte* failed to live up to the expectations which Bloch held of it. Two concrete examples of this failure are afforded by the record of Bloch's relations with two revisionist intellectuals – Kurt Eisner and Eduard Bernstein. With the neo-Kantian Eisner, Bloch failed absolutely, for Eisner simply refused to be co-opted by the *Monatshefte*. With Bernstein, the high priest of revisionism, Bloch enjoyed greater success, at least until December 1914 when Bernstein severed his connections with the *Monatshefte* after a head-on collision with Bloch over the war issue. Yet here, too, Bloch never really succeeded in manipulating the father of revisionism, for Bernstein found other means of giving expression to views which were unwelcome in the *Monatshefte*.

A Miscarriage of the Blochian Tactic: The Case of Kurt Eisner

Ethical or neo-Kantian Socialism

One of the many heterodoxies which Bloch strove to rally to the *Monatshefte* was ethical or neo-Kantian socialism. Bloch was not particularly worried by the competition of Bernstein's two short-lived journalistic endeavours – the *Neues Montagsblatt* (May to November 1904) and his monthly *Dokumente des Sozialismus* (1901–5) – but he was concerned that his thunder might be stolen by Heinrich and Lily Braun's *Neue Gesellschaft*. Strongly ethical in tendency, the *Neue Gesellschaft* attacked the party Marxism of the centre-orthodoxy for its dogmatism while attempting to elevate the intellectual tone of the movement by attracting disinterested intelligence to the movement and seeking to enrich the cultural life of the entire nation. At the same time, it tolerated chauvinism while working to forge a partnership between theoretical revisionism and leading reformists and *Praktiker* from the trade unions. Among its regular contributors were Eduard David, Kurt Eisner, Edmund Fischer, Paul Göhre, Wolfgang Heine, Otto Hué, Wilhelm Kolb, Johann Leimpeters, Theodor Leipart, Karl Leuthner, Paul Löbe, Max Maurenbrecher, Adolf Müller, August Müller, Wilhelm Schröder, Carl Severing, Friedrich Stampfer, Albert Südekum and Paul Umbreit. It was closely connected with Georg von Vollmar, the Bavarian reformist leader, whom it acknowledged as its 'godfather' (see Fricke, 1976, pp. 468–70). By October 1907, the Brauns' *Neue Gesellschaft* had to close for want of financial support – much to Bloch's relief, Arons refused to back it – and because it seemed too extreme for the time. (As noted above, even Bloch felt obliged to adopt a relatively moderate line until about 1907, which did not save several of his earlier 'swallows', most notably Calwer and Schippel, from being subjected to punitive measures by the party.) The conclusion which Bloch drew from this episode was that he must fill the void left by the *Neue Gesellschaft* and make a determined effort to win over to the *Monatshefte* those neo-Kantians and other ethical socialists who had formerly been associated with the rival revisionist publication.

The ethical socialists were regarded at the time, as they have been ever since, as a major component of the right wing of pre-1914 German Social Democracy. This particular heresy had its roots in the neo-Kantian revival which got under way in the 1870s. Primarily, though not exclusively, German in origin – for it is also apparent in the doctoral dissertation of Jean Jaurès (1891) – neo-Kantianism had a pedigree going back to Friedrich Albert Lange and Otto Liebmann in the 1860s. It was 'partly a reaction to the "vulgar" materialism of the natural scientists [and in part] an attempt to restore unity and cohesion to the liberal world-view' (Lichtheim, 1964, p. 290). Academic in nature from the start, it was posited on the hope that philosophy and science might be reintegrated on the basis of Kantian critical thinking shorn of its purely personal and historically outmoded metaphysical and ethical notions. Politically, it ranged from moderate liberalism to moderate socialism. Although their objective was to rescue what remained of German liberalism after the depredations of Bismarck's solution to the German question, a number of neo-Kantian philosophers, principally those of the Marburg school (Hermann Cohen, Paul Natorp and epigones like Karl Vorländer), allowed their sympathy for socialism to carry them to the point of suggesting a possible synthesis of philosophical idealism and Marxism. In the oppressive atmosphere of Wilhelmine Germany it was not possible for members of the professoriate to go further without forfeiting their places in respectable society. Nor were they encouraged to do so by the initially cool response of the socialists, although as late as 1898 Kautsky still thought that such a synthesis might be profitable (Kautsky to Plekhanov, 22 May 1898, cit. Steinberg, 1972, p. 99). In Germany, and in contrast with Austrian Social Democracy, neither the party centre nor the radical left concerned itself greatly with the problem of ethics. Only when the ethical question, through its association with revisionism, became integral to the debate over tactics did radical and orthodox Marxists perceive a need to find a substitute for the proletariat (see Kamenka, 1972, pp. xv, 8–9, 165).

By the turn of the century, when the revisionist debate erupted, there had also emerged within the socialist camp a number of active Social Democrats who professed Kantian inclinations – Ludwig Woltmann, Franz Staudinger (editor of the philosophical review section of the *Monatshefte* from 1905 onwards), Conrad Schmidt (Bloch's social sciences editor from 1908 to 1930), Karl Vorländer, Paul Kampffmeyer (also one of Bloch's coeditors) and Kurt Eisner. These ethical socialists attempted to fuse Kantian ethics with Marxian politics, but they did so in a wide variety of ways. Some neo-Kantain socialists, like the Austro-Marxist Max Adler, were also considered radical Marxists. Others, like Conrad Schmidt, adhered stubbornly to historical materialism and expressly rejected the notion that Kantian moral philosophy could be employed as a fruitful adjunct to received socialist theory. Schmidt's Kantianism in fact scarcely went beyond recognition of Kant's philosophy of history as prefiguring that of Marx (see Sandkühler and de la Vega, eds, 1974, pp. 87–106, 199–204). Ludwig Woltmann, who saw himself as an 'unadulterated orthodox Kantian' (although he was, in fact, far removed from seeking to substitute ethical idealism for materialism as the philosophical foundation of socialism) (ibid., pp. 107–18), was criticised by Franz Staudinger who, like Eisner, attempted to play a mediating role between Kant and Marx. Paul Kampffmeyer, whose position was probably closest to that of Bernstein, argued that socialism was defensible only on the basis of its ethical desirability, never on the grounds of its alleged historical inevitability (1909a, pp. 90–4; 1909b, pp. 490–5; 1911, pp. 33–7). Some neo-Kantians, such as Karl Vorländer, made their way to socialism from ethical idealism; others, like Bernstein himself, made this transition in reverse. All agreed that Marxism, as they knew it, both lacked and needed an adequate ethical foundation; all sought in some degree to confront this desideratum by drawing on the resources of the neo-Kantian revival.

It is quite true that 'not all neo-Kantians were supporters of Bernstein, and vice versa. Some prominent revisionists managed to remain both Kantians and Marxians.' It is also true that 'down to 1914 . . . orthodox Marxism tended to go hand in hand with political intransigence or "radicalism" [and philosophical materialism], while the reformist wing, by and large, came to shelter those who toyed with idealism in philosophy' (Lichtheim, 1964, pp. 293–4). Much as Joseph Bloch might lament the 'deplorable misunderstanding' through which people like Kurt Eisner had come to be regarded as revisionists (SMP, vol. 8: Bloch to Leuthner, 10 May 1907), ethical socialists were shepherded willy-nilly into the revisionist fold as a last refuge from the barbs and strictures of the radical left and orthodox centre. The question is whether ethical socialists like Eisner are accurately described as revisionists. Certainly, Leninists have no doubts on this point: neo-Kantianism, both academic and socialist, was a 'Trojan horse of revisionism' (Sandkühler and de la Vega, eds, 1974, p. 33).[2] The validity of this thesis may be tested by reference to the pre-1914 position of Kurt Eisner.

Kurt Eisner's Kantian Socialism

Among active Social Democrats before 1914, the foremost representative of the neo-Kantian position – and more specifically of the Marburg school – was undoubtedly Kurt Eisner (1867–1919), who subsequently came to fame as an anti-war radical, author of the Munich Putsch on 7 November 1918, Prime

Minister of the Bavarian Republic and one of the early martyrs of the November Revolution. Even before the war, Eisner had made a name for himself as an able, witty and reputedly revisionist journalist,[3] having succeeded Wilhelm Liebknecht as *de facto* managing editor of *Vorwärts* until his dismissal, as one of the revisionist 'noble six', in 1905 (see Schade, 1961, pp. 27–8; A. Mitchell, 1965, p. 53, n. 30; F. Eisner, 1979, pp. 36–40). After 1907 he attained some prominence as one of the anti-Prussian gadflies of the Bavarian party, as a popular literary critic and as a voluble opponent of Wilhelmine world policy. In his youth, Eisner had studied philosophy and *Germanistik* for eight semesters in Berlin, and as a political editor with the *Hessische Landeszeitung* (1893–7) he became acquainted with the leading philosopher of the Marburg school, Hermann Cohen, who made a deep and lasting impression on Eisner's thought. It was not until December 1898, after nine months' imprisonment for *lèse-majesté*, that Eisner joined the SPD. Financially, he survived this difficult period with the aid of a substantial personal loan from Charles Hallgarten of Frankfurt (Fricke, 1974*a*, p. 1057, n. 37), the same benefactor whose generosity embarrassed Bloch in 1909.

Although an intellectual, and one who prided himself on being a 'true' Marxist, Eisner's claim to theoretical orthodoxy was probably rather thin. This, at least, is the view of Allan Mitchell:

For all his talk of the 'scientific' aspects of Marxist thought, he had never demonstrated more than a rudimentary appreciation of economics and economic theory. And, after all, only in a very general sense could his political views be identified as either Marxist or Kantian; he accepted the common notion that society was divided into two 'armed camps', and he shared the fundamentally uncomplicated belief that society was wrong and that it ought somehow to be set right. (1965, pp. 70–1).

Although Freya Eisner strongly objects to this characterisation of her grandfather, most authorities would agree with Mitchell that Kurt Eisner was more a gifted *littérateur* than a clear-thinking theorist and that he 'tended to define socialism simply as social justice' (ibid., p. 40). Yet he saw himself, in 1918 as in 1904, as being in substantial agreement with Kautsky on all questions of political theory and practice. Of crucial importance to Eisner's position was his conviction that there was no logical inconsistency in holding that socialism was both scientifically determined and ethically desirable, that it was possible to marry Marx with Kant without doing violence to either. Eisner chose to regard Marx as having 'completed' Kant by adding the necessary economic and historical flesh and blood to the skeleton of Kantian ethics. It is hardly surprising, then, that the centre-orthodoxy and the radical left considered him tainted by revisionism in the sense that his grasp of Marxist doctrine was tenuous and friable, his revolutionary idealism being of an altogether different stamp from the radicalism of a Kautsky or a Luxemburg.

There was some basis to this charge. On 2 September 1903, for instance, Eisner wrote to Victor Adler and implored the respected and influential Austrian labour leader to use his authority with Bebel to forestall the imminent anti-revisionist witch-burning at Dresden. Defending Bernstein's position in the Reichstag vice-presidency imbroglio, Eisner described the royal audience issue as a mere 'pretext', such a 'promenade' having no meaning in itself. 'The Belgrade officers', he added, in a reference to the murder of the Serbian royal family, 'also went to court.' Possibly hinting at a future revisionist backlash against the party zealots, he suggested that the way to deal with the situation was to 'give the revisionists the correct orientation and establish to what extent their tendencies have or have not struck firm root within the party'. Bebel, in particular, he considered 'petty' (AA, file 174a). To be sure, this was before Eisner had become preoccupied with the threat of world war and before the *Monatshefte* had emerged as the plaything of apologists for the Prussian Moloch, and it could also be argued that Eisner was merely mediating to avert a mutually damaging public blood-letting. Yet he asked Adler to 'do something for us', which, since only the revisionists stood in need of deliverance, warrants the supposition that on this occasion, at least, Eisner identified himself with the revisionist camp.

Yet Eisner was never a thoroughgoing revisionist and repeatedly declined to accept the tag of revisionism. On 2 September 1907 he wrote to Joseph Bloch condemning factionalism *per se*, be it left or right. He added, 'Having always held myself aloof from all clique sentiment and conflicted most frequently with my best personal friends, I am not at all surprised that I have made myself downright unpopular in both camps.' Eisner explained his lone-wolf position as

a coherently conceived system of action which does not rule out day-to-day reform while not shrinking from any means, neither from compromise nor from revolution. This is also the attitude of Jaurès [who was, together with Wilhelm Liebknecht, one of Eisner's lifelong idols], whose opponents therefore charge him with inconsistency, just as you do me. Thus, I am, for example, 'ultra-radical' on the [Prussian] suffrage and militarism issues, in regard to colonialism and the trade union question, but 'ultra-revisionist' on questions of ministerialism or budget approval. That, in consequence, both camps are annoyed with me, that they don't know what to make of me, is as irksome for them as it is agreeable to me. (SMP, vol. 4)

Eisner spurned identification with the revisionists not only because he relished his independence and his eclecticism, which he viewed as being more 'truly Marxist' than the petty-minded sectarianism of both left and right, but also because he was congenitally incapable of accepting the principal tenet of revisionism, namely the proposition that time and economic change had overtaken the class struggle and made a reconciliation of classes both possible and necessary. 'We [Germans] will not be spared our revolution', he told Bloch in his letter of 2 September 1907. 'We will not have it any better than the English, the French or the Russians. And so I am in favour not only of the mass strike but also of taking to the streets. Had I the responsibility for such measures, I would accept it, with all its consequences, without the slightest hesitation.' His study of Prussian history had convinced Eisner that the incurably reactionary and expansionist Junker state had by-passed its bourgeois revolution, if not industrialism, so that the socialist revolution would assume the form of a head-on collision with the Junkers rather than with the capitalist class. Kautsky and Bernstein both envisaged Social Democracy as a surrogate bourgeoisie whose task was to complete the bourgeois revolution as the necessary prerequisite to socialism in Germany. It was Eisner's view, as much as that of Kautsky or Bernstein, that the defeat of Napoleon had facilitated the preternatural survival of Prussian absolutism into the age of industrialism, thereby obviating the need for social and political concessions to an eviscerated bourgeoisie. Where Eisner diverged from Kautsky and Bernstein was his conviction that the nature of the Prussian state made a direct confrontation between Junkerdom and socialism inevitable: after Leipzig and Waterloo the intermediate stage of bourgeois revolution had become superfluous and impossible in Germany (K. Eisner, 1907).

The central concerns of Eisner's journalistic output in the last decade of peace were his hatred of Prussian 'prison-state patriarchalism' and his fear of world war. At first he had been opposed to the use of the political mass strike, which formed part of the background to his removal from the editorial board of *Vorwärts*. But his study of German policy in the Moroccan crisis of 1905 convinced Eisner that 'German imperialism [was] merely awaiting the right moment to revolutionise the map of the globe'. Germany was grasping not only for Morocco but 'for Asia Minor, even Brazil and India'. It meant to get what it wanted, at the price of a global conflagration if need be, and its motivation owed at least as much to traditional Prussian cupidity as to the dynamics of capitalism: the key to the unsolved riddle of 'the sphinx of *Weltpolitik*' was to be found in 'the one salient fact that in Germany there never has been any public, any active popular participation in politics'. Since Germany was at best a mockery of a constitutional state, 'what the bourgeoisie [had] neglected [would] have to be conquered by the proletariat itself . . . By struggling for basic political rights, for the conquest of parliament, for the democratic electoral system in all legislative bodies, the German proletariat simultaneously works for the peace and civilisation of Europe' as well as its own emancipation (K. Eisner, 1906, pp. 6, 70–1). From 1905, when he wrote these words, Eisner never departed from this view of Prussia-Germany as a beast of prey lurking in the jungle of international politics in wait for an opportunity to establish its domain over all and sundry. It was then that Eisner became a proponent of the mass strike and of every other means that might contribute, however marginally, to the confounding and frustration of the Prussian juggernaut and its eventual conquest by the organised proletariat. Eisner later claimed of this study that it was 'probably the first brochure in the modern era of German Social Democracy to concern itself with concrete events of foreign policy' (K. Eisner, 1919a, Vol. 1, p. 328). Regardless of whether this claim was justified, as it possibly was, Eisner had no illusions as to the impact of his Moroccan brochure, for he frankly admitted that his efforts to enlighten his comrades on the nature and aims of Prusso-German policy had passed 'completely unnoticed' (ibid.).

The threat of world war, which to Eisner, as to almost every other socialist of the day, was synonymous with Armageddon, emanated pre-eminently from piratical Prussianism, for 'the Prussian state pursues one single purpose: to forward the crudest material power of the crown and the ruling Junker class in every way, unrestrained by moral scruples, national considerations or cultural ideals' (K. Eisner, 1907, pp. 71–2). In Bavaria, where censorship was lax and particularism strong, Eisner had a field-day with his anti-Prussian hobby-horse. As editor of the *Fränkische Tagespost* in Nuremberg (1907–10) he sought to conduct a one-man crusade against Wilhelmine *Weltpolitik*, but in the end he went too far. Lampooning the Prussians was one thing; it was quite another to tax the patience of provincials with never-ending articles on matters in which there was little interest and still less understanding. Eisner's anxiety was prompted not exclusively by the menace of war as such; he was as much concerned at its possible domestic repercussions, fearing a repetition of what had happened a century previously, when military victory abroad had enabled the Hohenzollern Moloch to devour the infant reform movement at home. Should the Prusso-German military monarchy actually wage and win a war of conquest, the revolutionary aspirations of Social Democracy might be stifled for generations to come. Worse still, they might perish ingloriously in a tidal wave of bloody counter-revolution (ibid., pp. iii–viii, 127).

Eisner's anxieties in respect of an imminent global catastrophe were augmented by his growing fears of Russian militarism. In 1904 he had published a polemic in which he had pilloried Russia as a menace to progress and peace the world over. The defeat of tsarism in the Russo-Japanese War and the 1905 Revolution in Russia temporarily assuaged his fears of tsarist aggression, but by 1912 Eisner felt that the eastern colossus had recovered its nerve and its power and was now planning an attack on Germany (Schade, 1961, p. 110, n. 298). He had apparently been taken in by the Bavarian government, which in November 1912 persuaded leading Bavarian Social Democrats that it was in possession of reliable and confidential information, including details of an alleged Russian plan of campaign, pointing to an imminent Russian attack on Germany (K. Eisner, 1919*a*, Vol. 1, p. 20). However vehement in expression, Eisner's Bavarian separatism and his hatred of Prussian reaction were never a match for his German patriotism, with the result that he was all too easily duped by such official canards. He therefore had no hesitation in giving unreserved support to the German war effort in August 1914. On August 2 he wrote:

> Now tsarism has attacked Germany, now we have no choice, now there is no looking back. Now the German proletariat has to annihilate the hereditary enemy of European civilisation. As Germans, as democrats, as socialists, we take up arms for the just cause. (ibid., pp. 15–16)

Upon more careful consideration of the facts, Eisner soon came to his senses and courageously denounced the conflict as a skilfully stage-managed Prusso-German war of aggression. For years the German left-wing radicals had also been thundering, in somewhat vague and abstract terms, against the iniquities and dangers of imperialism and militarism. But in the years immediately preceding the First World War Kurt Eisner had been one of those rare Social Democrats who, like Bernstein, worked tirelessly to bring home to the German masses the danger of war, not by drenching them in a heady brew of theoretically

nourishing slogans but by illuminating in detail the concrete events of international relations and of German policy in particular. What is noteworthy
of Eisner's endeavours is not that his warnings fell on deaf ears but rather that
such an informed and indefatigable commentator, committed to believing
the very worst of grasping Prussian chicanery, could so readily fall victim
to the Achilles' heel of prewar socialist foreign policy thinking – the Russian
bogey.

Bloch's Response
What did Bloch make of all this? As to ethical socialism generally, he had
mixed feelings. Believing himself to be an idealist, he welcomed an idealist
critique of what he regarded as the materialistic dogmatism of orthodox or
radical Marxism. Thus he had a lot of time for individual neo-Kantians like
Conrad Schmidt, Ludwig Woltmann, or Franz Staudinger. Even Eisner was
not entirely bereft of redeeming qualities – his love and admiration of
Napoleon, for instance (SMP, vol. 8: Bloch to Leuthner, 11 June 1908).
Indeed, Bloch admitted to Leuthner that he liked 'a lot of things about Eisner',
whom he found 'most congenial in several respects' (ibid., 10 May 1907). Nor
was Bloch above borrowing from the terminology of the neo-Kantians, as the
occasion demanded. But his grasp of Kantian philosophy was probably more
fragmentary than that of either Eisner or Bernstein. In 1907 he expressed
interest in both Cohen and Cassirer, particularly in the former, asking Eisner
to send him books on Cohen's logic: 'His ethics I also find interesting, but not
so important . . . I regard Cohen very highly, especially his outlook (*Gesinnung*)' (SMP, vol. 4: Bloch to Eisner, 27 May 1907, June 1907). In any event,
Bloch seems to have smelt a liberal rat in neo-Kantianism, which, after all, was
in a sense 'an academic version of the idealist-liberal *Weltanschauung*' (Lipton,
1978, p. 16). He judged the tumult over Kantianism to be far in excess of its
importance. 'For a time', he wrote sarcastically in 1908, 'it seemed as though
Goethe's position on Kantianism was the most topical of all party issues.' And
he lamented the Marxists' habit of pilfering its tones of 'moral indignation'
(Bloch, SMR, 1908, pp. 572, 574). He was certainly less interested in its
philosophical aspect than in its tactical and foreign policy implications.
Tactically, neo-Kantianism implied gradualism and co-operation. Bloch could
approve of that. But the *enfant terrible* of revisionism was essentially a *Realpolitiker*, and as such he emphatically resisted any attempt to smuggle the
categorical imperative into practical politics. To his way of thinking, the
international situation did not permit Germany the luxury of treating other
nations as anything but means to the larger end of German greatness. Invariably much closer to Nietzsche than to Kant, Bloch permitted himself inconsistencies which tended more towards Social Darwinism than in the direction
of ethical idealism. By and large, his private attitude towards neo-Kantianism
was one of qualified hostility. On the other hand, Bloch was intent on mobilising for the 'programme of the *Monatshefte*' all forms of socialist dissent which
might be useful either as bridges to suitable non-socialist allies (it is significant
that Hermann Cohen was among those who were caught up in the wave of
nationalist euphoria in 1914), or as a weapon in his campaign to replace the
Marxist revolutionary leadership of Social Democracy with men who, like

himself, aimed at integrating the labour movement into the nation under the aegis of imperialistic nationalism.

Accordingly, relations between Bloch and Eisner were far from amicable. For his part, Eisner made no secret of his dislike of the Blochian imperialists. In 1907 he wrote to Bloch describing Richard Calwer as 'a pig-headed driveller' and a 'nonentity' (*Mann ohne Absätze*) whose views on the tariff question were as ludicrously indefensible as they were contrary to the interests of Social Democracy. Calwer's presence within the party, which for years had been 'most singularly unpleasant' as well as 'superfluous' and 'disruptive', would 'in no way be missed' (SMP, vol. 4: Eisner to Bloch, 2 September 1907). On another occasion Bloch chortled over a letter he had just received from Eisner, who was 'livid with rage' at Leuthner's latest article in the *Monatshefte* (SMP, vol. 8: Bloch to Leuthner, 31 July 1908). Bloch reciprocated this antipathy in full measure. Eisner's sins were both general and specific. In the latter category was Eisner's role in the Krupp affair of November 1902 and his gratuitous defence of the party's refusal to re-endorse Calwer as an SPD Reichstag candidate in 1907. Eisner's general offences were his flirtations with radicalism, his inappropriate moralising and, above all, his disastrous influence on foreign policy thinking within the party. Eisner was convinced, so he wrote to Bloch, that 'not only shall we not be able to evade violent confrontation [with the Prussian state], but even in bloody defeats there is far greater value for the future than in all the rest of our bustling idleness' (SMP, vol. 4: 2 September 1907). Such obduracy on the efficacy and inevitability of class struggle and revolution was interpreted by Bloch as contumelious and meretricious humbug: Eisner was a case of that 'Putsch romanticism' which 'makes revolution behind editorial desks and proclaims anti-militarist general strikes in a filing cabinet' (SMP, vol. 8: Bloch to Leuthner, 29 June 1907). He belonged to that 'hybrid breed [by radicalism out of revisionism], politically incapable of living or dying, whose goodness and niceness knows no bounds' (*deren Bravheit nun einmal keine Überraschungen geben kann*) (ibid., 5 January 1907).

In Bloch's estimation, the second great fault of this 'ethical aesthete', his penchant for contemplating politics as an exercise in moral philosophy, had a highly dangerous catch: it predisposed Eisner to a particularist anti-Prussianism that was in flagrant violation of the German national interest. Eisner's 'freshly baked Bavarian anti-Prussian policy' (ibid., 31 July 1908) betrayed a complete lack of understanding of Prussia and subsumed the whole of Prussian history under sweeping and asinine generalisations against 'mad Junkerdom' (ibid., 11 June 1908). Bloch was convinced that Prussian grit (*Forsche*) had nothing to learn from South German slovenliness (*Schlamperei*) (SMR, 1908, p. 953; SMR, 1913, p. 1519), and in response to Eisner's complaints against Leuthner as 'a crank' and 'your Old Prussian in Vienna' (SMP, vol. 4: Eisner to Bloch, 25 July 1908, 15 June 1909), Bloch informed Eisner that he regarded the latter's polemics on foreign relations questions as 'pernicious, particularly because of the conclusions drawn from them for the party' (ibid., 14 June 1909). Believing that Eisner attributed to the Bavarians a culture they did not really possess (ibid., Bloch to von Elm, 8 October 1908), Bloch had Eisner in mind when he first urged Leuthner to break a lance on behalf of 'Prussia's mission' so that German socialists might, at length, begin to appreciate the weight of the bonds which anchored the interests of all Germany to the material interests of the Junker class. In a masterpiece of understatement, Bloch subsequently confessed to Leuthner that on this point he diverged sharply from 'our party' (SMP, vol. 8: Bloch to Leuthner, 19 January 1910). The howls of indignation which Leuthner's Prussian articles elicited from people like Eisner and Stampfer – Bloch regarded Stampfer as being dyed in the same wool as Eisner – not only gratified Bloch but also gave birth to the idea that Leuthner should be brought to Berlin on a *Monatshefte* grant. Eisner's morally based attacks on the reaction and aggression of incorrigible Prussia were an abomination in Bloch's eyes because Eisner's policy was calculated to undermine both national integration at home and the pursuit of national greatness abroad.

Particularly galling to Bloch was Eisner's popularity and influence. The bohemian expatriate Berliner had been in Bavaria barely a year when Bloch groaned that 'the spirit of Eisner is hovering over the waters of Bavarian politics'. Thanks to Eisner and, to some extent, also to David, Bloch saw heavy weather ahead in his struggle to nurture a Pan-German and socialist foreign policy viewpoint in the south: 'In the long term it will probably be just as impossible to conduct politics among the South Germans, whose political outlook is enclosed by the state border (and certainly not by the national frontier), as it is with the mulish Berlin ranters' (ibid., 28 September 1908).

Eisner was more than a regional pest. In January 1907, on the eve of the Hottentot elections, where the national slogan was used to such telling effect against the SPD, Bloch's grudge against the 'ethical aesthetes' was that in questions of foreign relations, *Weltpolitik*, colonialism and tariff policy, they foolishly parroted the inanities of the orthodox party line (ibid., 5 January 1907). After 25 January, when the party lost almost half its seats in the Reichstag, Bloch thought he saw a glimmer of light at the end of the tunnel. He hoped that the *Monatshefte* would be able to stiffen the backbone of the party centre against 'the radical clique' and encourage the party *Vorstand* to go further in its salutary change of course (ibid., 21 February 1907). Social Democracy, it seemed, was coming to realise that it ignored foreign policy at its peril; it was at long last beginning to grope its way towards the elaboration of a specifically socialist foreign policy viewpoint. 'Unfortunately, it is groping in quite the wrong direction – more in the sense of the policy of Eisner and company' (ibid., 31 July 1908). The wormwood and gall or 'special force of the Eisner–Stampfer policy' was the insouciant manner in which it ridiculed the blunders of German *Weltpolitik*, which allegedly enhanced the threat of war by exposing to enemy eyes the weakness and dissension besetting the Reich, for Bloch regarded all anti-patriotic agitation as 'sabotage against one's own country' (SMR, 1907, p. 881). The would-be revisionist Catilina was appalled to note that 'the rest of the party press and the Reichstag deputies as well' were now 'skipping along the trail blazed by Eisner and his cronies' (SMP, vol. 8: Bloch to Leuthner, 17 December 1908). At the very moment when the party centre showed signs of modulating its radicalism, if only in the realm of international relations, and Bloch girded himself to burst through the breach with 'the programme of the *Monatshefte*', along came Eisner, the grandstanding poetaster out of his depth in politics, yet posing as the head of a picaresque band of 'ethical aesthetes' and seeking to plug the gap with nationally suicidal anti-Prussian follies masked as Bavarian particularism.

Bloch was not amused. So little did Eisner's quixotic sorties in the field of *Weltpolitik* titillate Bloch's sense of the absurd that the self-appointed Catilina of revisionism ever after reserved a special spleen for this wanton obstructionist. Bloch's correspondence with Leuthner and others is replete with lachrymose lamentations against Eisner as 'nothing but style', a posturing windbag whose persiflage passed for wit, a bumptious adept at sententious cerebration without a single positive or concrete idea to offer (see Fletcher, 1980a, p. 475, n. 163). As early as May 1907 Bloch had, therefore, made it a rule 'never to publish anything political by Eisner' (SMP, vol. 8: Bloch to Leuthner, 10 May 1907), although he was pleased to avail himself of Eisner's talents as a literary critic. To this end, he bombarded Eisner with communications soliciting material. Most, but not all, went unanswered.

Bloch and Eisner had more in common than either would have cared to admit. In origin and training, both were bourgeois. Both were intellectuals with a penchant for philosophical idealism and a profound concern with Prussia and foreign policy problems. Each had a Jewish background and pursued a similar career in political journalism. They each saw the need for tactical flexibility if Social Democracy should ever break free of its partly self-imposed impasse of verbal radicalism and practical *attentisme*. Neither made the impact he desired. But here the similarities end. The superficiality of all such analogies may be illustrated by reference to Eisner's position on the Jewish question. Eisner, too, was a thoroughly assimilated German Jew. Although of Jewish parentage, he never attended the synagogue, married a Gentile and never considered himself as being other than a German. Indeed, he was fiercely patriotic. In religious matters a latitudinarian, he remained aloof from anti-clericalism without ever formally renouncing the faith of his fathers, for he declined to dissociate himself from Judaism out of solidarity with such a despised and persecuted community (see Schade, 1961, p. 105, n. 209), although this did not inhibit him from accusing Jewish businessmen of an unseemly preoccupation with 'money-grubbing' (F. Eisner, 1979, p. 98). In fact, his attitude seems to have closely paralleled that of Bernstein. As a professing Marxist internationalist, Eisner probably shared a lot of common ground with left-wing Jews like Rosa Luxemburg, who condemned Jewish nationalism, as she did all nationalism, as an inalienably bourgeois weapon in the all-important class war. But Eisner was not an 'Easterner' – despite the Kosmanowsky rumours concerning his alleged Galician origins – and he undoubtedly shared the widespread view among socialists of the Second International that the Jewish problem was an issue of quite secondary importance. Such personal detachment combined with his German patriotism and his socialist internationalism to neutralise his emotional identification with the Jewish underdog, producing in Eisner a sort of half-way position between anti- and philo-Semitism that resulted in almost total silence on the Jewish question. Yet it is difficult to believe that his unique blend of pacifism, Enlightenment progressivism and passionate humanism was not deeply indebted to his Jewish religious heritage.

Such parallels show Bloch and Eisner as having differed profoundly on all essentials. Bloch's idealism was always leavened by a hard-headed Machiavellism; Eisner lived and died a Kantian. Bloch viewed the Junkers as an indispensable, if intractable, pillar of the German state; Eisner hounded them as the Cossacks of Hohenzollern militarism and reaction. Bloch set his cap at a working-class share in the cake of Prusso-German greatness; Eisner set his face against war and would have set an axe to Prussia in order to build a people's state on the Hohenzollern catafalque. Bloch was a German nationalist, Eisner was a patriotic revolutionary. Finally, Eisner believed in humanity and liberty whereas Bloch prized security and sufficiency. Even where the ingredients were similar, as in the case of their common Jewish roots, the end-products were vastly dissimilar. Whereas Bloch's assimilationism provided psychological nourishment to his Prusso-German nationalism, Eisner's humanist universalism seems to have nurtured his almost prophetic zeal to remake man and society in a more perfect mould.

Despite these differences, Bloch tried for years to make use of Eisner. He obviously hoped to win Eisner for the *Monatshefte* in order to avail himself of the latter's academic and literary contacts, such as Hermann Cohen and the anarcho-socialist Gustav Landauer, for whom Bloch had the greatest respect. Although he would not accept anything political from the pen of Kurt Eisner, Bloch was more than willing to publish Eisner contributions that might fit in with his own programme. It was for this reason that he badgered Eisner over a period of years to write for the *Monatshefte* a hymn of praise to Napoleon I, for which purpose Bloch took the trouble to send Eisner a number of books (some were review copies, others were borrowed from libraries or from friends like Scheidemann, and most were apparently never returned). By thus linking Eisner's name with the revisionist organ, Bloch undoubtedly hoped to force the relatively isolated Berliner turned Bavarian gadfly into the camp of the *Monatshefte*. It would certainly have profited him to do so, for Eisner was the only neo-Kantian who was also an active socialist politician with a significant personal following. However improbable it may have seemed to some, Eisner did, after all, emerge as the leader of the USPD in Bavaria, the author of the November revolution in that state, and the first Prime Minister of the Bavarian Republic. Perhaps Bloch hoped to use Eisner eventually as his wedge into the South German wing of the SPD. He certainly had need of some such cat's-paw, for his relations with the South Germans generally varied between lukewarm and mutual antipathy.

Bloch unquestionably failed in this instance. He never got his Napoleon article and had great trouble getting his books returned. Try as he might, Bloch received no more from Eisner than an occasional reply to some of his many missives. Eisner was no fool and had no intention of being co-opted by Bloch. He had nothing to gain from an association with the revisionist organ. It had not saved his job in 1905 when Eisner had been forced to resign as editor-in-chief of *Vorwärts* because of his alleged revisionism and, in any event, Eisner had his own political ambitions for which he believed he had found an appropriate base in Bavaria. Moreover, and in contrast to Bernstein, Eisner was fully aware of the enormous ideological and political differences which separated him from the *Monatshefte*, and he was not only prepared to go outside the *Monatshefte* to find a platform for his own viewpoint; he also campaigned publicly and vigorously against the *Monatshefte*.

Although Bloch had some success with some neo-Kantian intellectuals (such as Woltmann and Staudinger), his relations with Eisner represent an unsuccessful attempt to co-opt for the *Sozialistische Monatshefte* an important socialist dissident and such mass support, or potential mass support, as this neo-Kantian revolutionary democrat may have commanded. Superficially, at least, Bloch had greater success with the reformists and the *Praktiker*, and although he managed, as early as 1899, to establish his journal as 'the official organ of the reformist oppositional group' (Rikli, 1936, p. 23), the story of his relations with Kurt Eisner illustrates some of the reasons why he was unable to use the *Monatshefte* as a vehicle for ensuring that 'Social Democracy [functioned] as a cultural force (*Kulturpartei*) to penetrate all possible social strata and [acquired] the broadest possible base' (SMP, vol. 4: Bloch to Elm, 17 August 1907) for his proposed integration of the German proletariat into the political nation via a 'revolution in world politics'.

Notes: Chapter 5

1 Admittedly, this observation conflicts with Geary's thesis that working-class militancy was rising before 1914 and culminated in radical attempts to improve the lot of the working class after 1917. This author makes no attempt to conceal his revolutionary bias, referring to the Third International as an attempt 'to sort out the sheep from the goats, the revolutionaries from their more feeble-minded and weaker-spirited colleagues' (1981, p. 148), and noting that French workers 'retained a charming predilection for threatening their employers with hanging well into the twentieth century' (1982, p. 224).

2 Schorske (1972, p. 70) and Groh (1973, p. 665) also consider Eisner to have been a revisionist, whereas Freya Eisner insists that her grandfather belonged to no faction (1979, p. 15).

3 Eisner's first book, *Psychopathia spiritualis* (1892), was a study of the work and influence of Friedrich Nietzsche, as well as a record of Eisner's own emancipation from that influence. For a very useful study of the profound impact which Nietzsche exerted on left-wing circles in Wilhelmine Germany, see R. Hinton Thomas (1983), who argues that Nietzsche initially appealed much more strongly to libertarian dissidents than to the radical right. While this may have been generally true, it was not universally so. I cannot, for example, accept Thomas's view that 'Leuthner's . . . relationship to Nietzsche was hardly more than marginal and incidental' (ibid., p. 36).

PART THREE

The Pursuit of International Integration: Eduard Bernstein and the English Model

Bernstein constructed his theory on the basis of English conditions. He sees the world through 'English spectacles'. In the party this has long been a byword.

(Rosa Luxemburg, 1899)

Bernstein was not only more intellectually honest than Kautsky (and, for that matter, Bebel as well), but he was also much more of a democrat than Marx.

(Helmut Schmidt, 1975)

In international affairs he [Bernstein] was freer of chauvinism than most of his colleagues. He became, and remained, a good European from the very first days of his conversion to socialism.

(Sidney Hook, 1963)

It is appropriate to inquire why Bernstein, in his observation of historical development, was so far ahead of all other devotees of Marx at that time, why the consciousness of confronting a new era with new challenges was manifestly most strongly developed in him. Without doubt this was related to his decades of expatriate experience, above all in England, where his observation of advanced industrial development enabled him to anticipate forces that were transforming capitalism in Germany as well. Yet it would be too coarse to dismiss this with Bernstein's 'English spectacles'.

(Helga Grebing, 1977)

6

The Father of Revisionism
'en famille'

We had expected a prophet but a mere doubter had come among us.
(Lily Braun, 1911)

Nowhere within Social Democracy was the Bernstein book greeted with
cheering. When it was very sharply attacked, a number of comrades came
along and said, 'First take a look at the book. Is it really as bad as all
that?' That is how it came to be discussed.
(Eduard David, Lübeck party congress, 1901)

On some political questions I am in real disagreement with Bernstein, and
we have often fought the most vigorous debates over single sentences in his
articles.
(Joseph Bloch to Adolf von Elm, 1908)

There is something touching in the care with which [Bernstein] subjects
problems to examination, analysis and prognosis . . . In his day, he
managed to resolve some completely ossified concepts, to give them new
life. He offers no lightning-flashes, but if he slowly plods along with his
lamp, he nevertheless illuminates many a shaded area and demonstrates
connections that had not previously been recognised as such.
(Karl Leuthner to Joseph Bloch, 1910)

My dear Ede, what you are recommending is not what one decides. You
don't say that sort of thing, you just do it. Our entire activity – even under
the shameful [anti-socialist] law – has been that of a Social Democratic
reform party. A party dealing with the masses can never be otherwise.
(Ignaz Auer to Eduard Bernstein, 1899)

Otto Bauer once divided the revisionists into two schools – 'the ignorant and
the confused' (KP, KDII 478: Bauer to Kautsky, 3 February 1908). Ever since
the problem of revisionism first became manifest as such, anti-revisionists
have had extreme difficulty separating definition and classification from
polemics and vituperation (see Lenin, 1966; Fülberth and Harrer, 1974,
pp. 7–24). In terms of its ideological components, revisionism has probably been
most simply and usefully categorised by H.-J. Steinberg, who identified four
main heterodoxies within classical German Social Democracy: Eduard Bernstein's attempt to 'revise' or update Marx in the light of economic and social
developments inadequately foreseen by Marx and Engels; ethical or neo-
Kantian socialism, which strove to provide the labour movement with an
ethical foundation – generally derived from Kant – which its adherents

believed to be lacking in classical or orthodox Marxism; the reformism of Georg von Vollmar, Eduard David and others, who either sought the integration of the proletariat into an improved version of the existing social order or worked to effect the piecemeal transformation of capitalism into socialism; and the theoretically indifferent *Praktizismus* of party practitioners and functionaries like Ignaz Auer, Friedrich Ebert and Gustav Noske who, as Eduard David complained during the war years, 'knew nothing and wanted nothing' but a better deal for the workers in the here-and-now (H.-J. Steinberg, 1972, pp. 87–124; Geary, 1981, p. 108). Of course, these groups overlapped so notoriously that their theoretical differentiation is only slightly less problematical than their sociological explanation, which is beyond the scope of this study and, as Sven Papcke observes, has yet to become the object of serious non-partisan study (1979, p. 14).[1] Steinberg's classification has at least the merit of being more discriminating than generalisations such as the definition of revisionism as 'an ideological tendency which seeks to provide reformism with a theoretical and ideological legitimation' (Frei, 1979, pp. 19–20), or the apodictic Leninist pronunciamentos which brand all revisionists as opportunistic betrayers of the working class and closet social imperialists. Yet some generalisation is unavoidable. Where it is necessary to give these forces on the moderate or right wing of prewar Social Democracy a collective label, it should now be obvious that they are here designated as revisionists, following the most widely accepted practice of the time – occasionally accepted, with reluctance, even by Bernstein (1913g, p. 949) – and distinguished from theoretical or Bernsteinian revisionism by the use of the qualifying adjective in the latter instance.

It has been argued that Joseph Bloch was a reformist of the integrationist rather than the revolutionary sort and that his attempt to rally the various forms of revisionism beneath the standard of the *Sozialistische Monatshefte* was ultimately a failure, conspicuously so in the case of Kurt Eisner. Consideration of the theoretical revisionism of Eduard Bernstein, and of his pre-1914 foreign policy views, provides a still more glaring example of Bloch's inability to successfully control and manipulate revisionism in the service of the *Monatshefte*. On both theory and international politics, Bernstein was poles apart from Bloch. If he remained an isolated intellectual who said very little that was new on theoretical matters after his return from exile in 1901, Bernstein had a great deal to say on issues of international relations, most of it appearing in outlets other than the *Monatshefte*.

Bernstein's Revisionism

Eduard Bernstein (1850–1932), rather than Bloch, was undoubtedly the 'father of revisionism' in the sense that he was the first and the most important theorist to offer a serious challenge to Marx from within the socialist movement. Almost all of this was presented in a series of articles entitled 'problems of socialism' which appeared in the *Neue Zeit* between 1896 and 1898 and in his *Presuppositions of Socialism* book published in Stuttgart in 1899.[2]

Philosophically, Bernstein began by rejecting 'the snare of the Hegelian dialectic', which, he felt, had misled Marx into a one-sided emphasis on the struggle of opposites, to the neglect of the importance of the co-operation of related forces in nature and society, in favour of a Blanquist veneration of force. In place of the dialectic, Bernstein offered a somewhat vague formulation of the ideal of ethical desirability. Where this led was not only to a renunciation of revolutionary violence in preference to co-operative parliamentary gradualism but also to a voluntarist, activist view of socialist tactics which contrasted with the practical quietism of the centre-orthodoxy while seemingly legitimising the activities of the South German reformists, the trade unions, co-operatives and *Praktiker* generally.

In economics, he implicitly, if evasively, recognised the flaws in the Marxist theory of value (defended then, as today, as the linchpin of any plausible Marxist system of economics) by maintaining that the labour and utility theorists were merely talking at cross-purposes, each saying essentially the same thing. He was less equivocal on the centralisation and concentration of capital. While admitting that Marx's prediction of increasing centralisation was correct as a tendency, he noted that countervailing, centrifugal forces had arisen, with the result that the propertied classes were not shrinking but growing, producing a rapidly expanding social cake. Pointing to the growth of the world market, improved transport and communications, the increased wealth of industrial states, the flexibility of the modern credit system and the rise of industrial cartels as counter-trends reducing the severity of factors tending towards capitalist breakdown, Bernstein envisaged a future of equilibrium rather than dislocation. He went so far as to predict that capitalism might well cure its own evils. Socialist revolution thus appeared unnecessary as well as improbable. Finally, he maintained that the intermediate social strata – the 'old' and the 'new' middle classes – were not vanishing, as Marx had anticipated, but were actually flourishing under advanced capitalism, and that these classes shared common interests with the industrial working class, not because the former were being proletarianised, which they were not, but because the proletariat was slowly acquiring a place in civil society.

Politically, everything pointed in the direction of parliamentary gradualism as the appropriate tactic for socialist movements. Citing such instances as British municipal 'gas-and-water' socialism and Bismarck's state socialism, Bernstein argued that the area of communal, collective action was already growing in size and significance, that a peaceful 'growing-into-socialism' was demonstrably at work in accord with the laws of 'organic evolutionism'. This was not the pessimistic and destructive interpretation of evolution which he discerned in Blanqui and many bourgeois Social Darwinists but the positive, optimistic evolutionism to be found in Herbert Spencer or Peter Kropotkin. Bernstein suggested that gradualism could be applied in a variety of ways – through the work of the trade unions and co-operatives as well as by socialist political parties divesting themselves of shop-worn slogans (these merely frightened away potential liberal and democratic allies), concentrating on the day-to-day practical work of the movement and striving to educate the masses to the responsibilities of power. Democracy he esteemed as both a means and an end, implying respect for minority rights, co-operation among classes, federalism and representative rather than direct democracy. Since he viewed socialism and democracy as 'one and the same thing', he could not envisage the one without the other. He defined socialism as 'a piece of the beyond', an abstract and, in its absolute form, largely unrealisable goal towards which society was gradually approximating. For all that, he was a socialist. He did argue for the socialisation of the means of production, distribution and exchange on a piecemeal basis, as economic and political conditions allowed. Although he denounced the dictatorship of the proletariat as a barbarian and counter-productive idea, he denounced with like vehemence the absolutism of private property, which he wanted and expected to see replaced by growing equality among all men and women, regardless of class, religion or nationality, in political and social as well as economic rights and opportunities. In essence, what he understood by socialism was equality.[3]

If the above thumb-nail sketch of Bernstein's revisionism errs in the direction of over-simplification or excessive schematisation it is, at least, in good company (see Gay, 1962; T. Meyer, 1977), and such failings may be offset by reference to Henry Pachter's perceptive article (1981, pp. 203–16). I do not wish to burden the reader unduly with the 'imported' ideas of socialist 'leaders', especially since we are now assured on every side that these ideas mattered far less than the values and norms which can be inferred from what ordinary workers ate, drank, wore, sang, stole, or otherwise did at work or at play (all filtered through what James Joll has called 'a blinding neo-Hegelian vision . . . of a totality in which everything interconnects with everything else and in which no detail is ever irrelevant, and which at the same time reveals to us the vast inexorable laws of the historical dialectic' [Joll, 1981, p. 46]). Yet I venture to suggest that such an outline, whatever its shortcomings, is a useful aid to clarification of Bernstein's position within the revisionist movement, for it is crucial to an understanding of why this 'father of revisionism' had so many children but so few followers. His theoretical work offered something for everyone. Ethical socialists, neo-Kantians, reformists of all shades (Blochian nationalists included), party bureaucrats, trade union and co-operative leaders and even rank-and-file militants could, if they chose, now cite Bernstein against the party Marxists as providing a respectably socialist, even Marxist, theoretical vindication of their own heretical aims and Sisyphus-like activities. Thus many of them applauded and defended what Bernstein had to say without necessarily understanding or accepting much of it, and with little or no intention of acknowledging him as their leader or spokesman – a position to which he wisely never aspired.

Bernstein and Ethical Socialism

A closer look at Bernstein's relations with his allies within the revisionist fold will fully bear out this contention. First, however, it seems appropriate to clarify the persistent misunderstanding which credits the Kantian democrat, Friedrich Albert Lange (1828–75), with having exerted a powerful, formative influence on Bernstein and his revisionism. Scholars who still consider Lange to have significantly, in some cases decisively, influenced Bernstein include Peter Gay (1962, p. 154) – still, by far, the best treatment of Bernstein in any language – J. W. Burrow (1966, p. 262), Thomas Meyer (1977, pp. 111–22), H.-J. Steinberg (1972, pp. 90–1), Sven Papcke (1979, pp. 76, 114) and Robert Steigerwald (1980, pp. 30, 33, 37). Unquestionably, an 'implicit though unspoken commitment to an ethical foundation of socialism . . . can be ascribed to Bernstein' (Pachter, 1981, p. 216), and this is a major reason why people like Georges Sorel, for a time, admired Bernstein's revisionism (Stanley, 1981, pp. 17, 108) – and perhaps also explains why Sorel contributed to the *Sozialistische Monatshefte*. But Bernstein's ethical inspiration did not derive from Kant, Lange, or the neo-Kantians of his own era.

Neither did it stem from an admiration of German liberalism. Although he constantly urged the creation of a parliamentary bloc of the left (socialists, National Liberals, left liberals and possibly the Catholic Centre Party as well), Bernstein had little affection for, and few illusions about, the character of German liberalism. In his estimation, Wilhelmine liberals of all shades were beyond redemption because, to varying degrees, they had abandoned free trade and democratic principles (1913*b*, p. 308; 1913*c*) and entirely succumbed to chauvinistic nationalism and militarism (1910*h*, p. 595; 1912*g*, p. 814). Through the pages of H. W. Massingham's *The Nation* he informed his British Radical friends that 'just as the rotting flesh offers the best nursery for certain microbes, the wretched state of middle-class party life in Germany makes the jingo game an easy one' (1911*m*, p. 94). Germany's middle-class parties, he warned his British readers, had all capitulated to militarism and *Weltpolitik* (1911*f*, pp. 349–51; 1913*f*, p. 142). Whereas the liberalism of the National Liberals was 'of the most diluted kind' and their chauvinism incurable (1913*b*, p. 308), the situation was hardly better among the left liberals, who were not to be confused with British Radicals (1907*j*, p. 13). By 1913 'German Radicals' had 'lost all power of resistance to the agitation of the Jingo section of the National Liberals, the Centre, and the Conservatives'. They 'raised hesitating, half-hearted objections' but had 'no Liberal foreign policy' (1911*f*, p. 551). Even the revolt of the Hansa-Bund against Junker and heavy-industry cupidity (see Mielke, 1976) gave him little encouragement, for it was not a force for a more liberal foreign policy or for democratic reform within the German Empire (1909*g*, p. 491): 'On all the important questions of our time, as between the leaders of the Hanse League and those of the Conservative groups, it has been at bottom a feud between "more" and "less" and not between "yes" and "no" ' (1912*d*, p. 659). In fact, he despised German liberalism for its timidity and class egoism both in theory and in practice (1907*b*, pp. 481, 486; 1913*e*, p. 568; 1914*c*, pp. 744–5; RTV, vol. 295 [15 May 1914], p. 8887).

Here Bernstein was caught in a dilemma. Although convinced that liberalism in Germany was more reactionary than elsewhere, and was becoming increasingly more so, he never ceased to urge a socialist alliance with this 'stinking corpse'. He held fast to this seemingly paradoxical course for three main reasons. In the first place, he had already nailed his colours to the mast of parliamentary democracy and he continued to believe that even the depressing situation in pseudo-constitutional Prussia-Germany afforded a better prospect of progress than did the revolutionary path. Secondly, he tended to generalise from British liberal experience. If Britain, 'whose political institutions [were] infinitely superior to those of Germany', manifesting numerous examples of 'more developed political manners' (1904*e*, pp. 893, 895), could achieve a Liberal–Labour alliance for progress and reform, in time Germany should be able to do likewise. Sooner or later, he felt, German liberals must begin to see that they had no political future unless they could appeal to the German working class (1912*g*, p. 814), and the conditions laid down by the SPD for its support were, after all, 'easy to fulfil', 'almost non-commital', such that 'any British Whig and many British Conservatives would countersign' them (1912*d*, p. 659). Finally, he believed that there remained a glimmer of hope as long as there were left liberals like Theodor Barth and Georg Gothein – 'preachers in the wilderness' certainly, but 'courageous and consistent' as well as 'men of free trade leanings and decided good feelings in regard to England' (1908*h*, p. 757; 1908*i*, p. 565). In February 1908, for example, he announced that such men were leading a 'Radical revolt' against the government which 'will this time bear fruit' (1908*j*, p. 705). He was to be disappointed, of course, and not for the last time. But the National Liberals, too, had a left wing which occasionally provided grounds for optimism. In 1909, for instance, Johannes Junck submitted a memorandum to Ernst Bassermann, the National Liberal leader (in Bernstein's view, a 'trimmer of trimmers' [1914*c*, p. 745]), in which Junck called for an 'opening to the left' on the Badenese model:

> He thought the Social Democratic 'danger' was waning despite its growth in mandates and placed his own hopes in an eventual triumph of the reformists; he attributed more importance to the revisionistic *Sozialistische Monatshefte* than to the official *Vorwärts* and eventually expected the Social Democrats to become a radical bourgeois party. He rightly felt that their working-class supporters were more interested in industrial growth and full employment than in revolution. (Heckart, 1974, p. 134; see also White, 1976, p. 191).

As F. A. Lange came from a similar stable to those which produced liberals like Barth, Gothein, Karl Schrader, Lujo Brentano, Walther Schücking and Rudolf Breitscheid, it is perfectly understandable that Bernstein found much that was congenial in this Kantian democrat. Presumably, he warmed to Lange's empiricism, his hostility to speculative philosophy in general, and to Hegelianism in particular; his eclecticism, and especially his blending of Darwin, Malthus and Marx; his individualism, agnosticism, cosmopolitan patriotism, interest in the agrarian question; his anti-statism and insistence on working-class self-help; his moral idealism and humanism; his antipathy to German liberalism for its tepid defence of political principle and neglect of the social question; and, above all, his concept of socialism which, for Lange, was virtually identical with the co-operative idea and subsumed democracy (perceived both as a means and an end) and hence also gradualism and free associations. All this cannot have failed to strike a sympathetic chord with Bernstein.

Having said this, we are obliged to note that his writings 'do not indicate that he had either read or understood Kant' (Pachter, 1981, p. 215). In his autobiography he frankly admitted as much while firmly rejecting the Kantian tag (1924, p. 40). Karl Vorländer, a neo-Kantian philosopher intimately

acquainted both with Bernstein and with the Kantian revival, correctly concluded that Bernstein was 'far removed from Kant's method and Kantian
ethics' and that his call for a 'return to Kant' rested 'in the last resort, on a
misunderstanding' (Vorländer, 1911, p. 189, cf. Gay, 1962, p. 156; Grebing,
1977, p. 43; Willey, 1978, p. 176). Bernstein's alleged 'discovery of Lange'
dated not from the late 1870s, when he had been private secretary to Karl
Höchberg (his lasting influence on Bernstein has also been much exaggerated),
but from January 1892, when he informed Kautsky that he had been reading
books on and by Lange in the British Museum. The result was a series of
articles in the *Neue Zeit* (essentially an extended review of a popular biography
by O. A. Ellissen) 'On the appreciation of F. A. Lange' (1891/2*b*, pp. 68–78,
101–9, 132–41) which revealed how much 'Bernstein was still very reserved
towards neo-Kantianism' (H.-J. Steinberg, 1972, p. 90). In 1898 he used the
slogan 'back to Kant' but granted it only limited application to socialist theory
(1904*f*, Vol. 2, p. 124). The following year, in his 'bible of revisionism',
Bernstein cited Lange against the dialectic and translated 'back to Kant' as
'back to Lange', explaining what he meant by this as a call for emulation of 'the
distinguishing union in Lange of an upright and intrepid championship of the
struggle of the working classes for emancipation with a large scientific freedom
from prejudice' ([1899] 1921, pp. 54, 257). In fact, it is doubtful whether
Bernstein ever acquired a solid grasp of Lange, let alone Kant. In 1905, for
instance, he still referred to Lange as a *Kathedersozialist* (socialist of the lectern)
and in 1909 he believed that Lange 'gave materialism a prominent place', when
in reality his putative mentor had set out to demolish the materialist argument
and to demonstrate that it was inherently and fallaciously monistic (cit. T.
Meyer, 1977, p. 111, n. 14; Bernstein, 1909*n*, p. 576). As to Bernstein's
foreign relations views, there is no evidence of more than a certain compatibility of outlook with Lange and none whatever to suggest that Bernstein was
influenced by Lange. The only inference to be drawn is that Lange may have
functioned as a minor contributing factor in Bernstein's abandonment of
orthodox Marxism but at no stage exerted a significant influence on Bernstein's thought. To date, no one had seriously suggested that neo-Kantians
other than Lange exerted any notable impact on Bernstein's thought. Of
course, this is by no means to deny Lange all influence on Bernstein. Like
Engels, Bebel and Kautsky, Bernstein exhibited great respect for the man and
his work. At a time when he could no longer accept the validity of the collapse
theory, exemplars like Lange undoubtedly reinforced his hope, as did T. H.
Green, the later John Stuart Mill, Gladstone, Bright, David Lloyd George and
many others, that class war and revolution were not the sole avenue to radical
social transformation. Through Lange he probably discovered, in the words
of Thomas Willey, 'an affinity between revisionism and Marburg neo-
Kantianism which offered the possibility of a timely convergence of bourgeois
reformism with the working-class movement' (1978, p. 176). In short, he saw
Lange, at least in part, as a possible bridge to his tactical passe-partout, a
socialist–liberal alliance for the realisation of parliamentary democracy in the
authoritarian military monarchy that was Prussia-Germany. There can be little
doubt that Bernstein was desperately searching for such a bridge and that
Lange was admirably suited to the task.

That he could appreciate Lange's ethical approach to the social question without embracing neo-Kantianism may be explained by reference to his thirteen years of exile in London (1888–1901, that is, from his thirty-eighth year, when he had yet to publish his first major book, to the age of 51). During this period, the labour people with whom he had most contact (apart from fellow-émigrés) and whom he most admired were not the Marxist sectarians of H. M. Hyndman's Social Democratic Federation (SDF) or even the Fabians (as the 'best informed' of British socialists, they provided agreeable and stimulating company, much to Engels's annoyance) but ethical socialists like Keir Hardie, Ramsay MacDonald and John Bruce Glasier, whose roots and ambience were the Nonconformist chapel, the trade unions and the Independent Labour Party (ILP) (Bernstein, 1918a, p. 276; Pierson, 1973, pp. 140–73, 198–214, 257–71). Bernstein, incidentally, was the one foreign socialist present at the inaugural conference of the ILP held at Bradford in 1893 (Pelling, 1965, p. 118). From this source he gained a vastly different perspective on Christianity and religion generally from that acquired in Germany during his youth. In 1890 he informed his German comrades that British Christian Socialists were an altogether different species from Stöcker, Distelkamp Treitschke, many of them having participated actively in the workers' class struggle against capital and distinguished themselves in the organisation of the new unions (1890/1c, pp. 730–2).[4] In 1897 he maintained that 'if a large section of English democracy draws its ethics from the New Testament rather than from some atheistic treatise, these "bigots" and "pharisees", or whatever one wishes to call them, have performed infinitely greater services for liberty in Europe than we enlightened Germans have so far done' (1896/7b, p. 15). In 1904 he described Keir Hardie's socialism as exhibiting 'a much more pronounced *ethical* hue than that of German Social Democracy' (italics in original), commenting that 'emphasis of the ethical factor may be a sign either of a backward movement or of the more advanced conditions with which it has to deal. Here both factors coalesce' (1904e, pp. 893–4). At Chemnitz in 1912 he described Jesus Christ as 'the greatest reformer of all time' (SPD A.C., 1912, p. 421). In so saying, he was no doubt as mindful of the fact that Christian ethics had not only produced such admired figures as William Morris (1896, pp. 668–73; 1918a, pp. 185, 222–4, 249–56), John Bright and W. E. Gladstone (1907f, p. 341; 1911f, p. 550) as he was aware that the Nonconformist conscience formed 'the backbone of the Liberal Party' in Britain (1895/6c, p. 614). Clearly, Bernstein was more impressed by Lange's social activism than by his Kantianism, more by British than by German ethical socialism. Important as it undeniably was, ethical socialism was nevertheless, as we shall see, but one among several factors which conditioned Bernstein's thought.[5]

Not only was Bernstein *not* a neo-Kantian, but he appears to have had minimal contact and, at best, lukewarm relations with neo-Kantian and ethical socialists in prewar Social Democracy. The 'Marxism and ethics' debate coincided with the revisionist controversy and was fought out very largely in the pages of Bloch's journal, though also in the *Neue Zeit* and its Austrian equivalent, *Der Kampf*. Closest to Bernstein's position were Eduard David and Paul Kampffmeyer, but none of the 'ethical aesthetes' (Eisner, Otto Bauer,

Franz Staudinger, Ludwig Woltmann and Conrad Schmidt) was closely identified with Bernstein. Both intellectually and in their personal relations, these heterogeneous elements manifested very little internal unity. A case in point is the response of the feminist revisionist, Lily Braun (see Quataert, 1979, pp. 79–80, 107–33 and *passim*), to Bernstein's 'Kantian' address, given before an academic audience shortly after his return to Germany in 1901, on the possibility of scientific socialism. Lily Braun, daughter of a Prussian general, had come to socialism via the ethical culture movement. At the time of Bernstein's eagerly awaited address she was an ethical socialist married to Heinrich Braun (like Stampfer, Hilferding and many others, Braun was an Austrian Jewish intellectual who made a career for himself in the German party). Together they edited the short-lived revisionist organ, *Die Neue Gesellschaft* (regular contributors included Stampfer, Eisner and Karl Leuthner). Eventually, Lily Braun was to become a Nietzschean in her search for a socialist ethic, and in 1914 she staunchly defended the decision of 4 August. Most revealing, however, was her record of the impression made by Bernstein's 1901 address:

> He stepped up to the lectern. Behind his spectacles his short-sighted eyes peered, with a look of astonished embarrassment, at the throng of listeners. Then he spoke, with brittle voice, in broken sentences, a man accustomed to the confines of his study, not to popular assemblies. Already the shadow of disenchantment was beginning to cloud the glow of anticipation on the faces. Here and there, softly and diffidently, the question now arose, 'What's he on about?' . . . We had expected a prophet but a mere doubter had come among us. (Braun, 1911, pp. 386–7)

Even earlier, on reading Bernstein's *Presuppositions of Socialism*, this fundamentally sympathetic figure had registered doubts as to the practicability of Bernstein's revisionism:

> Where were the free-thinking bourgeois elements who might profitably be turned to good account in a common struggle for the implementation of democratic demands? . . . Where were all those on whom I had counted? A single one of them had since come over to us: [Paul] Göhre. All the rest stared transfixed at the *fata morgana* of Germany's future world power. (ibid., pp. 285–6)

Another liberal who 'came over', Rudolf Breitscheid, who worked for a time on Stampfer's private *Korrespondenz* and collaborated extensively with Bernstein during the war years (on Breitscheid's *Sozialistische Auslandskorrespondenz*, in the USPD, the German Peace Society, the Bund Neues Vaterland and the Zentralstelle Völkerrecht), registered a similar estimate of Bernstein as a 'traffic hazard' who was neither a statesman, a speaker, an activist nor a diplomat (cit. Papcke, 1979, p. 7). Stampfer himself, though hardly an intellectual, belonged to the 'ethical aesthetes' but was 'no supporter of Bernstein', whom he considered a 'donkey' (Stampfer, 1957, pp. 15, 70, 110), and with whom he differed profoundly on questions of free trade, Britain and the possibility of a liberal alliance (ibid., pp. 52, 65, 121, 130, 137, 154–7). His circle of friends, which encompassed revisionists of all kinds as well as radicals like Karl Liebknecht, did not include Bernstein.

Bernstein's Relations with the Reformists

Of a similar calibre were Bernstein's relations with the reformists, most of whom were South Germans. In the south, where stronger liberal traditions made a reformist tactic seem more viable, there existed an indigenous reformist tradition which anticipated Bernstein's revisionism by at least two decades. In June and July 1891, for example, the leader of Bavarian Social Democracy, Georg von Vollmar, gave expression to this tradition in his famous El Dorado speeches. Calling on Social Democrats to concentrate on the most immediate and pressing tasks, to put forward 'positive action programmes', to abandon the unfruitful 'absolutist tactic' by transferring their attention 'from the theoretical to the practical, from the general to the particular', Vollmar urged the party to 'utilise today's forms in order to acquire influence on the future' (1977, pp. 137–61). In 1899 he insisted, however, that the purpose of such piecemeal reform was not to convert Social Democracy to a 'social reform party in the bourgeois sense' but the acquisition of 'a practical lever for transforming capitalist society into a socialist one' (ibid., p. 184). On the latter occasion he criticised Bernstein on a number of points, accusing him of lack of moderation in his zeal for revision, of imprecise and confusing terminology, of generalising from British conditions, of overestimating German liberalism and of misreading changing forms of the class struggle as presaging a diminution in the intensity of the class struggle. He further disagreed with Bernstein on the importance of theory – the movement was defined, he believed, not by common theory but by common action towards a common goal (ibid., p. 129) – and he resented Bernstein's theorising as a gratuitous provocation of the party Marxists that could only embarrass himself and the reformists generally (H.-J. Steinberg, 1972, p. 100). Privately, he complained of Bernstein's 'hypertrophy of the conscience', of his 'urge to confess and to regale, without regard for the stomach of [his] guests' (VP, C2368: Vollmar to Bernstein, 28 October 1899). Thus, at the Dresden party congress in September 1903, where an anti-revisionist *and* anti-reformist resolution was carried by 288 votes against only 11 (including Bernstein's), Vollmar sided with the majority in 'the broadest condemnation of revisionism ever promulgated by the party' (Schorske, 1972, p. 24).

Thereafter, as Vollmar's back injury (he had been severely wounded while serving as a cavalry officer in the Franco-Prussian War) obliged him to retire more and more into the background, leadership of the South German reformists passed increasingly into the hands of a brilliant young Jewish lawyer from Mannheim named Ludwig Frank. Possessed of many talents (intellect, a sure political instinct, boundless energy, an admirable organising ability, a gifted and popular public-speaking facility), the Badenese 'wonder-boy' (only 40 when war broke out in 1914) quickly became not only 'the leading intellect of the South German reformists' (Walther, 1981, p. 270) and Vollmar's heir-apparent, but was widely mooted to succeed Bebel as well (Groh, 1973, pp. 478–9). In the last years of peace Frank had emerged as one of the leaders of the SPD Reichstag *Fraktion* and, according to Stampfer, 'influenced the party's policies more strongly than any other person' (1957, p. 142). (Briefly, he also edited a *Sozialistische Monatshefte* column on public hygiene.) It is not hard to imagine why Bernstein so admired him (Bernstein, 1911*i*, p. 306; idem, 1914*c*, p. 744). Thanks to his grand bloc policy in Baden (collaboration between National Liberals, Progressives and Social Democrats against clerical and conservative opposition), 'the Badenese were the first Social Democrats to exercise real influence in a state or national legislature' (Heckart, 1974, p. 150). Frank successfully defended this 'collaborationist' policy against the strictures of the Berlin radicals, thereby in a sense reversing the Dresden decision of 1903, and lobbied for a similar policy at the national level. Since this pre-supposed the democratisation of the Prussian suffrage, Frank urged the adop-tion of the political mass strike to enforce the necessary suffrage reform (see Frank, n.d. [1924], pp. 97–101; SPD A.C., 1913, pp. 304–6), which might have simultaneously helped build a revisionist bridge to the radical left, and to Karl Liebknecht in particular (Boll, 1980, p. 86), while paving the way externally, so Frank believed, for the formation of an Anglo-French-German alliance for peace and the reform of international law (Stampfer, 1957, pp. 103, 151; Miller, 1974, p. 244; Boll, 1980, p. 86; Trotnow, 1980, p. 136).[6]

Although Bernstein must have welcomed such views and initiatives, he did not inspire or control them. On the contrary, it was rather Frank who led and Bernstein who followed. In the rebel South German parties of Baden, Bavaria, Württemberg and Hesse, Frank possessed an independent reformist power base to which the Berlin revisionist spokesman was not privy. In 1910, when Frank was contemplating having the issue of budget approval raised at the Copenhagen congress of the Second International, he prevailed on Bernstein to write an appropriate article for the *Monatshefte* (1910*f*, pp. 1000–6) and to mobilise his international contacts on Frank's behalf (SMP, vol. 2: Bernstein to Bloch, 21 August 1910). In Berlin, Frank's political headquarters was the Café Josty, which was attended by a wide variety of socialists including Karl Hildenbrand (a right-winger and *Monatshefte* contributor), Karl Liebknecht, Rudolf Hilferding, Rudolf Breitscheid, Friedrich Stampfer and Philipp Scheidemann (Hanssen, 1955, p. 32; Stampfer, 1957, pp. 140–2, 173, 223). Here there was a great deal of revisionist collusion, if Stampfer is to be believed, between Stampfer as journalist and Frank and Scheidemann as the SPD's principal Reichstag speakers in Bebel's last years (Stampfer, 1957, pp. 140, 173), but Bernstein did not figure in any of this. Apart from the genera-tion gap separating him from Frank and the Café Josty, Bernstein valued party unity much too highly (Gay, 1962, pp. 287–8; T. Meyer, 1977, pp. 6–7; Pachter, 1981, p. 203) for him to sympathise with Frank's willingness to split the movement rather than accept Berlin control over the South German regional branches (Groh, 1973, pp. 168–9, n. 292; Heckart, 1974, p. 106). Nor was Bernstein sufficiently opportunistic or patriotic to go along with Frank's view, as expressed in a letter to Gustav Mayer in August 1914, that 'for the duration, the international idea is superseded by the reality of a national labour movement. Instead of a general strike, we are waging a war for the Prussian suffrage' (Frank, n.d. [1924], p. 133). Despite some, in a few instances, quite strong parallels in outlook, Bernstein's relations with Ludwig Frank, as with Vollmar, were not close, and the common label of revisionism actually masked a number of significant points of divergence.

The same is true of his relations with Eduard David, another prominent South German reformist. Both enjoyed fairly close links with the *Monatshefte* (David wrote for it, and his first wife, Gertrud David, edited the *Monatshefte* rubric on the co-operative movement from 1907 to 1916). Both were pro-British and 'amongst the most unyielding Free Traders in the ranks of the party' (Bernstein, 1907c, p. 46). Bernstein admired David's pioneering study of the agrarian question, *Sozialismus und Landwirtschaft* (Socialism and Agriculture) (1903, released through the *Monatshefte* publishing house), and he shared David's prewar foreign policy aim – the preservation of peace through an understanding with Britain and France (S. Miller, ed., 1966, pp. xxviii–xxix). On the other hand, David showed no interest in the theoretical aspects of Bernstein's work, was a staunch South German loyalist who took Vollmar rather than Bernstein as his model (ibid., pp. xvi, xviii, n. 6; Heckart, 1974, pp. 146–7), believed in the primacy of domestic politics in a way Bernstein definitely did not (S. Miller, ed., 1966, pp. xxx–xxxi) and adhered to 'the ideology of the "folk community" which permeated his later concept of Social Democracy as a national people's party and equally characterised his concept of the democratic state'. Wanting not 'to overthrow the existing order but to improve it' (ibid., pp. xiii, xxxi), David was closer, in essentials, to the position of Bloch, Leuthner, Schippel and Calwer than to that of Bernstein.

Relations between 'old Ede', as Bernstein was affectionately known to party intimates, and other prominent reformists were broadly of this kind. Albert Südekum, for example (SPD Reichstag member for Nuremberg and editor of the party's local government periodical, *Kommunale Praxis*), demonstrated his impeccably reformist credentials, as well as his desire for Anglo-German amity, when in a lecture delivered to the Fabian Society at Essex Hall on 1 November 1907 he told his British audience, *inter alia*, that socialist practical work in municipal government, in the state parliaments and in the trade unions was contributing enormously to 'the internal transformation of Germany . . . which alone can protect the country against the catastrophe of a terrible revolution' (SP, vol. 8, no. 91). Südekum's prewar Reichstag speeches on Wilhelmine world policy and international politics also cannot have failed to evoke a sympathetic response from Bernstein. Moreover, he was quite close to the *Monatshefte*. He was an *habitué* of the Café des Westens and was still receiving political reports from Bloch during his semi-official Italian journey in August and September 1914 (ibid., no. 152c [1912 diary entry, p. 62], no. 166 [diary entry of 16 September 1914, p. 7]). Yet a diary entry of 17 October 1914 illustrates that Südekum was neither personally close to 'old Ede' nor even remotely familiar with Bernstein's true position and character, for Südekum's assessment was that 'Bernstein has by no means abandoned the standpoint of 4 August. Will not fight publicly. Thus no possibility that he will make a common front with the others' (ibid., no. 165, p. 9).

A very different sort of reformist, of course, was that which Joseph Bloch gathered to his bosom on the *Sozialistische Monatshefte* in the decade or so preceding the First World War. It says much for Bernstein's naïveté that he greatly underestimated the influence of this group and until very late in 1914 failed to notice that these people enjoyed the full confidence and backing of Joseph Bloch. When he finally saw that he had been hoodwinked for almost two decades, Bernstein at once severed his connections with Bloch and the *Monatshefte* (S. Miller, ed., 1966, pp. 43, 50–1, 141, 210; Fricke, 1975*b*, pp. 454–68). Entirely characteristic of Bernstein was his letter to Bloch of 8 August 1901, in which he informed his putative 'Nothung' that he was 'frightfully upset' at the way in which Heinrich Cunow (a left-of-centre radical, later to join the chorus of extreme socialist nationalism) had poured scorn on Calwer in *Vorwärts*, although Bernstein added his firm conviction that Cunow was right and Calwer wrong (SMP, vol. 3). Other *Monatshefte* favourites whom Bernstein felt obliged to attack in the prewar era (in the *Neue Zeit*, the *Monatshefte* itself, the British Radical *Nation* and elsewhere) for their protectionism, militarism, Anglophobia and, above all, for their power-political approach to international relations were Max Schippel (Bernstein, 1898/9, p. 55; 1904*d*, p. 595; 1911*n*, pp. 829–32), Karl Leuthner (idem, 1909*e*, pp. 613–24), Ludwig Quessel (idem, 1913*d*, pp. 1492–9), Gerhard Hildebrand (idem, 1911*g*, pp. 301–11), Max Maurenbrecher (idem, 1912*c* pp. 1147, 1150) and Bloch's agrarian specialist, Arthur Schulz (idem, 1911*n*, pp. 827 ff.) – in brief, virtually all the standard-bearers of 'the programme of the *Sozialistische Monatshefte*'. Yet he apparently believed of these people that 'their number [was] very small, and their influence . . . equal to *nil*' (idem, 1907*d*, p. 224). Certainly, 'nil' is the only correct estimate of Bernstein's influence on them.

Bernstein's Relations with the *Praktiker*

In view of the high importance which Bernstein consistently attached to the day-by-day practical work of the labour movement, and especially to trade union and co-operative activity, it might be thought that here, if nowhere else, 'Ede' was not merely venerated but actually listened to. Nothing could be further from the truth. He was personally very close to leading *Praktiker* (Ignaz Auer and Carl Legien, for example), many of whom contributed regularly to the *Monatshefte* either as writers or as co-editors of its review section. Apart from Auer and Legien, these included Noske, Wilhelm Peus, Ernst Deinhardt, Adolf von Elm, Otto Hué, Theodor Leipart, Johannes Timm, Paul Umbreit, Rudolf Wissell and August Winnig. In turn, Bernstein lectured at the trade union school in Berlin, almost certainly contributed articles to the German Commission's newspaper, the *Correspondenzblatt* – 'the mouthpiece of the entire trade union movement, while also commanding great respect outside the Social Democratic labour movement' (Schönhoven, 1980, p. 22) – and generally did his utmost to defend and promote by word and deed the *Gegenwartsarbeit* of the trade unions, the co-operatives and the party's municipal politicians. But the ageing revisionist's relations with the *Praktiker* foundered on the rocks of circumstance and his unfortunate and widely misunderstood slogan, 'The movement is everything; the goal, nothing' (1897/8*a*, p. 556). In one sense, the de-radicalisation, or at least 'de-theorising', of the Wilhelmine labour movement was nothing new, for non-Marxist and untheoretical *Praktiker* had been with the movement since its inception. Yet the process was hastened and intensified in the Wilhelmine era by a confluence of factors that had little to do with Bernstein's, or any other theory. The relative relaxation in the repressive apparatus of the state after 1890 combined with the post-1895 industrial upsurge, accelerating urbanisation and bringing an upturn in working-class living standards (see Figures 1.3 and 1.4; pp. 31 and 32), facilitated a massive expansion in proletarian organisation (trade union membership alone grew from 300,000 in 1890 to 2.5 million by 1913) which resulted in a preoccupation with organisation as an end in itself, or as a means of securing immediate material benefits for the rank and file. Wage differentials created a 'labour aristocracy' of skilled workers who were relatively satisfied with their lot and looked forward to further improving it within the existing system. Since skilled workers predominated in the party and other socialist organisations, the bureaucratisation of the movement meant its increasing immunisation against programmatic and theoretical discussion. Growing SPD success at the polls (see Figures 1.1 and 1.2, pp. 28 and 29, for the national elections) also meant that the party as a whole ceased to regard parliamentary work as a mere propaganda forum and was progressively 'sucked into the system through . . . participation in municipal politics, co-operation with government institutions involved in welfare activities and the like' (Geary, 1981, p. 112).[7] Thus relative political liberalisation, growing working-class affluence and organisational developments placed more and more power in the hands of theoretically indifferent *Praktiker* and simultaneously marked 'the emancipation of Social Democracy from all theory' (H.-J. Steinberg, 1972, p. 124).

A typical response of the *Praktiker* to Bernstein's revisionism was Ignaz Auer's comment on one of Ede's 'problems of socialism' articles: 'My dear Ede, you don't *say* that sort of thing; you just *do* it' (Bernstein, 1907g, p. 63, italics in original). For his part, Bernstein agreed with Bloch that many of the *Praktiker* needed 'to have their ears boxed' (SMP, vol. 2: Bernstein to Bloch, 24 November 1909), for it was largely due to their influence that the movement was becoming 'not social democratic but rather a proletarian class movement' desiring nothing more than 'recognition and integration within the existing state' (Moses, 1982, pp. 107, 137). The job of the *Praktiker*, as Bernstein saw it, was not to indulge or pander to the masses but to educate them for democracy and socialism under the leadership of the most skilled, intelligent and class-conscious cadres. Far from seeing anything romantic or 'authentic' in working-class (as distinct from socialist) culture, this former bank clerk and son of a Berlin locomotive driver was thoroughly imbued with the values and norms of the dominant, bourgeois culture, as clearly emerges from his 1907 comparison of working-class housing in London and Berlin:

> Go into the poorest districts of Berlin, and, with very few exceptions, you will find in the flat houses you see there a certain, and on the whole, favourable mingling of social classes . . . This mingling of social strata has as a result an emulation in the tidiness of home and dress that also in other

respects makes for progress. Monsieur Hervé thought in Stuttgart to
ridicule the German Socialist movement, when he declared that the
Stuttgart workers looked like *petty bourgeois*. He could not better illustrate
the superficiality of his criticism. The seeming *petty bourgeois* surprise
friend and foe by their creative power. But whence shall creative power
come in the region of the monotonous brick boxes and the abominations
called working-class mansions in London? What is there, what *can* there
be, of emulation? . . . The political dullness and depravity of so large a
section of the London working classes is no mystery to him who has seen
those castles of dirt and neglect which the Thames metropolis owns in
numberless quantity . . . I feel always a strong inclination towards
anarchism when my way leads me through such districts. Violent destruction seems the only salvation here. (1907*l*, pp. 991–2)

Given the lack of communication between the socialist intellectual bent on
'creative emulation' and the practically minded party and trade union cadres
interested only in 'doing', it was perhaps inevitable that, in the words of
Heinrich Hirschfelder, 'Bernstein's revisionism evoked no response from the
rank and file; indeed, even the leading reformist *Praktiker*, in spite of their
agreement with him on many issues, did not appeal to his authority' (1979,
pp. 583–4; cf. H.-J. Steinberg, 1972, p. 106). Again it is symptomatic of his
lack of real influence that among the 288 delegates who voted against him at
Dresden in 1903 were Carl Legien and Ignaz Auer, each in his way the epitome
of *Praktizismus*.

The above discussion of Bernstein's revisionism and his relations with his
fellow-revisionists indicates that the 'father of revisionism' was very far from
being, as he is still described, 'the leader of the right-wing "revisionist" wing of
the party' (Carsten, 1982, p. 19). Among the revisionists, he was hardly more
than an occasionally useful embarrassment, a crutch of last resort. In the
movement generally, he was an isolated but respected figure, a party monu-
ment rather than a faction leader or a serious actor in party politics. If many
shared Wolfgang Heine's estimate of 'Bernstein's complete political ineptitude' (VP, C226: Heine to Vollmar, 6 July 1903), many others would probably
have concurred in Vollmar's own judgement, expressed in 1899:

Eduard Bernstein is one of our oldest comrades; he is a man who directed
the fighting organ of the party [the Zurich-based *Sozial-Demokrat*] under
the anti-socialist law, who for this activity is obliged to live in exile. If he
now sees the world through English spectacles, that is not his fault. It is
the consequence of a sacrifice he has made for the party. We have always
honoured such people. (Vollmar, 1977, p. 184)

In sum, most heterodox Social Democrats knew whom to flee but not whom to
follow. Most Wilhelmine Social Democrats, whatever their persuasion, found
Bernstein impossible to follow principally because, as Cicero said of Cato,
'with all his patriotism and integrity he is sometimes a political liability. He
speaks . . . as though he were living in Plato's Republic instead of Romulus's

cesspool' (Cicero, 1978, p. 80). When Bernstein triumphantly informed his British Radical readers in September 1913 that the German socialist party congress of that year marked a milestone in the revisionist conquest of the party (1913*g*, pp. 949–50), he must have been unaware of the full implications of the impending 'revisionist' capture of the party, for the coming men were not *his* men but apparatchiks like Ebert and Noske and reformists like Ludwig Frank and Eduard David, whom he misjudged as badly as they did him. Within a year of Jena, Ludwig Frank was dead, killed 'defending the fatherland in order to conquer it' (Frank to Stampfer, cit. Boll, 1980, p. 124), and on 11 February 1915 Kautsky was complaining to Victor Adler in Vienna:

> Those around David and the trade unionists believe the moment is opportune to rid the party of all 'Marxism' [Bernstein's included, if one may judge from their behaviour]. They will hardly get away with simply throwing us out, but they dominate the executive and fill one position after another with their people. In so doing, they practise a ruthless terrorism that is hard to bear. They are aiming at . . . condemning us to the role of dumb animals. (Adler, 1954, p. 611)

Was Bernstein, as Peter Gay has argued, essentially a critical naturalist? It is clear that he derived his ethical interpretation of socialism partly from the life of the movement and partly through the 'English spectacles' acquired during his 'best years' in London. Whatever else he may have been, he was no leader. 'If Bernstein is really the Messiah and leader of the revisionists', Auer informed the Dresden party congress, 'then you can sleep peacefully' (SPD A.C., 1903, p. 306). Though unwilling and unable to split the German labour movement, Bernstein was determined to be heard on matters which concerned him deeply. First among these, after his return to Germany in 1901, was the deteriorating international situation. Here, too, he remained largely a chieftain without a tribe, for he had eventually to recognise that in this field, more than in any other, Joseph Bloch and the *Sozialistische Monatshefte* represented not a refuge but a mortal foe.

Notes: Chapter 6

1   The same observation has been made, albeit from a very different standpoint, by Geoff Eley, who calls for closer examination of the material and cultural bases of labour reformism (1976*a*, p. 289) while denouncing 'dense empiricism' and 'theoretical eclecticism' (Eley and Nield, 1980, pp. 261, 262); more moderately by Dick Geary (1981, p. 14); and by Richard Evans who, none the less, opens his attack on structural-functionalism with the provocative statement, 'The historiography of the labour movement in Germany has been dominated not by historians, but by sociologists' (1982, ed., p. 15). Unfortunately, all these authors appear far more concerned to locate that elusive pimpernel and persistently pursued darling of middle-class university Marxists, the radical worker, than to address themselves to the real world of the Wilhelmine labour movement, which demands the explanation not only of why radical movements arise but equally of why some social movements fail. The *Sozialistische Monatshefte* group clearly falls into the latter category, although one of the purposes of this study is also to demonstrate that the *Monatshefte* revisionists occupied a position of much greater importance in prewar German Social Democracy than previous studies have recognised.

2   Indicative of the misinformation which still abounds, not only on the *Sozialistische Monatshefte*,

but on Bernstein as well, is the following cornucopia of inaccuracies: 'Eduard Bernstein, who had spent many years in London, gave voice to . . . doubts in a series of articles in the intellectual periodical, *Berliner Monatshefte* (1896–7), which he later published as *Die Voraussetzungen des Sozialismus*' (Stone, 1983, p. 192). In fact, Bernstein's doubts first appeared in the *Neue Zeit* and were later published, together with other material, as part of a 3-volume study on the history and theory of socialism (1904*f*). His *Voraussetzungen* book originated quite separately at Kautsky's suggestion that Bernstein set down a comprehensive statement of his convictions (see Gay, 1962, pp. 77–8).

3 It is no wonder, therefore, that the anonymous wits of the *Also-Socialist Monthly Circus* promised their readers a future article by Bernstein entitled 'Karl Marx never lived: revelation of an audacious Kautskyite mystification'. Yet there is no reason for doubting the sincerity of Bernstein's claim, maintained to his dying day, that he was and remained a Marxist (SPD A.C., 1903, p. 400; Bernstein, 1924, p. 31). Certainly, at the time, Eleanor Marx saw no reason to question his Marxist bona fides, although she did describe his revisionist writings as producing the effect of a 'wet blanket' (*Daughters of Karl Marx*, 1982, p. 300). Nor did Kautsky at first see any cause for alarm in his old friend's 'moulting', as Bernstein's change of heart was described in party circles (H.-J. Steinberg, 1972, pp. 77–86). By the same token, Victor Adler admitted to Kautsky in March 1899 that 'a whole string of Ede's views are also my own' as well as 'the basis of the political action of all of us'. Adler deemed 'Ede's follies' far less damaging than those of 'literati and fanatics' like Plekhanov and Parvus; his misfortune was 'a pathological sense of responsibility, a self-devouring mania for objectivity', which accounted for 'his pathetic penchant for tilting at windmills' (Adler, 1954, pp. 296–7).

4 More than a decade later he still felt obliged to explain for the benefit of his German readers that 'in Protestant England, politically speaking, religion has never been simply a governmental tool of the possessing classes against the propertyless; it was always at the same time also a shield of the political underdog in his struggles against the privileged' (1901*b*, p. 569).

5 For a discussion of the part played by British liberalism, Fabianism and Bernstein's sentimental Anglophilia, both in the genesis of his revisionism and in conditioning his view of international relations, see Fletcher, 1979*a*, pp. 349–75. As Christoph Schröder has rightly drawn to my attention, this essay is somewhat deficient in that it pays insufficient attention to the specifically Radical impact on Bernstein's thought. The title, too, is somewhat misleading, but it was neither chosen nor approved by myself. Naturally, the gestation of Bernstein's revisionism also owed much to French, Italian and other influences (Gustafsson, 1972, pp. 181–326), but this phenomenon was neither the home-grown product so artfully systematised by T. Meyer (1977) nor so exclusively a Fabian spin-off as depicted by Frei (1979).

6 In the 1912 Reichstag elections the SPD had won 32.1 per cent of the vote in Prussia. In the 1913 elections for the Prussian Lower House, the SPD gained 28.38 per cent of the vote but won only 10 (2.3 per cent) of the 443 seats. The pessimistic and fatalistic attitude of the party centre was aptly expressed by Bebel at Nuremberg: 'I don't know when we in Prussia will get the universal suffrage; I fear it is only to be had when we conquer more than the universal suffrage' (SPD A.C., 1908, p. 292). Ludwig Frank's Berlin-Wilmersdorf speech of 11 June 1913, and its support from Bernstein, suggests, as Geary rightly observes, that the conventional 'revolutionary/revisionist' dichotomy may be quite misleading, and that 'to a large extent it is the surrounding terrain which determines the appropriate form of action (or quiescence)' (1982, p. 225). Thus, when Frank and Bernstein demanded a change of tactic (not of theory) in 1913, they moved closer to the radical left and into conflict with the quiescent centre for two reasons. First, they realised that the intransigence of the Prussian ruling classes left the SPD no choice but to resort to extra-parliamentary methods if the Prussian suffrage was ever to be democratised, and all Social Democrats were in agreement that this represented the precondition to progress in Germany and in Europe. Secondly, failure to achieve progress on this issue would not only demonstrate that the socialist–liberal alliance (or grand-bloc) strategy was applicable only in the South German states but must also cast serious doubt on the credentials of the SPD as a 'party of movement' (whether revolutionary or reformist), leading to an inevitable decline in party morale and in voter support, to which several indicators already pointed. It was therefore for good 'revisionist' reasons that Bernstein and Frank urged the adoption of a tactic which the centre and the left regarded as nothing less than revolutionary.

7 Recently the concept of a labour aristocracy has also become a bone of contention, its critics questioning the validity of attempts to identify empirically a division between 'labour

aristocrats' (better paid, more moderate workers) and other workers, as well as the explanatory value of such attempts, particularly in relation to the historical roots of socialist 'de-radicalisation' or working-class 'integration'. Robert Gray (1981) offers a good introduction to the controversy in its British context; Schönhoven questions its applicability in the German trade union context (1980, pp. 221–60); Evans and Geary disagree as to its importance, in the form of bureau-cratisation, as an agent of Social Democratic (but not, of course, working-class) *embourgeoise-ment* (Geary, 1981, pp. 118–19; Evans, ed., 1982, p. 29).

7

The Revisionist 'Troublemaker': Eduard Bernstein's Ambivalent Radical Internationalism

> *We are in the unfortunate position that the German people as a nation never has had a foreign policy, and consequently possesses no redeeming traditions.*
>
> (*Eduard Bernstein, 1911*)

> *Secure popular government, in substance and in form, and you secure internationalism; retain class government, and you retain military imperialism and international conflicts.*
>
> (*J. A. Hobson, 1902*)

> *The saying, the worker has no fatherland, is not to be found in my political vocabulary. The working class has national commitments just as much as it has international commitments, and by the same token it also has national interests.*
>
> (*Eduard Bernstein, 1911*)

> *He [Bernstein] can be wholly comprehended only in the English context. In many ways he was a 'Radical' in the English sense.*
>
> (*H.-C. Schröder, 1978*)

In Britain, between 1888 and 1901, Bernstein fully expected never to be allowed to set foot on German soil again. As the warrants for his arrest were regularly renewed in Germany, all thoughts of returning to the fatherland were synonymous with the dismal prospect of a long period of imprisonment. The ageing party journalist and theoretician therefore made the best of his London exile by thinking, writing and adapting to his British environment. On his return to Germany in 1901, Bernstein at once, and for the first time in his life, became a practising party politician: he sat in the Reichstag as an SPD deputy between 1902 and 1928, was active in municipal government, taught at the trade union school in Berlin and generally did his utmost to live up to the maxim that for him the movement was everything, the goal nothing. Henceforth he was much less concerned with theory than with the great issues immediately confronting the German labour movement at home and abroad. Paradoxically, he now wrote more than ever before, but again on practical issues rather than theoretical questions.

One matter which gripped his attention more and more was the problem area of Germany's position among the great powers and how German socialists might contribute to the resolution of the mounting difficulties in this area. He was concerned, at times alarmed, both as a patriot and as a socialist. It disturbed him to see Germany so unloved in the world, still more because he regarded the German Empire as pursuing a foreign policy that endangered peace and jeopardised the vital interests of the German people. As a socialist, he was concerned that Social Democracy appeared either to have no coherent foreign policy position of its own (1907*d*, p. 550) or, worse still, was drifting into a no-man's land between the revolutionary 'Blanquism' of the party radicals and the social imperialism of Joseph Bloch and most of his *Monatshefte* colleagues. Although Bernstein's crusade to outline a socialist foreign policy alternative was closely related to his revisionism, it clearly had little in common with 'the programme of the *SM*' and normally found expression in outlets other than the *Monatshefte*. Ultimately, his campaign to enlighten his comrades and his compatriots had little influence on Social Democratic contemporaries. For example, in September 1915, when he submitted a set of proposals on SPD war aims for consideration by the Reichstag caucus and the party's central committee (*Ausschuss*), it was Eduard David's draft which the party debated, amended and finally adopted, while Bernstein's guidelines were not even discussed (Bernstein, 1918*b*, p. 6). Only during the war did it become apparent that Bernstein's consistently argued foreign policy views were closest to those of Kautsky and former left-wing critics and that he had few political friends apart from an equally uninfluential handful of non-socialist pacifists and bourgeois democrats. In the short term, Bernstein was as much a political failure as was Joseph Bloch, even if in the long term, as Professor Carlo Schmid has put it, Bernstein 'triumphed all along the line' (Papcke, 1979, p. 9) – both as a revisionist and as a foreign affairs analyst.

Our first task is to demonstrate that betwen 1900 and 1914 Bernstein also offered, beside his now widely known socialist alternative to revolutionary Marxism, a less frequently remarked but seriously elaborated, piecemeal and highly polemical critique of Wilhelmine world policy in the context of the 'new imperialism' which, if it occasioned little resonance then or subsequently, was none the less as distinguished by an exceptionally informed, sustained and discerning analysis as it was indicative of the extent to which his eclecticism mirrored the common intellectual currency of the era, reflecting, in particular, important elements in the dominant values of his late-Victorian British milieu. In both its dimensions, this analysis was firmly grounded in a liberal inter-nationalist commitment to free trade, 'pacificism'[1] and a cosmopolitan patriotism. Its more negative dimension exhibited a highly critical, yet generally ambivalent, view of imperialism and colonialism.

Tariff Policy

Basic to Bernstein's foreign policy thinking was his sweeping and unequivocal endorsement of free trade principles, and it is worth noting that as a Social Democratic Reichstag deputy after 1902 he functioned as one of the party's principal spokesman on both foreign relations and taxation policy (1924, p. 40). With the 1902 Bülow tariff as his target – he normally preferred domestic to foreign targets for, as he liked to say, 'criticism, like charity, is best done at home' (1911*a*, p. 804) – he waged a vigorous and unrelenting campaign against protectionism. Claiming that protectionism was inherently reactionary and indefensible on rational economic grounds, he argued that it was the wrong remedy for the ills of German agriculture and represented more a hindrance than a help to industry in that its alleged advantages, even for infant industries, were either mythical or ephemeral whereas the concomitant disadvantages were neither. In fact, his main objection was that by insulating Germany from the world economy, this neo-mercantilist regression was less economic in inspiration than a domestic political expedient designed to cement a conservative alliance against democracy and social reform within Prussia and the Reich. Abroad it retarded, but could not seriously impair, economic progress. Its external menace he considered to be more political than economic, for he acknowledged that protectionism sowed mistrust among nations and was intimately, though not causally, related to militarism, navalism, the colonial fever and popular Anglophobia. Thus he insisted that 'the great peril of our time' was not Wilhelm II 'hunting after a war', which Bernstein believed to be untrue, but the Kaiser's domestic policy, for 'his endeavour to uphold the squirearchy and the peasantry [made] him a supporter of Protection, and consequently . . . one of the causes of continuous friction between the nations' (1907*a*, p. 234). Yet in recognising its aggressive and destructive associations, Bernstein was still unprepared to join J. A. Hobson and Rudolf Hilferding in condemning protectionism as inherently expansionist or dangerously bellicose. Prior to the First World War he continued to insist that the protectionist blight was more psychological than material, more an ephemeral relapse than a necessary feature of advanced capitalism. Indeed, and in consonance with his stand on the question of value theory, he could hardly have accepted the Hobson–Hilferding argument without jeopardising important revisionist assumptions, including his belief that the market – the domestic, no less than the world market – was capable of unlimited expansion, the assumption that the attainment of socialism presupposed a flourishing rather than a moribund capitalist economy (1896/7*e*, pp. 334–5), and the conviction (shared by British Radicals like H. N. Brailsford, E. D. Morel, Norman Angell, and Richard Cobden before them) that Saint-Simon's 'industrious classes' (the bourgeoisie and the proletariat) had a common interest in peace and international intercourse that might form a golden bridge to a liberal–socialist alliance for democracy and social reform.

Bernstein continued this striking anticipation of J. A. Schumpeter in an equally broadly based defence of free trade, although he believed that free trade needed no defence because its pacifist tendency was self-evident (1917*b*, p. 170). Like the good Cobdenite that he was, Bernstein endorsed free trade primarily because it conduced to general prosperity, progress and internationalism, but he also took care to commend it as sound national and social policy. As a socialist, however, he went further than his 'middle-class Marxist' mentor, as Cobden has been described (Briggs, 1968, p. 127), in admitting the need for state intervention, and in his conditional approval of tariffs to foster infant industries he endeavoured to rebut the argument that free trade, by perpetuating Britain's industrial and commercial supremacy, functioned as a weapon of British imperialism. The advantages predicted as accruing to the German economy from a reversion to 'duty-free international intercourse' were none the less stock-in-trade Cobdenism. Free trade, he argued, lowered production costs, favoured export industry, and promoted efficiency through international specialisation. The removal of the existing high agrarian duties would stimulate consumer spending and domestic consumption as well as promote agricultural rationalisation, while the introduction of direct taxation would compensate for lost revenue and provide a surplus sufficient to facilitate necessary social reforms. The resulting freer movement of labour, far from flooding the Reich with 'coolies and similar backward workers' (1901f, p. 693), could easily be regulated through social policy and the immigration laws. Free trade merited working-class support because it benefited all classes and accorded with the 'cultural mission of the working class' to uphold and advance the cause of human progress. As a policy, it was pronounced politically viable in that there did exist, even in Imperial Germany, significant bourgeois elements with a real interest in free trade, and after 1909 Bernstein was able to point to the Hansa-Bund as a clearly perceived and concrete expression of such interest. Specifically working-class advantages to be derived from free trade included, in the short term, more jobs at higher wages, shorter hours, and lower living costs and, in the long term, better prospects for the attainment of socialism – for the richer the society, the more readily socialist gains could be realised. In any event, free trade was the natural policy of a socialist state, since in a socialised economy the state would tax only itself if it levied duties on exchange.

Bernstein's principal reason for supporting free trade really had little to do with such considerations, however. When he chided his fellow-socialists for being less than whole-hearted in their advocacy of free trade principles, he had in mind their lack of attention to the 'wider bearing' of the question – 'its reaction on the question of peace and war, and all the other political relations between the nations' (1907d, p. 225). German liberals were reproved on the same grounds: 'You can hardly find a consistent Free Trader among them', he wrote in December 1911. 'How can you expect to find a consistent peace politician?' (1911f, p. 551). In his mind, free trade was not just a tariff policy; it was a touchstone and a talisman, the great divide between the progressive principle of co-operation and the reactionary idea of domination. As he wrote in June 1915, 'here is the point at which the dividing lines intersect, separating the advocates of the idea of a liberated humanity from the representatives of the old and the new politics of mastery' (1915d, p. 6). In short, free trade merited support, above all, because it was seen as the keystone of a liberal-humanitarian world view.

The National Question

If on the tariff question Bernstein revealed his overriding indebtedness as being neither to Marx nor to German liberalism but to Cobdenite British Radicalism[2] – though not to the relatively pessimistic variety adumbrated by J. A. Hobson during his *Imperialism* phase (see Cain, 1978, pp. 565–84, 1979b, pp. 406–24) – Bernstein's internationalist commitment appeared far more eclectic, equivocal and temporising in his treatment of the nationality question. Here the salient influences on his thought were, apart from British Radicalism, the legacy of Marx and Engels, of Lassalle and Fichte, the democratic Russophobic tradition of 1848, and his own liberal Jewish background. In contrast to his inflexible attachment to free trade principles, Bernstein's views on the national question passed through a succession of stages. In the 1880s, and until the death of Engels in August 1895, his position was essentially that of an orthodox Marxist, reflecting strong elements of the Eurocentric and predominantly Social Darwinist ethos of the era which he imbibed above all from Engels (see Rosdolsky, 1964, pp. 87–282; Wehler, 1971, pp. 17–33; H. Mommsen, 1979, pp. 61–71; D. Paul, 1981, pp. 115–38). Over the next decade, as he struggled to emancipate himself from such influence, his position manifested considerable ambiguity, and it was only after 1911 that he consistently championed a more coherent and unmistakably Cobdenite cosmopolitan patriotism. What moved him to do so was the shock of the Agadir crisis and the influence of Alfred Fried of the German Peace Society, with whom he was in regular contact after 1911.[3]

Yet it is possible to identify certain basic assumptions and values which repeatedly surfaced in Bernstein's views on this issue over the two decades preceding the First World War. A constant factor was his distinction between nationalism and patriotism. The former he emphatically rejected as reactionary and racist – a barbaric, irrational, artificial and ephemeral regression to a primitive tribalism which had no place in the modern world (1907*k*, pp. 436–9; cf. 1915*d*, p. 5). Cut of this cloth, he maintained, was the patriotism of the non-socialist classes in all the great powers. Nowhere was this more true than in Germany, where all the non-socialist parties had been gripped by a dangerous 'social insanity'. Although Germany had made enormous economic progress, her social and political life was still dominated by aristocratic 'wastrels', 'idlers' and 'microbes' who had infected and corrupted the middle-class parties with nationalism in order to prop up their declining position in German society and government. This 'subterfuge' was not an occasional electoral option, as in Britain, but had become 'a regular instrument for working the [German] electorate' (1911*m*, pp. 93–4; see also 1911*i*, p. 306 and 1912*j*, p. 1057). The result was international anarchy and a reversion to the worst features of international relations in the seventeenth and eighteenth centuries. This kind of patriotism entirely justified Samuel Johnson's dictum that patriotism was 'the last refuge of a scoundrel' (1911*m*, p. 93; 1916*f*, p. 4).

Cut of the same cloth, in Bernstein's view, was Zionism, which he denounced for its cultural pessimism as vehemently as he deprecated anti-Semitism and the exaggerated assimilationism of Jewish anti-Semites like Paul Nikolaus Cossmann (1893/4*c*, pp. 233–7; 1913/14, pp. 744–52; 1915*f*, pp. 127–33; 1916*d*, pp. 243–8; 1916*f*, pp. 3–4; 1917*a*. On Cossmann, see Selig, 1967, pp. 66–8; Gay, 1978, p. 156). On the eve of the First World War he described Zionism as a product of despair at the slow eradication of anti-Semitism and a 'manifestation of the great wave of nationalist reaction gripping the bourgeois world and seeking admittance to the socialist world as well'. It could have only 'a retarding effect' on the progress of humanity but would surely vanish like the epidemic it was (1913/14, p. 752). In October 1916 Bernstein said of his co-religionists, 'their history assigns them the task of cultivating that which binds the peoples and of opposing whatever separates them and sows hatred between them'. Their assimilation into the nations in whose midst they lived was 'an historical and cultural necessity' (1916*f*, p. 4). He understood the phenomenon of marginality, which explained why Jews like Joseph Bloch were 'so Prussian-minded' that they might be 'mistaken for' German nationalists (Bernstein, cit. Wistrich, 1982, p. 166), but he neither condoned such excess nor pardoned Jewish nationalists for their recidivism to a 'tribal atavism'.[4]

Proletarian patriotism, on the other hand, elicited Bernstein's unqualified approval, for he judged it to be progressive in the sense of his Whiggish (and inaccurate) interpretation of the patriotism once championed by Fichte and Lassalle (1904*b*; RTV, vol. 295 [15 May 1914], p. 8890; 1915*i*, pp. 143–62).[5] Invoking the ideals of the French Revolution and Mazzini, Bernstein claimed that the proletariat could be, and was, 'national' in this sense, its patriotism being a mere extension of its pursuit of liberty and rationality and therefore complementary rather than antagonistic to other similar patriotisms (1907*k*, pp. 434–40). Such *progressive* patriotism, being founded on 'sociological necessities' rather than biological principles, accorded with the historical evolution of the nation-state and was inherently democratic (1909*e*, pp. 614–15; 1913*d*, p. 1498), which also meant that its adherents were, as demonstrated by British history, 'man enough, if need be, to take issue with national constraints and national prejudice' (RTV, vol. 285 [18 May 1912], p. 2114). Again and again Bernstein denied the validity of the saying, the worker has no fatherland (1896/7*c*, pp. 111–12; 1899, p. 204; 1909*e*, pp. 614–15; 1911*d*, p. 428; 1913*a*, p. 15; 1917*a*, p. 36). The worker, he insisted, had not only a fatherland but also a stake in the continued prosperity and progress of capitalism (1907*c*, p. 47). In this progressive sense, the SPD was 'the most decisively national party (*Reichspartei*) in all Germany' (1907*k*, p. 437). In this sense, too, Bernstein personally was every inch a German patriot. To his friend, H. W. Massingham, editor of the Radical weekly, *The Nation*, he wrote on 6 March 1913 giving expression to his opinion that the German army increase of 1913, the largest in the history of Imperial Germany, was fully justified in the light of Russian machinations and 'the present system of imperialistic nationalism', to which he added: 'This much I am bound to say to myself but I am very much loathe [sic] to recognize it in public' (MC 41/8). In fact, his journalistic work for *The Nation* – he also managed to attend some of the famous *Nation* luncheons (Havighurst, 1974, p. 145)[6] – affords countless examples of frank denunciation of German evils, together with equally numerous assurances to his British readers that all would soon be put right by German Social Democracy.

Here Bernstein was betrayed by his German patriotism. In 1914 his model patriots – men like John Bright and Jean Jaurès – turned out to be as uninfluential in parliamentary Britain and republican France as he and his few friends proved to be in undemocratic Germany. Moreover, as Bernstein himself never tired of observing, Imperial Germany was a long way from democracy. To tell the German workers that they had duties to the nation as well as a stake in the fatherland, while they had as good as no control over the actions of the German state, was to take a large lien on the future, to confuse an assumed trend with actual reality. For Bernstein, it was axiomatic that British and French parliamentary precedent was the road that Germany had before her (1890/1*c*, p. 666; 1904*e*, pp. 888–95; 1906*c*, pp. 57–9; 1912*e*, p. 656). We may not be entitled to assume that what happened in 1914, and subsequently, could not have happened otherwise, but the conclusion is inescapable that Bernstein's patriotism, combined with his Enlightenment progressivism, induced him to take dangerous, perhaps foolhardy, liberties with the peace of Europe.

He applied the same progressive–reactionary dualism in his perception of internationalism. One of its manifestations, which he deemed indefensible and moribund, was a rootless and parasitic aristocratic cosmopolitanism (1907*k*, p. 437; 1917*a*, pp. 32–3), but he also discerned what he believed to be an increasingly prevalent variety of progressive internationalism rooted in positive liberty and patriotism which was justifiably professed by the proletariat and in accord with the true interests of the industrious classes as a whole. His view of the natural and legitimate objectives of such progressive internationalism scarcely differed from that of Bentham or Cobden and was generally more British than Saint-Simonian or Continental (see Hinsley, 1963, pp. 101–13, 141–3; Holbraad, 1970, pp. 62–72, 107–13, 131–5, 153–98; Howard, 1978, pp. 31–72). Although he frequently upbraided the German government for its persistent refusal to defend, or even respect, the rights of oppressed peoples either at home or abroad, Bernstein was a non-interventionist in so far as his first priority remained domestic: the duties which this concept of internationalism imposed on its adherents derived, at bottom, from a demand that internationalists concentrate on the struggle for more democracy in their respective polities and greater democratic control over foreign policy within the respective nation-state (1909*e*, p. 622; 1910*f*, pp. 1000–6). Granting only limited validity to the principle of national self-determination – he maintained that 'you cannot emancipate nations beyond their capacity for emancipation' (1913*k*, p. 987) – he yet insisted on the sovereignty of the nation-state as the only sound basis of internationalism (1909*e*, pp. 614–15; 1913*j*, p. 319; 1917*a*, p. 17) and explicitly excluded the use of the mass strike as a possible means of enforcing the principles of internationalism (SPD A. C., 1903, pp. 394–5, 1904, pp. 193–4, 1913, p. 284; 1905*b*, p. 39; 1910*i*, p. 483).

In practical terms, Bernstein's patriotism thus fell rather more heavily in the scales than did his internationalism. At least in his case, and in marked contrast to the blatant nationalism systematically propagated by many of his fellow-revisionists, this imbalance owed less to conscious distinctions than to a blind spot that he shared with most nineteenth-century progressives, including such stalwarts of Marxist orthodoxy as Karl Kautsky (H.-J. Steinberg, 1972, pp. 48–53; Steenson, 1978, pp. 7, 23–33 and *passim*; Salvadori, 1979, pp. 23–6): so boundless and unquestioning was Bernstein's faith in the beneficence and authenticity of an unwritten law of unilinear progress that in respect of democracy and internationalism he abandoned his wonted revisionist voluntarism and slipped into the same fatalistic *attentisme* which characterised the centre-orthodox attitude towards socialist revolution. In fact, the only real exceptions to this rule in pre-1914 German Social Democracy were a few hard-headed radical Marxists like Rosa Luxemburg, who confronted nationalism in any guise, both theoretically and in practice, with a stony indifference that bespoke truly irreconcilable opposition, for even Rudolf Hilferding (author of the most impressive of prewar Marxist theoretical condemnations of finance capitalism) as editor of *Vorwärts* (the SPD official newspaper) normally sided with the centre-orthodoxy on questions of practical politics. It may well be significant that many of these radicals came originally from Eastern Europe, where the Enlightenment tradition had not struck popular roots to anywhere near the same extent as in the West.

Militarism

Bernstein's attachment to an optimistic Enlightenment progressivism combined with his theoretical eclecticism to produce a similarly ambivalent analysis when he turned his attention to the problem of militarism and war.[7] Here the major determinants of his attitude appear to have been his personal abhorrence of violence (among individuals, classes, or nations) and his commitment to the idea of progress, together with the shadow of Engels and a strong admixture of Social Darwinism. Not very helpful was his definition of militarism as a situation where the political constitution segregates the army from the nation ([1899] 1921, pp. 202–3; 1913*a*, pp. 2–3).

In his references to the causes of war he customarily placed heavy emphasis on psychological and ideological factors such as protectionism, nationalism and the influence of an artificially created war hysteria that tended to function as a self-fulfilling prophecy. Although he believed that 'the spirit of the German people as a whole [was] hardly more bellicose than that of the British people' (1914*e*, p. 673) and saw no reason to doubt the Bethmann government's sincerity in its protestations of peaceful intent (1913*e*, p. 569), he admitted that 'the conviction has taken deep root in the thoughts of a good many Germans that, sooner or later, serious conflicts . . . will become inevitable' (1907*d*, p. 224) and that the Imperial government was subordinating 'every other interest' so that Germany might be 'fully armed in currency, as well as in ships, guns and drilled men' (1913*h*, p. 210). The root cause of this war hysteria, in Bernstein's view, was that 'the Prussian Conservatives [had become] a diminishing quantity in the economic structure of the nation and [remained] a force only through their hold on the army' (1914*c*, p. 745). Among the material causes of war and militarism, which he generally rated as less important than ideological and psychological factors, for he was convinced that the 'material reasons for war [were] losing ground day by day' (1912*j*, p. 1057), were the existence of large military bureaucracies, the pressures of the arms race and, as he argued in the last two years of peace, the emergence of a military-industrial complex (cf. Berghahn, 1973*b*, pp. 47–69). The constituents of this complex included ambitious generals and admirals, the 'bankers of the great' who 'condemn whole nations to Penelope's work' (1913*a*, p. 17) and 'marauding' armaments manufacturers:

It is an almost admitted fact that those papers who most clamorously agitate for increases in armaments are financed by the big firms who manufacture guns, steel plates, and other material for armaments. But the influence on public opinion of these firms reaches much further than the circulation of their press. By their connection with the great financial houses, by their intercourse with military people in responsible positions, by their great staff of agents and sub-agents, they are able to circulate those views of State policy which serve their purposes in all circles of society. Their influence is especially strong amongst the upper and middle sections of the intellectuals. The fact that in those ranks the officer of the reserve abounds, makes them a fruitful ground for the propaganda in favor of increased armaments . . . The resources of those firms are to-day immense, and their profits enormous. By their concerted action – concerted in many cases internationally – they have succeeded in raising the military budgets to an incredible height, and driving the nations wild with fear of one another . . . In former years some of the firms at least were private. Now they are all limited liability companies. Their shares are more widely circulated, and the circle of those interested in armaments has greatly increased. This explains, in a degree, the silent consent of the middle classes to the exorbitant increases of the military Budgets now before the German Reichstag. (1913*f*, p. 142)

Most serious of all, in Bernstein's catalogue of potential causes of war, was that concatenation of evils which he subsumed under the label of *Staatenpolitik* (cabinet or state politics) – as opposed to *Völkerpolitik* (international or peoples' politics) – and condemned for precisely the same reasons as those advanced by British Radicals from Bentham and Cobden to C. P. Trevelyan, Hobson and E. D. Morel (see Weinroth, 1970, pp. 653–82; Morris, 1972; idem, ed., 1974, esp. chs 10–15; idem, 1977, pp. 99–117; Cline, 1980, pp. 68–97). This inherently violent system of power politics, founded on interests and powers rather than the will of peoples, was both incapable of preserving peace and productive, at best, of 'this silent war, this cold war' ([1899] 1921, p. 207; RTV, vol. 197 [12 December 1903], p. 110, vol. 289 [14 April 1913], pp. 4734–40, vol. 295 [15 May 1914], pp. 8884–8; 1912*a*, p. 344). As a consequence of this system, force had become 'the idol of the day', dominating 'public opinion to a dreadful degree' (1913*h*, p. 210).

For Germany, the result was nothing less than devastating. Militarism, with its constant army and navy increases, raised the cost of living, hampered commerce, produced 'a state of real anarchy in taxation', made 'a thorough and consistent policy of social reform an impossibility', resulted in the slump of 1913 and reversed the social and political development of Germany by 100 years (1913*a*, p. 16; 1913*f*, p. 141; 1913*h*, pp. 210–11; 1913*k*, pp. 988–9). In fact, 'all the parties except Social Democracy' had disarmed before 'almighty, all-devouring militarism' (1913*k*, p. 988):

Nobody in the ranks of the middle classes dares touch the root of the evil. They have disarmed before militarism. Some are intoxicated by Jingoism. But the majority have given up every idea of influencing the foreign policy of the Empire. (1913*a*, p. 16)

What was to be done? Against the engines of militarism and war the struggle for peace, in Bernstein's view, had to be waged not internationally but at the national level and under the slogan of 'justice'. Right up to the outbreak of the First World War in 1914 he insisted that this struggle could be waged with confidence, for he never ceased to believe that the 'grand panacea' of commerce was steadily transforming civilised society, in Herbert Spencer's terminology, from a militant to an industrial type in which warfare and its associated evils became increasingly obsolete and impractical or, as Norman Angell argued in *The Great Illusion* (1910), unprofitable and therefore impossible (see Spencer, 1969, pp. 499–571; Peel, 1971, pp. 192–223; Wiltshire, 1978, pp. 243–56). As Bernstein told the Reichstag on 14 May 1912,

> We [Social Democrats] have the great developments of the age, the broad development of history, on our side . . . In spite of all the armaments, all the tariff walls you erect, the whole of modern life is becoming more international from year to year, thanks to economic development, which, mightier than all the rest, breaks through all impediments. An intricate network of all manner of bonds – commercial, scientific, connections of every kind – today extends over the globe; the whole of modern life is becoming international. (RTV, vol. 285, p. 7996)

Across the Channel, Radicals like Hobson and Brailsford were saying exactly the same thing, insisting that 'the vast and increasing trade we have with France, Germany, Russia and the United States is the most potent guarantee of peace which we possess' (Hobson 1938*b*, p. 343). A generation later, J. M. Keynes was still arguing that the competitive struggle for markets as a cause of war could be eliminated, for

> if nations can learn to provide themselves with full employment by their domestic policy . . . there need be no important economic forces calculated to set the interest of one country against that of its neighbours . . . International trade would cease to be what it is, namely, a desperate expedient to maintain employment at home by forcing sales on foreign markets and restricting purchases, which, if successful, will merely shift the problem of unemployment to the neighbour which is worsted in the struggle, but a willing and unimpeded exchange of goods and services in conditions of mutual advantage. (Keynes, 1936, pp. 382–3)

Nor is this congruence in the least fortuitous. What Bernstein the revisionist had in common with Hobson, Keynes and others was an intellectual ancestry which went back to Cobden via Spencer, J. S. Mill, Gladstone and Bright. On many occasions Bernstein acknowledged his admiration of, and indebtedness to, Cobden (1907*d*, p. 225; SPD A.C., p. 420; 1918*f*, p. 28), as he also did in the case of Spencer and positivism (1909*k*, p. 1091; 1924, p. 40). Indeed, his prewar writings, including his German publications, are so replete with references to his British Radical mentors that the 'Anglo-Saxon' reader is, or ought to be, more than a little puzzled by the persistence with which Continental scholarship – Hans-Christoph Schröder being a notable exception (1978*a*, pp. 166–212) – either ignores this dimension to the mature Bernstein or forces it into the procrustean bed of his alleged Fabianism.

Pending the attainment of what Joseph Schumpeter (also, by his own admission, much indebted to Herbert Spencer) later idealised as 'pure capitalism', the appropriate remedy against militarism seemed to Bernstein to lie in educating public opinion, as well as socialist opinion, to the necessity of free trade and representative democracy. Only in this manner could the dualism of army and nation, this 'double-entry book-keeping' (1915c, pp. 2–3), be abolished and peace assured. Bernstein admitted, with regret, that 'the contagion of the *policy of power* [*Machtpolitik*] and its diplomatic principles' (italics in original) had acquired such a stranglehold on all the non-socialist parties in Germany that there remained, apart from Social Democracy, 'no party and no politician of standing who could be described as a guardian of the vital interests of the trade and commerce of his country and of the well-being of humanity at large' (1911f, p. 550). His solution was that of Hobson and Cobden: more democracy. Although there seemed to be 'no way out as long as the present organisation of society lasts', for which 'nothing short of a revolutionary upheaval [appeared] adequate' (1913a, p. 16), the masses, at least, were 'impregnated . . . with a sense of their mission as the guardians of peace between the nations' (1908h, p. 758). Setting little store by international peace action and declining to underwrite the use of the strike weapon for any purpose other than defence of the universal suffrage, his 'revolutionary upheaval' on behalf of peace amounted to no more than the attainment of full democracy in Prussia and the Reich (1892/3, p. 296; 1909a, pp. 928–9; 1909i, p. 784; 1911h, p. 56; 1919a, p. 134). Quite alien to his thinking was the belief of radical and orthodox Marxists that lasting peace would follow only in the wake of a socialist revolution induced by a capitalist breakdown. If Bernstein's prewar anti-militarism thus merits no more than the tag of 'pacificism', the conditionality of his pacifist internationalism emerges still more starkly from such concessions to militarism as his insistence on the duty to national defence, his approval of colonial wars and his condemnation of Karl Leibknecht's anti-militarist agitation as pandering to foreign chauvinists (see Fletcher, 1982c, pp. 27–9), all of which places Bernstein much closer to J. S. Mill and W. E. Gladstone than to mainstream Cobdenism (see Flournoy, 1946, pp. 195–217; Taylor, 1957, pp. 67–94; K. E. Miller, 1961, pp. 493–514; Summerton, 1977, pp. 151–78; Kennedy, 1981, pp. 102–3), much nearer the later Engels than Marx (see Kitchen, 1977, pp. 122–3).

After August 1914, Bernstein adopted a more explicit, systematic and consistent stance on this problem, even to the point of accepting much of the Hobson–Hilferding analysis and seriously considering active collaboration with anti-militarist revolutionaries like Karl Liebknecht. The practical outcome, however, was a reconciliation with the 'renegade' Kautsky and former centre-left spokesmen like Hugo Haase, leading to Bernstein's uncomfortable and brief membership (he rejoined the SPD immediately after the war) in the anti-war coalition of the Independent Social Democratic Party (USPD). During his long career as the principal ideologue of revisionism, it was only at this time that he came close to applying Marxist categories, as opposed to those of the later Engels. In general, Bernstein's theory of war, besides reflecting the inescapable influence of 'the general', as Engels was known to intimates – and Bernstein was certainly among these intimates[8] – suggests, above all, a strong affinity with the views of Cobden, Spencer and J. S. Mill. Yet in relation to British contemporary views on this particular issue, Bernstein probably occupied more common ground with the Liberal Imperialists, the Fabians and the 'national efficiency' group than with those recalcitrant Radicals who later formed the core of the Union of Democratic Control and eventually went over to the Labour Party.

Following the death of Engels, Bernstein plainly ceased to be a Marxist and became instead a liberal internationalist cast in the Cobdenite mould. His method was eclectic and empirical, and his views on tariff policy, the nationality question and militarism clearly betrayed a large measure of utopian optimism and idealism as well as an attachment to democracy as being no less grand a panacea than the free trade principle. The implications for his position within the SPD were considerable. Since most of his fellow-revisionists, from the rare intellectuals to the reformists and party practitioners or *Praktiker*, were protectionists and Anglophobes, if not nationalists and imperialists, Bernstein was at best tolerated as a useful figurehead for the revisionist movement. On the party left, Bernstein's Enlightenment progressivism filtered through a Cobdenite lens was greeted as reactionary apostasy, for Marxist radicals like Rosa Luxemburg and Karl Liebknecht, being interested only in the imperialism versus socialist revolution dualism, regarded protectionism, nationalism and militarism not as discrete aberrations but as inevitable concomitants of capitalism in the age of imperialism. Bernstein had most in common with the Janus-faced party centre, but as each side approached this median point via a different avenue, until August 1914 he continued to be pilloried as a heretic for daring to speak what the custodians of Marxist orthodoxy only practised. Yet his own position was also crammed with inconsistencies. Perhaps most damaging was Bernstein's assumption that it was possible to be at once a German patriot and a genuine internationalist, both a reasonable nationalist and a good European. Following the example of early and mid-Victorian free trade imperialists, he took it for granted that the world was large enough to accommodate a spiritually and economically conceived Greater Germany without involving the nation in undesirable collisions and entanglements with other European powers. As we now know, this assumption, posited on faith in the 'invisible hand' and what Hobson termed a sublime 'confidence in peaceful democracy as an accepted principle of political evolution' (Hobson, 1938a, p. 94), proved to be entirely unfounded.

Imperialism and Colonialism

Unlike Hobson, Hilferding, or Luxemburg, Bernstein never elaborated a coherent theory of imperialism, but he did attach major importance to the problem, manifesting an informed and continuing interest which related both to his revisionism and to his liberal internationalism. In general, he took an essentially benign view of the phenomenon, which appeared to him at worst as an expiring remnant of an ancient evil, at best as a less than ideal stepping-stone, if not to Kautsky's 'ultra-imperialism', then at least to greater international harmony.

Bernstein's phenomenology of imperialism is not easy to specify with any degree of precision. Part of the difficulty arises from his reluctance to 'synthesise' on the subject, for he believed, as he put it in 1900, that 'imperialism and imperialism are two quite (or completely) different things' (1900b, p. 241), by which he meant imperia were open to meaningful discussion only in their particular spatio-temporal and national configurations. Moreover, his views exhibited considerable vagueness and inconsistency on crucial points, including the novelty of imperialism, its relation to capitalism and its position on the progress-reaction continuum. Much of this ambiguity stems from the fact that his views, like those of J. A. Hobson, changed over time. Both Hobson and Bernstein appear to have found a starting-point in Herbert Spencer's distinction between militant and industrial societies. Bernstein not only expressed his own admiration of English positivism but claimed that in some respects Marx and Engels were similarly indebted, more so than to Hegel (1890/1c, p. 732; 1904f, vol. 3, p. 83; 1909k, p. 1091). Certainly, Hobson had no qualms about owning to Spencer's 'profound influence' on his early development (Hobson, 1938a, p. 23), and there can be no doubt that Bernstein knew Hobson personally (Hobson, 1938a, pp. 84–5) or that he was familiar with, and well-disposed towards, Hobson's early work,[9] although he never accepted the underconsumption argument, whether expounded by Hobson or Rodbertus. In Kautsky's *Neue Zeit* (1893/4, pp. 504–7), it was Bernstein who reviewed *The Evolution of Modern Capitalism* – on the whole, favourably, and in a manner which Hobson judged 'most thoughtful and cogent' (BP, D 280: Hobson to Bernstein, 21 September 1911 [sic]). By 1898, however, Hobson had shifted his perspective from a relatively positive attitude to the highly critical position which first gained expression in the *Contemporary Review* in 1898 (for which Bernstein also wrote), to be fully elaborated in his imperialism study of 1902. Bernstein did not follow him in this change and had already left Britain by 1902. In his 'bible of revisionism' Bernstein did not even use the term imperialism. At this point, his image of imperialism was still that of a largely progressive, novel, politically neutral phenomenon tending towards excess and paralleling capitalist development without being a necessary consequence of capitalism.

By November 1912, when he delivered a lecture before the Sociological Society in Vienna on 'the alternatives of imperialism' (reported in the Viennese *Arbeiter-Zeitung* of 15 November 1912 in an unsigned article entitled 'Imperialism, its significance and future'),[10] his views had altered to the extent that he now described imperialism as related to *some* capitalist interests, as possessing political and economic as well as cultural features, yet, at bottom, a timeless and archaic problem at odds with modern development, tending to socially and psychologically motivated excess, while still ultimately progressive in function. Here he defined imperialism as 'the urge to create political entities consisting of more than a single nationality or people' and identified its motive force as 'the drive to domination'. (In 1919 Schumpeter was to define it as 'the objectless disposition on the part of the state to unlimited forcible expansion' [1951, p. 7].) Its Achilles' heel was its immoderacy, for the capacity to rule was often outstripped by an inordinate 'lust to dominate'. Bernstein here distinguished two forms of imperialism – the ancient, of which Rome afforded the most familiar example, and the modern variety (already in its death-throes) exemplified by the British world empire. The twin forces destroying modern imperialism were indicated as the internationalisation of commerce, which was outgrowing the institutions of even the greatest of empires, and the rise of the international socialist labour movement, which represented a formidable obstacle to future wars of conquest. The progressive function of all imperialisms was discerned in their creation of a 'cosmopolitan consciousness' and of a broader material basis for peace and the rule of law. Out of the organic development of existing imperia, Bernstein predicted the emergence of a 'league of civilised peoples' incorporating 'the socialisation of humanity'. Such notions are customarily attributed to a Continental ancestry, such as Saint-Simon's *De la Réorganisation de la société européenne* (1814), but Tennyson's 'parliament of man, the federation of the world' (*Locksley Hall*, 1838), was also part and parcel of the British Radical tradition. In 1846 Richard Cobden had envisaged world government as a distant goal (Cobden, 1878, p. 187), and J. S. Mill, despite his greater pessimism, 'did hold out some slight hope for a federation among European nations [and] the establishment of a league of nations' (K. E. Miller, 1961, p. 503).

Bernstein's parallels with Cobden, Spencer and Schumpeter, as well as his contrast with the anti-imperialist Hobson, are too obvious to require further comment. The point from which Bernstein never wavered was his 1897 insistence on the impossibility of inferring an adequate explanation of the 'new imperialism' from untenable political generalisations based on artificial distinctions between industrial and finance capital or derived from an empirically false prognosis of the long-term viability of the capitalist system (1904*f*, vol. 2, pp. 110–22. See also [1899] 1921, pp. 72–128; TP, 543/10: Bernstein to P. J. Troelstra, 2 March 1915). He would most assuredly have agreed with Keynes that the 'taproot of imperialism' was to be found in the realm of ideas rather than in the catacombs of vested interests. Indeed, in April 1907 he dismissed the emerging neo-Marxist theory of imperialism as a pessimistic generalisation of peculiarly German and therefore atypical conditions, as being 'partly the outcome of a catastrophical conception of modern evolution in contradiction to the conception of progressive evolution, and partly the reflection of the political conditions of Germany and the nature of the German Government and the German Government parties' (1907*d*, p. 225). He would equally have agreed with Hobson's later diagnosis of his own anti-imperialist phase as the product of 'an excessive and too simple advocacy of the economic determination of history' (Hobson, 1938*a*, p. 63).

Bernstein was much more at home, and prolific, coping with particular imperialisms. One reason for his preference was perhaps the fact that, as he admitted with disarming frankness, his was very definitely an 'analytical' brain which experienced great difficulty with 'synthesis' (1924, p. 7). Another was his Anglophilia, for just as 'Marx, like Say, indicated a firm preference for the British over other empires' (Semmel, 1970, p. 210), Bernstein found it more comforting and historically valid to generalise from British experience which, if it be deemed a 'Kehrite' failing, placed him in the company of Marx and the vast majority of contemporary observers. He had no hesitation in taking as his model the progressive and democratic free trade imperialism of Britain, which he described as widening the world's free trade area and a mere tidying-up of the 'administrative Manchesterism' of earlier decades (1900*b*, p. 244). This vast emporium, if it was no more acquired 'in a fit of absent-mindedness' than were the empires of Periclean Athens or Republican Rome, impressed Bernstein as being beneficial to colonial peoples, in no way anti-German or otherwise exclusive, but still an object lesson in the pitfalls of 'immoderacy' (see Fletcher, 1979*b*, pp. 254–6).

He was especially prone to drawing unflattering comparisons between the liberal imperialism of Britain and the reactionary imperialist aspirations of undemocratic and semi-feudal Wilhelmine Germany. Although prepared to concede that *some* capitalist interests had acquired a stake in German imperialism, he saw its essential motive force in the anachronistic and ephemeral ideological climate of 'superpatriotism', militarism and protectionism, which he dismissed as having no vital or necessary link with capitalism as a system. In anticipation of the 'Kehrite' analysis he identified two basic and contradictory tendencies at work in this bellicose 'atavism': one was anti-Russian, the other anti-British, each nurturing overseas ambitions as well, and both were anti-modernist flanking manoeuvres against the social and political concomitants of economic and technological progress. For him, Kaiser Wilhelm II epitomised the central contradiction of German society:

William II is a shrewd observer, and knows well to appreciate the increasing industrialisation of society. He sees that the Prussia of old is fast dying out, and that the towns and industrial centres will in the long run not stand the political predominance of squire and parson. Thus he gives more and more heed to the counsels of the merchant-princes and the captains of industry whilst trying to educate his Prussian squires to a more modern conception of politics. For he cannot do without them. They and the peasantry form an indispensable element of the army, its very foundation, the upholder of its traditions, the cement that secures its cohesion in a crisis. Here you have the contradiction in William II's personality, and the antinomy in his Government. On the one hand he desires to go with the times. He sees all the changes that are proceeding around him, and to a certain degree he grasps their meaning, and tries to adapt his policy to them. On the other hand he wishes to retain the character of an institution of such a formidable complexion as the army of universal conscription. The army is to him still the first interest of the State. (1907*a*, p. 234)

Although even after 1914 Bernstein admitted that social imperialism, or 'the directing outwards of internally menacing tensions', was 'a device of government that [had] been known and practised long before Machiavelli' (1916*b*, p. 3), and although he continued to speak of the need to oppose only *aggressive* imperialism (1918*e*, p. 3), he was adamant that 'as an Empire Germany corresponds in a high degree to Bonapartist Imperialism'. 'Democratic control of the foreign policy of the country' was 'less fully realised in Germany than in any other European country, Russia excepted' (1913*a*, p. 16). For this reason, he flatly rejected as a matter of principle any suggestion that Wilhelmine world policy merited Social Democratic support. By 1911 he was expatiating on the bankruptcy of German policy, which had effectively painted itself into a corner without registering any worthwhile colonial or other gains. What began to alarm him was the resultant fatalistic acceptance of the topos of inevitable war, as manifested not only by the ruling élites but in the populace at large (see W. Mommsen, 1981, pp. 23–45). His solution, however, remained unaffected by such portents of impending catastrophe: although fully cognisant of the impediments to progress in Germany, he stubbornly adhered to his Radical credo of enlightening public opinion and advocacy of a bloc of the left to realise the magic wand of democracy in Prussia and the Reich (1912*b*, pp. 141–7; 1912*e*, pp. 650–6).

The Schumpeter analogy can also be extended to Bernstein's much more intensive treatment of the problem of colonialism. Schumpeter, in his 1919 imperialism essay, declined to regard colonies under free trade as features of imperialism, since they conferred no exclusive advantages on the metropolitan power and could not be seen as objects of exploitation (1951, p. 15). Not far removed from this was Bernstein's distinction between imperialism (condoned if conducted under democratic and free trade auspices) and colonialism, which he broadly approved, even in the case of protectionist, nationalistic and militaristic Germany. How is this seemingly artificial and casuistic dichotomy to be explained? It is not impossible that on this point Bernstein was simply confused, for he was unquestionably as well informed on the colonial issue as any socialist of the Second International. In the 1880s, as editor of the illegal SPD newspaper, *Der Sozial-Demokrat*, and one of the three individuals primarily responsible for the adoption of Marxism as the dominant and official ideology of German Social Democracy, he had implacably opposed colonialism in any shape or form, most notably during the steamship subvention crisis of 1884–5. After a few years in England, and under constant exposure to the direct influence not only of Engels but also of the Fabians, Radicals, 'Limps' (Liberal Imperialists, whose ranks included not a few Fabians), ethical socialists à la Keir Hardie and trade unionists, Bernstein suffered a nervous breakdown and had to be sent to Zurich for a cure. It is unlikely that the effects of this 'neurasthenia' proved to be 'of the long-lasting variety' (Kapp, 1976, p. 553n.), but it is conceivable that in the course of his subsequent rethinking of his Marxism Bernstein never succeeded in sorting out a fully coherent position on colonialism or in wholly integrating this with his newly acquired perspectives on other issues.

Formative influences on his colonial revisionism may nevertheless be identified. Since he did not believe in the existence of a realisation problem under capitalism, Bernstein was little impressed by the neo-Marxist argument that colonisation represented a safety-valve for a stagnating capitalist economy or an insurance against the vagaries of the business cycle. He may, however, have retained some sympathy with Marx's own view of colonialism as a hallmark of capitalism in its infancy, and he was not unmoved by the Hegelian and positivist view that for any society to leap over a stage of historical evolution was neither desirable nor possible. He certainly followed Marx in believing that the worldwide expansion of industrial capitalism was inevitable and objectively progressive, that the destruction of 'backward' economic and social systems was no cause for regret or humanitarian 'mawkishness' (1896/7c, p. 109; 1900c, p. 551), that the formation of large-scale economic and political entities was historically progressive and 'necessary', and that all this was ultimately to the benefit of humanity. On the other hand, Bernstein also contended that colonialism 'would exist even if there were no capitalism and no capitalist-feudal militarism' (1907h, p. 989).

A parallel which cannot be overlooked is John Stuart Mill's view that although colonies conferred little benefit on the colonising power, they were defensible, even desirable, in the broader interest of humanity and of progress (1867a, pp. 123, 131–41; 1867b, pp. 167–9). Among Bernstein's favourite phrases was the description of his own era as 'the age of global intercourse', and he evidently thought of colonialism, no less than free trade, as a cardinal ingredient in the *Zeitgeist*, so that where J. S. Mill rhapsodised on the benefactions of commerce, Bernstein would have interpreted colonisation as a sub-set of expanding international trade. Certainly Bernstein would have endorsed Mill's view that

> the economical advantages of commerce are surpassed in importance by those of its effects which are intellectual and moral. It is hardly possible to overrate the value, in the present low state of human improvement, of placing human beings in contact with persons dissimilar to themselves, and with modes of thought and action unlike those with which they are familiar. Commerce is now what war once was, the principal source of this contact. Commercial adventurers from more advanced countries have generally been the first civilizers of barbarians. And commerce is the purpose of the far greater part of the communication which takes place between civilized nations. Such communication has always been, and is peculiarly in the present age, one of the primary sources of progress . . . It is commerce which is rapidly rendering war obsolete, by strengthening and multiplying the personal interests which are in natural opposition to it. And it may be said without exaggeration that the great extent and rapid increase of international trade, in being the principal guarantee of the peace of the world, is the great permanent security for the uninterrupted progress of the ideas, the institutions, and the character of the human race. (Mill [1848], 1976, pp. 581–2; cf. Bernstein, 1897/8b, p. 751; 1897/8c, p. 556; 1906b, pp. 10, 63–4)

In contrast to the thought of mainstream classical economics, and despite his insistence that colonialism had nothing to do with capitalism *per se*, Bernstein clearly envisaged colonisation as an analogue and agent of trade, civilisation and progress.

An additional factor which appears to have entered into his ken was the traditional nineteenth-century British view that colonies and free trade imperialism represented a welcome alternative to European entanglements. A. J. P. Taylor has attributed this attitude exclusively to the Radicals or 'troublemakers': 'Imperialism was a product of radical enthusiasm. The imperialists were isolationists so far as Europe went. They wanted to ignore the

Continent and discharge the "British mission" in the rest of the world' (1957, p. 90). In fact, the true exponent of this position was Disraeli rather than Gladstone, although it was Gladstone, in his occupation of Egypt, who proved to be its more effective practitioner. Bernstein had no qualms in defending either Gladstone or British free trade imperialism as providing a bulwark against Russia and as having 'performed infinitely greater services to the cause of liberty in Europe than we enlightened Germans have so far done'. Contemplating expansion as an index of national vitality, he argued that

> every vigorous race and every robust economy, together with its cultural superstructure, strives towards expansion. In all ages this drive has been a potent factor in evolutionary progress . . . Violence and coercion have always existed in this world . . . In principle, I am in full agreement with those preaching a crusade against colonial chauvinism. But I am of the opinion that this crusade is condemned to futility as long as endeavours to enlarge by colonial expansion the economic sphere of one's own nation (endeavours such as do not involve the nation in conflicts with other civilised peoples) are not differentiated from the kind of colonial policy which is directed against one of the advanced nations of the civilised world. Only the latter merits thoroughgoing opposition. (1900*c*, pp. 552–3, 556)

Thus George Lichtheim's dictum that 'nationalism transformed itself into imperialism wherever the opportunity offered' (1971, p. 81) might be transcribed, in Bernstein's case, as patriotic progressivism transforming itself into colonialism wherever the opportunity for national expansion might be exploited without risk of great-power collisions. He remained implacably opposed to any 'alteration of the map of Europe, which under present circumstances could be achieved only at the price of bloody wars' (1907*k*, p. 439).

In Bernstein's definition, colonialism entailed territorial expansion, permanent settlement and the transference of a particular and higher culture (1900*c*, p. 550). *Vis-à-vis* the lower civilisation, he maintained, 'the higher culture always has the greater right on its side; if necessary, it has the historical right, even the duty, to subjugate the former' (ibid., p. 551), for

> Humanity is not yet advanced enough to forego the application of force under all circumstances. Where two civilisations clash, the lower must give way to the higher. This law of evolution we cannot overthrow, we can only humanise its action. To counteract it would mean to postpone social progress. (1907*c*, p. 47)

This much-vaunted *force majeure* of 'higher culture' was to be found 'where there exist the prerequisites for the optimal enlargement, on a given area of land, of the possibilities for sustaining human life, the preconditions for the greatest possible material, intellectual and aesthetic enrichment of human life, and for the attachment of the highest value to the worth of man as an individual personality' (1907*h*, p. 993). Elsewhere, to be sure, he appealed to a highly materialistic concept of progress and civilisation, advancing utility as the ultimate criterion of right ([1899] 1921, p. 211; 1900c, p. 553; 1915e, p. 537). The right of colonisation he derived equally from humanitarian and Social Darwinist considerations, thus offering, as he believed, 'at one and the same time a humanitarian and a rational concept of the struggle for existence between races and peoples' (1900c, p. 551).

He admitted that colonialism could prove deleterious, and he noted its most dangerous excesses as exorbitant territorial expansion (such as might threaten economic stability or retard social development in the metropolitan power), the possibility of peripheral problems reacting on the centre as great-power conflict, and failure to devote proper attention to the welfare of native peoples, who deserved to be 'afforded that measure of protection to which they are entitled by virtue of their cultural development and needs' (ibid., p. 561). Yet the existence of such excesses offered no argument against colonisation as such, for they were mere excrescences or aberrations, and 'the advantages of colonisation could be achieved without them' (ibid., p. 559).

When discussing these advantages, Bernstein was careful to emphasise his conviction that profitability could not be the sole or even the main criterion of a progressive and therefore legitimate colonialism. 'Whether the increased [colonial] expenditure will ever be justified by corresponding benefits for the nation that will have to pay them', he wrote in March 1907, 'only the future can show' (1907j, p. 13). Even so, he believed that colonies were beneficial not only to the ruling classes of the metropolitan powers but equally to the European workers, the native peoples and humanity as a whole. His concept of benefit, like J. S. Mill's, clearly transcended immediate material advantages. At all times, though with greater poignancy after 1911, Bernstein was at pains to underline the limits and relativity of these advantages. Thus he consistently argued that there was no intrinsic relationship between prosperity and empire (as there was between prosperity and socialism), that colonies could be as much a burden as a source of wealth, and that their economic value must be seen very largely in terms of future return on present investment. Although, as early as 1907, he noted 'the narrow connection of the Colonial policy of the Empire with the so-called *world policy* of increased armaments and international meddling' (italics in original), which he identified as 'the predominant reason' why German socialists would continue to oppose German colonial policy (1907c, p. 46), it was only after 1911 that he began to take this connection seriously. At about the same time he began to accentuate more heavily than previously the superior value of trade among advanced industrial nations over the modest returns to be had from commerce between colonial powers and their respective formal and informal dependencies (1911b, pp. 32–42). As he put this point in March 1912, 'If one country can serve as an object-lesson that a nation can grow strong and wealthy without big fleets and colonial possessions, it is Germany' (1912j, p. 1057). In the last years of peace he went further and took a leaf from the neo-Marxist[11] book of imperialist horrors to warn that, in view of the visibly awakening Third World liberation movements, the era of formal empire was already at an end (ibid., p. 1057; RTV, vol. 285 [14 May 1912], p. 1995, vol. 295 [15 May 1914], p. 8886).[12] However, like Schumpeter and others, he still failed to distinguish clearly between formal and informal empire, between colonialism and the imperialism of free trade. In short, once he perceived extra-European entanglements as exacerbating existing great-power tensions and reinforcing the negative features of 'atavistic' imperialism, Bernstein ceased to commend colonialism as a duty to progress. Coincidentally, J. A. Hobson also reverted to a more consistently Cobdenite position at this time (see Cain, 1979*b*, pp. 423–4), joining the 'Angellites' in their crusade for peace as a matter of economic rationality (see Hobson, 1913; Hollenberg, 1974, pp. 60–113; Chickering, 1975, pp. 309–17).

On the colonial question the essential Bernstein thus emerges as a creature of Darwinian progressivism inspired by a diversity of sources which included Marx and Engels while owing at least as much to elements of the British Radical tradition which had made such a deep and lasting impression on him during his London exile. Yet there was another, no less significant dimension to Bernstein as colonial 'realist', for the revisionist would-be bloc-builder also presented, during his pro-colonialist heyday (roughly 1896–1907), a largely Fabian-inspired set of *ad hoc* arguments tailored to a German working-class or socialist audience. To be sure, the Fabian Society did not adopt a definite and common position on the colonial question until 1900, and then only after much controversy, but the 'national efficiency' viewpoint of Shaw and the Webbs had long been common knowledge and was certainly known to Bernstein. When Shaw's *Fabianism and the Empire* appeared in 1900, Bernstein at once applauded it[13] and henceforth applied it as a buttress to his Social Darwinist authorities, 'the three great theorists of modern Socialism, Karl Marx, Frederic Engels, and Ferdinand Lassalle' (1907*c*, p. 47).

Obviously with an eye to the anticipated criticism of Kautsky and the party orthodoxy, the revisionist heretic frequently affirmed his belief that there could be no question of socialists supporting the colonial policies of the existing state: at issue was merely the appropriate vindication of socialist anti-colonialism ([1899] 1921, pp. 208–9; MISC, 1907, p. 28). He then customarily added the rider that colonies existed and therefore required a 'positive socialist colonial policy'. In determining such a policy, socialists were urged to take into account a multiplicity of considerations, all of them calculated to enlist socialist support for an active German *Kolonialpolitik* both in the present and in the future. Despite his scepticism regarding the actual worth of colonies, Bernstein occasionally employed the argument of economic need, presumably in deference to its widespread support in trade union circles ([1899] 1921, p. 211; 1900*a*, pp. 711–14). Socialists were advised to weigh in the scales the interests of civilisation and humanitarian duties to 'backward' peoples, and in so doing they were adjured not to overlook the question of race, for civilised peoples were competing for living space both with one another and with 'the Mongol peril' (1900*c*, pp. 560–1; 1907*h*, pp. 989, 996). All this was, of course, supported with quotations from the 'revered masters' – a game which could also be played by revisionist social imperialists, as he was to observe with disgust during the First World War (see, for example, 1915*g*, pp. 1–3). At the 1907 Stuttgart congress of the Second International, in a disingenuous attempt to tap even left-wing sympathies, Bernstein repeated his earlier appeal to the 'socialism in one country' argument: until the victory of the socialist world revolution, he argued, any single socialist state must of necessity look to its defences as an island in a turbulent and inhospitable capitalist sea, and in this context the inheritance of a colonial bulwark could prove an invaluable asset ([1899] 1921, pp. 205, 211; MISC, 1907, pp. 28–9). Not surprisingly, the party radicals failed to flock to his colonialist standard, for it had long been a revisionist article of faith that there could be no sudden qualitative leap into socialism, only a gradual 'growing into socialism', which would differ from capitalism chiefly in degree. What may seem more surprising is the fact that he deemed it worth the opprobrium he encountered to enter a bid for support from this quarter. Yet the ardour with which prominent centrists and leftists like Alexander Parvus-Helphand, Paul Lensch, Heinrich Cunow and Konrad Haenisch later threw their energies into the propagation of the 'German mission' suggests that the miscarriage of Bernstein's ploy was by no means a foregone conclusion.

The zealous lack of scruple with which Bernstein solicited all potential socialist support for the principle of colonial expansion, when viewed in conjunction with his concept of socialism as an incompletely attainable *ideal* to which society could but gradually approximate, suggests a solution to the apparent contradiction in his imperialism-colonialism dichotomy. Whereas the neo-Marxist or proto-Leninist apocalyptic vision differentiated sharply between present evils (colonialism, militarism, nationalism, protectionism, monopoly capitalism, etc., all subsumed under imperialism as the highest and final stage in the development of capitalism) and a future utopia where, following the radical surgery of socialist revolution, all such afflictions abruptly lost their *raison d'être* and entered the 'dustbin of history', Bernstein *qua* revisionist had no such crutch and was obliged to confront directly the problem of future needs in terms of existing realities. With near-perfect consistency, his 'made-in-England' nineteenth-century progressivism thus dovetailed with his simultaneous rejection of 'atavistic' imperialism and his tortuous defence of a 'realistic' colonialism as an essentially culturally conceived variable of his concept of progress. He considered colonialism as having a legitimate claim on socialist support for the same reason as free trade. Both marked the progress of humanity towards a higher evolutionary stage. Imperialism, as a temporary reversion to a more primitive stage of development, deserved only condemnation and opposition, especially where it presumed to emulate the work of progress (colonisation) by reactionary means (protectionism, nationalism and militarism) and in pursuit of reactionary ends (the 'lust to dominate', which was the polar opposite of that co-operative spirit which he regarded as the hallmark of the more advanced 'age of global intercourse'). It was this conceptual framework, borrowed from Herbert Spencer and anticipating Schumpeter, which enabled Bernstein to apparently square the circle by approving British imperialism and rejecting German imperialism while generally condoning colonialism.

The internal consistency of his views nevertheless fell well short of completeness, for his position revealed baneful contradictions and deficiencies. Thus there was obvious inconsistency in his arguing that Germany had no need of colonies while simultaneously welcoming the seizure of Kiaochow and demanding a 'positive socialist colonial policy' which presupposed the present and future necessity of a German colonial empire. To take another example, his distinction between imperialism and colonialism, as a failure to recognise the imperialism of free trade, is open to the same kinds of objections that have been raised against Schumpeter's theory (see Kemp, 1967, pp. 86–105; W. Mommsen, 1980, pp. 26–7). More serious was his inability to perceive the fateful bifurcation of the labour movement in consequence of the rise of a labour aristocracy suborned, if not by the superprofits of finance capitalism, then certainly by the blandishments of national egoism. Bernstein can fairly be accused of having inadvertently contributed to the latter process. At the very least, he sowed doubt and confusion – by his racist appeals against 'the Mongol peril', for instance, and by proselytising on behalf of a socialist colonial policy. Given his limited political following, his personal responsibility must not be exaggerated, and he was by no means alone in his ambivalent colonialism. Within the Second International his position was closely paralleled by that of Jean Jaurès (see H. Mitchell, 1966, pp. 22–45), and Karl Kautsky, despite his formally negative stance on the colonial issue, operated from similar premises to arrive ultimately, in his imperialism essay of 1914 (1913/14, pp. 909–22), at an analogous result. Within the revisionist camp there were many more blatant champions of German imperialism than Bernstein. Yet those socialist workers and trade union functionaries who read Bernstein (the intellectual revisionists thought their own thoughts) generally found him sandwiched in between writers like Gerhard Hildebrand, Ludwig Woltmann (an exponent of bio-logical nationalism), Karl Leuthner and Richard Calwer. They can hardly be blamed for detecting little significant difference between the qualified colonialism of the 'arch-revisionist' and the more overtly nationalistic imperialism of his nominal allies, particularly since the battle-lines were drawn against a bewildering backdrop of conflicting party and factional loyalties. In 1907, for instance, August Bebel was obliged to deny in the Reichstag that Bernstein and Calwer – as alike as chalk and cheese – supported colonialism and imperialism (RTV, vol. 227 [26 February 1907], p. 48), a thankless task since Bebel's closest parliamentary colleague, the centre-leftist Georg Ledebour, had years beforehand publicly branded Bernstein as a carrier of 'the imperialist plague' (Ledebour, SPD A.C., 1900, p. 167). For reasons of group solidarity Bernstein also found himself driven to defending outrageous chauv-inists like Hildebrand and Noske, although his private view was that such people needed to have their ears boxed (1912c, pp. 1147–50).

Bernstein won so little discerning appreciation of his views largely because of the alien quality of so much of his thought. On this point, he revealed little enough of Cobden or of Hobson, but his confusing mélange of J. S. Mill, W. E. Gladstone, Herbert Spencer, Fabianism, Liberal Imperialism and Lib–Lab thinking made him signally unintelligible to the vast majority of his German comrades. If they perceived a liberal dimension to Bernstein's heresy, as several did, this did not endear him to his German public, which had come to equate liberalism either with the 'hypocrisy' of 'Professor Gladstone' or with the class egoism and bellicose imperialism of German National Liberalism. In the final analysis, his colonial views bear comparison not with those of Hilferding, Luxemburg and Lenin, or even with Kautsky's, but with such writings as Shaw's *Fabianism and the Empire* (1900) and Ramsay MacDonald's *Labour and the Empire* (1907). That he was less consistent or less Marxist than a Hilferding or a Kautsky appears, when viewed in this light, less a source of wonderment than the fact that he ever bothered to clothe his British Radical-ism in pseudo-Marxist garb.

As to Bernstein's overall perspective on imperialism, one is drawn back to the Schumpeter parallel. Both Bernstein and Schumpeter were Anglophile free-traders who generalised from the British model. Accordingly, and regard-less of their respective deficiencies, what has been said of Schumpeter could be applied with equal validity to Bernstein, namely that his 'central point, that imperialism is predominantly an affair of politicians, courtiers and military men, [offers] the weightiest arguments against the Marxist theories of imperialism' (Kemp, 1967, p. 105). Coming from a Marxist, this is high praise indeed. Nor is it unwarranted, for Bernstein's admittedly inchoate theory proved in many respects astonishingly prescient, accurate and of considerable immediate utility, and it was unquestionably a far cry from the rantings of Karl Leuthner and others of that species. On the other hand, he offered no real remedy to the problem, merely a reiteration of Goethe's plea for 'more light' and a restatement of the old Benthamite call for greater democracy and a more enlightened public opinion. But neither, as it turned out, did those of more impeccably Marxist theoretical credentials. The revolutions which toppled thrones at the close of the First World War terminated neither capitalism, imperialism, nationalism nor militarism: with one exception, they were merely a reverberation of 1789. This exception was the Bolshevik Revolution of 1917. As Bernstein rightly objected at the time, Bolshevism was not an aberration born of revolutionary expediency but a consistent application of undemocratic principles that threatened to turn the first 'workers' state' into a reactionary and anti-social military despotism. Such a tyranny, he warned, could not lead humanity forward to democracy and socialism; it could issue only in yet another barbaric atavism harking back to the age of the Caesars (1918c, pp. 5–8).

Plainly, Bernstein was not at all a neo-Kantian but an eclectic empiricist and a Radical democrat much indebted to British inspiration. Nowhere is this more glaringly apparent than in his foreign policy thinking, his chief preoccupation between his return to Germany and the First World War. Like Marx and Engels, only still more so, he was very much a product of his age and his environment, which stamped him, above all else, as a transplanted British Radical. It is a simple truth, yet it bears repetition, for it is as widely ignored today as previously: 'Much of the work that socialism stood for in continental Europe was the work of Liberalism in England; conversely, in a country like Germany progress was represented by Social Democracy. This analysis was in effect reciprocated by Eduard Bernstein, [whose] own reading of what revisionism implied in an English context is unmistakable' (Clarke, 1978, p. 152). It was perfectly natural that many of the ambiguities in late-Victorian and Edwardian Radicalism found an echo in Bernstein, and especially in the ambivalent quality of his internationalism which, whether applied to tariff policy, the national question, militarism, imperialism or colonialism, was often heavily compromised either by his 'progressive' German patriotism or by his inveterate eclecticism. His receptivity to his English environment and contacts was indeed staggering in its range. Cobdenism and J. A. Hobson,

Mill, Spencer and positivism, Liberal Imperialism, Fabianism, the national efficiency standpoint, the New Liberalism and ethical or Nonconformist socialism were all superimposed on what he had learnt from Marx, Engels and Lassalle, to say nothing of F. A. Lange, Eugen Dühring and his liberal Jewish upbringing. What has been said of J. S. Mill – that 'in an age of eclectics, he has considerable claim to be regarded as the arch-eclectic' (K. E. Miller, 1961, p. 513, n. 65) – is manifestly at least as applicable to the 'arch-revisionist'. In August 1914, Bernstein was thus still tilting at aristocratic rather than bourgeois windmills, and in so doing he was probably more attuned to the realities of his age than were many of his Continental Marxist opponents.

Notes: Chapter 7

1   A. J. P. Taylor's term (1957, p. 51, n. 5) is an apt one in this case, for, as we shall see, Bernstein was a 'dove' but no pacifist in the absolute sense. Before 1914 there were virtually no pacifists in the modern sense apart from those, like the Society of Friends, motivated by religious scruples.

2   Marx's position on the tariff question was decidedly ambivalent (see Schröder, 1975, pp. 79–85). For a more detailed discussion of Bernstein's Cobdenism, see Fletcher, 1983a, pp. 561–78). A more thorough treatment of Bernstein's attitude towards the nationality question may be found in my article, 'Revisionism and nationalism' (Fletcher, 1984), Less satisfactory is the treatment of this question by H. Mommsen (1979, pp. 109–24), who regards Bernstein's attitude towards the national conflicts of his era as a mere 'side-track' (*Nebenpfad*).

3   At the same time Hobson abandoned his earlier pessimism and fell under the influence of Norman Angell (Ralph Lane), an 'unreconstructed Cobdenite' sharing an almost identical outlook with Fried (see Weinroth, 1974a, pp. 551–74; Cain, 1978, p. 580). The fruit of such influence was Hobson's pamphlet, *The German Panic* (1913), which on practically every point was identical with Bernstein's views from *Die englische Gefahr und das deutsche Volk* (1911b) onwards.

4   In May 1915 Victor Adler, himself of Jewish family, remarked that the nationalist wing of German Social Democracy 'simply teems with Jews, old and young, academics and non-academics, from Bloch and Cohen right through the alphabet' (cit. Wistrich, 1982, p. 348).

5   Although he rarely discussed J. S. Mill in any detail – an exception being an *SM* article in 1913 (1913d, pp. 1492–9) – Bernstein greatly admired Mill (1907d, p. 225), and his writings show definite traces of Mill's influence (cf. Mill, 1867a, pp. 120–4; 1867b, vol. 3, pp. 153–78).

6   Bernstein's association with Massingham went back to 1889, when as journalists they had gone to Paris to cover the founding of the Second International together (Havighurst, 1974, pp. 34–6).

7   Limitations of space make it impossible to do justice to Bernstein's views here. For a more detailed discussion, and guidance to the available literature, see Fletcher 1982c, pp. 23–36.

8   As executors of his literary estate, Engels nominated not Kautsky, the 'pope of socialism', but August Bebel and Eduard Bernstein, and this despite the fact that Engels was as well aware of the latter's theoretical meanderings as was Eleanor Marx.

9   It may well be the case that the Marxist–Leninist theory of imperialism is conceptually very different from Hobson's theory (Cain, 1978, p. 565, n. 3), but there is an abundance of evidence indicating that Hobson's earlier work was widely known, and translated, on the Continent as early as the 1890s. Perhaps Hobson's influence was much wider than Georges Haupt and others have maintained. Lenin, for one, believed that in Hobson's *Imperialism* 'may be found nearly all Kautsky's pacifist and "conciliatory" banalities' (Lenin, 1966, p. 322).

10 Joseph Schumpeter, though then teaching at the University of Graz, contrived to spend much of his time in the national capital' (Smithies, 1950, p. 630) and would almost certainly have been present at the Bernstein lecture, which represented a strikingly close anticipation of Schumpeter's imperialism essay (first published in German in 1918/19 under the title 'Zur Soziologie der Imperialismen' ('On the sociology of imperialisms')).

11 The term 'neo-Marxism', as used here, has nothing to do with Lukács, the Frankfurt school, the new left, and so on, but refers exclusively to those radicals of the Second International (such as Anton Pannekoek and Rosa Luxemburg) who appealed directly to Marx for a vindication of their revolutionary activism and their rejection of both theoretical revisionism and the practical immobilism of the centre-orthodoxy.

12 G. B. Shaw said as much in 1900 when he warned against 'a Yellow Muddle that may bring the Chinese war into our own streets' (1900, p. 49). Bernstein praised this work as containing more Marxism than the anti-colonialist resolution sponsored by the Marxist radicals and passed by the 1900 Paris congress of the International (1900a, pp. 713–14).

13 See note 12 above.

8

Bernstein's Alternative 'World Policy'

> This much, at least, is incontestable, the European revolution was justi-
> fied in long regarding Russia as the hereditary foe.
>
> (Eduard Bernstein, 1896)

> If Germany becomes a Liberal power that will be the greatest event in the
> history of Europe since the battle of Leipzig . . . I suppose that it depends
> on the degree of tactical skill shown by the Social-Democratic Party.
>
> (Graham Wallas to Eduard Bernstein, 1911)

> If Asquith's declaration contained a friendly tone towards Germany, the
> speeches of the English ministers were henceforth more and more finely
> tuned to this tone. At the same time, a number of great and influential
> English liberal newspapers — to say nothing of the socialist press —
> demanded that England should provide Germany with unmistakable
> evidence of an accommodating spirit . . . One could fill whole volumes
> with emphatically pro-German articles and letters from English papers
> over recent weeks and months. And these papers by no means confined
> their remarks to gestures of Platonic friendship. They stressed the many
> interests Germany and England have in common, they recognised the
> justice in Germany's desire for more elbow-room in the world and there-
> fore called for greater compliance with German colonial aspirations.
>
> (Eduard Bernstein, 1911)

> [Millions of Germans] fail to see that the matter of our relations with
> England is a question of two world views. He who is unable to
> comprehend that two great industrial nations might live together in har-
> mony without arming to the teeth against each other, does not believe in the
> possibility of creating an international solidarity of nations; he cannot be
> an unqualified supporter of democracy, cannot be even a consistent
> liberal. Here, indeed, is the dividing-line which sharply separates the
> obsolescent politics of national rivalries from the emerging politics of
> international solidarity. He who lacks the courage to stand up for the one
> lends aid and comfort to the other. But he who perceives that the German
> people has no greater enemy than those who are constantly declaiming
> "enemies all around us!", such a person finds the courage to stand with us
> [socialists] and here and now to struggle manfully for the creation of a true
> peace-league of nations, for the realisation of the one great republic of
> peoples.
>
> (Eduard Bernstein, 1911)

> I believed that this phase of militarism would pass when Imperial

Germany became a more mature nation. Indeed, it was passing under the growing influence of Social Democracy, which was greatly increased by the elections which took place while I was in Berlin in 1912.

(*R.B. Haldane, 1920*)

If Bernstein may fairly be accused, as he was so accused (by Belfort Bax, among others), of having used democracy as a magic wand, he, in turn, repeatedly berated the party Marxists for using the socialist *Endziel* or final objective in a similar manner. Opposing all that *was* in the name of that which *will be*, orthodox and radical Marxists were constantly embattled for their alleged refusal to put forward, or even contemplate, serious practical measures which might help the movement along its way to the ultimate objective. In common with the reformists and most of the *Praktiker*, Bernstein did not believe in the collapse theory, but even if it were true, he argued, socialists must prepare themselves for the responsibilities of power by pursuing an active tactic, which entailed formulating and as far as possible implementing realistic and practicable policies for the immediate and distant future. From the Erfurt Programme onwards (whereas Kautsky drafted its theoretical section, it had been Bernstein whom the SPD called upon for the framing of its practical demands), Bernstein therefore endeavoured to provide the party with practical policy proposals, including foreign policy proposals, while encouraging fellow-revisionists to do likewise.

This is not to say that he always succeeded, or that his proposals necessarily carried much weight, even among revisionists. But we are bound to ask whether he had anything more positive to offer than his basically liberal critical asides on the great issues of his era (tariff policy, the national question, militarism, imperialism and colonialism). Conventional wisdom has it that Bernstein presented no carefully elaborated exposition of a socialist foreign policy alternative before 1914. This view is well founded in as much as Bernstein's prewar writings contain no major studies along these lines. What they do contain, however, is a great many frequently recurring ideas from which the kernel of a revisionist foreign policy alternative may legitimately be inferred. During the war years, his vision was to assume more concrete and coherent form, but there was no significant change of direction in his post-1914 socialist internationalism.

Among the premises of Bernstein's alternative world policy was his belief in liberty and national self-determination as rights of civilised peoples, and the concomitant belief that the nation-state would long remain the basic organisational unit of humanity. He held that civilised states had two vital interests – peace (security against war or involvement in war) and the right to material and spiritual progress – for which they might claim protection from the international community and which they were entitled to defend and assert. But the settlement of disputes among civilised states must proceed by peaceful means and in accord with the principles of justice (*Gerechtigkeit*). Convinced that there did exist an international community, even if few institutions yet existed to embody that community, Bernstein was prepared to recognise circumstances where its claims might take precedence over those of the nation-state. He thought of freedom of trade, or 'duty-free international intercourse', as falling within this sphere, but the balance-of-power concept, on the other hand, had no place in a community of civilised states and must give way to a popularly based comity of nations. Like Gladstone, he also believed that there existed a common moral law which applied to states in their domestic and international actions. Intervention was therefore permissible not only against 'savages' but also, under certain conditions, against civilised states which transgressed against the international community or its moral code. Since he defined a civilised state as one exhibiting a high degree of industrialism, political democracy and liberal culture, his perspective was Eurocentric as well as 'Kehrite', but not rigidly so: after the 1911 Chinese Revolution, and despite his earlier warnings about the 'Mongol peril', he clearly envisaged the admission of non-European nations to the community of civilised states. Before the First World War, he regarded Germany, despite its democratic shortfall, as being unquestionably a civilised state and one, moreover, which might reasonably claim a place of prominence in the councils of the nations. After 1914, when he believed the German government 'the most guilty of all for this crime on [sic] Europe' (MC 41/9: Bernstein to Massingham, 12 August 1915), he was no longer so sure of Germany's credentials as a civilised state. In a review of Bülow's *Deutsche Politik* he asked, 'how can a people permeated by militarism, a people whose best quality . . . is their martial prowess, how can such a people develop a truly political culture? However high its cultural attainments might otherwise be, its political perception will never rise appreciably beyond that of barbarians in the sociological sense of the term' (1916/17, pp. 535–6). Yet in the prewar period, Bernstein believed German democracy to be just around the corner, which, as we have seen, enabled him to combine a critical patriotism with his other inconsistencies. On such a base, he erected an anti-Russian, pro-Western foreign policy programme which was much closer to that of Bebel, Kautsky and the party centre than to that purveyed by Bloch and his 'swallows' of the *Sozialistische Monatshefte*.[1]

Security against Russia

Since the whole of the European left had execrated Russia as the citadel of reaction from the Holy Alliance onwards, it was to be expected that Bernstein should exhibit pronounced tendencies towards Russophobia. Naturally, he described the 'Russian peril' in political, economic and geographic terms – the nature of tsarism, its alliance with France, its Balkan machinations, its frontier with Germany and its vast demographic and material resources. But unlike Leuthner, who reduced all this to the menace of Russian popular nationalism, Bernstein saw the root of the problem in Russian backwardness. Whereas Imperial Germany was an 'industrial' society manifesting alarming symptoms of a 'militant' recidivism, tsarist Russia had only recently taken the first steps towards becoming a society of the 'industrial' type. It was therefore a 'threat to the internal development of Germany and Europe . . . beside which all others pale into insignificance' (1896/7b, p. 13). In 1902, in his short-lived review, the *Dokumente des Sozialismus*, he referred to 'the peculiar mixture of softness and savagery which we so often encounter among Slavs, the distorted position arrived at even by those members of this predominantly barbarous country who have absorbed the highest cultural attainments of the civilised world and operate within the civilised world, yet without ever completely breaking the bond with their native barbarism' (*Dokumente des Sozialismus*, 1902, vol. 1, p. 99; cf. Bernstein, 1907*i*, p. 518). Bernstein, in fact, was a lifelong Russophobe who feared the Eastern giant as a menace to civilised Europe, the true conductor of the European Concert and a mortal foe of 'Germany, the German government, German popular representation and the German people' (1896/7*a*, p. 688; RTV, vol. 295 [15 May 1914], p. 8885). The tsarist empire represented 'a constant and direct hindrance to Germany's political development. With tsarist Russia at her back, Germany will never acquire real political freedom. She is not even free to operate in international affairs as a great power' (1896/7*c*, p. 112).

He was particularly concerned at Russian expansion in the Near and Middle East, interpreting the Balkan Wars of 1912–13 as a 'shifting of the centre of gravity in favour of the Slavonic nations' (1913*k*, p. 988) and blaming the German army increase of 1913 on 'Russia's intrigues during the Balkan war and the jingoism of the Balkan people' (MC 41/8: Bernstein to Massingham, 6 March 1913). Armenia and Persia were also believed to be gravely threatened (RTV, vol. 295 [15 May 1914], pp. 8884–5). What Germany should do to combat this danger was to bring its Habsburg and Turkish client states firmly under control and then, in collaboration with such other interested third parties as France, Britain and the USA, practise a kind of anti-Russian, free trade imperialism in the area. This policy would have a secure base if Germany made moral conquests among the Balkan peoples by standing up for the principle of national self-determination, which Bernstein regarded as the most effective counter to Russian pretensions as 'protector' of the southern Slavs (1896/7*a*, pp. 687–92; 1896/7*b*, pp. 10–20; 1896/7*c*, pp. 108–16; 1902, pp. 37–40; RTV, vol. 289 [14 April 1913], pp. 4733–6, vol. 295 [15 May 1914], pp. 8883–6). Like many of his contemporaries, both within and beyond official circles, Bernstein was greatly encouraged by the Anglo-German Near Eastern *détente* of 1912–13, for 'it was generally accepted that this exercise had been of great benefit to Europe in that it had . . . done something to improve the exceedingly strained relations between Britain and Germany' (Crampton, n.d. [*Hollow Détente*], p. 171).

But Bernstein was well aware that such a Near Eastern policy represented a holding operation rather than a solution to the problem posed by the incubus of Russian militarism. Only the destruction and dismemberment of the tsarist empire would satisfy that requirement. A Herculean task of this magnitude was beyond the resources of Germany alone, for 'there [was] no single power in Europe able to assume the role of "bulwark" against Russia' (1896/7*b*, p. 18). Nor was the Triple Alliance the appropriate remedy. In a book review in 1894, Bernstein revealed his optimal solution to the 'Russian peril' as 'a league of the West against the East, based on prior resolution of the internal difficulties besetting the West', at the same time ruminating on the 'beautiful thought' of 'compelling tsarism to throw its frontiers wide open to German colonists and German products' (*NZ*, 1893/4, vol. 2, p. 633). However desirable, this objective struck him as wishful thinking in 1894, but he by no means abandoned the idea altogether. Over the next two decades he adverted to it several times (1896/7b, pp. 13, 19; 1905c, p. 294; 1906a, p. 211), and in August 1914 he returned to it with a vengeance (for instance, in a three-part article in *Vorwärts*, 26–28 August 1914). In January 1918, one of the few hopes he entertained of the Bolshevik regime was that it might honour its pledge to grant full national autonomy to all the peoples comprising the former Russian Empire (1918d, pp. 1–4) – an excellent example of that blending of idealism with *Realpolitik* which he so admired in Jaurès.

Bernstein's astonishingly and uncharacteristically aggressive *Ostpolitik* may seem difficult to reconcile with his almost congenital 'pacificism' unless it is borne in mind that virtually every influence to which he was ever exposed – Marx and Engels, the British Radical tradition (David Urquhart, as well as Cobden), contemporary bourgeois opinion in Germany and the socialism of the Second International – shared, if little else, the most deep-seated fear and the most violent hatred of Russian power, Russian expansionism and Russian barbarism. On this point, there was very little difference between Bernstein, on the one hand, and Bebel, Luxemburg, Leuthner, Jaurès, Hyndman, Keir Hardie, Campbell-Bannerman, H. N. Brailsford or E. D. Morel on the other. What may have sharpened the cutting edge of Bernstein's Russophobia was his bitter resentment of Russia's maltreatment of the Jews (1906a, p. 213).

The True Triple Alliance of Britain, France and Germany

How this 'league of the West against the East' might be realised – as he put it in 1914, 'as an affair of the *civilised world*' (1914d, p. 1019, italics in original) – was a subject on which the 'father of revisionism' repeatedly expressed definite, if not invariably consistent, views in the prewar era. As a first step in this direction, he recommended, and worked for, the conciliation of France which, for him, turned almost exclusively on the problem of Alsace-Lorraine. He reminded his countrymen that a grave injustice had been done to the French nation and that, in French eyes, a war for the recovery of their lost territory would be comparable to the German war of liberation against Napoleon (1901c, p. 258; RTV, vol. 295 [15 May 1914], p. 8889). (Unlike Bloch, but in common with Jean Jaurès, he was, incidentally, no admirer of Napoleon I, whom he considered a rapacious and bloodthirsty megalomaniac who had abandoned all ideals for the sake of power [1915c, p. 2].) For the purpose of underlining the 'alliance-worthiness' of Germany in British eyes, he was capable of telling his British Radical friends that 'the question of Alsace-Lorraine has ceased to be a serious impediment to friendly relations between France and Germany' (1907j, p. 13), but he knew this to be untrue and told a very different tale on the European continent. As Marx had predicted, Bismarck's annexation of the border provinces had cost Germany dearly in terms of diplomatic manoeuvrability and opportunities for extra-European expansion while providing French *revanchiste* mischief-makers – Bernstein mentioned *Le Temps* as a particularly malevolent influence (1913b, p. 309) – with a ready-made excuse for disrupting the peace and progress of civilisation.

The problem could be eliminated, he believed, by 'the granting of Home

Rule to Alsace-Lorraine within the framework of the German Empire'. In January 1915 he claimed to have been assured by Jaurès (before the latter was murdered by a nationalist fanatic during the July crisis of 1914) that 'had this been achieved, the Franco-Russian alliance – for French democracy, at least – would have lost all meaning and the foundations would have been laid for a truly democratic foreign policy. It might, indeed, have been accompanied by a transformation of diplomacy itself in the democratic sense' (1917*b*, p. 31). The 1911 Constitution bestowed on the Alsatian *Reichsland*, granting the State Parliament the same suffrage as that for the Reichstag, evidently failed to measure up to Bernstein's notion of 'home rule', but he was reluctant to be too insistent on the subject for fear of giving encouragement to foreign chauvinists (1907*k*, p. 439; 1909*e*, p. 614). Even so, he professed to be enormously impressed by indices of Franco-German *rapprochement* such as the 1913 conference of French and German parliamentarians. Here, according to Bernstein, a resolution 'strongly condemning Chauvinistic incitement and declaring for the proposal of Mr. W. J. Bryan to settle questions of international dispute by arbitration . . . was unanimously accepted amidst a scene of indescribable enthusiasm'. Moreover, 'for Germans, it was the first occasion on which [14] representatives of the Social Democratic Party combined with representatives of other parties [a handful of Progressives] for work of this kind' (1913*b*, p. 309).[2] All in all, the price Bernstein would have been willing to pay for amicable relations with France was hardly more generous than Calwer's, for Bernstein also believed that the French could well make do with a much more modest colonial empire (1900*c*, p. 555).

For Bernstein, 'the great question of the hour in international politics' was 'the relief of the Anglo-German tension' (1911*f*, p. 551). Convinced that this issue held the key to Franco-German concord and provided the means which would deliver Germany from the 'political vice' in which she had been locked by the Franco-Russian alliance, Bernstein proclaimed himself 'a German who has always worked for the best possible relations between the two nations' (1908*h*, p. 757).

To this question Bernstein devoted greater attention than to any other issue between 1901 and 1914. He consistently argued that the Anglo-German conflict was founded on no natural or traditional antagonisms, that it began with the annexation of Alsace-Lorraine and Bismarck's adoption of protectionism (leading ultimately to colonial and naval friction as well) and that it was aggravated by the blustering style of German diplomacy and the machinations of the popular press in both countries. The legend of the 'English peril' and that of Entente encirclement, together with the wave of 'stupid Anglophobia' and the fatalistic expectation of an 'inevitable war' which resulted from this thinking, constituted, in Bernstein's view, a dangerous myth, and he worked tirelessly to expose it as such. Arguing that the British economy had nothing to fear from German competition, and pointing to the reality of Anglo-German economic interdependence as a force for peace and progress, he strove to demonstrate that Britain's alleged 'commercial envy' was neither objectively nor subjectively a source of friction. In reply to German colonialist Anglophobes, he maintained that Germany's limited colonial swag was not due to British obstruction, that a larger colonial empire was possible only with British collaboration, that, in any case, formal ownership of colonies was of secondary importance to the question of access under the auspices of free trade. At all times, he insisted Germany's world standing in 'the age of global intercourse' was not, and could not be, dependent on the size of its colonial swag.

The naval issue, on the other hand, he reluctantly recognised as representing a real problem, particularly after 1906. From its inception, he denounced the Tirpitz battlefleet as being outrageously expensive (and hence a serious obstacle to social reform within the Reich), useless for defence purposes (Germany needed an army against Russia, not a navy against Britain), unnecessary to commerce and, above all, a gratuitous provocation of Britain. But the Tirpitz navy was again a mere symptom. In Bernstein's estimation, the root cause of the widening rift between Berlin and London was ideological: it was, at bottom, a 'question of two world views' (1911*b*, p. 48). On the German side, there was great 'antipathy to the spirit of independence and the free institutions of the Anglo-Saxon peoples' (1897/8*a*, pp. 494–5) because the Junker hegemons feared for their future in an increasingly industrialised German society. The Junkers dominated Prussia, and 'it is in the last instance always Prussia that decides the policy of the Empire' (1907*d*, p. 863). Since the spirit of Junkerdom had feudalised the mind of the German bourgeoisie,

> A large contributor to this unsound condition of German feeling towards Great Britain is the anarchical condition of home policy. The middle class parties see and feel that they are losing ground again . . . There is very little hope of winning back the electors on programmes of home policy, and thus a foreign danger must be set at work. (1911*m*, p. 93)

So successful was this 'subterfuge' that Bernstein admitted, in a clear reference to Bloch and the revisionist *Monatshefte*, that anti-British sentiments had 'got hold of the minds of several of [his] political friends' (1907*d*, p. 224). Thus, German 'distrust of Great Britain' in 1911 was 'not one whit smaller than at any time before'. It was 'a sort of hypnotic vision' in which 'the average German' saw 'the fatal hand of Great Britain' in 'every international intrigue' (1911*m*, p. 93).[3]

Bernstein set himself the task of reversing this process of estrangement. To this end, he waged an unrelenting and almost single-handed campaign to promote a naval *détente*, to re-educate German public opinion and to secure democratic government in Prussia and the Reich. He did not deny Germany's right to a navy but he deplored the kind of navy planned and built by Tirpitz, with its anti-British, anti-parliamentary edge (see Berghahn, 1971, pp. 90–201), as he deplored the repeated failure of the German government to respond to British disarmament proposals. What he urged was a scaling-down of the Tirpitz fleet in agreement with Britain, or at least to a degree that would allay British fears, as a means of arriving at 'a satisfactory and lasting understanding between the two countries' (1911*a*, p. 803). Basically, all he was prepared to offer Britain was 'retrenchment in armaments' (1909*j*, p. 241). By 6 March 1913, when the Tirpitz naval plan had apparently been defeated by the proponents of a Continental strategy, Bernstein wrote to Massingham of his general satisfaction with the progress achieved in this area. Although 'not very convinced of the good intentions of our naval people', he expressed the hope that 'for the present their declarations [might] serve, and words have often had as much their consequences as deeds'. Even the Balkan squabble was seen to have its positive side, for it had allegedly 'led to a stop of the naval armaments and consequently to better feeling between Germany and Great Britain' (MC 41/8). One is tempted to conclude that in Bernstein's mind the question of naval *détente* was not qualitatively different from the discussion of 'software' or peripheral issues such as the Baghdad railway or the future of the Portuguese colonies. Yet he was mindful of the fact that it was out of discussions of this kind there had emerged Britain's *ententes* with France and Russia in 1904 and 1907.

He appeared undaunted by the mammoth task of enlightening German public opinion (led astray, he believed, by ignorance and a manipulated as well as manipulative 'yellow press') to the true interest of the German people in Anglo-German amity and friendship. Like the good British Radical that he was, he had no doubt that the goal could be accomplished by means of a gigantic extra-parliamentary combination of 'the democratic forces on both sides of the channel' striving 'to collect the voices of those papers and politicians who work for peace and goodwill, and make them known from country to country' (1911*a*, p. 804). Hence his extensive journalism on both sides of the North Sea, his participation in public meetings and petitions, his involvement with the German Peace Society and his contacts with visiting speakers like Angell and Hobson. Despite moments of well-founded pessimism, he seems genuinely to have believed that all this was producing the desired effect, for on many occasions he assured his British readers that Anglophobia was abating as a significant influence on public and official opinion in Germany, adding that 'in stating this [he was] not driven by a desire to palliate or suppress unpleasant realities' (1907*d*, p. 224; 1908*h*, p. 757; 1911*i*, p. 305). In fairness to Bernstein, it must be admitted that his British Radical friends were equally deluded. On the eve of the First World War, most Radicals believed they had captured Grey for what A. G. Gardiner, in the *Daily News* of 17 January 1914, called 'the true Triple Alliance of England, France and Germany' (cit. Weinroth, 1970, p. 680) or what H. N. Brailsford described, in March 1914, as the 'natural grouping of the more advanced Western Powers . . . an *entente* for peace . . . in the broad sense of the word, as the Liberal party' (Brailsford, 1914, p. 297).[4]

If Bernstein met the first measure of a nineteenth-century British Radical – a determination to expand the political nation by mobilising public opinion in massive extra-parliamentary campaigns – he also exhibited in abundance its second distinguishing feature, namely, 'the conviction that small groups of people ran the state in a self-interested way and, because they controlled Parliament by corruption, imposed taxation on the rest of the nation to finance this parasitism'. By widening and deepening the democratic process, Radicals sought 'to remove corrupt, tyrannical and expensive institutions, cut government down to size, and so reduce its cost' (I. J. Prothero, *Times Literary Supplement*, 21 January 1983, p. 65). Bernstein's real answer to the Anglo-German antagonism, as to the problem of militarism and most other ills besetting the Reich and the age, was thus to labour unstintingly for the materialisation of Bismarck's nightmare – the realisation of a 'Gladstonian Cabinet' in a fully democratised Prusso-German polity.

He had no illusions as to the Reichstag, referring to its 'growing impotence' and 'lack of power' (*Kompetenz*) (SPD A.C., 1905, p. 226) and to the 'compromise and backstairs influence' that marked all its activities (1913*e*, p. 569). The Imperial government had 'neither the will nor the backbone to effect any Liberal reforms', for 'the most formidable obstacle' to all progress in Germany was 'the influence of the Lords in Prussia' (1908*j*, p. 705). Since 'a real progressive Liberal policy in Imperial matters [could] only be assured by defeudalising Prussia' (1907*j*, p. 14), the first duty of German socialists was to put a stop to their revolutionary phrase-mongering and to win over non-socialist allies for vigorous extra-parliamentary action to secure the Reichstag suffrage for the Prussian Lower House. Thus, his comment on the Zabern incident was that although nothing was to be expected of the Reichstag, 'progress will work on other lines in this country' (1914*c*, p. 745). Despite his extremely low estimate of all shades of German liberalism, he never lost heart. As he commented in December 1911, 'The present situation will not last forever. New problems will in time arise and teach people reason' (1911*f*, p. 551). He was so encouraged by the 1912 Reichstag elections, both by the large SPD vote and still more by the socialist-left liberal co-operation in the run-off elections, as to predict that socialism and government would soon cease to be mutually exclusive categories, for Germany as elsewhere (see his introduction to MacDonald, 1912, pp. iv–v).

He enthusiastically endorsed, and quoted (in his foreword to the German translation of *Human Nature in Politics*), the observation of his friend, the Radical and former Fabian Graham Wallas, when the latter wrote to him on 19 May 1911, 'If Germany becomes a Liberal power that will be the greatest event in the history of Europe since the battle of Leipzig . . . I suppose that it depends on the degree of tactical skill shown by the Social-Democratic Party' (BP, D 809: Wallas to Bernstein). Translating Wallas's 'Liberal power' as a 'decisively liberal power', Bernstein did not agree with Wallas that the process might take a further generation of struggle (foreword, Wallas, 1911, p. vii). Like his Junker enemies, Bernstein thought of Anglo-German amity and German democracy as being mutually supportive siblings. In February 1912 he wrote that

> we are not yet face to face with the question of forming a genuine governmental Block. What has been obtained is – to repeat the word – an *entente*, a combination for the fight against reaction and for the conquest of political reform. It is not much, but it is a great step forward in the direction of a sound political cleavage. And if, during the time of its achievement, the tension between Germany and Great Britain can effectively be terminated, further steps will be made possible. (1912*g*, p. 814)

His 'confidence in peaceful democracy as an accepted principle of political evolution' and his faith in the inevitable restoration of Anglo-German amity both derived, in the end, from his unlimited confidence in John Bright's 'grand panacea' of commerce. He was convinced that sooner or later the German bourgeoisie would see the light and fall into line behind Social Democracy in its struggle for progress, which was the same struggle as that being waged by British Liberals with the Labour Party as their junior partner. His reading of the German census figures, showing a dramatic increase in the preponderance of industry over agriculture, thus allowed him to proclaim 'the historical invincibility of the class which can be assured anew, the future belongs to you' (1901*a*, p. 292). Which would come first – German democracy or an Anglo-German *entente* – was a question which he left open. Republican France and liberal Britain had both demonstrated in their dealings with reactionary Russia that ideological disparity represented no insuperable obstacle to amicable relations, which encouraged Bernstein to hope for an immediate improvement in Anglo-German relations. By July 1914 he seemed as convinced as Chancellor Bethmann Hollweg that a substantial improve-ment, amounting almost to an *entente*, had already been achieved via the Balkan question and other peripheral issues (RTV, vol. 289 [14 April 1913], p. 4738).

Bernstein was in no doubt as to what Germany might gain from such a realignment. Not only would it put an end to the crippling and anti-social arms race as well as terminate Germany's (in Bernstein's view, largely self-imposed) diplomatic isolation, an Anglo-German settlement simultaneously offered the best prospect of a rewarding and peaceful renegotiation of the global colonial cake. With liberal Britain at her side, a democratic or soon-to-be democratic Germany might finally resolve the knotty problem of Alsace-Lorraine and at last bring French *revanchisme* to heel. If a 'league of the West against the East' did not at once materialise, at the very least the spectre of general war would be dispelled and 'militant' Russia effectively contained. It is interesting to note that Kautsky's thinking at this time closely paralleled that of Bernstein, his 'ultra-imperialism' thesis, as expressed in his famous *Neue Zeit* article of September 1914 (actually written shortly before the war), holding out the possibility that capitalism might eliminate the menace of war through an extension of the cartel system to foreign relations (Kautsky, 1913/14, pp. 919–21). In arriving at this position, Kautsky could well have been influenced by Bernstein, for 'Ede' had been his friend and mentor in their Zurich days, and the two had begun to effect a reconciliation as early as 1912 (Steenson, 1978, pp. 45–6, 281 n. 7).

Be that as it may, Bernstein also expected far-reaching domestic political advantages to accrue from an Anglo-German *entente* – a much overused term in his political vocabulary during the years 1912–14. Since the principle of federal direct taxation had already been established by 1913, he welcomed the pros-pect of an early end to the arms race as opening a vista on an era of sweeping social reform in Germany. But this was unlikely to be sponsored, or even tolerated, by Bethmann Hollweg and the agrarian wire-pullers behind him. Bernstein was convinced that some powerful external stimulus was needed to jolt the cowered German middle-of-the-road parties into making a clean break with 'the agrarian and the priest'. Recognising that the German bourgeoisie had been neutered by its fear of socialism and its chauvinism, he felt that 'bourgeois democratic liberalism [would] only acquire the strength to resist [its agrarian overlords] through co-operation with working-class democracy, with Social Democracy' (1912*h*, pp. 371–2). For this reason, he stressed the importance of Great Britain retaining her position of moral leadership as the model liberal state: 'An anti-democratic English Government will not make the German jingoes England's friends, whilst it is sure to alienate the sympathies of the rising democratic forces. If England wants to make moral conquests on the Continent she can only succeed by trying to justify her renown as one of the leading nations in political and social progress' (1908*h*, p. 757). Failing an Anglo-German *entente*, British example was needed to stiffen the backbone of German democrats and so help break the domestic political log-jam barring the way to a democratic Germany, a peaceful Europe and the progress of humanity.

The task of the German labour movement, as prescribed by Bernstein, was to maintain its vigilance in respect of aggressive and barbaric Russia while supporting all reasonable measures for improved relations with Britain and France. Above all, German Social Democracy should leave no stone unturned in its labours for the earliest possible realisation of parliamentary democracy in Prussia and the Reich. His socialist foreign policy alternative, like his revisionism, clearly smacked of British liberalism, his excuse being that 'we are in the unfortunate position that the German people as a nation never has had a foreign policy, and consequently possesses no redeeming traditions' (1911*m*, p. 94). Except for his greater faith in the practicability of his revisionist alliance tactic, Bernstein's foreign policy position was virtually identical in essentials with that of Bebel, Kautsky and the party centre, which is not at all surprising in that both positions originated, via different avenues, in the tradition of Enlightenment progressivism. Obviously, Bernstein's foreign relations views had almost nothing in common with 'the programme of the *Sozialistische Monatshefte*', which explains why it is necessary to ferret out his reflections on international relations not only in the revisionist and the official party press but equally in non-socialist and foreign publications (such as the *Frankfurter Zeitung, Die Friedens-Warte, Dokumente des Fortschritts, The Nation* and the *Contemporary Review*). With rare exceptions, for some inexplicable reason German scholars have hitherto neglected almost entirely the rich vein presented by sources of the latter category.

International Government

There is a further dimension to Bernstein's prewar foreign policy thinking which deserves to be taken more seriously than has previously been the case, and that is his attempt to grope his way towards a clearer concept of how 'the grand idea of the solidarity of peoples and its concomitant humanitarian ideals' (1915*c*, p. 3) might eventually be embodied. Apart from its endorsement of arbitration as a means of settling international disputes, the Erfurt Programme said nothing on the subject, and socialists of the Second International were generally little interested in the question. Bernstein, however, took a keen interest in the issue, and the root of such interest is indicated by his citation of Jesus Christ and the 1789 Declaration of the Rights of Man and Citizen in support of his contention that 'it is oppression of the entire body of humanity, of the body of the association of nations, when so much as a single civilisable nation is oppressed and downtrodden' (1902, p. 40).

In August 1914, like the overwhelming majority of German socialists, Kurt

Eisner included, he allowed himself to be rushed by his hatred of Russia into unequivocally supporting the SPD war credits vote. Again like Kurt Eisner, he soon reversed his position and emerged as a prominent anti-war radical – making 'methods of barbarism' speeches, denouncing German war aims as imperialistic and repudiating the *Burgfrieden* as political folly. What he now urged as the prophylaxis against future catastrophies of this kind was democratic control of foreign policy and its materialisation in some form of supranational political association (1916*c*; 1917*b*; 1918*f*; 1919*a*). This brought about a final rupture with most of his erstwhile revisionist friends and, when he saw the party firmly under the control of David, Ebert, Scheidemann and company, a still more painful separation from the movement to which he had given a lifetime of service and sacrifice. His new political ambience was the USPD, which he joined in the company of a few former revisionists like Kurt Eisner, together with those intellectuals of the centre, centre-left and left who had long been his most trenchant critics. At the same time, he kept up and extended his contacts among bourgeois democrats and pacifists at home and abroad – the British Union of Democratic Control, the Dutch Anti-Oorlog Raad and in Germany the Bund Neues Vaterland, the Peace Society and its successor, the Zentralstelle Völkerrecht. When he rejoined the Majority SPD in 1918, which he did in recognition of the fact that only a united labour movement would be capable of securing a viable German democracy, he was already, as he put it, politically dead. The revolutionary left went its own way, soon to be captured by Bolshevism; the Eberts and the Scheidemanns never forgave him for having stigmatised them as opportunist fools and moral bankrupts (1915*a*, pp. 3–4; 1915*d*, pp. 4–5; 1916*e*, pp. 3–6; 1918*c*, p. 5); revisionism had meanwhile become such a non-issue that he was able to effect a reconciliation with Joseph Bloch, now, like the former Pan-German Stresemann, posing as a 'good European'.

Bernstein's final wartime step into political oblivion may be regarded as a logical extension of his prewar internationalism. He had always been highly critical of traditional diplomacy and the Concert of Europe which, by practising *Staatenpolitik* instead of *Völkerpolitik*, heaped one injustice on another while aggravating instead of solving international disputes (1895/6*c*, pp. 616–17; 1896/7*a*, pp. 687–92; 1908*m*, p. 737; 1909*i*, p. 784; 1911*f*, p. 550; RTV, vol. 285 [14 May 1912], p. 1995, vol. 289 [14 April 1913], pp. 4734–5, vol. 295 [15 May 1914], p. 8886). Typical was his comment on the Balkan War:

The part played by the so-called Concert of the Great Powers in the Balkan War is both shameful and laughable. They started with the programme of preventing the war, and they succeeded in making it bloodier and more devastating than it probably would have been without them. They stepped forward afterwards with a determination to stop and end it, and managed only to protract it. Instead of exorcising the war demon they have given birth to new hatreds and rivalries. All this because of the systematic setting aside of principles of right, all this because, again and again, questions of prestige and material interest were allowed to supersede the fundamental rights of self-government and free nationality. (1913*k*, p. 988)

Bernstein stressed repeatedly 'the necessity to break resolutely and finally' with the traditions of such costly folly (ibid., p. 988) and to put in its place 'the principles of democratic diplomacy [which] must needs be different from those of capitalist diplomacy' (1911*f*, p. 550). Deriving his belief in the need for supranational political organisation from his condemnation of power politics as 'the sacrifice of trade to considerations of foreign policy' (1913*h*, p. 210) and from his conviction that 'in our days of, happily, increasing international relationship, no step taken by one country leaves the others unaffected' (1908*h*, p. 757), Bernstein supported, in principle, the idea of a league of nations many times in the prewar period. He referred to it variously as 'a real international alliance of nations', 'a true peace league of nations for the realisation of the one great republic of peoples' and 'the one league of peoples, the one league of nations' (1900*b*, p. 249; 1909*i*, p. 784; 1911*b*, p. 48; RTV, vol. 289 [14 April 1913], p. 4742).

What he expected of such an association was nothing and everything: through the application of the democratic principle to international relations, humanity was to be assured of peace, justice and progress (1913*a*, p. 17). In the prewar period, he offered no clear suggestions as to how such a body might be constituted. One criterion of membership which he envisaged was the degree of civilisation manifested by the respective nations, but his views changed considerably within a single decade. In 1907 he considered a political association of civilised humanity to be still unattainable; by 1913 he believed it to be within reach; by 1918 he was calling for a 'world republic of free peoples' (1907*k*, p. 437; 1913*d*, p. 1498, 1918*f*, p. 29). A second criterion which he employed, in this instance with absolute consistency, was his injunction that the envisaged organisation be a popularly based league of free peoples rather than a confederation of states (RTV, vol. 289 [14 April 1913], p. 4740, vol. 295 [15 May 1914], pp. 8889–90). Here he was echoing Richard Cobden's plea for 'as little intercourse as possible between the *Governments*, as much connection as possible between the nations of the world' (cit. Hobson, 1919, p. 34, Cobden's italics). As to the precise form his proposed league of nations might assume, Bernstein was vaguer still. He apparently expected it to arise organically from his 'league of the West', but in the prewar era he confined his remarks to the broadest of generalities. The 'ultra-imperialist' possibility which Kautsky mooted in economistic Marxist jargon may not have been too far removed from what Bernstein had in mind beneath his Cobdenite homilies. Bernstein's more intensive wartime proselytising in this cause evidently left his compatriots and his comrades unmoved or bewildered. Fifty years after his death, a not unsympathetic German-American socialist commentator could still judge his books on this issue as merely 'embarrassing' (Pachter, 1981, p. 207).

The overall picture presented by Bernstein's foreign policy alternative is that of a mixture of idealism and *Realpolitik* which did not quite jell. Looking back with the wisdom of hindsight, most observers today would probably be willing to credit the revisionist cum international relations theorist with a realistic assessment of the 'Russian peril' and a great deal of perspicacity in his analysis of the Anglo-German antagonism. But thereafter he lost his compass, his eclecticism and his deep-seated ethical proclivity leading him up normative bypaths where his socialism and his realism got lost in a fog of mere wishful thinking. Like the British Radical 'troublemakers' whom he so admired and resembled, Bernstein was always 'more concerned to attack an existing policy than to state [an] alternative' (Taylor, 1957, p. 19), with the result that his alternative, in so far as it can be pieced together, was in many respects incomplete and inconsistent. Thus his thought was characterised by such priority conflicts as principle versus policy, ideal versus expediency, patriotism versus internationalism, peace versus freedom and peace versus world government. He posed a number of questions without seriously answering many of them: How were peoples to bypass governments? How were great-power interests to be neutralised? Could a 'partnership of Western humanity' lead to world government rather than to Hobson's collective parasitism? How was socialism to be related to world government? Were democracy and public opinion a sufficient guarantee of peace or a necessary foundation of international integration? Much of the explanation of his failure to come to grips with these questions lies, once again, in his eclecticism. The British Radical tradition to which he was so heavily indebted had aimed at peace rather than international government. Primarily economic in approach and organic in concept, this school of thought relied on commerce as the 'grand panacea' and sought peace through international law backed by the power of public opinion. But Bernstein also drew heavily on the fundamentally political and dynamic approach of Saint-Simon, Comte, Mazzini and other champions of European integration as the stepping-stone to peace. Later confederalist, Christian pacifist and legalist nostrums, which owed little to either tradition, likewise found a place in Bernstein's foreign policy deliberations. The end-product was confusion and contradiction.

Particularly unrealistic was his use of democracy as a *deus ex machina*. In common with his British Radical friends, he seriously miscalculated the influence of democracy on Sir Edward Grey's policy, and his proposals for a 'saner' German world policy were entirely dependent on the assumption that Germany would soon become a parliamentary democracy on the British model. But, as Professor Berghahn has remarked, 'it is difficult to see how the development of a British-style parliamentarism might have come about in Wilhelmine Germany without a political revolution . . . Given the structural anti-parliamentarism of the 1871 Constitution, reform was not a matter of tinkering, but required a qualitative leap' (Berghahn, 1982, pp. 22–3). On this point, Bernstein's position was less realistic than that of Kautsky and the party Marxists. Moreover, like Engels and the SPD centre-orthodoxy, Bernstein misinterpreted the movement's organisational and electoral successes, overlooking, for example, the discomforting fact that by 1914 the membership of the Navy League alone exceeded that of the SPD. As the work of Eley, Blackbourn and others has demonstrated, *vox populi* in Wilhelmine Germany was neither so inherently democratic nor so easily manipulated as Bernstein was wont to believe. The tensions and conflicts besetting German society were not to be banished by a few speeches, petitions and newspaper articles. It has been said of Edwardian Radicals that their error was their attempt 'to transfer the rules of British development into the sphere of international relations'

(Weinroth, 1970, p. 682). At bottom, this was also Bernstein's error, but not his only error.

One is obliged to conclude, with Gerhard A. Ritter, Hans Mommsen, J. P. Nettl, Gary Steenson and others, that Bernstein, as he himself readily admitted, was not, after all, a theoretician. This was as valid for his forays into international relations theory as it was of his attempt to revise Marx. Yet it is equally clear that he was no more effective as a practising politician. His few non-socialist friends and allies were outsiders like himself – totally without influence and not always in complete accord with Bernstein's Anglophile cosmopolitanism. Most of his fellow-revisionists either execrated him as an English agent or ignored him altogether. To Kautsky and the party left, he was simply 'that flour-sack Bernstein', there to be pummelled for the theoretical edification of a virtually non-existent radical rank and file. In fact, most of his compatriots found Bernstein intelligible, if at all, only as a case of 'hyper-trophy of the conscience'. He may have been, in the words of former SPD Chancellor Helmut Schmidt, 'not only more intellectually honest than Kautsky (and, for that matter, Bebel as well), but . . . also much more of a democrat than Marx' (Lührs *et al.*, 1975, p. ix). This, however, was a liability rather than an asset in the rough-and-tumble of Wilhelmine politics, for Bernstein was all too apt to forget that Berlin, 'that upstart capital town of the new German Empire' (Bernstein, 1907*l*, p. 991), was not Westminster,[5] that Plato's Republic was not Romulus's cesspool.

Notes: Chapter 8

1 For a more detailed treatment of Bernstein's alternative world policy, as well as more extensive documentation, see Fletcher, 1982*a*, pp. 339–70.
2 Bernstein was at pains to explain away the fact that the French delegates outnumbered the Germans by about five to one. On the one hand, he was perfectly frank in admitting to his British readers the true situation in Prussia-Germany, so aptly summed up by Charles Sarolea in 1912: 'a power which has been supreme for two centuries will not surrender without a struggle. The Prussian Junkers may be politically stupid, but they have not lost the fighting spirit, and they will not give way to the "mob". Before Prussian reaction capitulates, it will play its last card and seek salvation in a European conflagration' (Sarolea, 1912, pp. 304–5). On the other hand, Bernstein grasped desperately at any straw which might enable him to go on hoping against hope in what J. A. Hobson later described as 'an atmosphere of illusion' (1938*a*, p. 94).
3 For a more detailed discussion of Bernstein's analysis of the Anglo-German problem, see Fletcher, 1978, pp. 309–36.
4 The 1914 edition of this book also contained the prediction – omitted from subsequent editions – that 'there will be no more wars among the six Great Powers' (p. 35, cit. Taylor, 1957, p. 123). On several occasions prior to August 1914 Bernstein made the same prediction.
5 Nor was he always the model diplomat in making known his personal preferences. His writings are replete with complaints that in Germany 'the level of political controversy is very low. Rudeness does duty for vigor of argument and pharisaic abuse for satire' (1911*f*, p. 550). Throughout the First World War he continued to quote *The Nation* to his German readers and to hold up progressive Britain as a mirror to reactionary Germany (1916*a*, pp. 1–4; 1918*c*, p. 5). In 1918 he admitted that in 1900, when it became possible for him to return to Germany, his initial reaction to the good news was less one of joy than of terror (1918*a*, p. 304).

Conclusion

The leaders of the present-day, so-called 'Social Democratic' Party of Germany are justly called 'social imperialists', that is, socialists in words and imperialists in deeds.

(V. I. Lenin, 1916)

The most satisfying accounts of nationalism have related it to the uneven development of European capitalism, or (in an alternative notation) to problems of modernization.

(Geoff Eley, 1982)

Imperial Germany knew no such thing as a revisionist creed or a revisionist movement. In so far as it existed as a politically significant ideology or an organised and coherent movement in prewar Germany, revisionism owed its force and its direction not to Eduard Bernstein but to the quiet, backstairs labours of its forgotten impresario, Joseph Bloch, and to the generosity of its principal benefactor, Leo Arons. From 1907 to 1914 the ideological position uniformly favoured and consistently promoted by Bloch through his organ, the *Sozialistische Monatshefte*, aimed at integrating the German working class into the existing social order with the aid of a *Sammlung* or common front founded on an illiberal and anti-Marxist nationalism whose point was to be directed not against Social Democracy but rather outwards, towards the pursuit of a German superpower position of truly global and epoch-making dimensions. Unwilling to compromise on matters of principle, Bloch enjoyed only checkered relations with several of the major components comprising the revisionist faction, these ranging from trade union and co-operative *Praktiker* like Adolf von Elm, through reformists like David and Südekum to intellectuals like the neo-Kantian Kurt Eisner and the theoretical revisionist Bernstein. Despite the friction thus produced, until 1914 Bloch generally succeeded in averting an open revolt against the *Monatshefte* and in retaining the grudging co-operation even of antipathetic revisionist elements. Some were less easily duped than others. Eisner, for example, refused to be co-opted either by the party *Vorstand* or by the revisionist Catilina. Bernstein, on the other hand, continued his collaboration with Bloch until September 1914 when, believing that Germany was no longer in danger of being crushed beneath the Russian steamroller, he began to campaign both against the German conduct of the war and for an honest reappraisal of its origins (Fricke, 1974*b*, pp. 865–6; idem, 1975*b*, pp. 454–68). In this instance, however, the war issue was no more than the final straw: from the very beginning of their relationship, Bloch and Bernstein had been in fundamental disagreement on all important aspects of their respective world views.

Although by no means alone in so doing, Bernstein attempted to provide German socialism with a realistic theory for the gradual transformation of capitalism into a vaguely defined democratic socialism. Although he was never a neo-Kantian, the inspiration behind both his revisionism and his inter-national relations theory was essentially ethical, liberal-democratic and British. After his return to Germany in 1901, Bernstein theorised less as he threw himself into the practical work of the labour movement, which included a growing preoccupation with the problems of Germany's place in the world of states. Even more than in the case of his revisionism, his related foreign policy views gained only limited expression in the *Sozialistische Monatshefte*. In fact, a full and accurate picture of his views on foreign policy issues is to be found not in his *Monatshefte* articles but in his many books, brochures, speeches and in his articles for the non-socialist and foreign press, especially those written for the British Radical press. On all the major issues of the era (tariff policy, nationalism, militarism, imperialism and colonialism) he spoke with the facile and eclectic voice of a British Radical. He was particularly critical of Wilhelmine world policy, which he considered from a 'Kehrite' perspective as a device got up by the Junker-heavy industry symbiosis for evading popular pressure for a more democratic Germany, but he did have an alternative foreign policy programme, however sketchy, contradictory and illusory this may have been. Like his revisionism, it was eclectic, ethically inspired and strongly influenced by British Radicalism. If, as he complained, neo-Marxist theorists tended to generalise from Central and East European experience, which partly explains the greater success subsequently enjoyed by the Lenin-ists in the Third World, Bernstein had in common with Marx the fact that he took his models from the more advanced and exceptional conditions of Britain, which is an important reason why West European Social Democracy is today rediscovering its affinity with Bernsteinian socialism, for it was the conditions of advanced capitalism from which Bernstein constructed his theory.

We may well ask why Bernstein did not follow Eisner's example and break with Bloch and the *Monatshefte* before December 1914. Ideologically and politically, Bloch and Bernstein seemed to be poles apart. Bloch was a practi-tioner of *Machtpolitik*; Bernstein, a democrat and a liberal humanitarian. Bloch's 'productive socialism' appeared to aim at working-class integration via nationalism into the Prusso-German power-state; Bernstein's more optimistic 'evolutionary socialism' envisaged a profound transformation of existing society into a 'higher' social order facilitating greater justice, freedom, liberty and brotherhood than anything deemed possible by Bloch or Leuthner. From such fundamental differences arose their divergent attitudes towards tariff policy, liberalism, nationalism, militarism, imperialism, Britain, Prussia and their common Jewishness. Yet there were also sufficient ideological and poli-tical affinities to provide a basis for an uneasy partnership. Most obviously, both were revisionists: hostile to revolutionary Marxism, committed to the politics of gradualism and convinced that the way out of the socialist ghetto was to be found in the location of non-socialist allies, Bloch and Bernstein were both, to varying degrees, German patriots who were much indebted to the values and ideals of the 'dominant', non-socialist culture (in its eclectic idealism, *Realpolitik*, Social Darwinism, and so on). In their perspectives on the imperialism problem, differences were often counterbalanced by similari-ties. Both, for example, rejected the economic interpretation in favour of a political and psychological approach. Each was bewitched by the Russian bogey and each stressed the primacy of Continental over world policy. After 1911, each looked to an Anglo-German naval agreement as the indispensable first step towards a resolution of Germany's immediate foreign policy dilemma. Nor was Bernstein entirely impervious to the social imperialist arguments that so many of his *Monatshefte* colleagues found so compelling. In his affirmation of the workers' stake in the fatherland, in his insistence that working-class emancipation depended on expanding social wealth, including that to be extracted from colonies, and in stressing the need for defence preparedness and national solidarity against foreign chauvinists, Bernstein must have impressed the readers of the *Monatshefte*, who, it cannot be emphasised too strongly, evidently threatened the viability of Kautsky's *Neue Zeit* from the turn of the century onwards, as exhibiting considerable community of outlook with Blochian favourites like Leuthner, Schippel and Hildebrand. To some extent, this apparent community of outlook was needlessly and artificially enlarged by such personal factors as Bernstein's patience and tolerance, which frequently bordered on naïveté and gullibility, as when he protested against Hildebrand's expulsion from the party in 1912.

A no less important reason for Bernstein's continued collaboration with the *Monatshefte* was his political isolation. The arithmetic of the Dresden anti-revisionist resolution cannot have failed to drive home to him the magnitude of what Wolfgang Heine referred to as his 'complete political ineptitude', and the *Monatshefte* did at least provide him with a 'literary home'. Not until 1911 did Bernstein succeed in repairing his relations with the party centre or in establishing contacts among left-liberal groups like the German Peace Society, but the party centre was already losing control to the Davids and the Eberts while the German left liberals had even less political clout than the British Radicals.

Bernstein had no influence on the prewar SPD and none whatever on Joseph Bloch and the *Sozialistische Monatshefte*. When he broke with the revisionist organ in December 1914 the result was, as he put it, his 'political death', and he was obliged to return to the *Monatshefte* soon after the First World War. As a theorist and a practising politician, Bernstein fell on deaf ears, his failure being due, in the main, to his eclecticism, his naïveté and his propensity to generalise from inappropriate British models. His chief contribution to political debate in the dog-days of Imperial Germany was to confuse the masses. They were all dressed up and ready to go somewhere, either to the left or to the right. Even Leuthner was convinced in 1910 that 'radicalism has the masses' (SMP, vol. 8: Leuthner to Bloch, 21 September 1910), and in 1917 Bernstein still believed it was 'not true that the party leadership merely followed the masses in approving the war. The opposite was the case' (Bernstein, 1916/17, p. 527). The problem was that the masses lacked a clear theoretical orientation. Thanks to the centre-orthodoxy, they knew little enough of Marxism beyond a handful of radical shibboleths that were plainly at odds with what the party and trade union leadership expected, or would tolerate, of them. What Bernstein recommended, speaking from the same rostrum as Bloch and Leuthner, was a zigzag course that was generally right in tendency but with frequent liberal digressions to the left. Neither the masses nor his fellow-revisionists were able to digest the fare which he offered. His wartime membership of the USPD, in the company of Rosa Luxemburg and Karl Liebknecht, no doubt added to this confusion, but by 1917 few German socialists were still listening to Bernstein. If Bernstein had little to say to his contemporaries, it may be that the post-1945 Bernstein renaissance has granted him some retrospective vindication. But it is equally possible that this renaissance was no more than an optical illusion created by the ephemeral boom conditions of the postwar decades or a creation born of the West German Social Democrats' need of an icon to hold up against the East German Stalinists and their own fractious Jusos (the radical Marxist youth wing of the SPD).

Bernstein's short-term failure and ultimate deification mirrored Bloch's fate in reverse. As we have seen, Bloch had a programme and a strategy which, by comparison with those of the party centre and the radical left, were based on a realistic assessment of working-class needs and what the situation would allow. This provided his journal with a mass base and enabled him to function as one of the major regulators of German socialist opinion before 1914. There can be no doubt that his nationalism did reach the Social Democratic masses. On the other hand, his influence on party policy was, as his nephew has described it, none at all (C. Bloch, 1977, p. 164), and the passe-partout of revisionism, the bourgeois alliance, materialised only under 'the hammer blows of war', and then in the shadow of the Ebert–Groener alliance. Although the *Monatshefte* survived the war, the 'Catiline' conspiracy to emancipate the German proletariat by means of a 'revolution in world politics' plainly did not. Bloch's failure, perhaps even more than his limited success, helped to divide the German working class and to deliver Germany into the hands of Hitler. To a certain degree, it is possible to say that Bloch's 'conspiracy' actually anticipated National Socialism, for several of his followers – August Winnig, for example (see Ribhegge, 1973) – made this transition readily enough, and the very bitterness of Bloch's posthumously published attack on the German people suggests that the master himself was fully aware all along, as he intimated in his 1895 broadside against the Bismarck cult (J. Bloch, 1895*b*, pp. 121–7), that his 'Nothung' was a dangerous weapon, perhaps capable of cutting the Gordian knot of Wilhelmine politics but equally capable of inflicting far greater havoc and destruction than its Siegfried ever intended or desired.

Yet it is only in the context of the Nazi teleology that Bloch's anti-Marxist tactic of national integration appears so grotesque. Rather than dismiss Bloch, Leuthner and company as proto-fascists, we would do better to contemplate them in their actual historical context. The problem, as they and many of their contemporaries saw it, was Germany's predicament as an industrial and imperial latecomer which had been cheated at the imperial feast by the 'have' nations, just as the industrial proletariat was denied its proper place within the folk or nation. Their aims were a strong, independent and economically viable German nation and a more equitable share of the domestic cake for all segments of the national community. Bloch and his comrades hoped to use German nationalism as a social fixative to help overcome the problems of social and political backwardness at home while at the same time presenting to Germany's external competitors, most notably Britain, the face of a united German people determined to compel a renegotiation of global-power relationships in a manner which guaranteed the 'arrived' German nation a place of honour and a chance of survival in the twentieth century. Viewed in this light, Bloch's nationalism may be seen as an ideology of underdevelopment, similar in kind to that later employed by Third World leaders from Gandhi, Gaddafi and Khomeini to Mao Tse-tung and Ho Chi Minh. In this sense, he was indeed as much an 'idealist and a courageous fighter for the progress of humanity' (C. Bloch, 1974, p. 287) as later generations of modernisers and liberationists seeking to moderate, suspend or externalise certain kinds of disagreement within the national community. Only the most tenuous of links bound Bloch, Leuthner, Hildebrand and the others to Hitler and National Socialism.

Bloch's 'conspiracy' failed because Wilhelmine nationalism could not transcend political conflict and social contradiction. However strongly Bebel, Bernstein and others stressed their patriotic 'me-tooism', however assiduously Bloch strove to cultivate a socialist variant of the populist nationalism propagated by Keim and Hugenberg through the patriotic societies, acceptance of nationalist ideology was too weak a plank to bridge the abyss known as 'the social question'. All varieties of non-socialist patriotism were fundamentally opposed to admitting the proletarian movement to the altar of the national community. Official imperialists, Junker and big-business patriots as well as the rabble-rousing chauvinists among the lower middle classes, the *nationale Verbände* and the 'naval professors' were all vitally, perhaps (as the 'Kehrites' argue) primarily concerned with deploying nationalism as an ideology of containment and a suppressive mechanism against the social and political demands rising from the factory floor. Bloch was virtually alone in seeking to use nationalist ideology as an instrument of national reconciliation and integration. As the levers of power were in the hands of the Bethmanns, the Heydebrands and the Hugenbergs, Bloch really had no more chance of success than the 'grasshoppers' of the radical left.

More careful reflection might lead one to reject as excessive, even absurd, a comparison of Bloch with Gandhi or Mao. After all, the German experience of modernisation was part of a nineteenth-century European phenomenon: 'The process started in Britain and the industrialization of Europe took place on the British model; it was, as far as the Continent was concerned, a purely and deliberately imitative process' (Pollard, 1981, p. v). Whatever the mutations caused by varying circumstances, Wilhelmine 'Germans were actively and continuously trading in that enormous cultural bazaar that constituted nineteenth-century Western civilization' (Gay, 1978, p. 27). To this extent, the national perspective must be recognised as 'an inadmissible backward projection from a differently organized world on to an earlier Europe' (Pollard, 1981, pp. vii–viii). The point is that German questions were indeed much more than purely German questions. Wilhelmine socialism and its 'revisionist' offshoot, considered as a particular response to the challenge of modernity, were as international and multifarious as any other manifestation of modernism. When one looks at Bernstein, the German patriot *cum* British Radical, at Eisner the patriotic Jaurèsiste, and at the native illiberalism of Bloch and Leuthner (anti-liberal, nationalist and imperialist [see Stern, 1972, pp. xi–xliv; Jarausch, 1983, p. 280]), the common core is far broader than their German patriotism. Whether liberal humanitarians or illiberal chauvinists, these revisionists all belonged among those 'other Modernists who made their revolutions quietly, by returning again and again to the very tradition that nourished them and that they were . . . subverting forever' (Gay, 1978, p. 25). Whether reflecting the ideas of 1789 or comprising a peculiar socialist eddy in that confluence of anti-rationalism, experimentation and alienation which can also legitimately be seen as part of a manipulative 'outgrowth of the latter-day remobilization of Europe's *anciens régimes*' (A. J. Mayer, 1981, p. 4), both camps revealed in their foreign policy attitudes how oppressive, captivating and alluring the influence of dominant, non-socialist ideologies could be.

Abbreviations

AA	Adler Archive, VGA Vienna
ABP	August Bebel Papers, IISH Amsterdam
APD	Stenographische Protokolle des österreichischen Reichsrates (Haus der Abgeordneten) (Austrian Parliamentary Debates)
BP	Bernstein Papers, IISH Amsterdam
FES	Friedrich-Ebert-Stiftung, Bonn-Bad Godesberg
GSKK	German Socialists, Kleine Korrespondenz, IISH Amsterdam
IISH	International Institute of Social History, Amsterdam
ILP	Independent Labour Party
KP	Kautsky Papers, IISH Amsterdam
MC	Massingham Collection, Norfolk Record Office, Norwich
MEW	Marx-Engels Werke (1955–)
MISC	Verhandlungen und Beschlüsse, internationale Sozialistenkongresse (minutes of international socialist congress)
NG	*Die Neue Gesellschaft*
NZ	*Die Neue Zeit*
RTV	Stenographische Berichte über die Verhandlungen des Deutschen Reichstages (German Parliamentary Debates)
SAK	*Sozialistische Auslandspolitik. Korrespondenz*
SM	*Die Sozialistischen Monatshefte*
SMP	*Sozialistische Monatshefte* Papers, Bundesarchiv Coblenz
SMR	*Sozialistische Monatshefte* Rundschau (*SM* review section)
SP	Albert Südekum Papers, Bundesarchiv Coblenz
SPD	Sozialdemokratische Partei Deutschlands (German Social Democratic Party)
SPD A.C.	Protokolle über die Verhandlungen der SPD (proceedings of SPD annual congress)
SPÖ A.C.	Verhandlungen des Parteitages der deutschen Sozialdemokratischen Arbeiterpartei Österreichs (variously styled) (proceedings of the annual congress of the German Social Democratic Labour party of Austria)
TP	Troelstra Papers, IISH Amsterdam
USPD	Unabhängige Sozialdemokratische Partei Deutschlands (Independent SPD)
VGA	Verein für Geschichte der Arbeiterbewegung, Vienna
VP	Georg von Vollmar Papers, IISH Amsterdam

Bibliography

(1) Archival Materials

Bundesarchiv, Coblenz: *SM* Papers (SMP) (R 117); Albert Südekum Papers (SP); Eduard David Papers; Nachlasssplitter – Ignaz Auer (Kleine Erwerbung 122), Eduard Bernstein (Kleine Erwerbung 83), Lily Braun (Kleine Erwerbung 129).

Friedrich-Ebert-Stiftung, Bonn-Bad Godesberg (FES): Teil-Nachlass Carl Severing, Teil-Nachlass Ludwig Frank, Teil-Nachlass Paul Kampffmeyer.

International Institute of Social History, Amsterdam (IISG): Private Papers of Eduard Bernstein (BP), August Bebel (ABP), Karl Kautsky (KP), Georg von Vollmar (VP), Pieter Jelles Troelstra (TP); German Socialists, Kleine Korrespondenz (GSKK).

H. W. Massingham Collection (MC), Central Library, Norfolk Record Office, Norwich, UK.

Staatsarchiv, Hamburg: Politische Polizei, S 6306: *Sozialistische Monatshefte* (1897–1916); S 7600: Eduard Bernstein; S 7259: Kurt Eisner.

Verein für Geschichte der Arbeiterbewegung, Vienna (VGA): Adler Archive (AA); Teil-Nachlass Engelbert Pernerstorfer; das alte Partei-Archiv.

(2) Journals, Newspapers, Yearbooks

Arbeiter-Zeitung, Vienna.
Archiv für Sozialwissenschaft und Sozialpolitik.
Contemporary Review.
Dokumente des Fortschritts.
Dokumente des Sozialismus.
Die Friedens-Warte.
Justice.
Der Kampf, Vienna.
Leipziger Volkszeitung.
The Nation.
Neue Deutsche Rundschau (Freie Volksbühne).
Die Neue Gesellschaft (NG).
Die Neue Zeit (NZ)
Österreichischer Arbeiter-Kalender.
La Revue socialiste.
The Social Democrat.
Sozialistische Auslandspolitik. Korrespondenz (SAK).
Die Sozialistischen Monatshefte (SM) (Sozialistischer Akademiker, 1895–6; thereafter *Sozialistischer Monatshefte).*
Vorwärts.

(3) Minutes, Proceedings, Protocols

Protokolle über die Verhandlungen des Parteitages der Sozialdemokratischen Partei Deutschlands (SPD A.C.).

Protokolle über die Verhandlungen der sozialdemokratischen Arbeiterpartei Österreichs (variously titled) (SPÖ A.C.).

Stenographische Berichte über die Verhandlungen des Deutschen Reichstages (RTV).
Stenographische Protokolle über die Sitzungen des Hauses der Abgeordneten des österreichischen Reichsrates (APD).
Verhandlungen und Beschlüsse, internationale Sozialistenkongresse (MISC).

(4) Handbooks, lexicons, etc.

Archiv für publizistische Arbeit (Internationales Biographisches Archiv), 1931– , Vienna.
Carlson, A. R. (1970), *German Foreign Policy 1890–1914, and Colonial Policy to 1914: A Handbook and Annotated Bibliography* (Metuchen, NJ).
Historische Kommission bei der bayerischen Akademie der Wissenschaften (ed.) (1953–), *Neue Deutsche Biographe*, 11 vols (Berlin).
Klaus, G., and Buhr, M. (1974), *Philosophisches Wörterbuch*, 11th edn, 2 vols (Leipzig).
Maitron, J., and Haupt, G. (eds) (1971), *Dictionnaire biographique du mouvement ouvrier international*, vol. 1: *Autriche* (Paris).
Osterroth, F. (ed.) (1961), *Biographisches Lexikon des Sozialismus*, Vol. 1: *Verstorbene Persönlichkeiten* (Hanover).
Österreichisches Biographisches Lexikon (1954–), 5 vols (Vienna).
Paupié, K. (ed.) (1960), *Handbuch der österreichischen Pressegeschichte 1848–1959*, 2 vols (Vienna).

(5) Contemporary Published Sources

Adler, V. (1954), *Briefwechsel mit August Bebel und Karl Kautsky*, ed. F. Adler (Vienna).
Andler, C. (1913), 'Ce qu'il y a d' "impérialisme" dans le socialisme allemand d'aujourd'hui', *La Revue socialiste*, vol. 57.
Andler, C. (1918), *Le Socialisme impérialiste dans l'Allemagne contemporaine* (Paris).
Angell, N. (1910), *The Great Illusion* (London, first published as *Europe's Optical Illusion* (London 1909).
Angell, N. (1951), *After All: The Autobiography of Norman Angell* (London).
Barday, K., and Max, E. (1918), *Was will die Zeit?*, ed. E. Bernstein (Berlin).
Bauer, O. (1907a), *Deutschtum und Sozialdemokratie* (Vienna).
Bauer, O. (1907b), *Die Nationalitätenfrage und die Sozialdemokratie* (Vienna).
Bauer, O. [pseud. H. Weber] (1909), 'Nationale und internationale Gesichtspunkte in der auswärtigen Politik', *Der Kampf*, Jg. 2, Nr. 12.
Bebel, A. (1883), *Die Frau und der Sozialismus* (Zurich).
Bebel, A. (1885/6), 'Deutschland, Russland und die orientalische Frage', *NZ*, Jg. 4, Bd. 2.
Bebel, A. (1901/2), 'Nachklänge zum Lübecker Parteitag', *NZ*, Jg. 20, Bd. 1.
Bebel, A. (1904), *Woman under Socialism*, trans. Daniel de Leon (New York).
Bebel, A. ([1910] 1978), *Aus meinem Leben*, 5th edn (East Berlin)
Beer, M. (1897/8), 'Der moderne englische Imperialismus', *NZ*, Jg. 16, Bd. 1.
Beer, M. (1902/3), 'Imperialistische Politik', *NZ*, Jg. 21, Bd. 1.
Belfort Bax, E. (1896), 'Our Fabian German convert', *Justice*, 17 November.
Belfort Bax, E. (1902), 'Bernstein and the German party', *The Social Democrat*, April.
Bernstein, E. (1890/1a), 'Acht Stunden', *NZ*, Jg. 9, Bd. 2.
Bernstein, E. (1890/1b), 'Briefe aus England', *NZ*, Jg. 9, Bd. 2 (29 August).
Bernstein, E. (1890/1c), 'Carlyle und die sozialpolitische Entwicklung Englands', *NZ*, Jg. 9, Bd. 1.
Bernstein, E. (1891/2a), 'Nieuwenhuis über die deutsche Sozialdemokratie', *NZ*, Jg. 10, Bd. 2.

Bernstein, E. (1891/2*b*), 'Zur Würdigung Friedrich Albert Langes', *NZ*, Jg. 10, Bd. 2.

Bernstein, E. (1892/3), 'Die internationale Bedeutung des Wahlkampfes in Deutschland', *NZ*, Jg. 11, Bd. 2.

Bernstein, E. (1893/4*a*), 'Am Gedenktag der Internationale', *NZ*, Jg. 12, Bd. 2.

Bernstein, E. (1893/4*b*), 'Eine neue Geschichte der Trade Union-Bewegung in England', *NZ*, Jg. 12, Bd. 2.

Bernstein, E. (1893/4*c*), 'Das Schlagwort und der Antisemitismus', *NZ*, Jg. 12, Bd. 2.

Bernstein, E. (1895), *Sozialismus und Demokratie in der englischen Revolution* (Stuttgart).

Bernstein, E. (1895/6*a*), 'Deutschland als Konkurrent Englands', *NZ*, Jg. 14, Bd. 2.

Bernstein, E. (1895/6*b*), 'Die Kämpfe ums Burenland', *NZ*, Jg. 14, Bd. 1.

Bernstein, E. (1895/6*c*), 'Die Transvaalwirren und ihr internationaler Rückschlag', *NZ*, Jg. 14, Bd. 1.

Bernstein, E. (1896), 'William Morris: Eindrücke und Erinnerungen', *Der Sozialistische Akademiker*.

Bernstein, E. (1896/7*a*), 'Kreta', *NZ*, Jg. 15, Bd. 1.

Bernstein, E. (1896/7*b*), 'Kreta und die russische Gefahr', *NZ*, Jg. 15, Bd. 2.

Bernstein, E. (1896/7*c*), 'Die Sozialdemokratie und die türkischen Wirren', *NZ*, Jg. 15, Bd. 1.

Bernstein, E. (1896/7*d*), 'Eine Theorie der Gebiete und Grenzen des Kollektivismus', *NZ*, Jg. 15, Bd. 1.

Bernstein, E. (1896/7*e*), 'Zwei politische Programmsymphonien', *NZ*, Jg. 15, Bd. 2.

Bernstein, E. (1897/8*a*), 'Der Kampf der Sozialdemokratie und die Revolution der Gesellschaft', *NZ*, Jg. 16, Bd. 1.

Bernstein, E. (1897/8*b*), 'Kritisches Zwischenspiel', *NZ*, Jg. 16, Bd. 1.

Bernstein, E. (1897/8*c*), 'Zusammenbruchstheorie und Kolonialpolitik', *NZ*, Jg. 16, Bd. 1.

Bernstein, E. (1898/9), 'Stehendes Heer und Überproduktion', *NZ*, Jg. 17, Bd. 2.

Bernstein, E. ([1899] 1921), *Die Voraussetzungen des Sozialismus und die Aufgaben der Sozialdemokratie* (Stuttgart), English translation by Edith C. Harvey entitled *Evolutionary Socialism* (London, 1909).

Bernstein, E. (1900*a*), 'Paris und Mainz', *SM*.

Bernstein, E. (1900*b*), 'Sozialdemokratie und Imperialismus', *SM*.

Bernstein, E. (1900*c*), 'Der Sozialismus und die Kolonialfrage', *SM*.

Bernstein, E. (1900*d*), 'Zum Thema Sozialliberalismus und Kollektivismus', *SM*.

Bernstein, E. (1901*a*), 'Deutschlands soziale Gliederung', *SM*, Bd. 1.

Bernstein, E. (1901*b*), 'Eindrücke aus England', *Neue Deutsche Rundschau (Freie Volksbühne)*, Bd. 1.

Bernstein, E. (1901*c*), 'Einige Klippen der Internationalität', *SM*, Bd. 1.

Bernstein, E. (1901*d*), 'England und Dr A. Tilles Flegeljahre', *SM*, Bd. 1.

Bernstein, E. (1901*e*), 'Der gegenwärtige Stand der demokratischen Entwicklung Englands', *SM*, Bd. 2.

Bernstein, E. (1901*f*), 'Zum Kampf gegen die Zollschraube', *SM*, Bd. 2.

Bernstein, E. (1901*g*), 'Prinzipielles zur Frage der Agrarzölle', *SM*, Bd. 1.

Bernstein, E. (1901*h*), 'Der südafrikanische Krieg und die Sozialdemokratie', *SM*, Bd. 1.

Bernstein, E. (1901*i*), *Wie ist wissenschaftlicher Sozialismus möglich?* (Berlin).

Bernstein, E. (1902), *Die Leiden des armenischen Volkes und die Pflichten Europas* (Berlin).

Bernstein, E. (1903*a*), 'Zur Bilanz des Kampfes gegen den neuen Zolltarif', *SM*, Bd. 2.

Bernstein, E. (1903*b*), 'The growth of German exports', *Contemporary Review*, vol. 84.

Bernstein, E. (1903*c*), 'Was folgt aus dem Ergebnis der Reichstagswahlen?', *SM*, Bd. 2.

Bernstein, E. (1904*a*), 'Englands Wirtschaftsentwicklung im letzten Jahrzehnt', *SM*, Bd. 2.

Bernstein, E. (1904*b*), *Ferdinand Lassalle und seine Bedeutung für die Arbeiterklasse* (Berlin).

Bernstein, E. (1904*c*), 'German professors and protectionism', *Contemporary Review*, vol. 86.

Bernstein, E. (1904*d*), 'Der internationale Kongress in Amsterdam und die sozialistische Taktik', *SM*, Bd. 2.

Bernstein, E. (1904*e*), 'Nationale Besonderheiten und internationale Sprache', *SM*, Bd. 2.

Bernstein, E. (1904*f*), *Zur Theorie und Geschichte des Sozialismus: Gesammelte Abhandlungen*, 4th edn, 3 vols (Berlin).

Bernstein, E. (1904*g*), 'Was treibt England zum Reichszollverein?', *SM*, Bd. 2.

Bernstein, E. (1905*a*), 'Über Bernard Shaw', *SM*, Bd. 1.

Bernstein, E. (1905*b*), *Der politische Massenstreik* (Breslau).

Bernstein, E. (1905*c*), 'Revolutionen und Russland', *SM*, Bd. 1.

Bernstein, E. (1905*d*), 'Wird die Sozialdemokratie Volkspartei?' *SM*, Bd. 2.

Bernstein, E. (1906*a*), 'Fragen der Taktik in Russland', *SM*, Bd. 1.

Bernstein, E. (1906*b*), *Die neuen Reichssteuern* (Berlin).

Bernstein, E. (1906*c*), *Parlamentarismus und Sozialdemokratie* (Berlin).

Bernstein, E. (1906*d*), 'Politischer Massenstreik und Revolutionsromantik', *SM* Bd. 1.

Bernstein, E. (1906*e*), 'Zum sozialdemokratischen Parteitag in Mannheim', *SM* Bd. 2.

Bernstein, E. (1906*f*), *Der Streik* (Frankfurt-am-Main).

Bernstein, E. (1907*a*), 'The character of William II', *The Nation*, vol. 2, no. 7, 16 November.

Bernstein, E. (1907*b*), 'The German elections and the Social Democrats', *Contemporary Review*, vol. 91.

Bernstein, E. (1907*c*), 'German socialism and the colonial question', *The Nation*, vol. 2, no. 2, 12 October.

Bernstein, E. (1907*d*), 'Germany and the limitation of armaments', *The Nation*, vol. 1, no. 6, 6 April.

Bernstein, E. (1907*e*), 'Germany and the reform of the Prussian Diet', *The Nation*, vol. 1, no. 23, 10 August.

Bernstein, E. (1907*f*), 'Germany's Ireland', *The Nation*, vol. 2, no. 10, 7 December.

Bernstein, E. (1907*g*), *Ignaz Auer: Eine Gedenkschrift* (Berlin).

Bernstein, E. (1907*h*), 'Die Kolonialfrage und der Klassenkampf', *SM*, Bd. 2.

Bernstein, E. (1907*i*), 'Von Marx, Engels und ihrem Kreise', *SM*, Bd 2.

Bernstein, E. (1907*j*), 'The new Reichstag and its visions', *The Nation*, vol. 1, no. 1, 2 March.

Bernstein, E. (1907*k*), 'Patriotismus, Militarismus und Sozialdemokratie', *SM*, Bd. 1.

Bernstein, E. (1907*l*), 'After six years: a comparison of housing in London and Berlin', *The Nation*, vol. 1, no. 28, 7 September.

Bernstein, E. (1907*m*), 'Trade unionism in Germany', *Contemporary Review*, vol. 92.

Bernstein, E. (1908*a*), 'Arbeiterbewegung und Kultur', *Dokumente des Fortschritts*, Jg. 1, Bd. 1.

Bernstein, E. (1908*b*), 'Die Demokratie in der Sozialdemokratie', *SM*, Bd. 3.

Bernstein, E. (1908*c*), 'The German war peril', *The Nation*, vol. 3, no. 13, 27 June.

Bernstein, E. (1908*d*), 'Grundlinien des sozialdemokratischen Reformismus', *SM*, Bd. 3.

Bernstein, E. (1908*e*), 'Klassenpolitik und Gefühlspolitik', *SM*, Bd. 2.

Bernstein, E. (1908*f*), 'The land question in German towns', *The Nation*, vol. 2, no. 14, 4 January.

Bernstein, E. (1908*g*), 'Modernität im Kampf', *SM*, Bd. 3.

Bernstein, E. (1908*h*), 'The naval race and German finance', *The Nation*, vol. 2, no. 21, 22 February.

Bernstein, E. (1908*i*), 'The popular struggle in Prussia', *The Nation*, vol. 2, no. 16, 18 January.

Bernstein, E. (1908*j*), 'The revolt in German radicalism', *The Nation*, vol. 2, no. 20, 15 February.

Bernstein, E. (1908*k*), 'The struggle for German freedom', *The Nation*, vol. 4, no. 10, 5 December.

Bernstein, E. (1908*l*), 'The two heads of the Freisinn', *The Nation*, vol. 3, no. 6, 9 May.

Bernstein, E. (1908*m*), 'The Zeppelin movement and German nationalism', *The Nation*, vol. 3, no. 21, 22 August.

Bernstein, E. (1909*a*), 'Arms and the bill', *The Nation*, vol. 4, no. 25, 20 March.

Bernstein, E. (1909*b*), 'Clearing the air', *The Nation*, vol. 4, no. 26, 27 March.

Bernstein, E. (1909*c*), 'The electoral policy of German social democracy', *The Nation*, vol. 6, no. 11, 11 December.

Bernstein, E. (1909*d*), 'Der Freischälersozialismus wider die Arbeiterpartei Grossbritanniens', *SM*, Bd. 1.

Bernstein, E. (1909*e*), 'Die internationale Politik der Sozialdemokratie', *SM*, Bd. 2.

Bernstein, E. (1909*f*), 'Die Massen werden irre', *SM*, Bd. 2.

Bernstein, E. (1909*g*), 'The meaning of the Bülow crisis', *The Nation*, vol. 5, no. 4, 3 July.

Bernstein, E. (1909*h*), 'The new chancellor and the old game', *The Nation*, vol. 5, no. 17, 24 July.

Bernstein, E. (1909*i*), 'Peace and King Edward's visit', *The Nation*, vol. 4, no. 21, 20 February.

Bernstein, E. (1909*j*), 'The pull towards the left in Germany', *The Nation*, vol. 6, no. 6, 6 November.

Bernstein, E. (1909*k*), 'Das Recht des sozialdemokratischen Schriftstellers', *SM*, Bd. 2.

Bernstein, E. (1909*l*), 'Revisionismus und Programmrevision', *SM*, Bd. 1.

Bernstein, E. (1909*m*), *Der Revisionismus in der Sozialdemokratie* (Amsterdam).

Bernstein, E. (1909*n*), 'The revival of will in German literature', *The Nation*, vol. 4, no. 15, 9 January.

Bernstein, E. (1910*a*), 'The backwater of German jingoism', *The Nation*, vol. 7, no. 18, 30 July.

Bernstein, E. (1910*b*), 'The death of a deformed Reform Bill', *The Nation*, vol. 7, no. 10, 4 June.

Bernstein, E. (1910*c*), 'Die Demokratisierung Englands und der Fall Shackleton', *SM*, Bd. 3.

Bernstein, E. (1910*d*), 'The early days of August Bebel', *The Nation*, vol. 7, no. 9, 28 May.

Bernstein, E. (1910*e*), 'The eve of the Prussian revolution', *The Nation*, vol. 7, no. 1, 2 April.

Bernstein, E. (1910*f*), 'Internationale Beschlüsse und ihr Anspruch', *SM*, Bd. 2.

Bernstein, E. (1910*g*), 'Kulturverelendungstheorie', *SM*, Bd. 1.

Bernstein, E. (1910*h*), 'Political scene-shifting in Germany', *The Nation*, vol. 7, no. 17, 23 July.

Bernstein, E. (1910*i*), 'Die Potenz politischer Massenstreiks', *SM*, Bd. 2.

Bernstein, E. (1911*a*), 'Breakers ahead', *The Nation*, vol. 9, no. 23, 2 September.

Bernstein, E. (1911*b*), *Die englische Gefahr und das deutsche Volk* (Berlin).

Bernstein, E. (1911*c*), 'Das Finanzkapital und die Handelspolitik', *SM*, Bd. 2.

Bernstein, E. (1911*d*), 'Das Grundsätzliche in der Frage der Handelspolitik', *SM*, Bd. 1.

Bernstein, E. (1911*e*), 'Herr von Bethmann Hollweg's first success', *The Nation*, vol. 9, no. 11, 10 June.

Bernstein, E. (1911*f*), 'How the new Reichstag will look', *The Nation*, vol. 10, no. 13, 30 December.

Bernstein, E. (1911*g*), 'Der kanadisch-amerikanische Schicksalsschlag', *SM*, Bd. 1.

Bernstein, E. (1911*h*), 'The meaning of the German chancellor's speech', *The Nation*, vol. 9, no. 2, 8 April.

Bernstein, E. (1911*i*), 'The Morocco debates in the Reichstag', *The Nation*, vol. 10, no. 7, 18 November.

Bernstein, E. (1911*j*), 'Neue Englandhetze', *Vorwärts*, 1 September.

Bernstein, E. (1911*k*), 'Protestant heretics in Prussia', *The Nation*, vol. 9, no. 16, 15 July.

Bernstein, E. (1911*l*), *Von der Sekte zur Partei: Die deutsche Sozialdemokratie einst und jetzt* (Jena).

Bernstein, E. (1911*m*), 'Social insanity', *The Nation*, vol. 10, no. 2, 14 October.

Bernstein, E. (1911*n*), 'Zollfreier internationaler Verkehr', *SM*, Bd. 2.

Bernstein, E. (1912*a*), 'Allerhand moderner Spuk', *SM*, Bd. 1.

Bernstein, E. (1912*b*), 'Bedeutung und Aufgaben des Sieges', *SM*, Bd. 1.

Bernstein, E. (1912*c*), 'Darf Hildebrand ausgeschlossen werden?', *SM*, Bd. 3.

Bernstein, E. (1912*d*), 'Between the first and the second ballot in Germany', *The Nation*, vol. 10, no. 16, 20 January.

Bernstein, E. (1912*e*), 'Vom Parlament und vom Parlamentarismus', *SM*, Bd. 2.

Bernstein, E. (1912*f*), 'Politische Schwarzmalerei', *SM*, Bd. 1.

Bernstein, E. (1912*g*), 'The presidency of the Reichstag and Lord Haldane's visit', *The Nation*, vol. 10, no. 20, 17 February.

Bernstein, E. (1912*h*), 'Wie ist eine Kooperation der Parteien der Linken im Deutschen Reichstag möglich?', *Documente des Fortschritts*, Jg. 5, Bd. 1.

Bernstein, E. (1912*i*), 'Wie man Kriegsstimmung erzeugt', *Die Friedens-Warte*, Jg. 14, Bd. 1.

Bernstein, E. (1912*j*), 'Victrix insania', *The Nation*, vol. 10, no. 26, 30 March.

Bernstein, E. (1913*a*), 'Almighty, all-devouring militarism', *The Nation*, vol. 13, no. 1, 5 April.

Bernstein, E. (1913*b*), 'From Berlin to Berne', *The Nation*, vol. 13, no. 8, 24 May.

Bernstein, E. (1913*c*), 'Eine demokratische Bibliothek', *Frankfurter Zeitung*, 12–13 January.

Bernstein, E. (1913*d*), 'Geburtenrückgang, Nationalität und Kultur', *SM*, Bd. 3.

Bernstein, E. (1913*e*), 'The German army bill and the taxes', *The Nation*, vol. 13, no. 15, 12 July.

Bernstein, E. (1913*f*), 'The marauders', *The Nation*, vol. 13, no. 4, 26 April.

Bernstein, E. (1913*g*), 'The milestone of the Jena congress', *The Nation*, vol. 13, no. 26, 27 September.

Bernstein, E. (1913*h*), 'The nemesis of force', *The Nation*, vol. 14, no. 5, 1 November.

Bernstein, E. (1913*i*), 'Regierung und Sozialisten', *SM*, Bd. 2.

Bernstein, E. (1913*j*), 'The result of the second Krupp trial', *The Nation*, vol. 14, no. 7, 15 November.

Bernstein, E. (1913*k*), 'A sacrifice to folly', *The Nation*, vol. 12, no. 24, 15 March.

Bernstein, E. (1913/14), 'Der Schulstreit in Palästina', *NZ*, Jg. 32, Bd. 1.

Bernstein, E. (1914*a*), 'Abrechnung mit Russland', *Vorwärts*, 26–28 August.

Bernstein, E. (1914*b*), 'Ein Beispiel', *Vorwärts*, 14 November.

Bernstein, E. (1914*c*), 'The German Chancellor's reply and after', *The Nation*, vol. 14, no. 18, 31 January.

Bernstein, E. (1914*d*), 'Der Krieg, sein Urheber und sein erstes Opfer', *SM*, Bd. 2.

Bernstein, E. (1914*e*), 'The meaning of the Strassburg verdict', *The Nation*, vol. 14, no. 16, 17 January.

Bernstein, E. (1914*f*), 'Die politische Krise in England', *SM*, Bd. 1.

Bernstein, E. (1914*g*), *Die Steuerpolitik der Sozialdemokratie* (Berlin).

Bernstein, E. (1914*h*), 'Was hat die sozialdemokratische Presse während des Krieges zu tun?', *Leipziger Volkszeitung*, 3 November.

Bernstein, E. (1914/15), 'Der englische Radikalismus und der Krieg', *NZ*, Jg. 33, Bd. 1.

Bernstein, E. (1915*a*), 'Eine Erinnerung', *SAK*, Jg. 1, Nr. 15, 20 July.

Bernstein, E. (1915*b*), *Die Internationale der Arbeiterklasse und der europäische Krieg* (Tübingen).

Bernstein, E. (1915*c*), 'Jean Jaurès' Erbe. Zum Gedächtnis seines Todestages', *SAK*, Jg. 1, Nr. 16, 27 July.

Bernstein, E. (1915*d*), 'Revisionismus und Internationalismus', *SAK*, Jg. 1, Nr. 7, 16 June.

Bernstein, E. (1915*e*), 'Die sogenannten nationalen Lebensfragen', *Internationale Rundschau*, Jg. 1.

Bernstein, E. (1915*f*), 'Überschätzte Friedensmächte', *Die Friedens-Warte*, Jg. 17, Bd. 4.

Bernstein, E. (1915*g*), 'Verfehlte Ausschlachtung der Klassiker des Sozialismus', *SAK*, Jg. 1, Nr. 12, 13 July.

Bernstein, E. (1915*h*), *Wesen und Aussichten des bürgerlichen Radikalismus* (Munich).

Bernstein, E. (1915*i*), 'Wie Fichte und Lassalle national waren', *Archiv für die Geschichte des Sozialismus und der Arbeiterbewegung*, Jg. 5.

Bernstein, E. (1915/16), 'Irland – eine Lehre', *NZ*, Jg. 34, Bd. 2.

Bernstein, E. (1916*a*), 'Die Bedeutung von Bristol', *SAK*, Jg. 2, Nr. 6, 16 February.

Bernstein, E. (1916*b*), 'Eine neue Theorie, warum der Weltkrieg kam', *SAK*, Jg. 2, Nr. 40, 12 October.

Bernstein, E. (1916*c*), *Die parlamentarische Kontrolle der auswärtigen Politik* (The Hague).

Bernstein, E. (1916*d*), 'Vom Patriotismus der Juden', *Die Friedens-Warte*, Jg. 18, Bd. 8/9.

Bernstein, E. (1916*e*), 'Unsere parlamentarischen Abstimmungen', *SAK*, Jg. 2, Nr. 3, 27 January.

Bernstein, E. (1916*f*), 'Weltbürgertum, Judentum und Patriotismus', *SAK*, Jg. 2, Nr. 42, 25 October.

Bernstein, E. (1916/17), 'Revenant Bülow', *NZ*, Jg. 35, Bd. 2.

Bernstein, E. (1917*a*), *Die Aufgaben der Juden im Weltkriege* (Berlin).

Bernstein, E. (1917*b*), *Sozialdemokratische Völkerpolitik* (Leipzig).

Bernstein, E. (1918*a*), *Aus den Jahren meines Exils* (Berlin).

Bernstein, E. (1918*b*), 'Ein Beitrag zum kommenden Friedenskongress', *SAK*, Jg. 4, Nr. 42, 17 October.

Bernstein, E. (1918*c*), 'Betrachtungen über das Wesen der Sowjetrepublik', *SAK*, Jg. 4, Nr. 38, 19 September.

Bernstein, E. (1918*d*), 'Friedensvertrag und Friedenszustand', *SAK*, Jg. 4, Nr. 3, 13 January.

Bernstein, E. (1918*e*), 'Rhetorik und Politik mit doppeltem Boden', *SAK*, Jg. 4, Nr. 33, 15 August.

Bernstein, E. (1918*f*), *Völkerbund oder Staatenbund?* (Berlin).

Bernstein, E. (1918*g*), *Was ist Sozialismus?* (Berlin).

Bernstein, E. (1919*a*), *Völkerrecht und Völkerpolitik* (Berlin).

Bernstein, E. (1919*b*), *Die Wahrheit über die Einkreisung Deutschlands* (Berlin).

Bernstein, E. (1921), *Wie eine Revolution zugrunde ging* (Berlin).

Bernstein, E. (1924), *Entwicklungsgang eines Sozialisten* (Berlin).

Bernstein, E. (1928), *Sozialdemokratische Lehrjahre* (Berlin).

Bernstein, E. (1929), 'Ferdinand Lassalles Kampf um Bismarck', *Die Gleichheit*, Jg. 6, Bd. 1.

Bernstein, E. (1976), *Ein revisionistisches Sozialismusbild*, 2nd edn, ed. H. Hirsch (Berlin).

Bernstein, E. (1977), *Texte zum Revisionismus*, ed. H. Heimann (Bonn).
Bernstein, E. (n.d.), *England and Germany: Reflections on the Possibility of an Under-standing* (The Hague).
Bloch, J. [pseud. Catilina] (1895*a*), 'Die anarchistischen Lehren und ihr Verhältnis zum Kommunismus', *Der Sozialistische Akademiker*.
Bloch, J. [pseud. Catilina] (1895*b*), 'Zum 80. Geburtstag des Fürsten Otto von Bismarck' *Der Sozialistische Akademiker*.
Bloch, J. [pseud. Catilina] (1895*c*), 'Einiges über die deutsche Sozialdemokratie', *Der Sozialistische Akademiker*.
Bloch, J. (1901), 'An den Abgeordneten Stadthagen', *Vorwärts*, 17 September.
Bloch, J. (1906), 'Bernard Shaw über seine Stellung zur deutschen Sozialdemokratie', *SM*, Bd. 2.
Bloch, J. (1910), 'Zurück zur Negation?', *SM*, Bd. 2.
Bloch, J. (1914), 'Der Krieg und die Sozialdemokratie', *SM*, Bd. 2.
Bloch, J. (1938), *Revolution der Weltpolitik. See under* Stössinger.
Blumenberg, W. (ed.) (1965), *August Bebels Briefwechsel mit Friedrich Engels* (The Hague).
Brailsford, H. N. (1914), *The War of Steel and Gold* (London).
Braun, L. (1911), *Memoiren einer Sozialistin: Kampfjahre* (Munich).
Broda, R. (1910), 'Das englische Kolonialreich', *Documente des Fortschritts*, Jg. 3, Bd. 2.
Bülow, Fürst B. von (1914), *Imperial Germany*, trans. Marie A. Lewenz (New York).
Calwer, R. (1900), 'Mitteleuropäische Handelspolitik', *Neue Deutsche Rundschau* (*Freie Volksbühne*), Jg. 11, Bd. 2.
Calwer, R. (1904), 'Der britische Reichszollverein', *SM*, Bd. 1.
Calwer, R. (1905), 'Englands Absichten und die deutsche Sozialdemokratie', *SM*, Bd. 2.
Calwer, R. (1906), *Einführung in die Weltwirtschaft* (Berlin).
Calwer, R. (1907*a*), 'Der 25. Januar', *SM*, Bd. 1.
Calwer, R. (1907*b*), 'Kolonialpolitik und Sozialdemokratie', *SM*, Bd. 1.
Calwer, R. (1908), 'Deutsch-französische Annäherung', *SM*, Bd. 2.
Catilina. *See* Bloch, J.
Cobden, R. (1878), *Speeches on Questions of Public Policy*, ed. J. Bright and J. E. Thorold Rogers (London).
Cunow, H. (1899/1900), 'Handelsvertrags- und imperialistische Expansionspolitik', *NZ*, Jg. 18, Bd. 2.
Daughters of Karl Marx. Family Correspondence 1866–1898, The (1982), commentary and notes by O. Meier, translated and adapted by F. Evans, introduction by S. Row-botham (London).
David, E. (1905*a*), 'Schrittmacher der Internationalität', *NG*, Bd. 1.
David, E. (1905*b*), 'Sozialdemokratische Briefe über Vaterlandsliebe', *NG*, Bd. 1.
David, E. (1909), 'In Sachen Leuthner', *Vorwärts*, 6 May.
David, E. (1913), 'Die Rüstungsmanie', *Dokumente des Fortschritts*, Jg. 6, Bd. 1.
David, E. (1922), *Sozialismus und Landwirtschaft*, 2nd edn (Leipzig).
Eckardstein, Baron von (1921), *Lebenserinnerungen und politische Denkwürdigkeiten*, 3 vols (Leipzig).
Eisner, K. (1892), *Psychopathia spiritualis: Friedrich Nietzsche und die Apostel der Zukunft* (Leipzig).
Eisner, K. (1904), *Der Geheimbund des Zaren* (Berlin).
Eisner, K. (1905), 'Zur Literatenpsychologie', *NG*, Bd. 1.
Eisner, K. (1906), *Der Sultan des Weltkrieges: Ein marokkanisches Sittenbild deutscher Diplomatenpolitik* (Dresden).
Eisner, K. (1907), *Das Ende des Reiches: Deutschland und Preussen im Zeitalter der grossen Revolution* (Berlin).

Eisner, K. (1919*a*), *Gesammelte Schriften*, 2 vols (Berlin).

Eisner, K. (1919*b*), *Schuld und Sühne* (Berlin).

Eisner, K. (1919*c*), *Unterdrücktes aus dem Weltkreig* (Munich).

Eisner, K. (1969), *Die halbe Macht den Räten*, ed. R. and G. Schmolze (Cologne).

Engels, F. (1890/1), 'Die auswärtige Politik des russischen Zarismus', *NZ*, Jg. 9, Bd. 1.

Fischer, E. (1913), 'Krieg und Sozialdemokratie', *SM*, Bd. 2.

Frank, L. (n.d. [1924]), *Reden, Aufsätze und Briefe: Ein Vorbild der deutschen Arbeiter-jugend*, ed. H. Wachenheim (Berlin).

Frantz, C. ([1882] 1966), *Die Weltpolitik, unter besonderer Bezugnahme auf Deutschland* (Osnabrück).

Frei, E. (1900), 'Zur Flottenpolitik', *SM*.

Gystrow, E. [pseud. W. Hellpach] (1900), 'Etwas über Nietzsche und uns Sozialisten', *SM*.

Haenisch, K., (1899/1900), 'Was lesen die Arbeiter?', *NZ*, Jg. 18, Bd. 2.

Haldane, R. B. (1920), *Before the War* (London).

Hanssen, H. P. (1955), *Diary of a Dying Empire*, trans. O. O. Winter, (Bloomington, Ind.).

Heilmann, E. (n.d. [1912]), *Geschichte der Arbeiterbewegung in Chemnitz und dem Erzgebirge* (Chemnitz).

Héritier, L. (1897), *Geschichte der französischen Revolution von 1848 und der zweiten Republik in volkstümlicher Darstellung*, ed. E. Bernstein and W. Eichhoff (Stuttgart).

Hildebrand, G. (1909), 'Weltpolitische Bilanz', *SM*, Bd. 2.

Hildebrand, G. (1910*a*), 'Die Entwicklung Persiens und das Interesse der deutschen Arbeiterklasse', *SM*, Bd. 3.

Hildebrand, G. (1910*b*), *Die Erschütterung der Industrieherrschaft und des Industrie-sozialismus* (Jena).

Hildebrand, G. (1911*a*), 'Die britische Reichskonferenz', *SM*, Bd. 2.

Hildebrand, G. (1911*b*), *Sozialistische Auslandspolitik: Betrachtungen über die weltpoli-tische Lage anlässlich des Marokkostreites* (Jena).

Hilferding, R. (1908/9), 'Der Revisionismus und die Internationale', *NZ*, Jg. 27, Bd. 2.

Hilferding, R. ([1910] 1974), *Das Finanzkapital*, 3rd edn (Frankfurt-am-Main).

Hirsch, H. (ed.) (1970), *Eduard Bernstein Briefwechsel mit Friedrich Engels* (Assen).

Hobhouse, L. T. (1911), *Liberalism* (London).

Hobson, J. A. (1900), *The War in South Africa: Its Causes and Effects* (London).

Hobson, J. A. (1901), *The Psychology of Jingoism* (London).

Hobson, J. A. (1901/2), 'Socialistic Imperialism', *International Journal of Ethics*, vol. 12, no. 1.

Hobson, J. A. (1904), *International Trade: An Application of Economic Theory* (London).

Hobson, J. A. (1913), *The German Panic* (London).

Hobson, J. A. (1915), *Towards International Government* (London).

Hobson, J. A. (1919), *Richard Cobden, The International Man* (London).

Hobson, J. A. (1938*a*), *Confessions of an Economic Heretic* (London).

Hobson, J. A. (1938*b*), *Imperialism: A Study*, 3rd rev. edn (London).

Kampffmeyer, P. (1909*a*), 'Marx und die wissenschaftliche Begründung des Marxis-mus', *SM*, Bd. 1.

Kampffmeyer, P. (1909*b*), 'Zur wissenschaftlichen Begründung des Sozialismus', *SM*, Bd. 1.

Kampffmeyer, P. (1911), 'Der ethische Ausgangspunkt des Marxismus', *SM*, Bd. 1.

Kautsky, K. (1897/8), 'Ältere und neuere Kolonialpolitik', *NZ*, Jg. 16, Bd. 1.

Kautsky, K. (1902), *Die soziale Revolution* (Berlin).

Kautsky, K. (1907*a*), *Patriotismus und Sozialdemokratie* (Leipzig).

Kautsky, K. (1907*b*), *Sozialismus und Kolonialpolitik* (Berlin).

Kautsky, K. (1910), *Der Weg zur Macht* (Berlin).

Kautsky, K. (1910/11), 'Krieg und Frieden', *NZ*, Jg. 29, Bd. 2.

Kautsky, K. (1911/12), 'Der erste Mai und der Kampf gegen den Militarismus', *NZ*, Jg. 30, Bd. 2.

Kautsky, K. (1912), *Weltpolitik, Weltkrieg und Sozialdemokratie* (Berlin).

Kautsky, K. (1913/14), 'Der Imperialismus', *NZ*, Jg. 32, Bd. 2.

Kautsky, K. (1914), *Der politische Massenstreik* (Berlin).

Keynes, J. M. (1936), *The General Theory of Employment, Interest and Money* (London).

Kliche, J. (1911), 'Arbeiterlektüre', *SM*, Bd. 1.

Laskine, E. (1915), *Les Socialistes du Kaiser* (Paris).

Lenin, V. I. (1955–), *Werke* (Berlin).

Lenin, V. I. (1966), *Against Revisionism*, 2nd edn (Moscow).

Lenin, V. I. (1972), *About the Press* (Prague), compiled by International Organization of Journalists.

Lenin, V. I. ([1916] 1978), *Imperialism, the Highest Stage of Capitalism* (Moscow).

Lensch, P. (1911/12), 'Miliz und Abrüstung', *NZ*, Jg. 30, Bd. 2.

Leuthner, K. (1902), *Arbeiterschaft und Zwischenhandel* (Vienna).

Leuthner, K. (1905), 'Die internationale Politik des deutschen Proletariats', *NG*, Bd. 1, Nr. 26.

Leuthner, K. (1906*a*), 'Ein Antimilitarist', *NG*, Bd. 3.

Leuthner, K. (1906*b*), 'Armee und Revolution', *NG*, Bd. 2, Nr. 36.

Leuthner, K. (1906*c*), 'Deutschtum und Socialdemokratie', *NG*, Bd. 2, Nr. 16.

Leuthner, K. (1906*d*), 'Hervorgang der Demokratie aus der Sozialdemokratie', *NG*, Bd. 2, Nr. 1.

Leuthner, K. (1906*e*), 'Die Internationale und der Krieg', *NG*, Bd. 2, Nr. 12.

Leuthner, K. (1906*f*), 'Jena', *NG*, Jg. 2, Nr. 3.

Leuthner, K. (1906*g*), 'Der Moskauer Kampf', *NG*, Bd. 2, Nr. 2.

Leuthner, K. (1906*h*), 'Eine Politik der vierten Dimension', *NG*, Jg. 2, Nr. 9.

Leuthner, K. (1906*i*), 'Der Sturz des österreichischen Wahlrechtsministers', *NG*, Bd. 2, Nr. 19.

Leuthner, K. (1906*j*), 'Volksautorität, *NG*, Jg. 2, Nr. 16.

Leuthner, K. (1907*a*), 'Friedens-Konferenzen und Friedens-Bürgschaften', *NG*, Bd. 4, Nr. 4.

Leuthner, K. (1907*b*), 'Die Haager Konferenz', *NG*, Bd. 5, Nr. 18.

Leuthner, K. (1907*c*), 'Kirche und Sozialdemokratie', *NG*, Bd. 3, Nr. 14.

Leuthner, K. (1907*d*), *Gegen die Klerikalen* (Vienna).

Leuthner, K. (1907*e*), 'Das Kolonialproblem', *NG*, Bd. 5, Nr. 8.

Leuthner, K. (1907*f*), 'Auf neuem Kampfboden', *NG*, Bd. 3, Nr. 20.

Leuthner, K. (1907*g*), 'Ein schweres Werk', *NG*, Bd. 3, Nr. 6.

Leuthner, K. (1907*h*), 'Sozialdemokratischer Antimilitarismus', *SM*, Bd. 2.

Leuthner, K. (1907*i*), 'Ursachen und Wesen der russischen Revolution', in *Österreichischer Arbeiter-Kalender 1907* (Vienna).

Leuthner, K. (1908*a*), 'Die Aufgabe der deutschen Sozialdemokratie in der auswärtigen Politik', *SM*, Bd. 3.

Leuthner, K. (1908*b*), 'Bilder im Hohlspiegel', *SM*, Bd. 1.

Leuthner, K. (1908*c*), 'Der Budgetstreit und was daran hängt', *SM*, Bd. 2.

Leuthner, K. (1908*d*), 'Demokratie und Selbstbehauptung der Nation', *SM*, Bd. 1.

Leuthner, K. (1908*e*), 'Deutscher Jammer', *SM*, Bd. 1.

Leuthner, K. (1908*f*), 'Das Ende der polnischen Reichsidee', *SM*, Bd. 2.

Leuthner, K. (1908*g*), 'Die Erneuerung der Türkei', *SM*, Bd. 2.

Leuthner, K. (1908*h*), 'Internationaler Lärm um nichts', *SM*, Bd. 3.

Leuthner, K. (1908*i*), 'Junker und Jude', *SM*, Bd. 2.

Leuthner, K. (1908*j*), 'Der Katholizismus als Kulturhemmung', *SM*, Bd. 1.

Leuthner, K. (1908*k*), 'Monarchismus und Macht des Reiches', *SM*, Bd. 3.

Leuthner, K. (1908*l*), 'Von der Verpreussung Deutschlands', *SM*, Bd. 2.
Leuthner, K. (1909*a*), 'Andere Verhältnisse', *SM*, Bd. 1.
Leuthner, K. (1909*b*), 'Der entblätterte Dreibund', *SM*, Bd. 3.
Leuthner, K. (1909*c*), 'Herrenvolk und Pöbelvolk', *SM*, Bd. 1.
Leuthner, K. (1909*d*), 'International und national', *SM*, Bd. 1.
Leuthner, K. (1909*e*), 'Klassengegensätze und Parteibündnisse', *SM*, Bd. 2.
Leuthner, K. (1909*f*), 'Notgedrungene Erklärung', *SM*, Bd. 1.
Leuthner, K. (1909*g*), 'Parteitagsnachklänge', *SM*, Bd. 3.
Leuthner, K. (1909*h*), 'Politische und humanitärische Idee', *SM*, Bd. 2
Leuthner, K. (1909*i*), 'Das serbische Problem', *SM*, Bd. 1.
Leuthner, K. (1909*j*), 'Stimmungs- und Realpolitik', *SM*, Bd. 2.
Leuthner, K. (1909*k*), 'Umlernen', *SM*, Bd. 1.
Leuthner, K. (1910*a*), 'Allgemeine Friedensbürgschaften', *SM*, Bd. 2.
Leuthner, K. (1910*b*), 'Einst und jetzt', *SM*, Bd. 1.
Leuthner, K. (1910*c*), 'Das Königtum und die Wahlreformaktion', *SM*, Bd. 1.
Leuthner, K. (1910*d*), 'Parlament und Demokratie', *SM*, Bd. 2.
Leuthner, K. (1910*e*), 'Parlament und Parlamentsreform', *SM*, Bd. 1.
Leuthner, K. (1910*f*), 'Ein Selbstporträt', *Arbeiter-Zeitung*, 1 March.
Leuthner, K. (1910*g*), 'Tolstois Leben und Werke', *Arbeiter-Zeitung*, 21 November.
Leuthner, K. (1910*h*), 'Wandlungen der Journalistik', *SM*, Bd. 1.
Leuthner, K. (1911*a*), 'Additionelle Lebenswerte', *SM*, Bd. 2.
Leuthner, K. (1911*b*), 'Der britische Imperialismus', *SM*, Bd. 1.
Leuthner, K. (1911*c*), 'Ein Nachwort zum Innsbrucker Parteitag', *SM*, Bd. 3.
Leuthner, K. (1911*d*), 'Der Niedergang einer Parteidespotie', *SM*, Bd. 2.
Leuthner, K. (1911*e*), 'Der Staat der Demagogie', *SM*, Bd. 2.
Leuthner, K. (1911*f*), 'Tripolitanischer Lehrkurs', *SM*, Bd. 3.
Leuthner, K. (1911*g*), 'Der Zwang zum Positiven', *SM*, Bd. 2.
Leuthner, K. (1912*a*), 'Das Balkanproblem und Österreich-Ungarn', *SM*, Bd. 3.
Leuthner, K. (1912*b*), 'Die Entente und das Ende des deutschen Orientpolitik', *SM*, Bd. 2.
Leuthner, K. (1912*c*), 'Vor geöffnetem Tor', *SM*, Bd. 1.
Leuthner, K. (1912*d*), 'Vom Seekrieg zum Landkrieg', *SM*, Bd. 1.
Leuthner, K. (1912*e*), 'Täuschung und Selbsttäuschung', *SM*, Bd. 3.
Leuthner, K. (1912*f*), 'Ein übersehenes Ereignis', *SM*, Bd. 2.
Leuthner, K. (1912*g*), 'Volksinteresse und Staatsschicksal', *SM*, Bd. 3.
Leuthner, K. (1912*h*), 'Die Weltherrschaft der Angstneurose', *SM*, Bd. 1.
Leuthner, K. (1912*i*), 'Wozu – wohin?', *SM*, Bd. 2.
Leuthner, K. (1913*a*), 'Die Angstneurose als Staatspolitik', *SM*, Bd. 2.
Leuthner, K. (1913*b*), *Bankerott unserer Balkanpolitik* (Vienna).
Leuthner, K. (1913*c*), 'Das kontinentale Deutschland', *SM*, Bd. 1.
Leuthner, K. (1913*d*), 'Der Krieg als eine moralische Anstalt betrachtet', *SM*, Bd. 1.
Leuthner, K. (1913*e*), 'Das Machtproblem und die Demokratie', *SM*, Bd. 3.
Leuthner, K. (1913*f*), 'Die Wiener Politik', *SM*, Bd. 1.
Leuthner, K. (1914*a*), 'Ist es noch der selbe Krieg?', *SM*, Bd. 3.
Leuthner, K. (1914*b*), 'Der sterbende Dreadnoughtwahn', *Der Kampf*, Jg. 7, Nr. 10.
Leuthner, K. (1915), *Russischer Volksimperialismus* (Berlin).
Leuthner, K. (1926), 'Erinnerungen an Victor Adler', *Arbeiter-Zeitung*, 7 November.
Lilienthal, E. (1910*a*), 'Deutschlands Feinde: Ein Wort in Sachen Dänemarks', *Documente des Fortschritts*, Jg. 3, Bd. 2.
Lilienthal, E. (1910*b*), 'Internationalismus und Nationalgefühl', *Documente des Fortschritts*, Jg. 3, Bd. 1.
Lloyd George, D. (1911), *Bessere Zeiten*, ed. E. Bernstein, trans. H. Simon (Jena).
Luxemburg, R. (1899*a*), 'Die englische Brille', *Leipziger Volkszeitung*, 9–10 May.

Luxemburg, R. (1899*b*), 'Verschiebungen in der Weltpolitik', *Leipziger Volkszeitung*, 13 March.

Luxemburg, R. (1963), *The Accumulation of Capital*, trans. A. Schwarzschild, intro. J. Robinson (London).

Luxemburg, R. (1979), *Comrade and Lover: Rosa Luxemburg's Letters to Leo Jogiches*, ed. and trans. E. Ettinger (Cambridge, Mass.).

MacDonald, J. R. (1907), *Labour and the Empire* (London).

MacDonald, J. R. (1908), 'England und Deutschland', *SM*, Bd. 2.

MacDonald, J. R. (1912), *Sozialismus und Regierung*, ed. E. Bernstein, trans. O. Peterssen (Jena).

Marx, K., and Engels, F. (1975–   ), *Collected Works*, 50 vols (Moscow and London).

Maurenbrecher, M. (1907), 'Was heisst Antimilitarismus?', *NG*, Bd. 5.

Maurenbrecher, M. (1909), 'Englische und proletarische Politik', *SM*, Bd. 2.

Mehring, Fr. (1898–9), 'Bernstein und der Zürich-Londoner *Sozial-Demokrat*', *NZ*, Jg. 17, Bd. 2.

Michels, R. (1907), 'Die deutsche Sozialdemokratie im internationalen Verbande', *Archiv für Sozialwissenschaft und Sozialpolitik*, Bd. 25.

Michels, R. (1911), *Zur Soziologie des Parteiwesens in der modernen Demokratie* (Leipzig).

Mill, J. S. (1867*a*), *Considerations on Representative Government* (London).

Mill, J. S. (1867*b*), *Dissertations and Discussions*, Vol. 3 (London).

Mill, J. S. (1924), *Autobiography*, ed. J. J. Coss (New York).

Mill, J. S. ([1848] 1976), *Principles of Political Economy*, reprint of 1909 edn (Fairfield, N J).

Mundt, M. (1909), 'Zur Angelegenheit der *Sozialistischen Monatshefte*', *Vorwärts*, 26 June.

Nitschke, W. (1913), 'Wie und nach welcher Richtung entwickelt sich das Lesebedürfnis der Arbeiterschaft?', *SM*, Bd. 1.

Noske, G. (1947), *Erlebtes aus Aufstieg und Niedergang einer Demokratie* (Offenbach-am-Main).

Pannekoek, A. (1911/12), 'Das Wesen unserer Gegenwartsforderungen', *NZ*, Jg. 30, Bd. 2.

Pannekoek, A. (1913/14), 'Deckungsfrage und Imperialismus', *NZ*, Jg. 32, Bd. 1.

Parvus-Helphand, A. I. (1900/1), 'Die Industriezölle und der Weltmarkt', *NZ*, Jg. 19, Bd. 1.

Parvus-Helphand, A. I. (1907), *Die Kolonialpolitik und der Zusammenbruch* (Leipzig).

Pease, E. R. (1905), 'Ist England Deutschlands Feind?', *NG*, Bd. 1.

Pease, E. R. (1925), *The History of the Fabian Society*, 2nd edn (London).

Pernerstorfer, E. (1905), 'Der nationale und der internationale Gedanke', *SM*, Bd. 2.

Quessel, L. (1912*a*), 'Die Furcht vor dem Imperialismus', *SM*, Bd. 1.

Quessel, L. (1912*b*), 'Die ökonomische Bedeutung des Imperiums', *SM*, Bd. 2.

Quessel, L. (1913*a*), 'Die Stellung der sozialdemokratischen Fraktion zu den Wehr- und Deckungsvorlagen', *SM*, Bd. 2.

Quessel, L. (1913*b*), 'Verständigung und Imperialismus', *SM*, Bd. 1.

Quessel, L. (1913*c*), 'Auf dem Weg zum Weltreich', *SM*, Bd. 2.

Quessel, L. (1914), 'Das parlamentarische Regierungssystem und der Imperialismus', *SM*, Bd. 1.

Radek, K. (1911/12), 'Zu unserem Kampfe gegen den Imperialismus', *NZ*, Jg. 30, Bd. 2.

Renner, K. (1909), 'Bebels *Frau*: Zur 50. Auflage des Buches', *Der Kampf*, Jg. 3, Nr. 3.

Renner, K. (1911), 'Nach Innsbruck', *Der Kampf*, Jg. 5. Nr. 3.

Renner, K. (1915), 'Sozialistischer Imperialismus oder internationaler Sozialismus?', *Der Kampf*, Jg. 8, Nr. 3.

Riezler, K. (1972), *Tagebücher, Aufsätze, Dokumente*, ed. K.-D. Erdmann (Göttingen).

Rother, E. (1899), 'Zur Theorie der Flottenfrage', *SM*.

Saint-Simon, H. (1975), *Selected Writings on Science, Industry and Social Organisation*, ed. K. Taylor (London).

Sarolea, C. (1912), *The Anglo-German Problem* (London).

Sarolea, C. (1917), *German Problems and Personalities* (London).

Scheidemann, P. (1930), *Memoiren eines Sozialisten*, 2 vols (Dresden).

Schifrin, A. (1933), 'Eduard Bernstein', *Deutsche Republik*.

Schippel, M. (1902), *Grundzüge der Handelspolitik* (Berlin).

Schippel, M. (1904), 'Die englischen Arbeiter und die Chamberlainsche Schutzzollagitation', *SM*, Bd. 1.

Schippel, M. (1908*a*), 'Manchestertheorie und englische Kolonialpraxis', *SM*, Bd. 1.

Schippel, M. (1908*b*), 'Tropenerschliessung und europäische Wirtschaftsentwicklung', *SM*, Bd. 1.

Schippel, M. (1909), 'England, Deutschland und Arbeiterparteien', *SM*, Bd. 1.

Schippel, M. (1912*a*), 'Britisches Weltreich und Reichsgedenktag', *SM*, Bd. 2.

Schippel, M. (1912*b*), 'Der Imperialismus auf dem Chemnitzer Parteitag', *SM*, Bd. 3.

Schippel, M. (1912*c*), 'Imperialismus und Manchestertum', *SM*, Bd. 3.

Schippel, M. (1913*a*), 'Flottenabkommen und handelspolitische Bedingungen?', *SM*, Bd. 3.

Schippel, M. (1913*b*), 'Das Grundgeheimnis des Imperialismus', *SM*, Bd. 1.

Schippel, M. (1913*c*), 'Kolonialpolitisches aus dem britischen Weltreich', *SM*, Bd. 2.

Schippel, M. (1913*d*), 'Radikales Durcheinander', *SM*, Bd. 1.

Schippel, M. (1914), 'Chamberlain, Manchestertum und Imperialismus', *SM*, Bd. 2.

Schmidt, C. (1900), 'Sozialismus und Ethik', *SM*.

Schmidt, C. (1908), 'Zur Erinnerung an Karl Marx', *SM*, Bd. 1.

Schmidt, R. (1932), 'Eduard Bernstein', *Gewerkschafts-Zeitung*, Jg. 42, Nr. 52.

Schumpeter, J. A. (1951), *Imperialism and Social Classes*, trans. P. M. Sweezy and H. Norden (New York).

Shaw, G. B. (1900), *Fabianism and the Empire* (London).

Shaw, G. B. (1976), *Practical Politics: Views on Politics and Economics*, ed. L. J. Hubenka (Lincoln, Neb.).

Sombart, W. (1908), *Sozialismus und soziale Bewegung*, 6th edn (Jena).

Spencer, H. (1969), *The Principles of Sociology*, ed. A. Andreski, abridged edn (Hamden, Conn.).

Stampfer, F. (1905), 'Die auswärtige Politik der Sozialdemokratie', *NG*, Bd. 1, Nr. 28.

Stampfer, F. (1906), 'Die Weltpolitik des Proletariats', *NG*, Bd. 3, Nr. 11.

Stampfer, F. (1957), *Erfahrungen und Erkenntnisse* (Cologne).

Staudinger, F. (1901), 'Sozialismus und Ethik', *SM*.

Staudinger, F. (1904), 'Kant und der Sozialismus: Ein Gedenkwort zu Kants Todestag', *SM*.

Stössinger, F. (in collaboration with Joseph Bloch) (1938), *Revolution der Weltpolitik: Joseph Blochs Vermächtnis* (privately printed, Prague)

Stössinger, F. (in collaboration with Joseph Bloch) (1939), *Revolution der Weltpolitik* (Paris). (Reissue of above, with differing pagination; both editions are cited in text.)

Stössinger, F. (1953), 'Bolschewismus oder revolutionärer Revisionismus', *Frankfurter Hefte*, Jg. 3.

Tirpitz, A. von (1919), *Erinnerungen* (Leipzig).

Trotsky, N. (1908/9), 'Nationalpsychologie oder Klassenkampf?' *NZ*, Jg. 27, Bd. 1.

Vollmar, G. von (1977), *Reden und Schriften zur Reformpolitik*, ed. W. Albrecht (Berlin).

Vorländer, K. (1911), *Kant und Marx* (Leipzig).

Wallas, G. (1889), 'An Economic Eirenicon', *Today*, no. 64, March.

Wallas, G. (1911), *Politik und menschliche Natur*, ed. E. Bernstein, trans. F. Leipnik (Jena).

Webb, S. and B. (1895), *Die Geschichte des britischen Trade Unionismus*, ed. E. Bernstein, trans. R. Bernstein (Stuttgart).
Woltmann, L. (1900), 'Die Begründung der Moral', *SM*.
Woltmann, L. (1903), *Politische Anthropologie* (Leipzig).

(6) Secondary Literature

Abendroth, W. (1964), *Aufstieg und Krise der deutschen Sozialdemokratie* (Mainz).
Aldcroft, D. H. (ed.) (1968), *The Development of British Industry and Foreign Competition, 1875–1914* (London).
Allett, J. (1981), *New Liberalism: The Political Economy of J. A. Hobson* (Toronto).
Anderson, P. (1939), *The Background of Anti-English Feeling in Germany, 1890–1902* (Washington, DC).
Angel, P. (1961), *Edouard Bernstein et l'évolution du socialisme allemand* (Paris).
Angel, P. (1963), 'L'évolution d'un militant socialiste: Edouard Bernstein. Un cas d'espèce et un cas-typ', *Le Mouvement social*, no. 42.
Ascher, A. (1957), 'National solidarity and imperial power: the sources and early development of social imperialist thought in Germany, 1871–1914', PhD thesis, Columbia University.
Ascher, A. (1960/1), 'Imperialists within German Social Democracy prior to 1914', *Journal of Central European Affairs*, vol. 20, no. 4.
Ascher, A. (1961), ' "Radical" imperialists within German Social Democracy, 1912–1918', *Political Science Quarterly*, vol. 76, no. 4.
Avineri, S. (1968), *The Social and Political Thought of Karl Marx* (Cambridge).
Avineri, S. (1972), *Hegel's Theory of the Modern State* (London).
Barber, W. J. (1967), *A History of Economic Thought* (Harmondsworth, Middx).
Barkin, K. D. (1970), *The Controversy over German Industrialization 1890–1902* (London).
Bartel, H. (1963a), *August Bebel: Eine Biographie* (East Berlin).
Bartel, H. (1963b), 'August Bebels Stellung zur Vaterlandsverteidigung', *Beiträge zur Geschichte der deutschen Arbeiterbewegung*, vol. 5.
Bathrick, D., and Breines, P. (1978), 'Marx und/oder Nietzsche', in *Karl Marx und Friedrich Nietzsche*, ed. R. Grimm and J. Hermand (Königstein).
Berger, M. (1977), *Engels, Armies and Revolution* (Hamden, Conn.).
Berghahn, V. R. (1971), *Der Tirpitz-Plan: Genesis und Verfall einer innenpolitischen Krisenstrategie unter Wilhelm II.* (Düsseldorf).
Berghahn, V. R. (1973a), *Germany and the Approach of War in 1914* (London).
Berghahn, V. R. (1973b), *Rüstung und Machtpolitik* (Düsseldorf).
Berghahn, V. R. (1982), *Modern Germany: Society, Economy and Politics in the Twentieth Century* (Cambridge).
Bieber, H.-J. (1981), *Gewerkschaften in Krieg und Revolution*, 2 vols (Hamburg).
Blackbourn, D. (1980), *Class, Religion and Local Politics in Wilhelmine Germany: The Centre Party in Württemberg before 1914* (New Haven, Conn. and London).
Blackbourn, D., and Eley, G. (1980), *Mythen deutscher Geschichtsschreibung: Die gescheiterte bürgerliche Revolution von 1848* (Frankfurt-am-Main).
Bley, H. (1975), *Bebel und die Strategie der Kriegsverhütung 1904–1913* (Göttingen).
Bloch, C. (1974), 'Der Kampf Joseph Blochs und der *Sozialistischen Monatshefte* in der Weimarer Republik', *Jahrbuch des Instituts für Deutsche Geschichte*, vol. 3 (Tel Aviv).
Bloch, C. (1977), 'Joseph Bloch – der jüdische Vorkämpfer für Kontinental-Europa', *Jahrbuch des Instituts für Deutsche Geschichte*, vol. 6 (Tel Aviv).
Bloom, S. F. (1941), *The World of Nations: A Study of the National Implications in the Work of Karl Marx* (New York).

Böhm, E. (1972), *Überseehandel und Flottenbau: Hanseatische Kaufmannschaft und deutsche Seerüstung 1879–1902* (Düsseldorf).

Boll, F. (1980), *Frieden oder Revolution? Friedensstrategien der deutschen Sozialdemokratie vom Erfurter Programm 1891 bis zur Revolution 1918* (Bonn).

Bon, F., and Burnier, M.-A. (1974), 'Edouard Bernstein et le triangle socialiste', *Le Mouvement Social*, no. 87.

Bourne, K. (1970), *The Foreign Policy of Victorian England, 1830–1902* (Oxford).

Bowen, R. (1947), *German Theories of the Corporative State* (New York).

Bracher, K.-D. (1964), *Deutschland zwischen Demokratie und Diktatur* (Munich).

Bramsted, E. K., and Melhuish, K. J. (1978), *Western Liberalism: A History in Documents from Locke to Croce* (London).

Braunthal, J. (1961), *Geschichte der Internationale*, 3 vols (Hanover).

Braun-Vogelstein, J. (1967), *Heinrich Braun: Ein Leben für den Sozialismus*, 2nd rev. edn (Stuttgart).

Briggs, A. (1968), *Victorian Cities* (Harmondsworth, Middx).

Bry, G. (1960), *Wages in Germany 1871–1945* (Princeton, NJ).

Bunsen, V. de (1947), *Charles Roden Buxton* (London).

Burrow, J. W. (1966), *Evolution and Society* (Cambridge).

Buse, D. K. (1973), 'Friedrich Ebert and German socialism, 1871–1919', PhD thesis, University of Oregon.

Cain, P. J. (1978), 'J. A. Hobson, Cobdenism and the Radical theory of economic imperialism, 1898–1914', *Economic History Review*, vol. 31, no. 4.

Cain, P. J. (1979a), 'Capitalism, war and internationalism in the thought of Richard Cobden', *British Journal of International Studies*, vol. 5, no. 3.

Cain, P. J. (1979b), 'International trade and economic development in the work of J. A. Hobson before 1914', *History of Political Economy*, vol. 11, no. 3.

Cain, P. J. (1980), *The Economic Foundations of British Overseas Expansion 1815–1914* (London).

Calkins, K. R. (1979), *Hugo Hasse: Democrat and Revolutionary* (Durham, NC).

Calleo, D. (1978), *The German Problem Reconsidered* (Cambridge).

Carlebach, J. (1978), *Karl Marx and the Radical Critique of Judaism* (London).

Carroll, E. M. (1966), *Germany and the Great Powers, 1866–1914: A Study in Public Opinion and Foreign Policy* (Hamden, Conn.).

Carsten, F. L. (1972), *Revolution in Central Europe 1918–1919* (London).

Carsten, F. L. (1977), *Fascist Movements in Austria: From Schönerer to Hitler* (London).

Carsten, F. L. (1982), *War against War: British and German Radical Movements in the First World War* (London).

Chickering, R. (1975), *Imperial Germany and a World without War: The Peace Movement and German Society, 1892–1914* (Princeton, NJ).

Chickering, R. (1979a), 'Der "Deutsche Wehrverein" und die Reform der deutschen Armee 1912–1914', *Militärgeschichtliche Mitteilungen*, vol. 28, no. 1.

Chickering, R. (1979b), 'Patriotic societies and German foreign policy, 1890–1914', *International History Review*, vol. 1, no. 4.

Cicero (1978), *Cicero's Letters to Atticus*, trans. D. R. Shackleton Bailey (Harmondsworth, Middx.)

Clarke, P. (1978), *Liberals and Social Democrats* (Cambridge).

Cline, C. A. (1963), *Recruits to Labour* (Syracuse, NY).

Cline, C. A. (1974), 'E. D. Morel: From the Congo to the Rhine', in A. J. A. Morris (ed.), *Edwardian Radicalism* (London).

Cline, C. A. (1980), *E. D. Morel* (Belfast).

Cocks, F. S. (1920), *E. D. Morel: The Man and his Work* (London).

Cole, M. (1961), *The Story of Fabian Socialism* (London).

Colletti, L. (1972), *From Rousseau to Lenin: Studies in Ideology and Society*, trans. J. Merrington and J. White (London).

Crampton, R. J. (1973), 'August Bebel and the British Foreign Office', *History*, vol. 58, no. 193.

Crampton, R. J. (n.d.), *The Hollow Detente: Anglo-German Relations in the Balkans 1911–1914* (London).

Crew, D. F. (1979), *Town in the Ruhr: A Social History of Bochum 1860–1914* (New York).

Cummins, I. (1980), *Marx, Engels and National Movements* (London).

Davis, H. B. (1967), *Nationalism and Socialism: Marxist and Labour Theories of Nationalism to 1917* (New York).

Dayan-Herzbrun, S. (1967), 'Nationalisme et socialisme chez Ferdinand Lassalle', *L'Homme et la société*, vol. 16, no. 5.

Dehio, L. (1965), *Germany and World Politics in the Twentieth Century* (London).

Deist, W. (1976), *Flottenpolitik und Flottenpropaganda: Das Nachrichtenbureau des Reichsmarineamtes 1897–1914* (Stuttgart).

Derry, J. W. (1967), *The Radical Tradition* (London).

Deutscher, I. (1954), *The Prophet Armed: Trotsky 1879–1921* (London).

Dorpalen, A. (1957), *Heinrich von Treitschke* (New Haven, Conn.).

Droz, J. (1966), *Le Socialisme démocratique 1864–1960* (Paris).

Düding, D. (1972), *Der Nationalsoziale Verein* (Munich).

Earle, E. M. (ed.) (1943), *Makers of Modern Strategy: Military Thought from Machiavelli to Hitler* (Princeton, NJ).

Eisner, F. (1976), 'Humanität in der Realpolitik: Kurt Eisners Konzeption des demokratischen Sozialismus', *L'76*, vol. 11, no. 1.

Eisner, F. (1979), *Kurt Eisner: Die Politik des libertären Sozialismus* (Frankfurt-am-Main).

Eley, G. (1974), 'Sammlungspolitik, social imperialism and the Navy Law of 1898', *Militärgeschichtliche Mitteilungen*, vol. 15, no. 1.

Eley, G. (1976a), 'Defining social imperialism: use and abuse of an idea', *Social History*, vol. 1, no. 3.

Eley, G. (1976b), 'Social imperialism in Germany: reformist synthesis or reactionary sleight of hand?', in J. Radkau and I. Geiss (eds), *Imperialismus im zwanzigsten Jahrhundert* (Munich).

Eley, G. (1978a), 'Capitalism and the Wilhelmine state: industrial growth and political backwardness in recent German historiography, 1890–1918', *Historical Journal*, vol. 21, no. 3.

Eley, G. (1978b), 'Die "Kehrites" und das Kaiserreich: Bemerkungen zu einer aktuellen Kontroverse', *Geschichte und Gesellschaft*, vol. 4, no. 1.

Eley, G. (1978c), 'Reshaping the right: radical nationalism and the German Navy League, 1898–1908', *Historical Journal*, vol. 21, no. 2.

Eley, G. (1978d), 'The Wilhelmine right: how it changed', in R. J. Evans (ed.), *Society and Politics in Wilhelmine Germany* (London).

Eley, G. (1980), *Reshaping the German Right: Radical Nationalism and Political Change after Bismarck* (New Haven, Conn. and London).

Eley, G. (1981), 'Nationalism and social history: review essay', *Social History*, vol. 6, no. 1.

Eley, G. (1982), 'State formation, nationalism and political culture in nineteenth-century Germany', in R. Samuel and G. Stedman Jones (eds), *Culture, Ideology and Politics* (London).

Eley, G., and Nield, K. (1980), 'Why does social history ignore politics?', *Social History*, vol. 5, no. 2.

Elm, L. (1968), *Zwischen Fortschritt und Reaktion: Geschichte der Parteien der liberalen Bourgeoisie in Deutschland 1893–1918* (East Berlin).

Evans, R. J. (ed.) (1978), *Society and Politics in Wilhelmine Germany* (London).

Evans, R. J. (ed.) (1982), *The German Working Class 1888–1933* (London).

Fieldhouse, D. K. (1973), *Economics and Empire, 1830–1914* (London).

Fischer, F. (1969), *Krieg der Illusionen: Die deutsche Politik von 1911 bis 1914* (Düsseldorf).

Fischer, F. (1974), *World Power or Decline: The Controversy over Germany's Aims in the First World War* (London).

Fischer, F. (1979), *Bündnis der Eliten: Zur Kontinuität der Machtstrukturen in Deutschland 1871–1945* (Düsseldorf).

Fletcher, R. A. (1978), 'An English advocate in Germany: Eduard Bernstein's analysis of Anglo-German relations 1900–1914', *Canadian Journal of History*, vol. 13, no. 2.

Fletcher, R. A. (1979a), 'Bernstein in Britain: revisionism and foreign affairs', *International History Review*, vol. 1, no. 3.

Fletcher, R. A. (1979b), 'A revisionist looks at imperialism: Eduard Bernstein's critique of imperialism and *Kolonialpolitik*', *Central European History*, vol. 12, no. 3.

Fletcher, R. A. (1979c), 'World power without war: Eduard Bernstein's proposals for an alternative *Weltpolitik* 1900–14', *Australian Journal of Politics and History*, vol. 25, no. 2.

Fletcher, R. A. (1980a), 'A revisionist dialogue on Wilhelmine *Weltpolitik*: Joseph Bloch and Kurt Eisner 1907–1914', *Internationale wissenschaftliche Korrespondenz zur Geschichte der deutschen Arbeiterbewegung*, vol. 16, no. 4.

Fletcher, R. A. (1980b), 'Revisionism and empire: Joseph Bloch, the *Sozialistische Monatshefte* and German nationalism 1907–1914', *European Studies Review*, vol. 10, no. 4.

Fletcher, R. A. (1982a), 'British Radicalism and German revisionism: the case of Eduard Bernstein', *International History Review*, vol. 4, no. 3.

Fletcher, R. A. (1982b), 'Karl Leuthner's Greater Germany: the pre-1914 Pan-Germanism of an Austrian socialist', *Canadian Review of Studies in Nationalism*, vol. 9, no. 1.

Fletcher, R. A. (1982c), 'Revisionism and militarism: war and peace in the pre-1914 thought of Eduard Bernstein', *Militärgeschichtliche Mitteilungen*, vol. 31, no. 1.

Fletcher, R. A. (1982d), 'Socialist nationalism in Central Europe before 1914', *Canadian Journal of History*, vol. 17, no. 1.

Fletcher, R. A. (1983a), 'Cobden as educator: the free-trade internationalism of Eduard Bernstein', *American Historical Review*, vol. 88, no. 3.

Fletcher, R. A. (1983b), 'In the interest of peace and progress: Eduard Bernstein's socialist foreign policy', *Review of International Studies*, vol. 9, no. 2.

Fletcher, R. A. (1984), 'Revisionism and nationalism: Eduard Bernstein and the national question, 1900–1914', *Canadian Review of Studies in Nationalism*, vol. 11, no. 1.

Flournoy, F. R. (1946), 'British Liberal theories of international relations, 1848–98', *Journal of the History of Ideas*, vol. 7, no. 2.

Freeden, M. (1978), *The New Liberalism: An Ideology of Social Reform* (Oxford).

Frei, H. (1979), *Fabianismus und Bernstein'scher Revisionismus 1884–1900* (Berne).

Fremantle, A. (1960), *This Little Band of Prophets: The Story of the Gentle Fabians* (London).

Fricke, D. (1962), *Zur Organisation und Tätigkeit der deutschen Arbeiterbewegung 1890–1914* (Leipzig).

Fricke, D. (1973), 'Eine Musterschrift des Opportunismus: Die *Sozialistischen Monatshefte* am Ende der relativ friedlichen Entwicklung des Kapitalismus in Deutschland (1909)', *Zeitschrift für Geschichtswissenschaft*, vol. 21, no. 10.

Fricke, D. (1974a), 'Die Gründung der revisionistischen Zeitschrift Die Neue Gesellschaft 1900 bis 1909', *Beiträge zur Geschichte der deutschen Arbeiterbewegung*, vol. 16, no. 5.

Fricke, D. (1974b), 'Opportunismus und Nationalismus: Zur Rolle Wolfgang Heines in der deutschen Sozialdemokratie bis zum Beginn des Ersten Weltkrieges', *Zeitschrift für Geschichtswissenschaft*, vol. 22, no. 8.

Fricke, D. (1974c), 'Zur Rückkehr Eduard Bernsteins in das Deutsche Reich 1901', *Zeitschrift für Geschichtswissenschaft*, vol. 22, no. 12.

Fricke, D. (1975a), 'Die *Sozialistischen Monatshefte* und die imperialistische Konzeption eines Kontinentaleuropa (1905–1918)', *Zeitschrift für Geschichtswissenschaft*, vol. 23, pt 1, no. 5.

Fricke, D. (1975b), 'Zum Bruch Eduard Bernsteins mit den *Sozialistischen Monatsheften* im Herbst 1914', *Beiträge zur Geschichte der deutschen Arbeiterbewegung*, vol. 17, no. 3.

Fricke, D. (1976), *Die deutsche Arbeiterbewegung 1869 bis 1914: Ein Handbuch über ihre Organisation und Tätigkeit im Klassenkampf* (East Berlin).

Fricke, D. (1977), 'Auf dem Weg nach Mannheim', *Zeitschrift für Geschichtswissenschaft*, vol. 25, no. 4.

Friederici, H. J. (1979), 'Der Feind unserer Feinde: Ferdinand Lassalle', *Beiträge zur Geschichte der deutschen Arbeiterbewegung*, vol. 21, no. 1.

Frölich, P. (1940), *Rosa Luxemburg: Her Life and Work*, trans. E. Fitzgerald (London).

Fry, M. G. (1977), *Lloyd George and Foreign Policy*, vol. 1 (Montreal).

Fülberth, G. (1971), 'Zur Genese des Revisionismus in der deutschen Sozialdemokratie vor 1914', *Das Argument*, no. 63.

Fülberth, G., and Harrer, J. (1974), *Die deutsche Sozialdemokratie 1890–1933* (Darmstadt).

Gallie, W. B. (1978), *Philosophers of Peace and War* (Cambridge).

Gay, P. (1962), *The Dilemma of Democratic Socialism: Eduard Bernstein's Challenge to Marx*, Collier edn (New York).

Gay, P. (1978), *Freud, Jews and Other Germans* (New York).

Geary, D. (1976), 'The German labour movement 1848–1919', *European Studies Review*, vol. 6, no. 3.

Geary, D. (1981), *European Labour Protest 1848–1939* (London).

Geary, D. (1982), 'Identifying militancy: the assessment of working-class attitudes towards state and society', in R. J. Evans (ed.), *The German Working Class 1888–1933* (London).

Gemkow, H. (1969), 'Grossbourgeois und musterhafter Sozialdemokrat: Paul Singer', *Beiträge zur Geschichte der deutschen Arbeiterbewegung*, vol. 11, no. 1.

Gifford, P., and Louis, W. R. (eds) (1971), *Britain and Germany in Africa: Imperial Rivalry and Colonial Rule* (New Haven, Conn.).

Ginsberg, M. (1961), *Evolution and Progress* (Melbourne).

Gneuss, C. (1957), 'Über den Einklang von Theorie und Praxis', in I. Fetscher (ed.), *Marxismusstudien*, 2nd ser. (Tübingen).

Gottschalch, W. *et al.* (1969), *Geschichte der sozialen Ideen in Deutschland*, ed. H. Grebing (Munich).

Gray, R. (1981), *The Aristocracy of Labour in Nineteenth-Century Britain c. 1850–1914* (London).

Grebing, H. (1969), *The History of the German Labour Movement: A Survey* (London).

Grebing, H. (1970), *Geschichte der deutschen Arbeiterbewegung*, DTV edn (Munich).

Grebing, H. (1977), *Der Revisionismus: Von Bernstein bis zum 'Prager Frühling'* (Munich).

Grenville, J. A. S. (1964), *Lord Salisbury and Foreign Policy: The Close of the Nineteenth Century* (London).

Grimm, R., and Hermand, J. (eds) (1978), *Marx und Nietzsche: Acht Beiträge* (Königstein).

Groh, D. (1973), *Negative Integration und revolutionärer Attentismus: Die deutsche Sozialdemokratie am Vorabend des Ersten Weltkrieges* (Frankfurt-am-Main).

Grunenberg, A. (ed.) (1970), *Die Massenstreikdebatte* (Frankfurt-am-Main).

Guratzsch, D. (1974), *Macht durch Organisation: Die Grundlegung des Hugenbergschen Presseimperiums* (Düsseldorf).

Gustafsson, B. (1972), *Marxismus und Revisionismus: Eduard Bernsteins Kritik des Marxismus und ihre ideengeschichtlichen Voraussetzungen*, 2 vols (Frankfurt-am-Main).

Gustafsson, B. (1978), 'A new look at Bernstein: some reflections on reformism and history', *Scandinavian Journal of History*, vol. 3, no. 4.

Guttsman, W. L. (1981), *The German Social Democratic Party 1875–1933* (London).

Hall, A. (1977), *Scandal, Sensation and Social Democracy: The SPD Press and Wilhelmine Germany 1890–1914* (Cambridge).

Hallgarten, G. W. F. (1963), *Imperialismus vor 1914*, 2nd rev. edn, 2 vols (Munich).

Hamburger, M. (1962), 'A craving for hell: Nietzsche and the Nietzscheans', *Encounter*, vol. 19, no. 4.

Haupt, G. (1972), *Socialism and the Great War: The Collapse of the Second International* (Oxford).

Haupt, G., Lowy, M. and Weill, C. (1974), *Les Marxistes et la question nationale 1848–1914* (Paris).

Hautmann, H., and Kropf, R. (1974), *Die österreichische Arbeiterbewegung vom Vormärz bis 1945: Sozialökonomische Ursprünge ihrer Ideologie und Politik*, 2nd edn (Linz).

Havighurst, A. F. (1974), *Radical Journalist: H. W. Massingham, 1860–1924* (Cambridge).

Heckart, B. (1974), *From Bassermann to Bebel: The Grand Bloc's Quest for Reform in the Kaiserreich, 1900–1914* (New Haven, Conn.).

Heimann, H., and Meyer, T. (eds) (1978), *Bernstein und der Demokratische Sozialismus* (Berlin).

Henderson, W. O. (1962), *Studies in German Colonial History* (London).

Hermes, I. (1979), *Gegen Imperialismus und Krieg: Gewerkschaften und II. Internationale* (Cologne).

Hickey, S. (1978), 'The shaping of the German labour movement: miners in the Ruhr', in R. J. Evans (ed.), *Society and Politics in Wilhelmine Germany* (London).

Hinsley, F. H. (1963), *Power and the Pursuit of Peace: Theory and Practice in the History of Relations between States* (Cambridge).

Hirsch, H. (1977), *Der 'Fabier' Eduard Bernstein* (Bonn).

Hirschfelder, H. (1979), *Die bayerische Sozialdemokratie 1864–1914*, 2 vols (Erlangen).

Hobsbawm, E. J. (1964), *Labouring Men* (London).

Hoffman, R. J. S. ([1933] 1964), *Great Britain and the German Trade Rivalry* (New York).

Höhle, T. (1958), *Franz Mehring: Sein Weg zum Sozialismus* (East Berlin).

Höhn, R. (1969), *Sozialismus und Heer*, 3 vols (Bad Harzburg).

Holbraad, C. (1970), *The Concert of Europe: A Study in German and British International Theory 1815–1914* (London).

Holl, K., and List, G. (eds) (1975), *Liberalismus und imperialistischer Staat* (Göttingen).

Hollenberg, G. (1974), *Englisches Interesse am Kaiserreich: Die Attraktivität Preussen-Deutschlands für konservative und liberale Kreise in Grossbritannien 1860–1914* (Wiesbaden).

Howard, M. (1978), *War and the Liberal Conscience* (London).

Hulse, J. W. (1970), *Revolutionists in London: A Study of Five Unorthodox Socialists* (Oxford).

Irrlitz, G. (1966), 'Bemerkungen über die Einheit politischer und theoretischer Wesenszüge des Zentrismus', *Beiträge zur Geschichte der deutschen Arbeiterbewegung*, vol. 8, no. 1.

Jacobsen, H.-A. (1979), *Karl Haushofer: Leben und Werk*, 2 vols (Boppard-am-Rhein).

Jansen, R. (1958), *Georg von Vollmar: Eine politische Biographie* (Düsseldorf).

Jarausch, K. (1972), *The Enigmatic Chancellor: Bethmann Hollweg and the Hubris of Imperial Germany* (London).

Jarausch, K. (1982), *Students, Society, and Politics in Imperial Germany: The Rise of Academic Illiberalism* (Princeton, NJ).

Jarausch, K. (1983), 'Illiberalism and beyond: German history in search of a paradigm', *Journal of Modern History*, vol. 55, no. 2.

Jerussalimski, A. S. (1968), *Der deutsche Imperialismus: Geschichte und Gegenwart* (East Berlin).

Johannsen, H. (1954), 'Der Revisionismus in der deutschen Sozialdemokratie 1890–1914', diss., University of Hamburg.

Joll, J. (1974), *The Second International 1889–1914*, 2nd rev. edn (London).

Joll, J. (1976), *Europe since 1870: An International History*, 2nd edn (Harmondsworth, Middx).

Joll, J. (1981), 'Walther Rathenau – intellectual or industrialist', in V. R. Berghahn and M. Kitchen (eds), *Germany in the Age of Total War* (London).

Jordan, G. H. S. (1974), 'Pensions not Dreadnoughts: the Radicals and naval retrenchment', in A. J. A. Morris (ed.), *Edwardian Radicalism 1900–1914* (London).

Kamenka, E. (1972), *The Ethical Foundations of Marxism*, 2nd edn (London).

Kapp, Y. (1976), *Eleanor Marx*, 2 vols (London).

Kaufmann, W. (1974), *Nietzsche: Philosopher, Psychologist, Antichrist*, 4th edn (Princeton, NJ).

Kautsky, J. H. (1961), 'J. A. Schumpeter and Karl Kautsky: Parallel theories of imperialism', *Midwest Journal of Political Science*, vol. 5, no. 2.

Keck, T. R. (1977), 'The Marburg school and ethical socialism: another look', *Social Science Journal*, vol. 14, no. 3.

Kehr, E. (1930), *Schlachtflottenbau und Parteipolitik 1894–1901* (Berlin).

Kehr, E. (1977), *Economic Interest, Militarism and Foreign Policy*, ed. G. A. Craig, trans. G. Heinz (Berkeley, Calif.).

Kemp, T. (1967), *Theories of Imperialism* (London).

Kennedy, P. M. (1972), 'German colonial expansion: has the "manipulated social imperialism" been ante-dated?' *Past and Present*, no. 54.

Kennedy, P. M. (1976), *The Rise and Fall of British Naval Mastery* (London).

Kennedy, P. M. (1980), *The Rise of the Anglo-German Antagonism 1860–1914* (London).

Kennedy, P. M. (1981), *The Realities behind Diplomacy* (London).

Kiernan, V. G. (1974), *Marxism and Imperialism* (London).

Kitchen, M. (1968), *The German Officer Corps 1890–1914* (Oxford).

Kitchen, M. (1977), 'Friedrich Engels' theory of war', *Military Affairs*, vol. 41, no. 3.

Kitchen, M. (1978), *The Political Economy of Germany 1815–1914* (London).

Kitchen, M. (1980), *The Coming of Austrian Fascism* (London).

Klein, F. (1976), *Deutschland 1897/8–1917* (East Berlin).

Koch, H. W. (ed.) (1972), *The Origins of the First World War* (London).

Koch, H. W. (1973), *Der Sozialdarwinismus: Seine Genese und sein Einfluss auf das imperialistische Denken* (Munich).

Kocka, J. (1981), *Die Angestellten in der deutschen Geschichte 1850–1980* (Göttingen).

Koebner, R., and Schmidt, H. D. (1965), *Imperialism: The Story and Significance of a Political Word* (Cambridge).

Kolakowski, L. (1978), *Main Currents of Marxism*, 3 vols (Oxford).

König, E. (1964), *Vom Revisionismus zum 'demokratischen Sozialismus': Zur Kritik des ökonomischen Revisionismus in Deutschland* (East Berlin).

Korsch, K. (1929), *Die materialistische Geschichtsauffassung* (Leipzig).

Korsch, K. (1970), *Marxism and Philosophy* (London).

Koss, S. (1969), *Lord Haldane: Scapegoat for Liberalism* (New York).

Koss, S. (1973a), *Fleet Street Radical: A. G. Gardiner and the 'Daily News'* (London).

Koss, S. (1973b), *The Pro-Boers* (Chicago).

Koss, S. (1975), *Nonconformity in British Politics* (Hamden, Conn.).

Kotowski, G. (1963), *Friedrich Ebert: Eine politische Biographie* (Wiesbaden).
Krieger, L. (1957), *The German 'Idea' of Freedom: History of a Political Tradition* (Chicago).
Kulemann, P. (1979), *Am Beispiel des Austromarxismus: Sozialdemokratische Arbeiterbewegung in Österreich von Hainfeld bis zur Dollfuss-Diktatur* (Hamburg).
Kunz, R. (1949), 'Die Geschichte der "Arbeiter-Zeitung" von ihrer Gründung bis zur Jahrhundertwende', diss., (University of Vienna).
Labedz, L. (ed.) (1962), *Revisionism: Essays on the History of Marxist Ideas* (London).
Lamberti, M. (1970), 'The attempt to form a Jewish bloc: Jewish notables and politics in Wilhelmine Germany', *Central European History*, vol. 3, nos 1/2.
Langerhans, H. (1957), 'Richtungsgewerkschaft und gewerkschaftliche Autonomie 1890–1914', *International Review of Social History*, vol. 2.
Langewiesche, D., and Schönhoven, K. (1976), 'Arbeiterbibliotheken und Arbeiterlektüre im Wilhelminischen Deutschland', *Archiv für Sozialgeschichte*, vol. 16.
Laschitza, A. (1967), 'Kurt Eisner – Kriegsgegner und Feind der Reaktion', *Beiträge zur Geschichte der deutschen Arbeiterbewegung*, vol. 9, no. 3.
Laschitza, A., and Schumacher, H. (1965), 'Thesen über die Herausbildung der deutschen Linken von der Jahrhundertwende bis zur Gründung der Kommunistischen Partei Deutschlands (Spartakusbund)', *Beiträge zur Geschichte der deutschen Arbeiterbewegung*, vol. 7, no. 1.
Lauterbach, A. (1977), 'Changing concepts of imperialism', *Weltwirtschaftliches Archiv*, vol. 113, no. 2.
Lee, A. J. (1970), 'A study of the social and economic thought of J. A. Hobson', PhD, University of London.
Lee, A. J. (1976), *The Origins of the Popular Press, 1855–1914* (London).
Lees, A. (1979), 'Critics of urban society in Germany, 1854–1914', *Journal of the History of Ideas*, vol. 40, no. 1.
Lehnert, D. (1977), *Reform und Revolution in den Strategiediskussionen der klassischen Sozialdemokratie* (Bonn).
Leser, N. (ed.) (1964), *Werk und Widerhall: Grosse Gestalten des österreichischen Sozialismus* (Vienna).
Leser, N. (1968), *Zwischen Reformismus und Bolschewismus: Der Austromarxismus als Theorie und Praxis* (Vienna).
Leuschen-Seppel, R. (1978), *Sozialdemokratie und Antisemitismus im Kaiserreich* (Bonn).
Levinthal, F. M. (1974), 'H. N. Brailsford and the search for a new international order', in A. J. A. Morris (ed.), *Edwardian Radicalism 1900–1914* (London).
Lichtheim, G. (1964), *Marxism: An Historical and Critical Study* (London).
Lichtheim, G. (1971), *Imperialism* (Harmondsworth, Middx.)
Lidtke, V. L. (1964), 'German social democracy and German state socialism', *International Review of Social History*, vol. 9, no. 2.
Lidtke, V. L. (1966), *The Outlawed Party: Social Democracy in Germany, 1878–1890* (Princeton, NJ).
Lidtke, V. L. (1972), 'Revisionismus', in *Sowjetsystem und demokratische Gesellschaft: Eine vergleichende Enzyklopädie*, vol. 5 (Freiburg).
Lidtke, V. L. (1974), 'Naturalism and socialism in Germany', *American Historical Review*, vol. 79, no. 1.
Lipgens, W. (1974), 'Staat und Internationalismus bei Marx und Engels', *Historische Zeitschrift*, vol. 217, no. 3.
Lipton, D. R. (1978), *Ernst Cassirer: The Dilemma of a Liberal Intellectual in Germany 1914–1933* (Toronto).
Lison, R. (1978), *Reform als Strategie: Die Entstehung des Reformismus in der deutschen Gewerkschaftsbewegung* (Hamburg).
Lösche, P. (1967), *Der Bolschewismus im Urteil der deutschen Sozialdemokratie 1903–1920* (Berlin).

Lösche, P. (1969), 'Arbeiterbewegung und Wilhelminismus', *Geschichte in Wissenschaft und Unterricht*, vol. 20, no. 9.

Low, A. D. (1974), *The Anschluss Movement 1918–1919 and the Paris Peace Conference* (Philadelphia, Pa).

Lübbe, H. (1964), *Politische Philosophie in Deutschland* (Basle).

Lührs, G. *et al.* (1975), *Kritischer Rationalismus und Sozialdemokratie* (Berlin).

Lunn, E. (1973), *Prophet of Community: The Romantic Socialism of Gustav Landauer* (Berkeley, Calif.).

Lyons, F. S. L. (1963), *Internationalism in Europe 1815–1914* (Leyden).

McBriar, A. M. (1962), *Fabian Socialism and English Politics 1884–1918* (Cambridge).

McClelland, C. E. (1971), *The German Historians and England: A Study in Nineteenth-century Views* (Cambridge).

McClelland, C. E. (1980), *State, Society and University in Germany 1700–1914* (Cambridge).

McGrath, W. J. (1967), 'Student radicalism in Vienna', *Journal of Contemporary History*, vol. 2, no. 3.

McGrath, W. J. (1974*a*), *Dionysian Art and Populist Politics in Austria* (New Haven, Conn.).

McGrath, W. J. (1974*b*), 'Freud as Hannibal: the politics of the brother band', *Central European History*, vol. 7, no. 1.

MacKenzie, N. (ed.) (1978), *The Letters of Sidney and Beatrice Webb*, 3 vols (Cambridge).

MacKenzie, N. and J. (1977), *The First Fabians* (London).

Maehl, W. H. (1973), 'Russian imperialism and the emergence of a German socialist foreign policy, 1890–1900', *New Review*, vol. 13, no. 3.

Maehl, W. H. (1978), 'German socialist opposition to the Tirpitz Plan: Bebel and the Naval Law of 1900', *The Historian*, vol. 40, no. 4.

Maguire, J. (1972), *Marx's Paris Writings* (Dublin).

Mandelbaum, K. (1926), 'Die Erörterungen innerhalb der deutschen Sozialdemokratie über das Problem des Imperialismus 1895–1914', diss., (University of Frankfurt-am-Main).

Marks, H. J. (1939), 'Sources of reformism in the Social Democratic Party of Germany', *Journal of Modern History*, vol. 11, no. 3.

Marquand, D. (1977), *Ramsay MacDonald* (London).

Marxismus und deutsche Arbeiterbewegung, (1970), ed. Institut für Marxismus-Leninismus beim ZK der SED (East Berlin).

Matthew, H. C. G. (1973), *The Liberal Imperialists: The Ideas and Politics of a Post-Gladstonian Elite* (Oxford).

Matthias, E. (1954), *Die deutsche Sozialdemokratie und der Osten 1914–1945* (Tübingen).

Matthias, E. (1957), 'Kautsky und der Kautskyanismus', in I. Fetscher (ed.), *Marxismusstudien*, 2nd ser. (Tübingen).

Matthias, E., and Pikart, E. (1966), *Die Reichstagsfraktion der deutschen Sozialdemokratie 1898–1918* (Düsseldorf).

Mayer, A. J. (1981), *The Persistence of the Old Regime: Europe to the Great War* (London).

Mayer, G. (1936), *Friedrich Engels: A Biography* (London).

Mayer, G. (1972), *Arbeiterbewegung und Obrigkeitsstaat* (Bonn).

Meyer, H. C. (1955), *Mitteleuropa in German Thought and Action 1815–1945* (The Hague).

Meyer, T. (1977), *Bernsteins konstruktiver Sozialismus: Eduard Bernsteins Beitrag zur Theorie des Sozialismus* (Berlin).

Mielke, S. (1976), *Der Hansa-Bund für Gewerbe, Handel und Industrie 1909–1914: der gescheiterte Versuch einer antifeudalen Sammlungspolitik* (Göttingen).

Miliband, R. (1961), *Parliamentary Socialism* (London).

Miller, K. E. (1961), 'John Stuart Mill's theory of international relations', *Journal of the History of Ideas*, vol. 22, no. 4.

Miller, K. E. (1967), *Socialism and Foreign Policy: Theory and Practice in Britain to 1931* (The Hague).

Miller, S. (1964), *Das Problem der Freiheit im Sozialismus: Freiheit, Staat und Revolution in der Programmatik der Sozialdemokratie von Lassalle bis zum Revisionismusstreit* (Frankfurt-am-Main).

Miller, S. (ed.) (1966), *Das Kriegstagebuch des Reichstagsabgeordneten Eduard David 1914 bis 1918* (Düsseldorf).

Miller, S. (1967), 'Critique littéraire de la Social-Démocratie allemand à la fin du siècle dernier', *Le Mouvement social*, no. 59.

Miller, S. (1971), 'Das Ringen um "die einzige grossdeutsche Republik": Die Sozialdemokratie in Österreich und im Deutschen Reich zur Anschlussfrage 1918–1919', *Archiv für Sozialgeschichte*, vol. 11.

Miller, S. (1974), *Burgfrieden und Klassenkampf: Die deutsche Sozialdemokratie im Ersten Weltkrieg* (Düsseldorf).

Miller, S., and Potthoff, H. (1981), *Kleine Geschichte der SPD: Darstellung und Dokumentation 1848–1980*, 4th rev. edn (Bonn).

Mitchell, A. (1965), *Revolution in Bavaria 1918–1919: The Eisner Regime and the Soviet Republic* (Princeton, NJ).

Mitchell, A. (1977), 'Bonapartism as a model for Bismarckian politics', *Journal of Modern History*, vol. 49, no. 2.

Mitchell, H. (1965), 'Hobson revisited', *Journal of the History of Ideas*, vol. 26, no. 3.

Mitchell, H. (1966), 'Jean Jaurès: socialist doctrine and colonial problems', *Canadian Journal of History*, vol. 1, no. 1.

Mittmann, U. (1976), *Fraktion und Partei: Ein Vergleich von Zentrum und Sozialdemokratie im Kaiserreich* (Düsseldorf).

Mogk, W. (1972), *Paul Rohrbach und das 'Grössere Deutschland'* (Munich).

Molin-Pradel, M. (1963), 'Friedrich Austerlitz, Chefredakteur der "Arbeiter-Zeitung" ', diss., University of Vienna.

Mommsen, H. (1963), *Die Sozialdemokratie und die Nationalitätenfrage im Habsburgischen Vielvölkerstaat* (Vienna).

Mommsen, H. (1979), *Arbeiterbewegung und Nationale Frage* (Göttingen).

Mommsen, W. (1973), 'Domestic factors in German foreign policy before 1914', *Central European History*, vol. 6, no. 1.

Mommsen, W. (1980), *Theories of Imperialism* (London).

Mommsen, W. (1981), 'The topos of inevitable war in Germany in the decade before 1914', in V. R. Berghahn and M. Kitchen (eds), *Germany in the Age of Total War* (London).

Morgan, K. O. (1975), *Keir Hardie: Radical and Socialist* (London).

Moring, K.-E. (1968), *Die sozialdemokratische Partei in Bremen 1890–1914: Reformismus und Radikalismus in der sozialdemokratischen Partei Bremens* (Hanover).

Morris, A. J. A. (1972), *Radicalism Against War 1906–1914* (London).

Morris, A. J. A. (ed.) (1974), *Edwardian Radicalism 1900–1914* (London).

Morris, A. J. A. (1977), *Charles Philip Trevelyan 1870–1958* (Belfast).

Moses, J. A. (1975), *The Politics of Illusion: The Fischer Controversy in German Historiography* (London).

Moses, J. A. (1982), *Trade Unionism in Germany from Bismarck to Hitler 1869–1933*, 2 vols (London).

Mosse, G. L. (1964), *The Crisis of German Ideology: Intellectual Origins of the Third Reich* (New York).

Mosse, W. E. (1974), *Liberal Europe: The Age of Bourgeois Realism 1848–1875* (London).

Mosse, W. E. (ed.) (1976), *Juden im wilhelminischen Deutschland 1890–1914: Ein Sammelband* (Tübingen).

Mrossko, K. D. (1972), 'Richard Calwer: Wirtschaftspolitiker und Schriftsteller 1868–1927', in R. Uhland (ed.), *Lebensbilder aus Schwaben und Franken*, Vol. 12 (Stuttgart).

Müller, D. H. (1975), *Idealismus und Revolution: Zur Opposition der Jungen gegen den Sozialdemokratischen Parteivorstand 1890 bis 1894* (Berlin).

Na'aman, S. (1961), 'Die theoretischen Grundlagen der Aktion Lassalles im Briefwechsel mit Rodbertus', *International Review of Social History*, vol. 6, no. 3.

Na'aman, S. (1962), 'Lassalles Beziehungen zu Bismarck – ihr Sinn und Zweck', *Archiv für Sozialgeschichte*, vol. 2.

Na'aman, S. (1963), 'Lassalle – Demokratie und Sozialdemokratie', *Archiv für Sozialgeschichte*, vol. 3.

Na'aman, S. (1970), *Ferdinand Lassalle: Eine neue politische Biographie* (Hanover).

Nettl, J. P. (1965), 'The German Social Democratic Party, 1890–1914, as a political model', *Past and Present*, no. 30.

Nettl, J. P. (1966), *Rosa Luxemburg*, 2 vols (London), abridged edn in one volume, 1969.

Nipperdey, T. (1961), *Die Organisation der deutschen Parteien vor 1918* (Düsseldorf).

Nipperdey, T. (1975), 'Wehlers "Kaiserreich": Eine kritische Auseinandersetzung', *Geschichte und Gesellschaft*, vol. 1, no. 4.

O'Boyle, L. (1950), 'Theories of socialist imperialism', *Foreign Affairs*, vol. 28, no. 2.

Offermann, T. (1979), *Arbeiterbewegung und liberales Bürgertum in Deutschland 1850–1863* (Bonn).

Owen, R., and Sutcliffe, B. (eds) (1972), *Studies in the Theory of Imperialism* (London).

Owtscharenko, N. (1970), 'Zur Herausbildung der aussenpolitischen Konzeption der Sozialdemokratie im Kampf gegen die imperialistische "Weltpolitik" an der Wende vom 19. zum 20. Jahrhundert', in Deutsche Akademie der Wissenschaft (ed.), *Marxismus und deutsche Arbeiterbewegung* (East Berlin).

Pachter, H. (1981), 'The ambiguous legacy of Eduard Bernstein', *Dissent*, Spring.

Padfield, P. (1974), *The Great Naval Race: The Anglo-German Naval Rivalry 1900–1914* (New York).

Papcke, S. (1979), *Der Revisionismusstreit und die politische Theorie der Reform* (Stuttgart).

Paul, D. (1981), 'In the interests of civilization: Marxist views of race and culture in the nineteenth century', *Journal of the History of Ideas*, vol. 42, no. 1.

Paul, H.-H. (1978), *Marx, Engels und die Imperialismustheorie der II. Internationale* (Hamburg).

Peel, J. D. Y. (1971), *Herbert Spencer: The Evolution of a Sociologist* (London).

Pelling, H. (1965), *The Origins of the Labour Party 1880–1900*, 2nd edn (Oxford).

Petit, I. (1969), 'Kautsky et les discussions autour du problème de l'impérialisme dans le parti Social-démocrate allemand de 1907 à 1914', *La Revue d'Allemagne*, vol. 1, no. 3.

Pierson, S. (1973), *Marxism and the Origins of British Socialism* (Ithaca, NY and London).

Pierson, S. (1979), *British Socialists: The Journey from Fantasy to Politics* (Cambridge, Mass.).

Platt, D. C. (1968), *Finance, Trade and Politics in British Foreign Policy 1815–1914* (Oxford).

Pollard, S. (1981), *Peaceful Conquest: The Industrialization of Europe 1760–1970* (Oxford).

Porter, B. (1968), *Critics of Empire: British Radical Attitudes to Colonialism in Africa 1895–1914* (London).

Price, R. (1972), *An Imperial War and the British Working Class: Working-class Attitudes and Reactions to the Boer War 1899–1902* (London).

Puhle, H. J. (1966), *Agrarische Interessenpolitik und preussischer Konservatismus im wilhelminischen Reich (1893–1914)* (Hanover).

Quataert, J. H. (1979), *Reluctant Feminists in German Social Democracy 1885–1917* (Princeton, NJ).

Ratz, U. (1966), 'Karl Kautsky und die Abrüstungskontroverse in der deutschen Sozialdemokratie 1911–1912', *International Review of Social History*, vol. 11, no. 2.

Ratz, U. (1967), 'Briefe zum Erscheinen von Karl Kautskys *Weg zur Macht*', *International Review of Social History*, vol. 12, no. 3.

Ratz, U. (1969), *Georg Ledebour 1850–1947: Weg und Wirken eines sozialistischen Politikers* (Berlin).

Rauh, M. (1972), *Föderalismus und Parlamentarismus im Wilhelminischen Reich* (Düsseldorf).

Rauh, M. (1977), *Die Parlamentarisierung des Deutschen Reiches* (Düsseldorf).

Read, D. (1967), *Cobden and Bright: A Victorian Political Partnership* (London).

Reichard, R. W. (1953), 'The German working-class and the Russian Revolution of 1905', *Journal of Central European Affairs*, vol. 13, no. 2.

Reichard, R. W. (1969), *Crippled from Birth: German Social Democracy 1844–1870* (Ames, Iowa).

Reichel, E. (1947), *Der Sozialismus der Fabier: Ein Beitrag zur Ideengeschichte des modernen Sozialismus in England* (Heidelberg).

Reisberg, A. (1970), *Lenins Beziehungen zur deutschen Arbeiterbewegung* (East Berlin).

Ribhegge, W. (1973), *August Winnig: Eine historische Persönlichkeitsanalyse* (Bonn).

Rich, N. (1965), *Friedrich von Holstein*, 2 vols (Cambridge).

Rikli, E. (1936), 'Der Revisionismus: Ein Revisionsversuch der deutschen marxistischen Theorie (1890–1914)', diss., University of Zurich.

Ringer, F. (1969), *The Decline of the German Mandarins* (Cambridge, Mass.).

Ritter, G. A. (1963), *Die Arbeiterbewegung im Wilhelminischen Reich: Die Sozialdemokratische Partei und die Freien Gewerkschaften 1890–1900*, 2nd rev. edn (Berlin).

Ritter, G. A. (1973), *Die deutschen Parteien vor 1918* (Cologne).

Ritter, G. A. (1978), 'Workers' culture in Imperial Germany: problems and points of departure for research', *Journal of Contemporary History*, vol. 13, no. 2.

Ritter, G. A., and Kocka, J. (eds) (1982), *Deutsche Sozialgeschichte 1870–1914: Dokumente und Skizzen*, 3rd rev. edn (Munich).

Robbins, K. (1976), *The Abolition of War: The Peace Movement in Britain, 1914–1919* (Cardiff).

Robbins, K. (1979), *John Bright* (London).

Robinson, R., Gallagher, J., and Denny, A. (1961), *Africa and the Victorians: The Official Mind of Imperialism* (London).

Rohr, D. G. (1963), *The Origins of Social Liberalism in Germany* (Chicago).

Rolling, J. D. (1979), 'Liberals, socialists and city government in imperial Germany: the case of Frankfurt-am-Main, 1900–1918', PhD, University of Wisconsin-Madison.

Rosdolsky, R. (1964), 'Friedrich Engels und das Problem der "geschichtslosen" Völker (die Nationalitätenfrage in der Revolution von 1848–1849 im Lichte der *Neuen Rheinischen Zeitung*)', *Archiv für Sozialgeschichte*, vol. 4.

Roth, G. (1963), *The Social Democrats in Imperial Germany: A Study in Working-Class Isolation and National Integration* (Totowa, NJ).

Rothman, S., and Isenberg, P. (1974), 'Sigmund Freud and the politics of marginality', *Central European History*, vol. 7, no. 1.

Royle, E., and Walvin, J. (1982), *English Radicals and Reformers 1760–1848* (Brighton, Sussex).

Sagarra, E. (1977), *A Social History of Germany 1648–1914* (London).

Salvadori, M. (1979), *Karl Kautsky and the Socialist Revolution 1880–1938*, trans. J. Rothschild (London).

Sandkühler, H.-J., and de la Vega, R. (eds) (1974), *Marxismus und Ethik* (Frankfurt-am-Main).

Saul, K. (1974), *Staat, Industrie, Arbeiterbewegung im Kaiserreich: Zur Innen- und Aussenpolitik des wilhelminischen Deutschland 1903–1914* (Düsseldorf).

Scally, R. J. (1975), *The Origins of the Lloyd George Coalition: The Politics of Social Imperialism 1900–1918* (Princeton, NJ).

Schade, F. (1961), *Kurt Eisner und die bayerische Sozialdemokratie* (Hanover).

Scharlau, W. B., and Zeman, Z. A. B. (1965), *The Merchant of Revolution: The Life of Alexander Israel Helphand (Parvus) 1867–1924* (London).

Schenk, W. (1967), *Die deutsch-englische Rivalität vor dem Ersten Weltkrieg in der Sicht deutscher Historiker: Missverstehen oder Machtstreben?* (Aarau).

Schieder, T. (1978), 'Typologien und Erscheinungsformen des Nationalstaates in Europa', in H. A. Winkler (ed.), *Nationalismus* (Königstein).

Schoenbaum, D. (1966), *Hitler's Social Revolution: Class and Status in Nazi Germany 1933–1939* (New York).

Schoenbaum, D. (1982), *Zabern 1913: Consensus Politics in Imperial Germany* (London).

Schoeps, J. H. (1976), 'Aron Bernstein – ein liberaler Volksaufklärer, Schriftsteller und Religionsreformer', *Zeitschrift für Religions- und Geistesgeschichte*, no. 4.

Schönhoven, K. (1980), *Expansion und Konzentration: Studien zur Entwicklung der Freien Gewerkschaften im Wilhelminischen Deutschland 1890 bis 1914* (Stuttgart).

Schorske, C. E. (1972), *German Social Democracy 1905–1917: The Development of the Great Schism*, Harper Torchbook edn (New York).

Schorske, C. E. (1980), *Fin-de-siècle Vienna: Politics and Culture* (London).

Schottelius, H., and Deist, W. (eds) (1972), *Marine und Marinepolitik im kaiserlichen Deutschland 1871–1914* (Düsseldorf).

Schröder, H.-C. (1973), *Sozialistische Imperialismusdeutung: Studien zu ihrer Geschichte* (Göttingen).

Schröder, H.-C. (1975), *Sozialismus und Imperialismus: Die Auseinandersetzung der deutschen Sozialdemokratie mit dem Imperialismusproblem und der Weltpolitik vor 1914*, 2nd rev. edn (Hanover).

Schröder, H.-C. (1978*a*), 'Eduard Bernsteins Stellung zum Imperialismus vor dem Ersten Weltkrieg', in H. Heimann and T. Meyer (eds), *Bernstein und der Demokratische Sozialismus* (Berlin).

Schröder, H.-C. (1978*b*), *Imperialismus und antidemokratisches Denken: Alfred Milners Kritik am politischen System Englands* (Wiesbaden).

Schröder, H.-C. (1979), *Gustav Noske und die Kolonialpolitik des Deutschen Kaiserreichs* (Berlin).

Schulz, G. (1954), 'Die deutsche Sozialdemokratie und die Entwicklung der auswärtigen Beziehungen vor 1914', diss., Free University of Berlin.

Schumacher, H. (1964), 'Zum 50. Jahrestag der Herausgabe der *Sozialdemokratischen Korrespondenz*', *Beiträge zur Geschichte der deutschen Arbeiterbewegung*, vol. 6, no. 1.

Schwabe, K. (1969), *Wissenschaft und Kriegsmoral: Die deutschen Hochschullehrer und die politischen Grundfragen des Ersten Weltkrieges* (Göttingen).

Searle, G. R. (1971), *The Quest for National Efficiency 1899–1914* (Berkeley, Calif.).

Seeber, G. (ed.) (1978), *Gestalten der Bismarckzeit* (East Berlin).

Selig, W. (1967), *Paul Nikolaus Cossmann und die Süddeutschen Monatshefte 1914–1918* (Osnabrück).

Semmel, B. (1960), *Imperialism and Social Reform: English Social-Imperialist Thought 1895–1914* (London).

Semmel, B. (1970), *The Rise of Free Trade Imperialism* (Cambridge).

Shaw, W. H. (1978), *Marx's Theory of History* (London).

Sheehan, J. J. (1966), *The Career of Lujo Brentano* (Chicago).

Sheehan, J. J. (1978), *German Liberalism in the Nineteenth Century* (Chicago).

Siemsen, A. (1954), *Ein Leben für Europa: In memoriam Joseph Bloch* (Frankfurt-am-Main).

Sigel, R. (1975), 'Die Lensch-Cunow-Haenisch Gruppe: Ihr Einfluss auf die Ideologie der deutschen Sozialdemokratie im Ersten Weltkrieg', *Internationale wissenschaftliche Korrespondenz zur Geschichte der deutschen Arbeiterbewegung*, vol. 11, no. 3.

Sigel, R. (1976), *Die Lensch-Cunow-Haenisch Gruppe: Eine Studie zum rechten Flügel der SPD im Ersten Weltkrieg* (Berlin).

Skinner, Q. (1969), 'Meaning and understanding in the history of ideas', *History and Theory*, vol. 8, no. 1.

Smithies, A. (1950), 'Joseph Alois Schumpeter 1883–1950', *American Economic Review*, vol. 40, no. 4.

Snell, J. L., and Schmitt, H. A. (1976), *The Democratic Movement in Germany 1789–1914* (Chapel Hill, NC).

Sontag, R. J. (1964), *Germany and England: Background to Conflict 1848–1894* (New York).

Spender, J. A. (1924), *The Life of Sir Henry Campbell-Bannerman* (Boston, Mass.).

Stanley, J. L. (1981), *The Sociology of Virtue: The Political and Social Theories of Georges Sorel* (Berkeley, Calif.).

Steenson, G. P. (1978), *Karl Kautsky 1854–1938: Marxism in the Classical Years* (Pittsburgh, Pa).

Stegmann, D. (1970), *Die Erben Bismarcks. Parteien und Verbände in der Spätphase des wilhelminischen Deutschland: Sammlungspolitik 1897–1918* (Cologne).

Steigerwald, R. (1980), *Bürgerliche Philosophie und Revisionismus im imperialistischen Deutschland* (Frankfurt-am-Main).

Steinberg, H.-J. (1972), *Sozialismus und deutsche Sozialdemokratie: Zur Ideologie der Partei vor dem Ersten Weltkreig*, 3rd edn (Bonn).

Steinberg, H.-J. (1976), 'Workers Libraries in Germany before 1914', *History Workshop*, vol. 1, no. 1.

Steinberg, J. (1968), *Yesterday's Deterrent: Tirpitz and the Birth of the German Battlefleet* (London).

Steiner, Z. S. (1977), *Britain and the Origins of the First World War* (London).

Stern, F. (1965), *The Politics of Cultural Despair: A Study in the Rise of the Germanic Ideology* (Garden City, NY).

Stern, F. (1972), *The Failure of Illiberalism: Essays on the Political Culture of Modern Germany* (New York).

Stern, F. (1977), *Gold and Iron: Bismarck, Bleichröder and the Building of the German Empire* (New York and London).

Stirner, H. (1979), *Die Agitation und Rhetorik Ferdinand Lassalles* (Marburg).

Stone, N. (1983), *Europe Transformed 1878–1919* (Glasgow).

Strausz-Hupé, R. (1941), *Geopolitics: The Struggle for Space and Power* (New York).

Strutynski, P. (1976), *Die Auseinandersetzungen zwischen Marxisten und Revisionisten in der deutschen Arbeiterbewegung um die Jahrhundertwende* (Cologne).

Struve, W. (1973), *Elites against Democracy: Leadership Ideals in Bourgeois Political Thought in Germany 1890–1933* (Princeton, NJ).

Summerton, N. W. (1977), 'Dissenting attitudes to foreign relations, peace and war, 1840–90', *Journal of Ecclesiastical History*, vol. 28, no. 2.

Swartz, M. (1971), *The Union of Democratic Control in British Politics during the First World War* (Oxford).

Talmon, J. L. (1980), *The Myth of the Nation and the Vision of Revolution: The Origins of Ideological Polarisation in the Twentieth Century* (London).

Tampke, J. (1978), *The Ruhr and Revolution: The Revolutionary Movement in the Rhenish-Westphalian Industrial Region 1912–1919* (London).

Taylor, A. J. P. (1957), *The Trouble Makers* (London).

Taylor, A. J. P. (1967), *Germany's First Bid for Colonies 1884–85: A Move in Bismarck's European Policy* (Hamden, Conn.).

Theodor, G. (1957), *Friedrich Naumann oder der Prophet des Profits* (East Berlin).

Thomas, R. Hinton (1983), *Nietzsche in German Politics and Society 1890–1918* (Manchester).

Thompson, E. P. (1963), *The Making of the English Working Class* (London).

Thompson, L. (1971), *The Enthusiasts: A Biography of John and Katherine Bruce Glasier* (London).

Trotnow, H. (1975), 'The misunderstood Karl Liebknecht', *European Studies Review*, vol. 5, no. 2.

Trotnow, H. (1980), *Karl Liebknecht: Eine politische Biographie* (Cologne).

Tsuzuki, C. (1961), *H. M. Hyndman and British Socialism* (Oxford).

Tsuzuki, C. (1967), *The Life of Eleanor Marx 1855–1898* (Oxford).

Victor, M. (1928), 'Die Stellung der deutschen Sozialdemokratie zu den Fragen der auswärtigen Politik (1869–1914)', *Archiv für Sozialwissenschaft und Sozialpolitik*, vol. 60.

Viner, J. (1951), *International Economics* (Glencoe, Ill.).

Vital, D. (1975), *The Origins of Zionism* (Oxford).

Wachenheim, H. (1967), *Die deutsche Arbeiterbewegung 1844 bis 1914* (Cologne).

Wallach, J. (1968), *Die Kriegslehre von Friedrich Engels* (Frankfurt-am-Main).

Walther, R. (1981), '. . . aber nach der Sündflut kommen wir und nur wir.' 'Zusammenbruchstheorie', *Marxismus und politisches Defizit in der SPD, 1890–1914* (Frankfurt-am-Main).

Wank, S. (ed.) (1978), *Doves and Diplomats* (Westport, Conn.).

Weber, H. *See* Bauer, O.

Wegner, K. (1968), *Theodor Barth und die Freisinnige Vereinigung: Studien zur Geschichte des Linksliberalismus im wilhelminischen Deutschland (1893–1910)* (Tübingen).

Wehler, H.-U. (1962), *Sozialdemokratie und Nationalstaat: Die Sozialdemokratie und die Nationalitätenfrage in Deutschland von Karl Marx bis zum Ausbruch des Ersten Weltkrieges* (Würzburg).

Wehler, H.-U. (1969), *Bismarck und der Imperialismus* (Cologne).

Wehler, H.-U. (ed.) (1970*a*), *Der Imperialismus* (Cologne).

Wehler, H.-U. (1970*b*), *Krisenherde des Kaiserreichs* (Göttingen).

Wehler, H. U. (1971), *Sozialdemokratie und Nationalstaat*, 2nd rev. edn of 1962 work cited above (Göttingen).

Wehler, H. U. (1973), *Das deutsche Kaiserreich 1871–1918* (Göttingen).

Weinberger, G. (1967), 'Die deutsche Sozialdemokratie und die Kolonialpolitik', *Zeitschrift für Geschichtswissenschaft*, vol. 15, no. 3.

Weinroth, H. S. (1970). 'The British Radicals and the balance of power, 1902–1914', *Historical Journal*, vol. 13, no. 4.

Weinroth, H. S. (1974*a*), 'Norman Angell and *The Great Illusion:* An episode in pre-1914 pacifism', *Historical Journal*, vol. 17, no. 3.

Weinroth, H. S. (1974*b*), 'Radicalism and nationalism: an increasingly unstable equation', in A. J. A. Morris (ed.), *Edwardian Radicalism 1900–1914* (London).

Wernecke, K. (1970), *Der Wille zur Weltgeltung: Aussenpolitik und Öffentlichkeit im Kaiserreich am Vorabend des Ersten Weltkrieges*, 2nd edn (Düsseldorf).

Wette, W. (1971), *Kriegstheorien deutscher Sozialisten* (Stuttgart).

White, D. S. (1976), *The Splintered Party: National Liberalism in Hessen and the Reich, 1867–1918* (Cambridge, Mass.).

Whiteside, A. G. (1975), *The Socialism of Fools: Georg Ritter von Schönerer and Austrian Pan-Germanism* (Berkeley, Calif.).

Whittlesey, D. (1971), 'Haushofer: the geopoliticians', in E. M. Earle (ed.), *Makers of Modern Strategy: Military Thought from Machiavelli to Hitler* (Princeton, NJ).

Willey, T. E. (1978), *Back to Kant: The Revival of Kantianism in German Social and Historical Thought 1860–1914* (Detroit, Mich.).

Wiltshire, D. (1978), *The Social and Political Thought of Herbert Spencer* (Oxford).

Winslow, E. M. (1948), *The Pattern of Imperialism* (New York).

Winzen, P. (1976), 'Prince Bülow's *Machtpolitik*', *Australian Journal of Politics and History*, vol. 22, no. 2.

Winzen, P. (1977), *Bülows Weltmachtkonzept: Untersuchungen zur Frühphase seiner Aussenpolitik 1897–1901* (Boppard-am-Rhein).

Wistrich, R. S. (1976*a*), 'German Social Democracy and the problem of Jewish nationalism', *Leo Baeck Institute Yearbook*, vol. 21.

Wistrich, R. S. (1976*b*), *Revolutionary Jews from Marx to Trotsky* (London).

Wistrich, R. S. (1977), 'The SPD and antisemitism in the 1890's, *European Studies Review*, vol. 7, no. 2.

Wistrich, R. S. (1978), 'Back to Bernstein?', *Encounter*, vol. 50, no. 6.

Wistrich, R. S. (1979*a*), 'Dilemmas of assimilation in *fin-de-siècle* Vienna', *Wiener Library Bulletin*, vol. 32, nos 49/50 (new series).

Wistrich, R. S. (1979*b*), 'Eduard Bernstein and the Jewish problem', *Jahrbuch des Instituts für Deutsche Geschichte*, vol. 8 (Tel Aviv).

Wistrich, R. S. (1982), *Socialism and the Jews: The Dilemmas of Assimilation in Germany and Austria-Hungary* (E. Brunswick, NJ).

Witt, P. C. (1970), *Die Finanzpolitik des Deutschen Reiches von 1903 bis 1913* (Lübeck).

Wittwer, W. (1964), *Streit um Schicksalsfragen: Die deutsche Sozialdemokratie zu Krieg und Vaterlandsverteidigung* (Berlin).

Woodward, E. L. (1935), *Great Britain and the German Navy* (Oxford).

Young, H. F. (1977), *Prince Lichnowsky and the Great War* (Athens, Ga.).

Zmarzlik, H.-G. (1975), 'Das Kaiserreich als Einbahnstrasse?', in K. Holl and G. List (eds), *Liberalismus und imperialistischer Staat* (Göttingen).

Index